HOW TO BREW

Everything you need to know to brew beer right the first time

brewers publications

A Division of the
Brewers Association
Boulder, Colorado

Brewers Publications
A Division of the Brewers Association
PO Box 1679, Boulder, Colorado 80306-1679
BrewersAssociation.org

Printed in the United States of America.

10 9 8

ISBN-13: 978-0-937381-88-5
ISBN-10: 0-937381-88-8

Library of Congress Cataloging-in-Publication Data

Palmer, John J., 1963-
   How to brew : ingredients, methods, recipes and equipment
for brewing beer at home / by John J. Palmer.-- 3rd ed.
      p. cm.
   Includes bibliographical references and index.
   ISBN-13: 978-0-937381-88-5
   1. Brewing--Amateur's manuals. I. Title.

   TP570.P275 2006
   641.8'73--dc22

      2006004807

Publisher: Ray Daniels
Technical Editor: Randy Mosher
Copy Editor: Daria Labinsky
Index: Daria Labinsky
Production & Design Management: Stephanie Johnson
Cover and Interior Design: Julie Lawrason
Cover photo: Souders Studios/Square Pixels
Interior photos: Naomi K. Palmer and John Palmer

TABLE OF CONTENTS

SECTION III—ALL-GRAIN BREWING

SECTION IV—RECIPES, EXPERIMENTING, AND TROUBLESHOOTING

LIST OF TIPS, TABLES, AND SIGNIFICANT FIGURES

Inside Front Cover

°SRM Color Scale Swatches

SECTION I—BREWING WITH MALT EXTRACT

SECTION IV—RECIPES, EXPERIMENTATION, AND TROUBLESHOOTING

Appendix G Brewing Metallurgy

Appendix H Metric Conversions

Inside Back Cover

ACKNOWLEDGEMENTS

This book is dedicated to all my brewing friends all over the world. I couldn't have done it without your enthusiasm and support.

I am constantly overwhelmed by the generosity of brewers in sharing information, their time, and their passion for beer and brewing. There are so many people I need to thank for making this third edition possible.

My wife, for raising an eyebrow and saying, "Well…? (Get going!)"

My friends in the Crown of the Valley Brewing Club: Tim Aberle, Herb Adams, Michael Babcock, JT Blancett, Brian Dearden, Jeff Crowell, Bob Curtiss, Brian Dellosa, Bob Gunner, Erik Kobulnick, Dale Lauterbach, Shawn Olsson, Doug Parker, Mike Peterson, Todd Peterson, James Reynolds, Andrew Sayeg, Jamie Smith, Robert Streutker, Paul Valvidiez, Scott Velasquez, Vitol Wiacek, for friendship, project support, and good beers.

There are several people that I would pester with phone calls and late night emails to answer tough questions, and they had a real hand in helping me develop this book:

A.J. deLange
Steve Alexander
Bob Hansen of Briess Malt & Ingredients Company
Brian Kern
Berne Jones, Ph.D, of the U.S. Department of Agriculture
Evan Evans, Ph.D, of the Tasmanian Institute of Agricultural Research
Greg Doss of Wyeast Laboratories Inc.
Chris White of White Labs Inc.
Mark Jilg and Todd Peterson of Craftsmen Brewery
Matt Brynildson of Firestone Walker Brewery

And I want to thank Ray Daniels and Randy Mosher for enthusiastically getting behind the third edition and asking the tough questions that made it better.

John
October 5, 2005

Notes on the Third Edition

How to Brew Your First Beer was created in 1993 as a twelve-page electronic document that contained everything that a beginning brewer would need to know to get started. It contained equipment descriptions, process descriptions, and some of the whys of homebrewing. I posted it to electronic bulletin boards and homebrewing ftp sites such as sierra.stanford.edu. (Would you believe that the World Wide Web didn't exist back then?) It was written to help the first-time brewer produce a foolproof beer—one he or she could be proud of. That document apparently served quite well; it was requested and distributed to every continent (including Antarctica) and translated into Spanish, Italian, Czech, Korean, and Japanese. Glad I could help.

As time went by, I received requests from brewers to write how-to's for the more complex brewing methods, such as extract-and-specialty-grain and all-grain brewing. There is a lot to talk about with these methods, though, and I realized that it would be best done with a book. After years and years of writing and rewriting, I published the first edition of *How to Brew* online with the help of the Real Beer Page in June 2000. But I immediately started receiving requests for hard copy. Of course, in the process of laying it out, I couldn't resist the chance to improve it. The second edition was self-published in 2001. It added different sparging techniques and a more technical discussion of fluid flow in the lauter tun, as well as more pictures and data tables than the online edition.

Since that time, there have been a couple of changes in the state-of-the-art of homebrewing:

- The brewing quality of malt extract has been improving for more than a decade and is, in fact, excellent, but the basic extract brewing methods have gone unchanged since we brewed with baker's extract.
- Batch sparing and no-sparge methods for all-grain brewing are now as popular as the continuous-sparging method, which used to be the only method discussed in the literature.

To give these changes their due, I had to rework most of the chapters of the book. Sometimes it was just a sentence or two, other times it was the entire presentation of the chapter.

This was also an opportunity to improve on topics I had only touched on before:

- Brewing sugars other than maltose
- Beer clarity and controlling beer haze
- Beer color and how to estimate it in a recipe
- Acid calculations for controlling mash and sparge pH.

I also re-took a few pictures.

Cheers!
John

INTRODUCTION

Perhaps you have heard this before:

"You brew your own beer?"

"Yes."

"Really? Wow ... what does it taste like?"

"It's really good."

"Can you make Budweiser?"

"Yes, and every other kind of beer, too."

"You know, I have always wanted to try doing that. ..."

Hello and welcome to the third edition of *How to Brew*. This book is going to introduce you to the art and science of brewing, great beer, and a fascinating hobby. You will truly "amaze your friends!" Brewing good beer is not hard.

This is how the brewing process works:

1. Malted barley is soaked in hot water to create fermentable sugars.
2. The malt sugar solution is boiled with hops for seasoning.
3. The solution is cooled, and yeast is added to begin fermentation.
4. The yeast ferments the sugars, releasing carbon dioxide and ethyl alcohol.
5. When the main fermentation is complete, the beer is bottled with a little bit of added sugar to provide the carbonation.

Sounds fairly simple, doesn't it? It really isn't any harder than baking a batch of cookies. What is difficult is understanding how to make cookies when you have never seen it done before. The goal of this book is to teach you how to brew beer in as logical and straightforward a manner as possible without burying you in scientific details. When you have read this book, you will understand what you are doing, why you are doing it, and how to do it easily.

In this first section of the book, we are going to lay the groundwork for the rest of your brewing education. As with every new skill, it helps to learn to do things the right way the first time, rather than learning via short cuts that you will have to unlearn later on. On the other hand, you don't need to know how an internal combustion engine works when you are learning how to drive. You just need to know that it needs gas and oil to work.

To learn to brew beer, you don't need to learn how the yeast metabolize the malt sugars, but you do need to understand that eating sugar is what they do, and you need to understand what they need from you to get the job done. Once you understand that, you can do your part, they can do theirs, and good beer will happen. As you gain some familiarity with the brewing processes, you can delve deeper into the inner workings and probably make your beer even better.

So, in Brewing With Malt Extract, you will learn to drive. Chapter 1—A Crash Course in Brewing will provide an overview of the entire process for producing a beer. You can use this single chapter to brew a beer right now—today. Chapter 2—Brewing Preparations explains why good preparation, including sanitation, is important, and how to go about it. Chapter 3—Malt Extract and Beer Kits examines the key ingredient of do-it-yourself beer and how to use it properly. Chapter 4—Water for Extract Brewing cuts to the chase with a few do's and don'ts about a very complex subject. Chapter 5—Hops covers the different kinds of hops, why to use them, how to use them, and how to measure them for consistency in your brewing. The last ingredient chapter in Section I, Chapter 6—Yeast, explains what yeast are, how to prepare them, and what they need to grow.

From there, Section I moves into the physical processes of brewing. Chapter 7—Boiling and Cooling walks you through a typical brew day: mixing the wort, boiling it, and cooling it to prepare it for fermentation. Chapter 8—Fermentation examines how the yeast ferments wort into beer so you will understand what you are trying to do, without going into excruciating detail. Chapter 9—Fermenting Your First Beer does just what it says: It takes what you have just learned and walks you through the practical application.

Everybody wants to brew their favorite beer that they buy at the store, and it's usually a lager. So, Chapter 10—What Is Different About Brewing Lager Beer? examines the key differences of lager brewing, building on what you have already learned about ale brewing. Section I finishes with Chapter 11—Priming and Bottling, explaining each step of how to package your five gallons of new beer into something you can really use.

It is a long section, but you will learn to brew, and brew right the first time. Later sections of the book will delve deeper into malted barley, so you can take greater control of the ingredients, and thus, your beer. A later section, Section IV—Recipes, Experimentation, and Troubleshooting, will give you the road maps, the tools, and the repair manual you need to always achieve your goals.

It is my sincere hope that this book will help you to derive the same sense of fun and enthusiasm that I have experienced, and that it will enable you to brew some really outstanding beer.

Good Brewing!

SECTION 1

BREWING WITH MALT EXTRACT

A CRASH COURSE IN BREWING

What Do I Do?

If you are like me, you are probably standing in the kitchen wanting to get started. Your beer kit and equipment are on the counter, and you are wondering how long this will take and what to do first. I would recommend that you read all of Section I—Brewing With Malt Extract. This section will teach you the fundamentals of how to brew beer, so you won't be confused by incomplete instructions on a beer kit, and you will have an outstanding first batch.

But if you *are* like me, you probably want to do this right now while you have some time. (It's going to take about three hours, depending.) So, in this first chapter, I will walk you through the steps necessary to get your first batch bubbling in the fermenter and give you an overview of what you will do to ferment and bottle your beer.

The instructions in this chapter may not explain why you are doing each step or even what you are doing. To understand the whats and whys of brewing, you will need to read the rest of this section. Each of the chapters in Section I discuss the brewing steps in detail, giving you the purpose behind each step. You will know what you are doing, rather than doing it that way just because "that's what it said . . . ." You will know how long to boil the wort, how to really use hops, why to bother cooling the wort, why to bother rehydrating the yeast, why to wait two weeks before bottling . . . get the picture?

But if you can't wait, this chapter should see you through. Beer production can be broken down into three main events: Brew Day, Fermentation Week(s), and Bottling Day. If you have questions about terminology, check the Glossary at the back of the book.

Figure 1 Here you see all the usual equipment a beginning brewer might use. Fermenters, brewpot, funnel, hydrometer, bottle brush, bottle capper, bottle caps, sanitizer, racking cane/siphon, and a bottle. But you don't have to have all of these things to get started.

Brew Day

Equipment Needed

Here is a list of the minimum equipment you will need today for this first batch:

Airlock. Two basic kinds are available: the single-piece or "bubbler," and the three-piece. They are filled with water or sanitizer to prevent contamination from the outside atmosphere. The three-piece has the advantage of disassembly for cleaning but can inadvertently allow the water to be sucked back into the fermenter, which can happen if the internal pressure drops due to a drop in temperature, or from lifting the plastic bucket. The bubbler type will not suck liquid back inside but is more easily clogged by fermentation gunk and cannot be disassembled for cleaning.

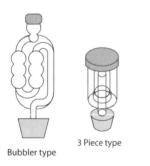

Bubbler type

3 Piece type

Boiling pot. The pot must be able to comfortably hold a minimum of 3 gallons; bigger is better. A 5-gallon home canning pot (those black, speckled ones) is the least expensive and a good choice for getting started, although it is more prone to scorching and will rust if chipped. A 5-gallon, thick-walled aluminum stockpot is a very good choice, because it heats well and won't scorch or rust. Stainless steel is easier to maintain but is also more expensive and does not conduct heat as well as aluminum.

Can opener. It is very annoying to stare in frustration at a full can of malt extract.

Fermenter. The 6-gallon food-grade plastic pail is recommended for beginners. It is very easy to work with. Glass

bucket   carboy

carboys are also available, in 3- , 5- , and 6.5-gallon sizes. The carboy is shown with a blowoff hose, which ends in a bucket of water and takes the place of an airlock.

Glass measuring cup. The quart-sized or larger measuring cup will quickly become one of your most valuable tools for brewing. The heat-resistant glass ones are best, because they can be used to measure boiling water and are easily sanitized.

Plastic wrap or aluminum foil. Very handy for keeping jars or fermenters clean and sanitized.

Sanitizer. Chemical sanitizers are necessary to ensure that yeast are the only microorganisms growing in your beer. Popular no-rinse sanitizers are iodophor and acidic sanitizers like StarSan and Final Step. Common household bleach can also be used, but it can cause off-flavors if not rinsed or used at too strong a concentration.

Stirring spoon. Food-grade plastic or metal spoon for stirring the wort during the boil.

Thermometer. Obtain a thermometer that can be immersed safely in the wort and has a range of at least 40 to 180° F (4 to 82° C). The floating dairy thermometers work very well. LCD digital thermometers also work well and are inexpensive. (Always calibrate your thermometer with boiling water or another known temperature before using it for the first time.)

Hydrometer (optional). A hydrometer measures the difference in specific gravity between pure water and water with dissolved sugar. A hydrometer is used to gauge the progress of fermentation by measuring one aspect of it, attenuation. As the fermentation progresses, the yeast consume the sugar and the original wort gravity (OG) decreases towards an anticipated final gravity (FG). Hydrometers are necessary when making beer from scratch (all-grain brewing) or when designing recipes. Beginning brewers usually don't need one, but it can be a useful tool. See Appendix A for more information.

Preparation

(45 minutes)

1. Assemble ingredients. Gather together the ingredients for the brew. You may have purchased a brewing kit at a home-brewing shop, and it will contain the ingredients needed to brew a particular style of beer. A typical kit consists of a single can of hopped malt extract and a packet of yeast. This type of kit is usually combined with a couple of pounds of table sugar or plain malt extract to make 5 gallons of beer. These

---

RECIPE
Cincinnati Pale Ale

OG = 1.045 (11.2 °P), 30 IBUs

Ingredients for a 5-gallon (19-liter) batch

- 3.3 lbs. (1.5kg) pale malt extract syrup, unhopped

- 2.5 lbs. (1.1kg) amber dry malt extract

- 6 AAUs of bittering hops (any variety) For example, 0.5 oz. (14g) of 12% AA Nugget, or 0.75 oz. (21g) of 8% AA Northern Brewer

- 5 AAUs of finishing hops (Cascade or other) For example, 1 oz. (28g) of 5% Cascade or 1.25 oz. (36g) of 4% Liberty

- 2 new packets of dry ale yeast

Figure 4   Hydrometer and Hydrometer Jar

Alpha Acid Unit (AAU)

AAU is a measurement unit for hops, which add a balancing bitterness to the malt in beer. The actual unit for measuring bitterness in beer is the IBU (International Bittering Unit), for which the AAU is a constituent. The AAU is obtained by multiplying the alpha acid rating of the hop (a percentage value) by the weight (ounces) that you intend to use. For example, 2 ounces of a 6% alpha acid hop equals 12 AAUs.

Every package of hops you buy will list the hop's alpha acid rating. To figure out how much of a hop you will need for this recipe, just divide the AAU target by the alpha acid percentage on your hops. For example, 12 AAUs divided by 12% alpha equals 1 ounce; 12 AAUs divided by 8% alpha equals 1.5 ounces.

kits do not require boiling and are the simplest to make. The other type of kit uses unhopped malt extract, and the extract is boiled with hops to give the beer its bitterness.

If you don't have a kit, then head to a homebrew supply store and buy the ingredients outlined in the Cincinnati Pale Ale recipe on p.7. You will notice that the recipe calls for various quantities of hops measured in AAUs. AAU stands for alpha acid unit. (See the AAU sidebar and Chapter 5 for more info.)

2. Boil water. You will need at least a gallon of sterile water for a variety of small tasks. Start by boiling about 1 gallon of water for 10 minutes, and let it cool, covered, to room temperature.

3. Clean and sanitize. It may seem strange to the first-time brewer, but probably the most important factor for success in brewing is good cleaning and sanitization. Clean all equipment that will be used during the brew with a mild, unscented dishwashing detergent, and be sure to rinse well. Some equipment will need to be sanitized for use after the boiling stage as described below.

You can easily sanitize most of your equipment by filling the fermenter bucket with 5 gallons of water and adding the recommended amount of no-rinse chemical sanitizer. Soak all items that need to be sanitized in this bucket for at least the minimum recommended time. Longer times will not hurt.

TABLE 1
Cleaning and Sanitization Checklist

Brewpot	❏ Clean	
Stirring spoon	❏ Clean	
Tablespoon	❏ Clean	❏ Sanitize
Measuring cup	❏ Clean	❏ Sanitize
Yeast starter jar	❏ Clean	❏ Sanitize
Fermenter and lid	❏ Clean	❏ Sanitize
Airlock	❏ Clean	❏ Sanitize
Thermometer	❏ Clean	❏ Sanitize

Figure 6 Start boiling the water and get your ingredients ready. Do you have yeast?

After soaking, dump the sanitizing solution and cover the fermenter with the lid to keep it sanitary. Place the small spoon and the thermometer in the measuring cup, and cover it with plastic wrap to keep them sanitary. (See Chapter 2 for more info.)

Making Wort

(1½ hours)

Now we begin the fun part of the work, creating the wort. Wort is what brewers call the sweet, amber liquid extracted from malted barley that the yeast will later ferment into beer.

4. Boil the brew water. In the brewpot, bring about 2 gallons (7.6 liters) of water to a boil. You will be boiling the extract in this water and diluting this concentrated wort with the water in the fermenter to make the total 5 gallons (19 liters). Some water will evaporate during the boil, and some will be lost to the trub (hop and protein crud). (See Chapter 7 for more info.)

Note: If your beer kit includes some crushed specialty grain, you will need to steep that in the hot water first, before adding the extract. See Chapter 13 for more info.

5. Rehydrate the dried yeast. While you are waiting for the brew water to boil, rehydrate one packet (about 11 grams) of dried ale yeast. Put 1 cup (237 milliliters) of warm (95 to 105° F, 35 to 40° C), preboiled water into your sanitized jar, and stir in the yeast. Cover with plastic wrap, and wait 20 minutes before pitching. (See Chapter 6 for more info.)

6. Add malt extract. When the water in the brewpot is boiling, turn off the stove and stir in the malt extract. Be sure the extract is completely dissolved (if your malt extract is the dry variety, make sure there are no clumps; if the extract is syrup, make sure that none is stuck to the bottom of the pot).

Figures 7 and 8 Rehydrating the yeast

Here is a decision point: Do you need to boil the wort? The boil time for extract beers depends on three things: pasteurizing the extract, waiting for the "hot break" (see Step 8), and boiling for hop additions. In a nutshell, if you are using hopped extract without any added hops, then you may not need to boil at all, because the hot break has already occurred during the extract manufacturing process. If you are using hopped extract but adding flavoring or aroma hops, then you will want to boil it for 15 to 30 minutes. If you are using unhopped extract, then you will need to add multiple hop additions for bittering, flavor, and aroma, and you will boil for an hour. (See Chapters 3, 5, and 7 for more info.)

Figure 11 Chilling the wort in an ice bath

Figure 12 Pouring the chilled wort

7. Add hops. If you are using unhopped extract, add the first (bittering) hop addition and begin timing the hour-long boil. (See Chapter 5 for more info.)

8. Watch for boilovers. As the wort boils, foam will form on the surface. This foam will persist until the wort goes through the "hot break" stage. The wort will easily boil over during this foaming stage, especially when hops are first added, so stay close by and stir frequently. Blow on it, and turn the heat down if it begins to boil over. Put a few copper pennies into the pot to help prevent boilovers. (See Chapter 7 for more info.)

9. Add finishing hops (optional). If you are using unhopped malt extract or want to add more character to hopped extract, add finishing hops during the last 15 minutes of the boil. (See Chapter 5 for more info.)

10. Cool the wort. After the boil, the wort must be cooled to yeast-pitching temperature (65 to 77° F, 18 to 25° C) as quickly as possible. To do this, immerse the pot in a cold water or ice bath. A sink, bathtub, or a handy snowbank all work well. Be sure to keep the lid on the pot while cooling to prevent any cooling water or other potential contaminants from getting in. (See Chapter 7 for more info.)

Fermentation Week(s)

The science of fermentation is discussed in Chapter 8. The next chapter walks you through the application of that science, so that you, too, will be able to amaze your family and friends with a bubbling airlock! (You laugh now . . . .)

1. Pour the cooled wort. Pour the cooled wort into the fermentation bucket aggressively, so that it splashes and churns in the bucket. This action adds the oxygen yeast need for growth. For best results, pour some back into the boiling pot, and then pour it into the fermenter again. *This is the only time during the brewing process that you want the beer to be aerated or exposed to oxygen.* All other transfers should be done quietly, using a sanitized siphon, and with very little disturbance in the flow and minimal contact with the air.

If you had added hops during the boil, you can remove them during this step by pouring the wort into the fermenter through a strainer. It is not necessary to remove the hops, however.

2. Add water. Add enough clean water to the fermenter to bring the volume up to 5 gallons (19 liters). If your tap water has a strong chlorine smell, you will probably want to run it through a carbon filter or use bottled water. Aerate the wort again by pouring it back and forth to the brewpot a few times. Or use a clean and sanitized egg beater or whisk.

3. Pitch the yeast. Pour the rehydrated yeast solution into the fermentation bucket.

4. Store the fermenter. Put the lid tightly on the fermenter, and carry the bucket to a secure location where it will be undisturbed for two weeks. Choose a location that has a stable temperature of 65 to 70° F (18 to 21° C). A warmer temperature of 75° F (24° C) is OK, but above 80° F (26° C) the flavor of the beer will be affected. As soon as you have finished moving it, insert the airlock and fill the airlock with clean water or sanitizer solution.

5. Leave it alone! After about 24 hours, the airlock will be bubbling steadily, the exciting evidence of fermentation. (At right, you can see what it looks like inside.) The fermentation will proceed like this for two to four days, depending on the conditions of your fermentation. The activity will decrease as the yeast consume most of the malt sugars, although fermentation continues long after the bubbling diminishes. Leave the beer in the fermenter for a total of two weeks.

6. Clean up. Now is the time to wash out your brewpot and other equipment. Only use mild unscented dishwashing detergents or the cleaners recommended in Chapter 2, and rinse well.

Bottling Day

The second big day in your career as a homebrewer comes two weeks later, after fermentation is complete. Everything outlined below is thoroughly discussed in Chapter 11.

To bottle your beer, you will need:

Bottles. You will need 48 recappable 12-ounce bottles for a typical 5-gallon batch. Alternatively, 30 of the larger 22-ounce bottles may be used to reduce capping time. Twist-offs do not recap well and are more prone to breaking. Used champagne bottles are ideal if you can find them.

Bottle capper. Two styles are available: hand cappers and bench cappers. Bench cappers are more versatile, and are needed for the champagne bottles, but are more expensive.

Bottle caps. Either standard or oxygen-absorbing crown caps are available.

Bottle brush. A long-handled nylon bristle brush is necessary for the first, hardcore cleaning of used bottles.

Siphon. Available in several configurations, it usually consists of clear plastic tubing with a racking cane and optional bottle filler.

Racking cane. Rigid plastic tube with sediment standoff used to leave the trub behind when siphoning.

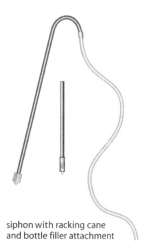

siphon with racking cane
and bottle filler attachment

Bottling Bucket
with fill tube attached

Bottle filler. Rigid plastic (or metal) tube, often with a spring-loaded valve at the tip, for filling bottles.

Bottling bucket (optional). A 6-gallon food-grade plastic pail with attached spigot and fill-tube. The finished beer is racked into this for priming prior to bottling. Racking into the bottling bucket allows clearer beer with less sediment in the bottle. The spigot is used instead of the bottle filler, allowing greater control of the fill level and no hassles with a siphon during bottling.

1. Prepare your bottles. A typical 5-gallon batch requires two cases (48) 12-ounce bottles for bottling. Thoroughly clean and sanitize the bottles before use. If you are using old bottles, check them inside for dirt or mold deposits. They may need to be scrubbed with a bottle brush to get them really clean. Always clean first, then sanitize.

2. Prepare your bottle caps. The bottle caps should at least be clean before you use them, and it doesn't hurt to sanitize them too. Some brewers use swing-top (Grolsch-style) bottles. The ceramic part of the swing-tops can be sanitized along with the bottles. The rubber seals can be sanitized like the bottle caps.

3. Prepare your priming sugar. We add a priming solution just before bottling to provide carbonation to the beer in the bottle. Boil ¾ cup (4 ounces by weight) of corn sugar or ⅔ cup (3.8 ounces by weight) of table sugar in two cups of water. Cover the pan and allow it to cool.

4. Combine beer and priming sugar. The best method for preparing the beer and priming sugar solution is to use a separate container the same size as your fermenter as a "bottling bucket." Clean and sanitize it, and gently pour the priming solution into it. Next, siphon the beer from the fermenter into the bottling bucket. Don't simply pour the beer into the bucket, and don't let the beer splash as you siphon it in. Instead, put the end of the siphon under the surface of the beer as it fills. The swirling motion of the beer as it enters the bucket will be sufficient to mix the priming solution into the beer evenly without aeration. See Figure 19.

If you don't have a bottling bucket, you can gently pour the priming solution into the fermenter and gently stir it. Allow the sediment in the fermenter to settle for 15 to 30 minutes before proceeding. You can fill the bottles using the bottle filler attachment on your siphon. See Figure 20.

5. Bottle. Carefully fill the bottles with the primed beer, place a sanitized bottle cap on each bottle, and crimp it using the bottle capper. At this stage it is helpful to have a friend operate the capper, while you fill the bottles.

6. Store the bottles. Place the capped bottles out of the light in a warm environment (room temperature—65 to 75° F, 18 to 24° C). The bottles will take about two weeks to carbonate. The bottles will have a thin layer of yeast on the bottom.

Serving Day

At last, you get to sample the fruit of your labors. It has been about a month since Brew Day, and you are ready to open your first bottle and see what kind of wonderful beer you have created. During the past two weeks, the yeast still swimming around in the beer have consumed the priming sugar, creating just enough carbon dioxide to carbonate your beer perfectly.

OK, so maybe you couldn't wait that long, and you already opened a bottle. You may have noticed the beer wasn't fully carbonated, or that it seemed carbonated but the bubbles had no staying power. You may have also noticed a "green" flavor. That flavor is the sign of a young beer. The two-week "conditioning" period not only adds carbonation but also gives the beer flavors time to meld and balance out.

1. Chill your beer. The bottled beer does not need to be stored cold. It will keep for about six months, depending on how well you managed to avoid exposure to oxygen during the last stage of fermentation and the bottling process. You will probably want to chill it before serving, however. The optimal temperature for serving beer depends on the style, varying from 40 to 55° F (4 to 12° C). In general, the darker the beer, the warmer you serve it.

2. Pouring your beer. To pour the beer without getting yeast in your glass, tip the bottle slowly to avoid disturbing the yeast layer on the bottom of the bottle. With practice, you will be able to pour everything but the last quarter-inch of beer without getting any yeast in your glass.

3. Savor the flavor. Finally, take a deep drink and savor the flavor of the beer you created. Take time to evaluate the aroma, the flavor, its bitterness qualities, its sweetness, and the level of carbonation. These observations are your first steps to beer appreciation and designing your own recipes.

Figure 19 Filling bottles from the bottling bucket

Figure 20 Filling bottles from a siphon with a bottle filler attachment

But Wait! There's More!

If you want to learn more about brewing beer—how it works, why it works, and how to have fun creating your own recipes and trying advanced techniques—then I encourage you to keep reading. The next chapters in this book will lead you through extract brewing again, but this time with more explanation. They include descriptions of the great variety of hops, yeast strains, and malts that can make each brewing session and every beer unique.

BREWING PREPARATIONS

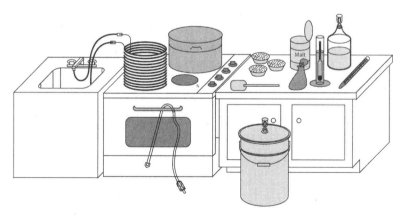

The Road to Good Brewing

There are three important things to keep in mind every time you brew: preparation, sanitation, and good recordkeeping. Good preparation prevents nasty surprises. You don't want to be halfway through your brewing and realize that you don't have any yeast. You don't want to pour good wort into a fermenter that you forgot to clean. Cleaning and sanitizing are part of your preparation but are the most important factors for assuring a successful batch of beer. During an

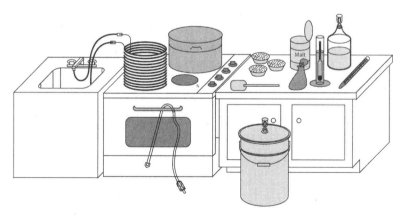

Figure 22 All the equipment and ingredients for the day's brew are set out on the counter and ready to go. The crushed specialty malt is tied in a muslin grain bag, and the hops have been weighed and put in three separate bowls.

interview, Bob Brandt, the head brewer at a very successful brewpub, told me, "Good brewing is 75 percent cleaning." And I agree.

Likewise, there are two types of brewers—lucky and consistent. The lucky brewer will sometimes produce an outstanding batch of beer, but just as often, one that is not. He brews from the seat of his pants, innovating and experimenting, with mixed results. The consistent brewer has more outstanding batches than poor ones. He may be an innovator and an experimenter; the difference is that he takes note of what he did and how much he did of it, so that he can always learn from his results. Good recordkeeping will make the difference between luck and skill.

Preparation

Preparing your brewing equipment is principally a matter of cleaning and sanitizing, but organization is a part of the process, too. For each of the brewing processes, some preparation can be done to make the process work better. Consider what you are going to do:

Check the recipe. Make a shopping list of your ingredients and amounts. Plan ahead on how you are going to measure them. Do you need extra bowls or measuring cups? Do you have good water out of the tap, or should you buy some?

Equipment. Make a checklist of the equipment you will be using, and note whether it needs to be sanitized or only cleaned. Don't try to clean something at the last minute just as you need it; you are inviting trouble. Use a checklist to organize your thoughts and see if you have overlooked anything. You may want to purchase utensils expressly for brewing, so that you don't stir the wort with a spatula often used to cook onions. More instruction on cleaning is given later in this chapter.

TABLE 1 Cleaning and Sanitization Checklist		
Brewpot	❏ Clean	
Stirring spoon	❏ Clean	
Tablespoon	❏ Clean	❏ Sanitize
Measuring cup	❏ Clean	❏ Sanitize
Yeast starter jar	❏ Clean	❏ Sanitize
Fermenter and lid	❏ Clean	❏ Sanitize
Airlock	❏ Clean	❏ Sanitize
Thermometer	❏ Clean	❏ Sanitize

Sanitizing. Anything that touches the cooled wort must be sanitized. This includes the fermenter, airlock, and any of the following, depending on your transfer methods: funnel, strainer, stirring spoon, and racking cane. Sanitizing techniques are discussed later in this chapter.

Preparing the yeast. This step is paramount. Without yeast, you cannot make beer. The yeast should be prepared ahead of the brewing session, especially if you need to make a yeast starter to increase the cell count. If you spend time preparing the equipment and making the wort, but have nothing to ferment it with, you will be very disappointed. See Chapter 6 for detailed information on yeast preparation.

The boil. Weigh out your hop additions, and place them in separate bowls for the different addition times during the boil. If you are going to steep crushed specialty grain (see Chapter 13), then weigh it, bag it, and steep it before adding your extract to the boiling pot.

Cooling after the boil. If you plan to chill the wort using a water bath, e.g., by setting the pot in the sink or bathtub, make sure you have enough ice on hand to cool the wort quickly. A quick chill from boiling is necessary to help prevent infection and to generate the cold break in the wort. A good cold break precipitates proteins, polyphenols (tannins), and beta-glucans that are believed to contribute to beer instability during storage. A good cold break also reduces the amount of chill haze in the final beer.

All this preparation will make your brewing go smoothly and reduce the likelihood of disasters like missed steps, boilovers, forgotten ingredients, or unwilling yeast. In short, having the equipment ready and the process planned out will make the whole operation simple and keep it fun. Your beer will probably benefit, too. As in all things, a little preparation goes a long way toward improving the end result.

Sanitation

Cleanliness is the foremost concern of the brewer. Providing good growing conditions for the yeast in the beer also provides good growing conditions for other microorganisms, especially wild yeast and bacteria. Cleanliness must be maintained through every stage of the brewing process.

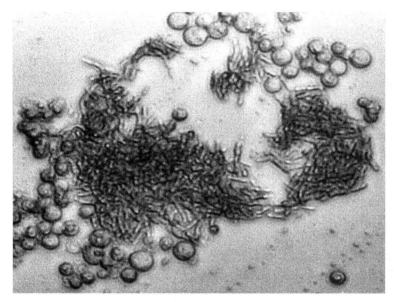

Figure 23 The yeast cells are the round things, the worms are the bacteria. (Sample was taken from fermenting wort that was spit into.) 500x

The definition and objective of sanitization is to reduce bacteria and contaminants to insignificant or manageable levels. The terms clean, sanitize, and sterilize are often used interchangeably but should not be. Items may be clean but not sanitized or vice versa. Here are the definitions:

Clean   To be free from dirt, stain, or foreign matter.

Sanitize To kill/reduce spoiling microorganisms to negligible levels.

Sterilize To eliminate all forms of life, especially microorganisms, either by chemical or physical means.

Cleaning is the process of removing all the dirt and grime from a surface, thereby removing all the sites that can harbor bacteria. Cleaning is usually done with a detergent and elbow grease. None of the sanitizing agents used by homebrewers are capable of eliminating all bacterial spores and viruses. The majority of chemical agents homebrewers use will clean and sanitize but not sterilize. However, sterilization is not necessary. Instead of worrying about sterilization, homebrewers can be satisfied if they consistently reduce these contaminants to negligible levels.

All sanitizers are meant to be used on clean surfaces. A sanitizer's ability to kill microorganisms is reduced by the presence of dirt, grime, or organic material. Organic deposits can harbor bacteria and shield the surface from being reached by the sanitizer. So it is up to you to make sure the surface of the item to be sanitized is as clean as possible.

Cleaning Products

Cleaning requires a certain amount of scrubbing, brushing, and elbow grease. It is necessary because a dirty surface can never be a completely sanitized one. Grungy deposits can harbor bacteria that will ultimately contaminate your beer. The ability of a sanitizing agent to kill bacteria is reduced by the presence of any extra organic matter, so prior cleaning is necessary to assure complete sanitization. Several cleaning products available to the homebrewer are discussed below. Cleaning recommendations for the equipment you will be using follow.

Detergents. Dishwashing detergents and cleansers should be used with caution when cleaning your brewing equipment. These products often contain perfumes that can be adsorbed onto plastic equipment and released back into the beer. In addition, some detergents and cleansers do not rinse completely and often leave behind a film that can be tasted in the beer. Several rinses with hot water may be necessary to remove all traces of the detergent. Detergents containing phosphates generally rinse more easily than those without, but because phosphates are pollutants, they are not used in most household products. A mild, unscented dishwashing detergent like Ivory is a good choice for most of your routine equipment cleaning needs. Only stubborn stains or burned-on deposits will require something stronger.

Bleach. Bleach is one of the most versatile cleaners available to the homebrewer. When dissolved in cold water, it forms a caustic solution that is good at breaking up organic deposits like food stains and brewing gunk. Bleach is an aqueous solution of chlorine, chlorides, and hypochlorites. These chemical agents all contribute to bleach's bactericidal and cleaning powers but are also corrosive to a number of metals used in brewing equipment. Bleach should not be used for cleaning brass and copper, because it causes blackening and excessive corrosion. Bleach can be used to clean stainless steel, but you need to be careful to prevent corrosion and pitting.

There are a few simple guidelines to keep in mind when using bleach to clean stainless steel:

- Don't leave the metal in contact with chlorinated water for extended periods of time (no more than an hour).
- Fill vessels completely, so corrosion does not occur at the water line.
- After the cleaning or sanitizing treatment, rinse the item with boiled water and dry the item completely if it is going to be stored.

Percarbonates. Sodium percarbonate (e.g., OxyClean) is sodium carbonate (e.g., Arm and Hammer Super Washing Soda) reacted with hydrogen peroxide. It is an effective cleaner for all types of brewing equipment, and it rinses easily. Several products containing percarbonates are approved by the Food and Drug Administration as cleaners in food-manufacturing facilities. Use these cleaners according to the manufacturer's instructions, but generally use 1 tablespoon per gallon (or 4 milliliters per liter) and rinse after cleaning.

In my opinion, percarbonate-type cleaners are the best choice for equipment cleaning, and PBW (Powder Brewery Wash) from Five Star Chemicals and Straight-A from Logic are the best of them. These products combine the percarbonate with sodium metasilicate, which increases its effectiveness on proteins and prevents the corrosion of metals (like copper and aluminum) that strong alkaline solutions can cause.

Note: These cleaners will throw a chalky haze on surfaces in hard water if left sitting for several days, which can only be removed with an acid rinse or acidic cleaner like CLR from Jelmar.

Automatic dishwashers. Using dishwashers to clean equipment and bottles is a popular idea among homebrewers, but there are a few limitations:

- The narrow openings of hoses, racking canes, and bottles usually prevent the water jets and detergent from effectively cleaning inside.
- If detergent does get inside these items, there is no guarantee that it will get rinsed out again.
- Dishwasher drying additives (Jet Dry, for example) can ruin the head retention of beer. Drying additives work by putting a chemical film on the items that allows them to be fully wetted by the water, so droplets don't form, preventing spots. The wetting action destabilizes the proteins that form the bubbles.

With the exceptions of spoons, measuring cups, and widemouthed jars, it is probably best to use automatic dishwashers only for heat sanitizing, not for cleaning. Heat sanitizing is discussed later in this chapter.

Oven cleaner. Every once in a while, brewers will scorch the bottom of their brewpots, resulting in a black, burned deposit that is difficult to remove. The easiest solution is to apply oven cleaner and allow it to dissolve the stain. After the burned-on area has been removed, it is important to thoroughly rinse the area of any oven cleaner residue to prevent subsequent corrosion of the metal. This is usually the only situation where you would need to use it. Usually, percarbonate cleaners should be all that is needed to clean even tough deposits.

Spray-on oven cleaner is the safest and most convenient way to use sodium hydroxide. Commonly known as lye, sodium hydroxide (NaOH) is the caustic main ingredient of most heavy-duty cleaners like oven and drain cleaner. Potassium hydroxide (KOH) is also commonly used. Even in moderate concentrations, these chemicals are very hazardous to skin and should only be used when wearing rubber gloves and goggle-type eye protection. Vinegar is useful for neutralizing sodium hydroxide that gets on your skin, but if sodium hydroxide gets in your eyes it could cause severe burns or blindness. Caustic can cause a lot of damage to skin without much pain (at first). That slippery feeling is the oils and lipids in your skin turning into soap. Sodium hydroxide is very corrosive to aluminum and brass. Copper and stainless steel are generally resistant. Pure sodium hydroxide should not be used to clean aluminum brewpots, because the high pH causes the dissolution of the protective oxides, and a subsequent batch of beer might have a metallic taste. Oven cleaner should not affect aluminum adversely, if it is used properly.

Cleaning Your Equipment

Cleaning plastic. There are basically three kinds of plastic that you will be cleaning: opaque white high-density polyethylene (HDPE), hard clear polycarbonate, and clear soft vinyl tubing. You will often hear the polyethylene referred to as "food-grade plastic," though all three of these plastics are. Polyethylene is used for utensils, fermenting buckets, and fittings. Polycarbonate is used for racking canes and measuring cups. The vinyl tubing is used for siphons and the like.

The main thing to keep in mind when cleaning plastics is that they may absorb odors and stains from the cleaning products you use. Dish detergents are your best bet for general cleaning, but scented detergents should be avoided. Bleach is useful for light duty cleaning, but the odor can remain, and bleach tends to cloud vinyl tubing. Percarbonate cleaners (see above) have the benefit of cleaning as well as bleach without the odor and clouding problems. Dishwashers are a convenient way to clean plastic utensils, but the heat might warp polycarbonate items.

Figure 25

Cleaning glass. Glass has the advantage of being inert to everything you might use to clean it with. The only considerations are the danger of breakage and the potential for stubborn lime deposits when using bleach and percarbonates in hard water areas, but an acid rinse takes care of the problem. When it comes to cleaning your glass bottles and carboys, you will probably want to use bottle and carboy brushes so you can effectively clean the insides.

Cleaning copper. For routine cleaning of copper and other metals, percarbonate-based cleaners like PBW are the best choice. For heavily oxidized conditions, acetic acid is very effective, especially when hot. Acetic acid is available in grocery stores as white distilled vinegar at a standard concentration of 5% acetic acid by volume. Acid cleaners such as CLR (Calcium, Lime & Rust Remover), or "dairy rinse" (a phosphoric acid-based cleaner for dairy equipment), or even StarSan are also very effective when diluted.

Brewers who use immersion wort chillers are always surprised by how bright and shiny the chiller is the first time it comes out of the wort. If the chiller wasn't bright and shiny when it went into the wort, guess where the grime and oxides ended up? Yep, in your beer. The oxides of copper are more readily dissolved by the mildly acidic wort than is the copper itself. By cleaning copper tubing with acetic or phosphoric acid once before the first use, and rinsing with water immediately after each use, the copper will remain clean with no oxide or wort deposits that could harbor bacteria. Cleaning copper with vinegar should only occasionally be necessary.

Cleaning and sanitizing copper and brass with bleach solutions is not recommended. The chlorine and hypochlorites in bleach cause oxidation and blackening of copper and brass. If the oxides come in contact with the mildly acidic wort, the oxides will quickly dissolve, possibly exposing yeast to unhealthy levels of copper during fermentation.

> **Brewing Tip: Cleaning and Sanitizing Bottles**
>
> Dishwashers are great for cleaning the outside of bottles and heat sanitizing, but will not clean the insides effectively.
>
> If your bottles are dirty or moldy, soak them in a mild bleach solution or sodium percarbonate-type cleaner (e.g., PBW) for an hour or two to soften the residue. You'll still need to scrub them thoroughly with a bottle brush to remove any stuck residue.
>
> To eliminate the need to scrub bottles in the future, rinse them thoroughly after each use.

Note: I discuss the cleaning of metals more thoroughly in Appendix G.

Cleaning brass. Some brewers use brass fittings in conjunction with their wort chillers or other brewing equipment and are concerned about the lead that is present in brass alloys. The amount of lead on the surface of brass parts is minuscule and not a health concern. However, a solution of two parts white vinegar to one part hydrogen peroxide (common 3% solution) will remove tarnish and surface lead from brass parts when they are soaked for 5 to 15 minutes at room temperature. The brass will turn a buttery yellow color as it is cleaned. If the solution starts to turn green, then the parts have been soaking too long, and the copper in the brass is beginning to dissolve. The solution has become contaminated, and the part should be re-cleaned in a fresh solution.

Cleaning stainless steel and aluminum. For general cleaning, mild detergents or percarbonate-based cleaners are best for steel and aluminum. Bleach should not be used to clean stainless steel and aluminum, because it is just too corrosive. Do not clean aluminum shiny bright, because this removes the protective oxides and can result in a metallic taste. This detectable level of aluminum is not hazardous. There is more aluminum in a common antacid tablet than would be present in a batch of beer made in an aluminum pot.

There are oxalic acid-based cleansers available at the grocery store that are very effective for cleaning stubborn stains, deposits, and rust from stainless. They also work well for copper. Examples are Bar Keeper's Friend Cleanser, Revere Ware Copper and Stainless Cleanser, and Kleen King Stainless Steel Cleanser. Use according to the manufacturer's directions, and rinse thoroughly with water afterwards. These cleansers are more effective than any other method for removing stains, heat tint, and corrosion from stainless steel and other brewing metals.

Beerstone removal. Beerstone is a composite coating of protein and calcium oxalate that is more difficult to remove than typical hard water scale. It precipitates from beer over time to deposit a film onto stainless steel and glass. It is undesirable not only because the coating is rough and can harbor bacteria, but it can also initiate crevice corrosion of stainless steel around the edges of the deposit. Cleaning of beerstone requires a two-step process: a detergent or wetting agent to break up the protein binders, and then a second acidic cleaner to dissolve the exposed oxalates and carbonates. A blend of nitric acid and phosphoric acid is commonly used in the brewing industry, but that solution is fairly hazardous to handle. A safer and more accessible solution for the homebrewer is to soak the item with a strong solution of PBW for a couple of hours or overnight, and follow that with an acid soaking to dissolve the exposed salts. Phosphoric acid, acetic acid, or CLR can be used for the final step.

Sanitizing Products

Once your equipment is clean, it is time to sanitize it before use. Only items that will contact the wort after the boil need to be sanitized, namely, fermenter, lid, airlock, rubber stopper, yeast starter jar, thermometer, funnel, and siphon. Your bottles will need to be sanitized also, but that can wait until bottling day. There are two very convenient ways to sanitize your equipment: chemical and heat. When using chemical sanitizers, the solution can usually be prepared in the fermenter bucket, and all the equipment can be soaked in there. Heat-sanitizing methods depend on the type of material being sanitized.

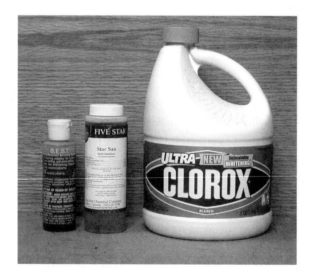

Figure 26 The most commonly used chemical sanitizers: iodophor, StarSan, and bleach

Bleach. The cheapest and most readily available sanitizing solution is made by adding 1 tablespoon of bleach to 1 gallon of water (4 milliliters per liter). Let the items soak for 20 minutes, and then drain. Rinsing is supposedly not necessary at this concentration, but many brewers, myself included, rinse with some boiled water anyway to be sure of no off-flavors from the chlorine. NEVER soak stainless steel in bleach solution.

Iodophor. Iodophor is a solution of iodine complexed with a polymer carrier that is very convenient to use. One tablespoon in 5 gallons of water (15 milliliters in 19 liters) is all that is needed to sanitize equipment with a 2-minute soak time. This produces a concentration of 12.5 ppm of titratable iodine. Soaking equipment longer, for 10 minutes, at the same concentration will disinfect surfaces to hospital standards. At 12.5 ppm the solution has a faint brown color that you can use to monitor the solution's viability. If the solution loses its color, it no longer contains enough free iodine to work. There is no advantage to using more than the specified amount of iodophor. In addition to wasting the product, you risk exposing yourself and your beer to excessive amounts of iodine. Iodine is a halogen, like chlorine, but it is less corrosive to stainless steel.

Iodophor will stain plastic with long exposures, but that is only a cosmetic problem. The 12.5 ppm concentration does not need to be rinsed, but the item should be allowed to drain before use. Even though the recommended concentration is well below the taste threshold, I rinse everything with a little bit of cooled boiled water to avoid any chance of off-flavors, but that's me.

Phosphoric/anionic surfactants. Acidic sanitizers like StarSan, from the makers of PBW, and Final Step from Logic were developed especially for sanitizing brewing equipment. They require only 30 seconds of contact time and do not require rinsing. These sanitizers work by opening the bacterial cell membranes and rupturing cell walls. Unlike bleach and iodophor, they will not contribute off-flavors at higher-than-recommended concentrations. The recommended usage is 1 fluid ounce per 5 gallons of water. The solution can be put in a spray bottle and used as a spray-on sanitizer for glassware or other items that are needed in a hurry. The foam is just as effective for sanitizing as immersion in the solution.

StarSan and Final Step are my preferred sanitizers for all usages except those that I can conveniently do in the dishwasher. These solutions have a long usage life, and an open bucket of it will remain active for several days. It will keep indefinitely in a closed container, such as a spray bottle. The viability of the solution can be judged by its clarity; it turns cloudy as the viability diminishes.

StarSan is only effective when the pH of the solution is less than 3.5. At a pH above 3.5, the solution turns cloudy and loses its bactericidal properties. This is also the reason it is a no-rinse sanitizer: When the fermenter or bottle has been drained and filled with wort or beer, the higher pH of the wort and beer neutralizes the sanitizing capability, so that the yeast are unaffected. As a matter of fact, even though there can be a huge amount of foam in vessels like carboys after draining, it will have no effect on fermentation or flavor. I have proven this to myself by intentionally fermenting in a carboy that had been full of foam, and the fermentation, flavor, and head retention of the beer were fine.

One last note on this product: Because it is listed as a sanitizer and bactericide by the FDA and EPA, the container must list disposal warnings that are suitable for pesticides. Do not be alarmed; it is less hazardous to your skin than bleach.

Heat

Heat is one of the few means by which the homebrewer can actually sterilize an item. Why would you need to sterilize an item? Homebrewers who grow and maintain their own yeast cultures want to sterilize their growth media to assure against contamination. When a microorganism is heated at a high-enough temperature for a long-enough time, it is killed. Both dry heat (oven) and steam (autoclave, pressure cooker, or dishwasher) can be used for sterilizing.

Oven. Dry heat is less effective than steam for sanitizing and sterilizing, but many brewers use it. The best place to do dry heat sterilization is in your oven. To sterilize an item, refer to Table 2 for the temperatures and times required.

TABLE 2 Dry Heat Sterilization	
Temperature	**Duration**
338° F (170° C)	60 minutes
320° F (160° C)	120 minutes
302° F (150° C)	150 minutes
284° F (140° C)	180 minutes
250° F (121° C)	12 hours

The times indicated begin when the item has reached the indicated temperature. Although the durations seem long, remember this process kills all microorganisms, not just most as in sanitizing. To be sterilized, items need to be heat proof at the given temperatures. Glass and metal items are prime candidates for heat sterilization.

Some homebrewers bake their bottles using this method and thus always have a supply of clean, sterile bottles. The opening of the bottle can be covered with a piece of aluminum foil prior to heating to prevent contamination after cooling and during storage. They will remain sterile indefinitely if kept wrapped.

One note of caution: bottles made of soda lime glass are much more susceptible to thermal shock and breakage than those made of borosilicate glass and should be heated and cooled slowly (e.g., 5° F per minute). Put the bottles in the oven when the oven is cold. You can assume all beer bottles are made of soda lime glass and that any glassware that says Pyrex or Kimax is made of borosilicate.

Autoclaves, pressure cookers, and dishwashers. Typically when we talk about using steam, we are referring to the use of an autoclave or pressure cooker. These devices use steam under pressure to sterilize items. Because steam conducts heat more efficiently, the cycle time for such devices is much shorter than when using dry heat. The typical amount of time it takes to sterilize a piece of equipment in an autoclave or pressure cooker is 20 minutes at 257° F (125° C) at 20 pounds per square inch (psi).

Dishwashers can be used to sanitize, as opposed to sterilize, most of your brewing equipment; you just need to be careful that you don't warp any plastic items. The steam from the drying cycle will effectively sanitize all surfaces. Bottles and other equipment with narrow openings should be pre cleaned. Run the equipment through the full wash cycle without using any detergent or rinse agent; we want to avoid having any residue drying onto the items. Dishwasher rinse agents will destroy the head retention on your glassware. If you pour a beer with carbonation and no head, this might be the cause.

Cleaning and Sanitizing Final Thoughts

Clean all equipment as soon after use as possible. This means rinsing out the fermenter, tubing, etc., as soon as they are used. It is very easy to get distracted and come back to find that the syrup or yeast has dried hard as a rock, and the equipment is stained. If you are pressed for time, keep a large container of water handy, and just toss things in to soak until you can clean them later.

You can use different methods of cleaning and sanitizing for different types of equipment. You will need to decide which methods work best for you in your brewery. Good preparation will make each of the brewing processes easier and more successful.

TABLE 3
Cleaning Products Summary Table

Cleaners	Amount	Comments
Detergents	(squirt)	It is important to use unscented detergents that won't leave any perfume odors behind. Be sure to rinse well.
PBW, Straight-A	1/4 c. per 5 gal. (<1 tbsp./gal.)	Best all-purpose cleaners for grunge on all brewing equipment. Most effective in warm water.
Sodium percarbonates	1 tbsp./gal.	Effective cleaner for grungy brewing deposits. Will not harm metals.
Bleach	1–4 tbsp./gal.	Good cleaner for grungy brewing deposits. Do not allow bleach to contact metals for more than an hour. Corrosion may occur.
Dishwasher	Normal amount of automatic dish washer detergent	Recommended for utensils and glassware. Do not use scented detergents or those with rinse agents.
Oven cleaner (Spray-on)	Follow product instructions	Useful for dissolving burned-on sugar from a brewpot.
White distilled vinegar	Full strength as necessary	Most effective when hot. Useful for cleaning copper wort chillers.
Vinegar and hydrogen peroxide	2:1 volume ratio of vinegar to peroxide	Use for removing surface lead and cleaning tarnished brass.
Oxalic acid-based cleansers	As needed with scrubby	Sold as stainless steel and copper cookware cleanser. Use for removing stains and oxides.

TABLE 4
Sanitizers Summary Table

Sanitizer	Amount	Comments
StarSan, Final Step	2 tbsp. per 5 gal.	Can be used via immersion or spraying. Will sanitize clean surfaces in 30 seconds. Allow to drain before use; does not need to be rinsed.
Iodophor	12.5-25 ppm 1 tbsp. per 5 gal. = 12.5 ppm	Iodophor will sanitize in 10 minutes at 12.5 ppm and does not need to be rinsed. Allow to drain before use.
Bleach	1 tbsp. per gal.	Bleach will sanitize equipment in 20 minutes. It should be rinsed to prevent chlorophenol flavors.
Dishwasher	Full wash and heat dry cycle without detergent	Bottles must be clean before being put in dishwasher for sanitizing. Place upside down on rack.
Oven	340° F (170° C) for 1 hour	Renders bottles sterile, not just sanitized. Allow bottles to heat and cool slowly to prevent thermal shock and cracking.

Note: 1 tablespoon per gallon equals 4 milliliters per liter.

Recordkeeping

Always keep good notes on what ingredients, amounts and times were used in the brewing process. There are several brewing spreadsheets and software programs available over the Internet that can be a big help; or if you want to keep things simple, paper forms work just fine. A brewer needs to be able to repeat good batches and learn from poor ones. If you have a bad batch and want to ask another brewer for their opinion, they are going to want to know all the brewing details: ingredients and amounts, how long you boiled, how you cooled, the type of yeast, how long it fermented, what the fermentation looked like, what the temperature was, etc. There are so many possible causes for "it tastes funny" that you really need to keep track of everything that you did so you can figure where it might have gone wrong and fix it the next time. Chapter 22—Is My Beer Ruined? will help you identify possible causes for most of the common problems.

Create a recipe form that will help you be consistent. See the example on the next page.

Example Recipe Form

Recipe Name: Cascade Ale

Recipe Volume: 5 gal.

Yeast: Safale US-56 Ale Yeast (rehydrated)

Malts:	**Amount**	**Type**
1. Muntons amber malt extract	2 lbs.	dry
2. Briess golden light malt extract	4 lbs.	liquid
Calculated Original Gravity	1.045	

Hops:	**Amount**	**Time**	**% Alpha Acid**
1. Perle	1.5 oz.	60 min.	6.4%
2. Cascade	0.5 oz.	30 min.	5%
3. Willamette	0.5 oz.	30 min.	4%
4. Cascade	0.5 oz.	15 min.	5%
Calculated IBUs	40		

Procedure

Boiled 3 gallons of water, turned off heat and stirred in extract.
Returned to boiling. Added first hop addition. Boiled 30 minutes and added Cascade and Willamette hops. Boiled another 15 minutes and added final addition of Cascade. Turned off heat and chilled the pot in an ice water bath to 70° F. Added the 2.5 gallons of wort to 2.5 gallons of water in the fermenter. Aerated by pouring back and forth five times. Pitched yeast.

Fermentation

Fermenter is sitting at 70° F and started bubbling within 12 hours.
Bubbled furiously for 36 hours, then slowed. After 4 days, bubbles had stopped completely. It remained in the fermenter for two weeks total. Racked to bottling bucket and primed with 3/4 cup of corn sugar (boiled). Bottles were allowed to condition for 2 weeks.

Results

Beer is Good! Strong hop taste and aroma. Perhaps a little too bitter. Tone down the bittering hops next time or add more amber malt extract to better balance the beer.

MALT EXTRACT, BEER KITS, AND BREWING SUGARS

3

What Is Malt Extract?

Malt extract is the concentrated and/or dried sugars extracted from malted barley. Most of the malt extract produced in the world is used in various food products: everything from malted milk, to breakfast cereals, to baking additives, to pet foods. There are two main grades of barley: malting grade and feed grade. There are also several subclasses within these grades. The barley that is used to make food extracts is a lower grade of malting barley, such as C and D grades and distiller's grade. These lower-grade malting barleys are typically smaller kernels with higher protein levels, less convertible starch, and a higher proportion of husk material by weight. The barley that is used for brewing beer is universally the highest grade, and to brew the best possible beer, you need to be sure you are using extract made from brewing-grade barley.

The malting process consists of soaking and draining the barley to initiate the germination of the plant from the seed. When the seed germinates, it activates enzymes that start converting its starch reserves and proteins into sugars and amino acids that the growing plant can use. The purpose of malting is to release these enzymes and starch reserves for use by the brewer. Once the seeds start to sprout, the grain is dried in a kiln to stop the enzymes until the brewer is ready to use the grain, which is generically referred to as malt. There are many specific types of malt that yield a wide range of flavors and aromas and are used to make different styles of beer. These include lager malts, pale malts, Vienna malts, Munich malts, toasted, roasted, and chocolate malts.

Figure 28 Brewhouse for production of malt extract *(Photo courtesy of Briess Malt & Ingredients Company)*

Malt extract starts out in the brewhouse just the same as if you were brewing an all-grain beer. The brewer crushes the malted barley and soaks it in hot water to reactivate and accelerate the enzyme activity, converting the barley's starch reserves into the fermentable sugar solution called *wort*. To make beer, the wort is boiled with hops and fermented with yeast. To make malt extract, the wort is transferred to evaporators after boiling instead of to a fermenter. Malt extract is simply concentrated wort. The malt extract may consist of a single malt or a combination of different types, depending on which style of beer is being made.

Brewers boil the wort to accomplish two things: to coagulate the hot break proteins that otherwise contribute to haze and long-term flavor stability problems, and to isomerize the hop alpha acids for bitterness. Manufacturers of malt extract for brewing do the same steps for the same reasons, although a lot of malt extract is manufactured unhopped. Those extracts are only boiled long enough to coagulate the proteins. The wort is then run into vacuum chambers for dehydration to make a shelf-stable product, at 80% solids, without the use of preservatives. By boiling off the water under a partial vacuum, the wort sugars are not caramelized by the full heat of boiling, and the original flavor and color of the wort is preserved. To make a hopped extract, hops can be added to the initial boil, or hop iso-alpha acid extracts can be added to the extract later. Malt extract takes a lot of the work out of homebrewing.

Malt extract is sold in both liquid (syrup) and powdered forms. The syrups are approximately 20% water, so 4 pounds of dry malt extract (DME) is roughly equal to 5 pounds of liquid malt extract (LME). Dry malt extract is produced by heating and spraying the liquid extract from an atomizer in a tall heated chamber. The small droplets dry and cool rapidly as they settle to the floor. DME is identical to LME except for the additional dehydration to about 2% moisture. DME is typically not hopped.

What Is Malt Sugar?

Brewing beer is all about working with sugars—glucose, fructose, sucrose, maltose, and all the rest. If you are like me, you want someone to explain it without getting too technical. Bear with me, as I need to lay some groundwork and describe the different building blocks. It won't take long, and once you understand what everything's made of, it becomes a lot easier to understand the answers. Sugars (technical name: saccharides) are made up of groups of one to nine carbon atoms. The common sugars like glucose and sucrose are made of groups of six carbon atoms and are therefore called "hexoses." A monosaccharide is a single sugar group, a disaccharide is composed of two sugar groups, a trisaccharide is three, etc. The most common type of sugar is the monosaccharide glucose (a.k.a. dextrose, blood sugar, corn sugar). Other monosaccharides relevant to brewing are fructose and galactose. Compositionally, these are all the same, but they are isomers of each other, i.e., their chemical structure/arrangement gives them different properties. For instance, fructose (also known as fruit sugar) is an isomer of glucose but tastes sweeter than glucose.

Table 5 lists the approximate levels of the different sugars found in a typical beer wort. The main constituent is maltose, followed by assorted dextrins, maltotriose, glucose, sucrose, and fructose. Maltose is a glucose disaccharide, which means that it is made up of two glucose molecules. Maltotriose is a trisaccharide consisting of three glucose molecules. Sucrose (commonly known as table sugar) is a disaccharide that is made of one glucose and one fructose, and occurs naturally in plants. Sources include sugar cane, beets, maple sap, and nectar. Dextrins (a.k.a. oligosaccharides) are larger sugars consisting of more than three monosaccharide groups. In general, monosaccharides are sweeter tasting than (poly) saccharides. In descending order of sweetness: fructose is

TABLE 5 Typical Sugar Profile Extracted From Malted Barley	
Sugar	Typical Percentage in Wort
Maltose	45%
Maltotriose	14%
Glucose	8%
Sucrose	6%
Fructose	2%
Unfermentable dextrins	25%

sweeter than sucrose, which is sweeter than glucose, which is sweeter than maltose, which is sweeter than maltotriose. (Not that it matters in fermentation; I just thought you would like to know.) The different types of common sugars and their use in brewing will be discussed in more detail in Section IV.

Fermentation of Sugars

Yeast are apparently very methodical creatures. Even though sucrose is usually a small percentage of the wort, studies have shown that most brewing yeast strains seem to work on it first, breaking it down into its glucose and fructose components. Once the sucrose has been broken down, the yeast cells consume the glucose first, followed by fructose, maltose, and finally maltotriose. Some yeast strains behave differently, eating maltose in parallel with the monosaccharides, but that would seem to be the exception. In addition, most strains are glucophilic, utilizing most of the glucose in the wort before consuming the other monosaccharides, and fermenting most of those before fermenting maltose, and subsequently, maltotriose. In fact, it is known that high levels of glucose and fructose in a wort (e.g., more than 15 to 20%) will inhibit the fermentation of maltose. This repressive behavior is probably a common cause of stuck fermentations in worts containing a lot of refined sugars—the yeast have fermented the monosaccharides and then quit, leaving more than half of the total sugars unfermented.

Yeast metabolize the different wort sugars in different ways. To consume the disaccharide sucrose, the yeast utilizes an enzyme called invertase, which works outside the cell to separate the molecule into its components—glucose and fructose. The glucose and fructose are then transported through the cell wall and metabolized inside the cell. Conversely, maltose and maltotriose are transported into the cell first and then are broken down into glucoses by the enzyme maltase. Even though the enzyme for both sugars is the same, maltose is typically consumed first, indicating that the cell wall transport mechanism for the two sugars is different. Maybe maltotriose is too big to get through the maltose door!

The take-home message is that all fermentable sugars are broken down into monosaccharides like glucose before being utilized by the yeast, and that yeast evidently prefer to eat their sugars one course at a time. This has big implications for choosing our malt extract and formulating recipes.

Shopping for Extracts

The freshness of the extract is important, particularly for the syrup. Liquid malt extract typically has a shelf life of about two years, depending on storage conditions, during which time its color will approximately double. The Maillard reactions that are responsible for the color change can generate off-flavors like licorice, molasses, and ballpoint pen aroma. Beer brewed with old extract syrup can also have a blunt, stale, or soapy flavor to it. These flavors are caused by the oxidation of the fatty acid compounds in the malt. These off-flavors are part of a group that is collectively known as extract twang. Homebrewers will often complain that they can't make good beer with extract, but it's just a matter of freshness. The bottom line is to use fresh extract by checking the "Use By" dates on the cans or by buying from a shop that has a high stock turnover. Dry malt extract has a better shelf life than liquid, because the extra dehydration slows the chemical reactions. If you can't get fresh liquid extract, use dry.

Another quality of an extract that can have a particularly strong effect on the quality of the finished beer is Free Amino Nitrogen (FAN). FAN is a measure of the amount of amino acid nitrogen that is available to the yeast for nutrition during fermentation. Without sufficient FAN, the yeast are less efficient and produce more fermentation by-products, which result in off-flavors in the beer. This is why it is important not to add sugar to the wort, which most canned kit instructions say to do; use more malt extract instead. Corn, rice, and cane sugar don't contain FAN. Adding large percentages of these adjuncts to the wort dilutes the FAN and deprives the yeast of the nutrients they need to grow and function. Yeast nutrient containing FAN can be added to the wort if necessary. See Chapter 6 for more information.

Malt extract is available as either hopped or unhopped. Hopped extracts are boiled with hops prior to dehydration and usually contain a mild to moderate level of bitterness. Alexander's, Briess, Coopers, Edme, Ireks, John Bull, Mountmellick, Muntons, Northwestern, and Weyermann are all high-quality brands.

Malt extract is commonly available in pale, amber, and dark varieties, and can be mixed depending on the style of beer desired. Wheat malt extract is also available, and new extracts tailored to specific beer styles are arriving all the time. The quality of extracts and beer kits has improved greatly in the last five years. All-extract brewers will be quite satisfied brewing entirely from beer kits as long as they ignore the instructions on the can and follow the guidelines in this book. With the variety of extract now available, there are few beer styles that cannot be brewed using extract alone. For more information on using extract to make different styles of beer, see Chapters 13 and 20.

Choosing a Good Kit

What is a beer kit? A typical beer kit consists of a yeast packet and one can of hopped malt extract that is designed to be diluted, pasteurized, and fermented into a reasonable example of a particular style of beer. Often the malt extract in the single can kits is brewed to a relatively low fermentability and is extended with highly fermentable adjuncts like corn or cane sugar. This type of kit is often referred to as "kit and kilo" brewing, because the instructions usually say to add 1 kilogram (about 2.2 pounds) of sugar to the extract before fermenting. These kits make an acceptable beer but usually don't taste just like the commercial example the homebrewer had hoped to make. And let's be frank about this: Commercial beers are not brewed from a dextrinous concentrate and highly refined sugars in small batches at the mercy of the household environment. So it's no wonder that these homebrew kits don't taste exactly the same. If you have purchased one of these kits, I recommend that you use pale malt extract in place of the sugar, and use fresh yeast. You will be much happier with the results.

But there are also better kits on the market that will taste more like the commercial beer that you are trying to copy. These all-malt kits consist of two cans of malt extract and are not meant to

HOW TO BREW

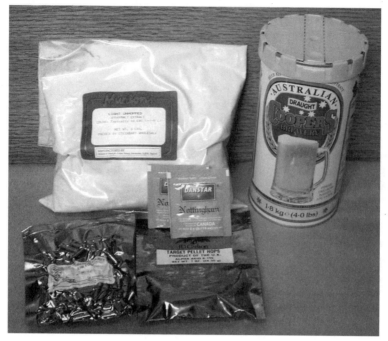

Figure 30 Building your own kit for Cincinnati Pale Ale

be extended with sugar. These all-malt kits will produce a very good beer that tastes more like what you would expect. There are also no-boil liquid wort kits that are simply diluted in the fermenter, and these make very good beer, too. There has been a revolution in home beermaking over the past decade, and beer kit manufacturers have responded by creating more interesting kits that can produce outstanding beers. I have talked with most of the top manufacturers in the past couple of years, and every time I was impressed by their passion for beer and their pride in their products.

In addition to the name-brand beer kits available, many of the better homebrew shops package their own kits and provide more comprehensive instructions. Kits assembled by homebrewers for homebrewers are probably the best way to get started. If your supply shop does not offer this type of kit, you can assemble your own. Cincinnati Pale Ale (see sidebar) is a basic American pale ale and quite tasty. You will be amazed at the full body and rich taste compared to most commercial beers. More recipes and style guidelines are given in Chapter 20. You can use any of those recipes for your first batch by choosing the all-extract option, or you can read Section II and try that easy additional step for a bit more liveliness in your first batch.

**RECIPE
Cincinnati Pale Ale**

OG = 1.045 (11.2 °P), 30 IBUs

Ingredients for a 5-gallon (19-liter) batch

- 3.3 lbs. (1.5kg) pale malt extract syrup, unhopped

- 2.5 lbs. (1.1kg) amber dry malt extract

- 6 AAUs of bittering hops (any variety). For example, 0.5 oz. (14g) of 12% AA Nugget, or 0.75 oz. (21g) of 8% AA Northern Brewer

- 5 AAUs of finishing hops (Cascade or other). For example, 1 oz. (28g) of 5% Cascade or 1.25 oz. (36g) of 4% Liberty

- 2 new packets of dry ale yeast

How Much Extract to Use

A rule of thumb is 1 pound of liquid extract per gallon of water for a light-bodied beer. One and a half pounds per gallon produces a richer, full-bodied beer. A pound of LME typically yields a gravity of 1.034 to 1.038, as measured by a hydrometer, when dissolved in water to form 1 gallon. DME yields about 1.040 to 1.043. These yield values are referred to as points per pound per gallon. If someone tells you that a certain extract or malt's yield is 36 points, it means that when 1 pound is dissolved in water to form 1 gallon, the gravity is 1.036. If that 1 pound is dissolved into 3 gallons, its gravity would be 36/3 = 12 or 1.012. The gravity is how the strength of a beer is described. Most commercial beers have an original gravity (OG) of 1.035 to 1.050.

Gravity vs. Fermentability

Different extracts have different degrees of fermentability. In general, the darker the extract, the more complex sugars it will contain, and the less fermentable it will be. Amber extract will typically have a higher finishing gravity than pale extract, and dark will be higher than amber. This is not always the case, though. By manipulating the mash conditions, the relative percentages of sugars that are extracted from the mash can be varied. A brewer can produce a wort that is almost entirely made up of highly fermentable sugars like maltose or one that has a higher percentage of unfermentable complex carbohydrates. Because these complex sugars are not very fermentable, the beer will have a higher finishing gravity. While most of the perception of a beer's body is due to medium-length proteins, the unfermentable complex sugars will lend some of the same feel.

For example, Laaglander's DME from the Netherlands is a high-quality extract that often has a finishing gravity (FG) as high as 1.020 from a common 1.040 OG. The heavier body is nice to have in a stout, for example; all-grain brewers would

> **CALCULATION**
> **Gravity (OG) Calculations**
>
> Total gravity points
> = an extract's yield x mass
> = specific gravity x total volume.
>
> If you want to brew 5 gallons of 1.040 gravity beer, this would call for:
> 5 lbs. of DME having 40 pts./lb./gal., or
> 5.5 lbs. of LME having 36 pts./lb./gal.
>
> 40 pts./gal. x 5 gal. = 200 pts. total
> 200 pts. = 36 pts./lb. x (?) lbs.
> => (?) lbs. = 200 / 36 = 5.55 lbs.
>
> 5.55 lbs. of 36 pts./lb./gal. LME are needed to make the same 5 gallons of beer.
>
> Note: The same concept can be used with the metric units of liter degrees per kilogram, i.e., l°/kg or pts./kg/L. The conversion factor between ppg and l°/kg is 8.3454 x ppg = l°/kg.

add a dextrin malt (e.g., Briess CaraPils) to their mash to produce the same effect. Brewers using extract have the alternative of adding maltodextrin powder, which is a concentrated form. Maltodextrin powder has no taste, i.e., it's not sweet, and is slow to dissolve. It contributes about 40 points per pound per gallon.

Summary

To summarize, malt extract is not some mysterious substance but simply a concentrated wort, ready for brewing. You don't need to agonize over which kit to buy, comparing labels and product claims; you can plan your own beer and buy the type of extract that you want to use to make it. Malt extract makes brewing easier by taking the work out of producing the wort. This lets a new brewer focus on the fermentation processes.

The next step in improving your brews and your control over recipes will be to get some of your flavor and color from specialty grains instead of just relying on whatever is in the malt extract. You will probably want to try it for your second or third batch, but it is certainly not difficult and could be done for a first beer. In Section II, we will examine this middle ground, which offers the benefits of grain brewing without an investment in a lot of new equipment.

Eventually, it will be useful to learn how to extract the sugars from the malted grain yourself. This process, called mashing, allows the brewer more control in producing the wort and tailoring the fermentability. This type of homebrewing is referred to as all-grain brewing, because the wort is produced from the grain without using any malt extract, and it is discussed in Section III.

WATER FOR EXTRACT BREWING

The Taste of Water

Water is very important to beer. After all, beer is mostly water. Some waters are famous for brewing: the soft water of Pilsen, the hard water of Burton, Midlands, and pure Rocky Mountain spring water. Each of these waters contributed to the production of a unique tasting beer. But what about your water? Can it make a good beer? When using malt extract, the answer is almost always "yes." If you are brewing with grain, the answer can vary from "sometimes" to "absolutely." The reason for this difference between the brewing methods is that the minerals in the water can affect the starch conversion of the mash, but once the sugars have been produced,
the effect of water chemistry on the flavor of the beer is greatly reduced. When brewing with malt extract, if the water tastes good to begin with, the beer should taste good.

There are three main aspects of water for extract brewing to be considered: pretreatment for off-odors and flavors, mineral additions to enhance the flavor of the beer, and necessary mineral levels for good fermentation.

Home Water Treatment

If your water tastes good, your extract-brewed beer should taste good. If your water does not taste good, then you probably need to pre-treat it before brewing. There are a couple of methods that can be used to improve the quality of your tap water for brewing.

Water for Extract Brewing

Boiling. If the water smells like a swimming pool, some odors (like chlorine) can be removed by boiling. Other odors, like chloramine, cannot.

Campden tablets. Chloramine is used instead of chlorine by many (most?) city water supplies to kill bacteria, because it is more stable than chlorine. The trouble is, "more stable" means that it is harder to get rid of than chlorine. Chloramine cannot be easily removed by boiling and will give a medicinal taste to beer. However, chloramine can be effectively removed by adding one Campden tablet (potassium metabisulfite). Campden tablets are used in winemaking and should be available at your brewshop. One tablet will treat 20 gallons, although using one tablet for only 5 gallons won't hurt anything. Crush it up and stir to help it dissolve. Both chlorine and chloramine are reduced to insignificant levels of sulfate and chloride ions (<10 ppm) within a couple of minutes at room temperature.

Activated charcoal filtration. Charcoal filters are a good way to remove most odors and bad tastes due to dissolved gases and organic substances like nitrates. These filters are relatively inexpensive and can be attached in-line to the faucet or spigot. Charcoal filtration alone will not affect dissolved minerals like iron, calcium, magnesium, copper, or bicarbonate, but some filters (e.g., Brita) contain ion exchange resins that will remove most of these ions. Pouring all of your brewing water through a Brita pitcher could be a bit tedious, though. Check the manufacturer's website for complete information on what a particular product will or won't filter. Carbon filtration should remove 80 to 90% of chlorine and chloramine, but a single Campden tablet added to the water before the boil is much more effective.

Water softeners. Water softening systems can also be used to remove bad-tasting minerals like iron, copper, and manganese, as well as the scale-causing minerals calcium and magnesium. Salt-based water softeners use ion exchange to replace these heavier metals with sodium. Softened water works fine for extract

---

How to Read a Water Report

Your local municipal water report provides the information you need as a brewer to take your beer to the next level. Water reports are mainly concerned with levels of chemical contaminants, but the Secondary or Aesthetic Standards will contain the mineral information that you need. There are six primary ions that can affect your fermentation and flavor.

Ion	Target Range	Purpose
Calcium	50-150 ppm	Calcium is a water hardness ion and is vital to many of the biochemical reactions in fermentation. In extract brewing, it should be adequately supplied by the malt extract.
Magnesium	10-30 ppm	Similar to calcium. Also a vital yeast nutrient but should be adequately supplied by the malt extract. High levels taste sour/bitter
Bicarbonate or (Total Alkalinity as CaCO₃)	0-250 ppm (0-200 ppm)	Bicarbonate is the principal alkalinity ion at normal drinking water pH of 7-8.5. Alkalinity as CaCO₃ = 50/61 of the bicarbonate concentration. Areas of high alkalinity are more likely to be affected by astringent tannins.
Sodium	0-150 ppm	Can be very high due to water softeners. Acts like salt to accentuate the malt flavor at moderate levels
Chloride	0-250 ppm	Acts like salt to accentuate the malt flavor at moderate levels. Excessive concentrations can lead to chlorophenol off-flavors.
Sulfate	50-150 ppm	Sulfate accentuates hop bitterness, making it seem drier and crisper. At high concentrations (>400) it is harsh and unpleasant.

Water reports and water chemistry adjustment are explained more fully in Chapter 15.

brewing but should not be used for all-grain brewing. The mashing process requires minimum levels of minerals like calcium and magnesium in the water that the softening process will remove.

Other water. Bottled drinking water is available from most grocery stores and supermarkets and typically has low levels of alkalinity and other minerals. Bottled water works very well for extract brewing. Reverse osmosis and distilled water can be added to your tap water to reduce the mineral levels as necessary. Generally, adding RO or distilled water will reduce the minerals at the same ratio as the dilution. You can also use distilled water alone when you are brewing with malt extract, because the extract will provide all the necessary minerals for yeast health.

Water Chemistry Adjustment for Extract Brewing

Burtonizing. A lot of people try to use brewing salts in the brewpot to imitate the water of a famous brewing region, like the Burton region of Britain. While some salts can be added to extract-based brews to improve the flavor profile, salts are more properly used to adjust the pH of the mash for all-grain brewing. Most tap water supplies are fine for brewing with extract and don't need adjustment. So, if you are brewing from an extract recipe that calls for the addition of gypsum or Burton salts, do not add it. The proper amount of a salt to add to your water depends on the mineral amounts already present, and the brewer who published the recipe probably had entirely different water than you do. You may end up ruining the taste of the beer by adding too much. Just leave it out; you probably won't miss it.

Decarbonation. Several areas of the United States are cursed with highly alkaline water. Normally this would only be a concern for all-grain brewers, because alkalinity greatly affects the mash chemistry and beer flavor, but it can also affect the flavor of extract beers. If your water is high in alkalinity, i.e., bicarbonate ion concentrate higher than 250 ppm or Total Alkalinity as $CaCO_3$ higher than 200 ppm, pale highly hopped beers may have a harsh astringent bitterness due to extraction of hop polyphenols from the cones.

To remove some of the alkalinity from the water:

1. Add 1 teaspoon (5 milliliters) of calcium carbonate to 3 to 5 gallons (11.4 to 19 liters) of brewing water, and stir. This will act as precipitation nucleation and growth sites, i.e., seed crystals.

2. If the total alkalinity is greater than the total hardness (see water report), you will need to add more calcium in the form of calcium sulfate (gypsum) or calcium chloride to equalize the two. See Chapter 15 for a complete discussion of how to determine this addition.

3. Boil for 10 minutes and allow to cool.

4. Pour the decarbonated water off the chalk sediment into another pot.

For a more complete discussion and other methods to reduce alkalinity, please read Chapter 15. Here are the main points to remember about water for extract brewing:

- You can't make good beer with bad-tasting water.
- Bad-tasting water can be treated by a variety of methods.
- Do not add brewing salts to your recipe until you know how much you have to start with from your water report.
- Decarbonation of your water for brewing pale, highly hopped beers may be necessary.

Water chemistry is even more important for all-grain brewing. The mineral profile of the water has a significant effect on the performance of the mash. Water reports, brewing salts, and their effects are discussed more fully in Chapter 15. I suggest you read that chapter if you want to get serious with your brewing water.

HOPS

5

What Are They?

Hops are the conelike strobiles of a climbing vine that is native to the temperate regions of North America, Europe, and Asia. The species has separate male and female plants. Only the female vines (known as bines) produce the cones. The vines will climb 20 feet or more up any available support and are commonly trained onto strings or wires when grown commercially. The leaves resemble grape leaves, and the cones vaguely resemble pinecones in shape but are light green, thin, and papery. At the base of the bracts are the yellow lupulin glands that contain

the essential oils and resins that are so prized by brewers for their bittering and aroma qualities.

Hops have been cultivated for use in brewing for more than 1,000 years. The earliest known cultivation was in Central Europe, and by the early 1500s, cultivation had spread to Western Europe and Great Britain. At the turn of the century, about one dozen varieties of hop were being used for brewing; today, there are more than one hundred. The focus of breeding programs has been to increase the alpha acid bittering compounds while improving yield and disease resistance.

What Do They Do?

Hops are a natural preservative, and part of the early use of hops in beer was to help preserve it. This is how one particular style of beer, India pale ale, was developed. At the turn of the 18th cen-

tury, British brewers began shipping strong ale with lots of hops added to the barrels to preserve it during the several-month voyage to India. By journey's end, the beer had acquired a depth of hop aroma and flavor—perfect for quenching the thirst of British personnel in the tropics.

Figure 33 Lupulin glands at the base of the bracts

Beer as we know it today wouldn't be beer without hops. Hops provide the balance and are the signature in many styles. The bitterness contributed by hops balances the sweetness of the malt sugars and provides a refreshing finish.

The main bittering agents are the alpha acid humulone resins, which are insoluble in water and not particularly bitter until isomerized by boiling. The longer the boil, the greater the percentage of isomerization and the more bitter the beer gets. One humulone constituent, called cohumulone, is easier to isomerize than the others, but it is also common-ly perceived to give a rougher bitterness to the beer. Even though this position is debatable, selection of low cohumulone character was encouraged as new varieties were developed. Many of today's high-alpha varieties, like Magnum and Horizon, have lower cohumulone than older, lower alpha varieties of the past, such as Galena and Cluster.

While most of the bitterness comes from isomerization of the alpha acid resins, the character-istic flavor and aroma compounds come from the essential oils, which are typically 1 to 2% of the dry weight of the cone. These are volatile and are lost to a large degree during the boil. The light aromatic oils (Myrcene, Linalol, Geraniol, Limonene, Terpineol, etc.) are responsible for the fresh hop aroma you smell when you open the bag, and what you can impart to your beer by dry-hop-ping. The heavier aromatic oils (e.g., Humulene, Caryophyllene, Farnesene) and their oxides/epox-ides are what you smell from the late hop additions to the boil, and it is these aromas as they man-ifest in the beer that are identified as "noble."

There are many varieties of hops, but they are usually divided into two general categories, bit-tering and aroma, although today there is a pretty clear-cut group of "dual-use" hops, which have both moderately high bitterness and good aromatic properties. Bittering hops are high in alpha acids, at about 10% by weight. Aroma hops are usually lower, around 5%, and contribute a more desirable aroma and flavor to the beer. Several hop varieties are in between and are used for both purposes. Bittering hops, sometimes called kettle hops, are added at the start of the boil and boiled for about an hour. Aroma hops are added toward the end of the boil and are typically boiled for 15 minutes or less. Aroma hops are also referred to as finishing hops. By adding different varieties of hops at different times during the boil, a more complex hop profile can be established that gives the beer a balance of hop bitterness, taste, and aroma. Descriptions of the five main types of hop addi-tions and their attributes follow.

For a good discussion of the essential hop oils, see Ray Daniels' *Designing Great Beers* (Boulder, Colo.: Brewers Publications, 1996).

First Wort Hopping

An old yet recently rediscovered process (at least among homebrewers), first wort hopping (FWH) consists of adding a large portion of the finishing hops to the boil kettle as the wort is received from the lauter tun. As the boil tun fills with wort (which may take a half-hour or longer), the hops steep in the hot wort and release their volatile oils and resins. The aromatic oils are normally insoluble and tend to evaporate to a large degree during the boil. By letting the hops steep in the wort prior to the boil, the oils have more time to oxidize to more soluble compounds, and a greater percentage are retained during the boil. A blind tasting among professional German brewers determined that the use of FWH resulted in a more refined hop aroma, a more uniform bitterness (i.e., no harsh tones), and a more harmonious beer overall compared to an identical beer produced without FWH.

Only low-alpha finishing hops should be used for FWH. The FWH addition should account for at least 30% of the total hops originally intended for finishing. The total bitterness of the beer is not increased substantially, even though the hops are in the boil longer, because they are low-alpha acid varieties. The popular consensus among homebrewers seems to be that the utilization of FWH equates to about a 20-minute boil.

Bittering

The primary use of hops is for bittering. Bittering hop additions are boiled for 45 to 90 minutes to isomerize the alpha acids, the most common interval being 1 hour. There is some improvement in the isomerization between 45 and 90 minutes (about 5%), but only a small improvement at longer times (less than 1%). The aromatic oils of the hops used in the bittering addition(s) tend to boil away, leaving little hop flavor and no aroma. Because of this, high-alpha varieties (which commonly have poor aroma characteristics) can be used to provide the bulk of the bitterness without hurting the taste of the beer. If you consider the cost of bittering a beer in terms of the amount of alpha acid per unit weight of hop used, it is more economical to use a half-ounce of a high-alpha hop rather than 1 or 2 ounces of a low-alpha hop. You can save your more expensive (or scarce) aroma hops for flavoring and finishing. See Table 7 (p. 58) for the percent utilization of the hops as a function of boiling time and boil gravity.

Flavoring

By adding the hops midway through the boil, a compromise between isomerization of the alpha acids and evaporation of the aromatics is achieved to yield moderate bitterness and characteristic flavors. These flavoring hop additions are added 20 to 40 minutes before the end of the boil, with the most common time being 30 minutes. Any hop variety may be used. Usually the lower alpha varieties are chosen, although some high-alpha varieties such as Northern Brewer and Challenger have pleasant flavors and are commonly used. Often small amounts (one-quarter to one-half ounce, 7 to 15 grams) of several varieties will be combined at this stage to create a more complex character.

Finishing

When hops are added during the final minutes of the boil, fewer of the aromatic oils are lost to evaporation, and more hop aroma is retained. One or more varieties of hop may be used, in amounts varying from ¼ to 4 ounces, depending on the character desired. A total of 1 to 2 ounces is typical. Finishing hops are typically added 15 minutes or less before the end of the boil, or are added "at knockout" (when the heat is turned off) and allowed to steep 10 minutes before the wort is cooled. In some setups, a "hopback" is used—the hot wort is run through a small chamber full of fresh hops before the wort enters a heat exchanger or chiller.

A word of caution when adding hops at knockout or using a hopback: Depending on several factors, e.g., amount, variety, freshness, etc., the beer may take on a grassy taste, probably due to tannins or other compounds that are usually neutralized by the boil. If short boil times are not yielding the desired hop aroma, or a grassy flavor is evident, then I would suggest using FWH or dry-hopping. High-quality, noble hop varieties are your best bet for fine hop aroma character.

Dry-Hopping

Hops can also be added to the fermenter for increased hop aroma in the final beer. This is called "dry-hopping" and is best done late in the fermentation cycle. If the hops are added to the fermenter while it is still actively bubbling, then a lot of the hop aroma will be carried away by the carbon dioxide. It is better to add the hops (usually about a half-ounce per 5 gallons) after bubbling has slowed and the beer is going through the conditioning phase prior to bottling. The benefit of adding hops at this stage is that the yeast are still active and can take up any oxygen that gets into the wort. On the other hand, the hop oils will absorb onto the yeast cells, and an appreciable fraction will be taken out of solution when the yeast settle out. The best way to utilize dry-hopping is to put the hops in a secondary fermenter or keg after the beer has been racked away from the trub and let it sit a couple of weeks before bottling, allowing the volatile oils to diffuse into the beer. The draw-back here is that the extended time allows for more hop polyphenols and tannins to leach into the wort, which can give the beer a dry aftertaste, like old tea. Many homebrewers put the hops in a nylon mesh bag—a "hop bag"—to facilitate removing the hops.

Many varieties of hop are appropriate for dry-hopping, and several varieties can be combined to give the beer a more complex character. While you may be tempted to use a large portion of noble hops in your beer, you need to consider that this will also add a lot of plant material to the beer, which can contribute to tannic/husky flavors. Even though this tannic quality will subside after a few weeks, a lot of craft- and microbrewers use higher alpha varieties, like Centennial, Columbus, and Horizon, because high-alphas often have higher oil content per pound, which means less vegetative matter in the tank. Choose your variety with care, because some are very citrusy, resiny, and/or assertive and are not appropriate for every beer style.

Don't worry about adding unboiled hops to the fermenter when you are dry-hopping. Infection and beer spoilage from the hops just doesn't happen.

Hop Forms—Pellets, Plug, and Whole

It's rare for any group of brewers to agree on the best form of hops. Each of the common forms has its own advantages and disadvantages. What form is best for you will depend on where in the brewing process the hops are being used and will probably change as your brewing methods change.

Whichever form of hops you choose to use, freshness is important. Fresh hops smell fresh, herbal, and spicy, like evergreen needles, and have a light green color like freshly mown hay. Old hops or hops that have been mishandled are often oxidized and smell like pungent cheese and may have turned brown. It is beneficial if hop suppliers pack hops in oxygen barrier bags and keep them cold to preserve the freshness and potency. Hops that have been stored warm and/or in non-barrier (thin) plastic bags can easily lose 50% of their bitterness potential in a few months. Most plastics are oxygen permeable, so when buying hops at a homebrew supply store, check to see if the hops are stored in a cooler or freezer and if they are stored in oxygen barrier containers. If you can smell the hops when you open the cooler door, then the hop aroma is leaking out through the packaging and they are not

TABLE 6
Hop Forms and Merits

Form	Advantages	Disadvantages
Whole	Easy to strain from wort, Best aroma, if fresh, Good for dry-hopping	They soak up wort, resulting in some wort loss after the boil. Bulk makes them more difficult to weigh
Plug	Retain freshness longer than whole form, Convenient half-ounce units, Plugs behave like whole hops in the wort	Can be difficult to break apart into smaller amounts. Soak up wort just like whole hops
Pellets	Easy to weigh, Small increase in utilization due to shredding, Best storability	Turns into hop sludge in bottom of kettle that is difficult to strain. Aroma content tends to be less than other forms due to amount of processing. Hard to contain when dry-hopping—creates floaters

well protected from oxygen. If the stock turnover in the brew shop is high, non-optimal storage conditions may not be a problem. Ask the shop owner, if you have any concerns.

Hop Types
Bittering Hop Varieties

Name:	**Brewers Gold**
Grown:	United Kingdom, United States
Profile:	Black currant, fruity, spicy aroma; sharp bittering hop
Usage:	Bittering for ales
AA range:	8-10%
Hop oil:	2.0-2.4ml/100g
Substitute:	Bullion

Name:	**Chinook**
Grown:	United States
Profile:	Heavy spicy/piney aroma, strong versatile bittering hop, cloying in large quantities
Usage:	Bittering
Examples:	Sierra Nevada Celebration Ale, Sierra Nevada Stout
AA range:	12-14%

Hop oil:	1.5-2.5ml/100g
Substitute:	Brewers Gold, Nugget, Target

Name:	**Galena**
Grown:	United States
Profile:	Strong, clean bittering hop, citrusy aroma
Usage:	General-purpose bittering
Example:	The most widely used commercial bittering hop in the United States
AA range:	12-14%
Hop oil:	0.9-1.2ml/100g
Substitute:	Cluster, Northern Brewer, Nugget

Name:	**Magnum**
Grown:	United States, Germany
Profile:	Clean bittering hop
Usage:	Good general-purpose bittering
AA range:	12-14%
Hop oil:	1.9-2.3ml/100g
Substitute:	Northern Brewer, Perle, Horizon

Name:	**Newport**
Grown:	United States
Profile:	Strong bittering hop
Usage:	New high-alpha bittering hop for ales
AA range:	13-17%
Hop oil:	1.6-3.6ml/100g
Substitute:	Galena, Nugget, Magnum

Name:	**Nugget**
Grown:	United States
Profile:	Heavy, spicy, herbal aroma; strong bittering hop
Usage:	Strong bittering, some aroma uses
Examples:	Sierra Nevada Porter and Bigfoot Barleywine Style Ale, Anderson Valley Belk's ESB
AA range:	12-14%
Hop oil:	1.7-2.3ml/100g
Substitute:	Galena, Magnum, Columbus

Name:	**Pacific Gem**
Grown:	New Zealand
Profile:	Pleasant blackberry aroma with woody undertones, good bittering hop
Usage:	Widely used bittering hop
AA range:	14-16%
Hop oil:	1.0-2.0ml/100g
Substitute:	

Name:	**Perle**
Grown:	Germany, United States
Profile:	Pleasant aroma; slightly spicy, almost minty bittering hop
Usage:	General-purpose bittering for all lagers
Example:	Sierra Nevada Summerfest
AA range:	7-9.5%
Hop oil:	0.7-1.3ml/100g
Substitute:	Northern Brewer, Cluster, Tettnang

Name:	**Pride of Ringwood**
Grown:	Australia
Profile:	Poor citric aroma, clean bittering hop
Usage:	General-purpose bittering
Examples:	Most Australian beers
AA range:	9-11%
Hop oil:	1.0-2.0ml/100g
Substitute:	Cluster

Name:	**Simcoe**
Grown:	United States
Profile:	Strong bittering hop, with unique fresh-cut-pine aroma
Usage:	Bittering and aroma in American pale ales
AA range:	12-14%
Hop oil:	2.0-2.5ml/100g
Substitute:	

Name:	**Warrior**
Grown:	United Kingdom
Profile:	Mild aroma; a clean bittering hop
Usage:	Growing acceptance as a good bittering hop for ales
AA range:	15-17%
Hop oil:	1.0-2.0ml/100g
Substitute:	Nugget, Columbus

Dual-Purpose Hop Varieties

Name:	**Amarillo**
Grown:	United States
Profile:	Floral and citrus, similar to Cascade
Usage:	Dual-purpose bittering and aroma hop for ales
Examples:	Old Dominion New River Ale, Rockies Mojo India Pale Ale, Hale's Pale American Ale
AA range:	8-11%
Hop oil:	1.5-2.0ml/100g
Substitute:	Cascade, Centennial

Name: **Centennial**
Grown: United States
Profile: Floral, citrus aroma, often referred to as Super Cascade
                because of the similarity; a clean bittering hop
Usage: General-purpose bittering, aroma, some dry-hopping
Examples: Sierra Nevada Celebration Ale, Sierra Nevada Bigfoot Ale
AA range: 9-11.5%
Hop oil: 1.5-2.3ml/100g
Substitute: Cascade, Columbus

Name: **Challenger**
Grown: United Kingdom
Profile: Medium, fine spicy aroma widely used for English bitters;
                a clean bittering hop
Usage: Excellent dual-purpose bittering, flavoring, and aroma hop
Examples: Full Sail India Pale Ale, Butterknowle Bitter
AA range: 6-8%
Hop oil: 1.0-1.7ml/100g
Substitute: Progress, Perle, Northern Brewer, Horizon

Name: **Cluster**
Grown: United States, Australia
Profile: Medium, spicy/floral aroma; sharp, clean bittering hop
Usage: General-purpose bittering (Aussie version has a
                better aroma and is used as a finishing hop)
Example: Winterhook Christmas Ale
AA range: 5.5-8.5%
Hop oil: 0.4-1.0ml/100g
Substitute: Galena, Northern Brewer

Name: **Columbus (a.k.a. Tomahawk)**
Grown: United States
Profile: Strong herbal flavor and aroma; solid, clean bittering hop
Usage: Good general-purpose bittering and aroma hop, often dry-hopped
Examples: Anderson Valley Hop Ottin' IPA, Full Sail Old Boardhead Barleywine Ale
AA range: 13-16%
Hop oil: 1.5-2.5ml/100g
Substitute: Nugget, Centennial, Chinook, Target

Name: **Horizon**
Grown: United States
Profile: Good floral, spicy aroma; excellent bittering dual-purpose hop
Usage: Bittering and finishing for all ales and lagers
Example: Lagunitas IPA

AA range:	10-14%
Hop oil:	1.5-2.0ml/100g
Substitute:	Northern Brewer, Northdown, Challenger

Name:	**Northern Brewer**
Grown:	United Kingdom, United States, Germany (called Hallertauer NB), and other areas (growing region affects profile greatly)
Profile:	Hallertauer NB has a fine, fragrant aroma; dual-purpose clean bittering hop
Usage:	Bittering and finishing for a wide variety of beers
Examples:	Old Peculier (bittering), Anchor Liberty (bittering), Anchor Steam (bittering, flavoring, aroma)
AA range:	7-10%
Hop oil:	1.5-2.0ml/100g
Substitute:	Perle, Horizon

Name:	**Northdown**
Grown:	United Kingdom
Profile:	Similar to Northern Brewer but with a better flavor and aroma than domestic NB; a clean bittering hop
Usage:	Dual-purpose bittering, flavor, and aroma for ales
Example:	Fuller's ESB
AA range:	7-8%
Hop oil:	1.5-2.5ml/100g
Substitute:	Northern Brewer, Target, Horizon

Name:	**Santiam**
Grown:	United States
Profile:	Floral, slightly spicy, noble characteristics
Usage:	Dual-purpose bittering and aroma hop for ales
Example:	(too new)
AA range:	5-7%
Hop oil:	1.0-1.5ml/100g
Substitute:	Tettnang, Spalt

Name:	**Sterling**
Grown:	United States
Profile:	Herbal, spicy, slight floral and citrus
Usage:	Dual-purpose bittering and aroma hop for ales and lagers
Example:	(too new)
AA range:	6-9%
Hop oil:	1.3-1.9ml/100g
Substitute:	Saaz, Mt. Hood

Name:	**Target**
Grown:	United Kingdom
Profile:	Strong herbal/floral aroma can be too strong for lagers; a clean bittering hop
Usage:	Widely used bittering and flavoring hop for strong ales
Example:	Fuller's Hock
AA range:	8-10%
Hop oil:	1.6-2.6ml/100g
Substitute:	Northdown, Fuggle, Willamette

Figure 35 Cascade hops on the vine

The next group includes common examples of aroma hops. Aroma hops can be used for bittering, also, and many homebrewers swear by this, claiming a finer, cleaner overall hop profile. I like to use Galena for bittering and save the good stuff for finishing. But making these decisions for yourself is what homebrewing is all about.

There is a category of aroma hops called "noble hops" that are considered to have the best aroma. These hops are principally four varieties grown in Central Europe: Hallertauer Mittelfrüh, Tettnanger Tettnang, Spalter Spalt, and Czech Saaz. Where a hop is grown has a definite impact on the variety's character, so only a Tettnanger/Spalter hop grown in Tettnang/Spalt is truly noble. There are other varieties that are considered to be noble-type, such as Perle, Crystal, Mt. Hood, Liberty, and Santiam. These hops were bred from the noble types and have very similar aroma profiles, having high humulone oil content and low cohumulone alpha acids. Noble hops are considered to be most appropriate for lager styles, because the beer and the hops grew up together. This is purely tradition, and as a homebrewer you can use whichever hop you like for whatever beer style you want. After all, we are doing this for the fun of it!

Aroma Hop Varieties

Name:	**British Columbia (BC) Goldings**
Grown:	Canada
Profile:	Earthy, rounded, mild aroma; spicy flavor
Usage:	Bittering, finishing, dry-hopping for British-style ales
	Used as a domestic substitute for East Kent Goldings
	Not quite as good as East Kent
AA range:	4.5-7%
Hop oil:	0.5-1.0ml/100g
Substitute:	East Kent Goldings

Name:	**Cascade**
Grown:	United States
Profile:	Strong spicy, floral, citrus (i.e., grapefruit) aroma
Usage:	The defining aroma for American-style pale ales
	Used for bittering, finishing, and especially dry-hopping
Examples:	Anchor Liberty Ale and Old Foghorn Barleywine Style Ale, Sierra Nevada Pale Ale
AA range:	4.5-8%
Hop oil:	0.8-1.5ml/100g
Substitute:	Centennial

Name:	**Crystal, a.k.a. CJF-Hallertau**
Grown:	United States
Profile:	Mild, pleasant, slightly spicy. One of three hops bred as domestic replacements for Hallertauer Mittelfrüh
Usage:	Aroma/finishing/flavoring
AA range:	2-5%
Hop oil:	1.0-1.5ml/100g
Substitute:	Hallertauer Mittelfrüh, Hallertauer Hersbrucker, Mt. Hood, Liberty

Name:	**East Kent Goldings (EKG)**
Grown:	United Kingdom
Profile:	Spicy/floral, earthy, rounded, mild aroma; spicy flavor
Usage:	Bittering, finishing, dry-hopping for British-style ales
Examples:	Young's Special London Ale, Samuel Smith's Pale Ale, Fuller's ESB
AA range:	4.5-7%
Hop oil:	0.5-1.0ml/100g
Substitute:	BC Goldings, Whitbread Goldings Variety

Name:	**Fuggles**
Grown:	United Kingdom, United States, and other areas
Profile:	Mild, soft, grassy, floral aroma
Usage:	Finishing/dry-hopping for all ales, dark lagers

Examples: Samuel Smith's Pale Ale, Old Peculier, Thomas Hardy's Ale
AA range: 3.5-5.5%
Hop oil: 0.7-1.5ml/100g
Substitute: East Kent Goldings, Willamette, Styrian Goldings

Name: **Glacier**
Grown: United States
Profile: Excellent earthy, spicy aroma
Usage: Aroma hop for ales
Example: (too new)
AA range: 5-6%
Hop oil: 0.5-1.5ml/100g
Substitute: Willamette, Fuggles, Styrian Goldings

Name: **Hallertauer Hersbrucker**
Grown: Germany
Profile: Pleasant, spicy/mild, noble, earthy aroma
Usage: Finishing for German-style lagers
Examples: Wheathook Wheaten Ale
AA range: 2.5-5%
Hop oil: 0.7-1.3ml/100g
Substitute: Hallertauer Mittelfrüh, Mt. Hood, Liberty, Crystal

Name: **Hallertauer Mittelfrüh**
Grown: Germany
Profile: Pleasant, spicy, noble, mild herbal aroma
Usage: Finishing for German-style lagers
Examples: Samuel Adams Boston Lager, Samuel Adams Boston Lightship
AA range: 3-5%
Hop oil: 0.7-1.3ml/100g
Substitute: Hallertauer Hersbrucker, Mt. Hood, Liberty, Crystal

Name: **Liberty**
Grown: United States
Profile: Fine, very mild aroma. One of three hops bred as domestic replacements for
                Hallertauer Mittelfrüh
Usage: Finishing for German-style lagers
Examples: Pete's Wicked Lager
AA range: 2.5-5%
Hop oil: 0.6-1.2ml/100g
Substitute: Hallertauer Mittelfrüh, Hallertauer Hersbrucker,
                Mt. Hood, Crystal

Name: **Mt. Hood**
Grown: United States
Profile: Mild, clean aroma. One of three hops bred as domestic replacements for Hallertauer Mittelfrüh
Usage: Finishing for German-style lagers
Example: Anderson Valley High Rollers Wheat Beer
AA range: 3.5-8%
Hop oil: 1.0-1.3ml/100g
Substitute: Hallertauer Mittelfrüh, Hallertauer Hersbrucker, Liberty, Tettnang

Name: **Progress**
Grown: United Kingdom
Profile: Assertive fruity aroma
Usage: Widely used for real cask ales
Examples: Hobson's Best Bitter, Mansfield Bitter
AA range: 5-6%
Hop oil: 0.6-1.2ml/100g
Substitute: Fuggles, Whitbread Goldings Variety

Name: **Saaz**
Grown: Czech Republic
Profile: Delicate, mild, floral aroma
Usage: Finishing for Bohemian-style lagers
Example: Pilsner Urquell
AA range: 2-5%
Hop oil: 0.5-1.0ml/100g
Substitute: Tettnang, Spalt, Sterling

Name: **Spalt**
Grown: Germany/United States
Profile: Mild, pleasant, slightly spicy
Usage: Aroma/finishing/flavoring, some bittering
AA range: 3-6%
Hop oil: 0.5-1.1ml/100g
Substitute: Saaz, Tettnang, Santiam

Name: **Styrian Goldings**
Grown: Yugoslavia (seedless Fuggles grown in Yugoslavia), also grown in United States
Profile: Similar to Fuggles
Usage: Bittering/finishing/dry-hopping for a wide variety of beers
Examples: Ind Coope Burton Ale, Timothy Taylor's Landlord
AA range: 4.5-7%
Hop oil: 0.5-1.0ml/100g
Substitute: Fuggles, Willamette

Name:	Tettnang
Grown:	Germany
Profile:	Fine, spicy aroma
Usage:	Finishing for German-style beers
Examples:	Gulpener Pilsener, Samuel Adams Oktoberfest, Anderson Valley Belk's ESB, Redhook ESB
AA range:	3-6%
Hop oil:	0.6-1.0ml/100g
Substitute:	Saaz, Spalt

Name:	Willamette
Grown:	United States
Profile:	Mild, spicy, grassy, floral aroma
Usage:	Finishing/dry-hopping for American- /British-style ales
Examples:	Sierra Nevada Porter, Ballard Bitter, Anderson Valley Boont Amber Ale, Redhook ESB
AA range:	4-7%
Hop oil:	1.0-1.5ml/100g
Substitute:	Fuggles

Name:	Whitbread Goldings Variety (WGV)
Grown:	United Kingdom
Profile:	Flowery, fruity, a cross between Goldings and a Fuggles
Usage:	Often combined with other varieties in bitters
Examples:	Whitbread Best Bitter
AA range:	4-5%
Hop oil:	0.8-1.2ml/100g
Substitute:	Progress, Fuggles, EKG

How to Measure Hops

Alpha Acid Units (AAUs). As noted in the glossary, there are two ways to measure hops for use in brewing. The first way measures the bittering potential of the hops going into the boil. Alpha Acid Units (AAUs) or Homebrew Bittering Units (HBUs) are the weight of hops (in ounces) multiplied by the percentage of alpha acids. This unit is convenient for describing hop additions in a recipe, because it indicates the total bittering potential from a particular hop variety while allowing for year-to-year variation in the percentage of alpha acids.

Whenever a brewer is using AAUs in a recipe to describe the quantity of hops, it is important to specify how long each addition is boiled. The boiling time has the largest influence on how bitter a hop addition makes the beer. If no times are specified, then the rule of thumb is that bittering hops are boiled for an hour, and finishing hops are boiled for the last 10 to 15 minutes. Many brewers add hops at 15- or 20-minute intervals and usually in multiples of a half-ounce (for ease of measurement).

International Bittering Units (IBUs). The second way to measure hops estimates how much of the alpha acid is isomerized and actually dissolved into the beer. The equation for International

Bittering Units (IBUs) takes the amount of hops in AAUs and applies factors for the boil gravity, volume, and boiling time. IBUs are independent of batch size and, to some extent, independent of the gravity of the beer, unlike the AAU.

Hop resins act like oil in water. It takes the boiling action of the wort to isomerize them, which means that the chemical structure of the alpha acid compounds is altered, so that the water molecules can attach and these compounds can dissolve into the wort. The percentage of the total alpha acids that are isomerized and survive into the finished beer, i.e., are utilized, is termed the "utilization." Under homebrewing conditions, utilization generally tops out at 30%.

Several factors in the wort boil influence the degree to which isomerization occurs. Unfortunately the way all these factors affect the utilization is complicated and not well understood. But empirical equations have been developed that give us at least some ability to estimate IBUs for homebrewing.

The utilization is influenced by the vigor of the boil, the total gravity of the boil, the time of the boil, and several other minor factors. The vigor of the boil can be considered a constant for each individual brewer, but between brewers there probably is some variation. The gravity of the boil is significant, because the higher the malt sugar content of a wort, the less room there is for isomerized alpha acids. The strongest bittering factors are the total amount of alpha acids you added to the wort, and the amount of time in the boil for isomerization. Therefore, most equations for IBUs work with these three variables (gravity, amount, and time) against a nominal utilization.

The Utilization Table (Table 7 in the following section) lists the utilization versus time and gravity of the boil. This allows you to estimate how much each hop addition is contributing to the total bitterness of the beer. By incorporating a factor for gravity adjustment, the IBU equation allows for direct comparisons of total hop bitterness across beer styles. For instance, 10 AAUs in a pale ale would taste pretty bitter, while 10 AAUs would hardly be noticed in an imperial stout. As the maltiness of the beer increases, so does the relative balance between hop bitterness and malt sweetness. A very sweet American amber ale needs about 40 IBUs to yield the same balance of flavor as a Bavarian Oktoberfest of the same gravity does with 30 IBUs. The ratio between the bitterness units and the starting gravity is a useful way to compare the bitterness between styles. The BU:GU ratios for several beer styles are plotted in Chapter 20.

So, how bitter is bitter? Well, in terms of IBUs, 20 to 40 is considered to be the typical international range. North American light beers, like Coors, have a bitterness of only 10 to 15 IBUs. More bitter imported light beers, like Heineken, have a bitterness closer to 20 to 25. American

Calculating Alpha Acid Units (AAU)

AAUs are a good way to state hop additions in your recipes. By specifying the amount of alpha acid for each addition, rather than just the weight, you don't have to worry about year-to-year variation in the hop.

An AAU is equal to the % AA multiplied by the weight in ounces.

For example:

1.5 ounces of Cascade at 5% alpha acid is 7.5 AAUs.

If next year the alpha acid percentage in Cascade is 7.5%, you would only need 1 ounce rather than 1.5 ounces to arrive at the same bitterness contribution.

microbrews like Samuel Adams Boston Lager have a bitterness of about 30 IBUs. Bitter India pale ales like Anchor Liberty Ale and Sierra Nevada Celebration Ale have bitterness of 50 or more.

There are several different bitterness equations/models for calculating IBUs currently in use among homebrewers. The Rager, Mosher, Daniels, Garetz, and Tinseth models are the most commonly used.[1] The Tinseth model is presented below. Everyone has their own preference, and your choice is not that critical, since the resolution of the human palate is only about 5 IBUs. (This was determined in a blind tasting study using beers that had their IBUs measured using high-performance liquid chromatography.) Therefore, everyone is in the same ballpark, and that is close enough for comparison.

Hop Bitterness (IBU) Calculations

For those of you who dislike math, I will make this as straightforward as possible. We will use the following "Joe Ale" recipe for our example:

The first step is to calculate the AAUs from the recipe.

$$\text{AAU Perle} = 1.5 \text{ oz.} \times 6.4\% = 9.6$$
$$\text{AAU Liberty} = 1 \text{ oz.} \times 4.6\% = 4.6$$

To calculate how much bitterness the final beer will have from these hop additions, we apply factors for the recipe volume (V), gravity of the boil, and the boil time. The time and gravity of the boil are expressed as the utilization (U). The equation for IBUs is:

$$\text{IBU} = \text{AAU} \times \text{U} \times 75 / \text{V}$$

Seventy-five is a constant for the conversion of English units to metric. The proper units for IBUs are milligrams per liter, so to convert from ounces per gallon a conversion factor of 75 (74.89) is needed. For the metric world, using grams and liters, the factor is 10. (For those of you paying attention to the units, the missing factor of 100 was taken up by the percentage in the AAU calculation.)

Gravity of the Boil

The recipe volume is 5 gallons. The gravity is figured by examining the amount and concentration of malt being used. As noted in the previous chapter, dry malt extract typically yields about 40 points per pound per gallon. Since this recipe calls for 6 pounds of extract to be used in 5 gallons, the calculated OG is:

$$\text{OG} = 6 \times 40 / 5 = 48 \text{ or } 1.048$$

But, since we are only boiling 3 of the 5 gallons due to the size of the pot, we need to take into account the higher gravity of the boil. The boil gravity becomes:

$$6 \times 40 / 3 = 80 \text{ or } 1.080$$

Example Recipe
Joe Ale

Ingredients for a 5-gallon (19-liter) batch

- 6 lbs. (2.7kg) of amber dry malt extract

- 1.5 oz. (43g) of 6.4% AA Perle hops (60 minutes)

- 1 oz. (28g) of 4.6% AA Liberty hops (15 minutes)

For a 5-gallon recipe, we will boil 1.5 ounces (43 grams) of Perle hops for 60 minutes for bittering, and 1 ounce (28 grams) of Liberty for 15 minutes for finishing. The recipe calls for 6 pounds (2.7 kilograms) of dry malt extract, and it will be boiled in 3 gallons (11.4 liters) of water because of the pot size. The remaining water will be added in the fermenter.

It is the gravity of the boil (1.080) that is used in figuring the utilization. As you will see in the next section, hop utilization decreases with increasing wort gravity. A higher concentration of sugars makes it more difficult for the isomerized alpha acids to dissolve. I use the initial boil gravity in my utilization calculation; others have suggested that the average boil gravity should be used (the average being a function of how much volume will be boiled away during the boiling time). This gets rather complicated with multiple additions, so I just use the initial boil gravity to be conservative. The difference is small—overestimating the total bitterness by one to three IBUs.

To increase your utilization, and thereby use less hops, you can boil your hops in a lower gravity wort using (for example) half of the total malt extract in the recipe. The other half of the extract can be added at the end of the boil to pasteurize it before cooling the wort and diluting it to the recipe gravity in the fermenter.

Utilization

The utilization is the most important factor. This number describes the efficiency of the isomerization of the alpha acids as a function of time. This is where a lot of experimentation is being conducted to get a better idea of how much of the hops are actually being isomerized during the boil. The utilization numbers that Glenn Tinseth published are shown in Table 7. To find the utilizations for boil gravities in between the values given, simply interpolate the value based on the numbers for the bounding gravities at the given time.

For example, to calculate the utilization for a boil gravity of 1.057 at 30 minutes, look at the utilization values for 1.050 and 1.060. These are 0.177 and 0.162, respectively. There is a difference of 15 between the two, and 7/10 of the difference is about 11, so the adjusted utilization for 1.057 would be 0.177 - 0.011 = 0.166

The utilizations for 60 minutes and 15 minutes at a boil gravity of 1.080 are 0.176 and 0.087, respectively. Inserting these values into the IBU equations gives:

IBU60 = 9.6 x 0.176 x 75 / 5 = 25 (rounded to nearest whole number)
and
IBU15 = 4.6 x 0.087 x 75 / 5 = 6

Giving a grand total of 31 IBUs.

Utilization numbers are really an approximation. Each brew is unique; the variables for individual conditions, e.g., vigor of the boil, wort chemistry, or losses during fermentation, are just too hard to get a handle on from the meager amount of published data available. Then why do we bother, you ask? Because if we are all working from the same model and using roughly the same numbers, then we will all be in the same ballpark and can compare our beers without too much error. Plus, when the actual IBUs are measured in the lab, these models are shown to be pretty close.

Hop Utilization Equation Details

For those of you who are comfortable with the math, the following equations were determined by Tinseth* from curve fitting a lot of test data and were used to generate Table 7. The degree of utilization is composed of a Gravity Factor and a Time Factor. The gravity factor accounts for reduced utilization due to higher wort gravities. The boil time factor accounts for the change in utilization due to boil time:

Utilization = $f(G) \times f(T)$
where: $\quad f(G) = 1.65 \times 0.000125^{(Gb - 1)}$
$\quad\quad\quad f(T) = [1 - e^{(-0.04 \times T)}] / 4.15$

TABLE 7
Utilization As a Function of Time vs. Boil Gravity

	1.030	1.040	1.050	1.060	1.070	1.080	1.090	1.100	1.110	1.120
0	0.000	0.000	0.000	0.000	0.000	0.000	0.000	0.000	0.000	0.000
5	0.055	0.050	0.046	0.042	0.038	0.035	0.032	0.029	0.027	0.025
10	0.100	0.091	0.084	0.076	0.070	0.064	0.058	0.053	0.049	0.045
15	0.137	0.125	0.114	0.105	0.096	0.087	0.080	0.073	0.067	0.061
20	0.167	0.153	0.140	0.128	0.117	0.107	0.098	0.089	0.081	0.074
25	0.192	0.175	0.160	0.147	0.134	0.122	0.112	0.102	0.094	0.085
30	0.212	0.194	0.177	0.162	0.148	0.135	0.124	0.113	0.103	0.094
35	0.229	0.209	0.191	0.175	0.160	0.146	0.133	0.122	0.111	0.102
40	0.242	0.221	0.202	0.185	0.169	0.155	0.141	0.129	0.118	0.108
45	0.253	0.232	0.212	0.194	0.177	0.162	0.148	0.135	0.123	0.113
50	0.263	0.240	0.219	0.200	0.183	0.168	0.153	0.140	0.128	0.117
55	0.270	0.247	0.226	0.206	0.188	0.172	0.157	0.144	0.132	0.120
60	0.276	0.252	0.231	0.211	0.193	0.176	0.161	0.147	0.135	0.123
70	0.285	0.261	0.238	0.218	0.199	0.182	0.166	0.152	0.139	0.127
80	0.291	0.266	0.243	0.222	0.203	0.186	0.170	0.155	0.142	0.130
90	0.295	0.270	0.247	0.226	0.206	0.188	0.172	0.157	0.144	0.132
100	0.298	0.272	0.249	0.228	0.208	0.190	0.174	0.159	0.145	0.133
110	0.300	0.274	0.251	0.229	0.209	0.191	0.175	0.160	0.146	0.134
120	0.301	0.275	0.252	0.230	0.210	0.192	0.176	0.161	0.147	0.134

*Utilization numbers taken from G. Tinseth, Glenn's Hop Utilization Numbers, www.realbeer.com/hops/, 1995.

The numbers 1.65 and 0.000125 in $f(G)$ were empirically derived to fit the boil gravity (Gb) analysis data. In the $f(T)$ equation, the number –0.04 controls the shape of the utilization vs. time curve. The factor 4.15 controls the maximum utilization value. This number may be adjusted to customize the curves to your own system. If you feel that you are having a very vigorous boil or generally get more utilization out of a given boil time for whatever reason, you can reduce the number a small amount, to 4 or 3.9. Likewise, if you think that you are getting less, then you can increase it by one- or two-tenths. Doing so will increase or decrease the utilization value for each time and gravity in Table 7.

IBU Nomograph for Hop Additions

To use the nomograph, start on the right and draw a straight line from the %Alpha Acids of your hop through the Weight of the addition to arrive at the AAUs for that addition. Next, draw a line from the AAUs through the Recipe Volume to arrive at the AAUs/gallon. Now move to the left-hand side of the chart, and draw a line from your Boil Gravity through your Boil Time to determine the Utilization. Finally, draw a line through the points from the Utilization and AAUs/gallon lines to determine the IBUs of that hop addition.

[1] Rager, J. Calculating Hop Bitterness in Beer, Zymurgy 13: 4 (1990). Garetz, M., *Using Hops: The Complete Guide to Hops for the Craft Brewer*, Danville, Calif.: HopTech, 1994. Daniels, R., *Designing Great Beers*, 91-106. Mosher, R., *The Brewers Companion*, Seattle: Alephenalia Publishing, 1995.

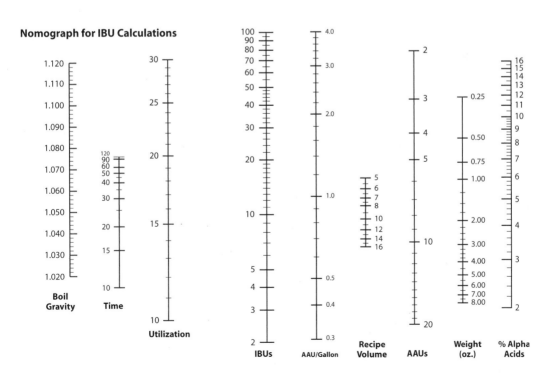

Nomograph for IBU Calculations

Nomograph for IBU Calculations
Grams and Liters

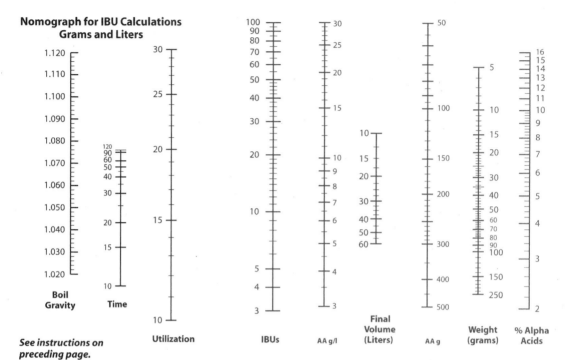

Boil Gravity · **Time** · **Utilization** · **IBUs** · **AA g/l** · **Final Volume (Liters)** · **AA g** · **Weight (grams)** · **% Alpha Acids**

See instructions on preceding page.

YEAST

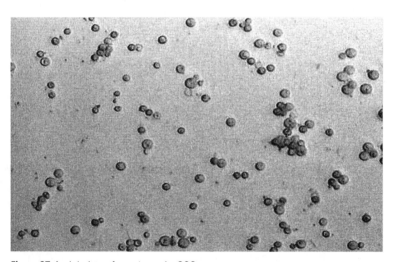

Figure 37 Aerial view of yeast ranch. 300x

There was a time when the role of yeast in brewing was unknown. In the days of the Vikings, each family had its own brewing stick, which was used for stirring the wort. These brewing sticks were family heirlooms, because it was the use of that stick that guaranteed that the beer would turn out right. Obviously, those sticks retained the family yeast culture.

The German Beer Purity Law of 1516, the *Reinheitsgebot*, listed the only allowable materials for brewing as malt, hops, and water. With the discovery of yeast and its function in the late 1860s by Louis Pasteur, the law had to be amended.

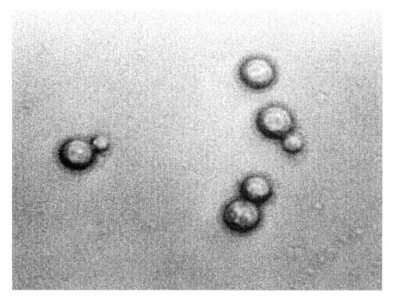

Figure 38 Budding yeast cells. 1,000x

Brewers' yeast (*Saccharomyces cerevisiae*) is a type of fungus. It reproduces asexually by budding—splitting off little daughter cells. Yeast are unusual in that they can live and grow both with or without oxygen. Most microorganisms can only do one or the other. Yeast can live without oxygen by a process that we refer to as fermentation. The yeast cells take in simple sugars like glucose and maltose and produce carbon dioxide and alcohol as waste products.

In addition to ethyl alcohol and carbon dioxide, yeast produce many other compounds, including esters, fusel alcohols, ketones, various phenolics, and fatty acids. Esters are the molecular compound responsible for the fruity notes in beer; phenols cause the spicy notes, and in combination with chlorine (chlorophenols), medicinal notes. Diacetyl is a ketone compound that can be beneficial in limited amounts. It gives a butter or butterscotch note to the flavor profile of a beer and is desired to a degree in heavier pale ales, Scotch ales, and stouts. Unfortunately, diacetyl tends to be unstable and can take on stale, raunchy tones due to oxidation as the beer ages. This is particularly true for light lagers, where the presence of diacetyl is considered to be a flaw. Fusel alcohols are heavier molecular weight alcohols and are thought to be a major contributor to hangovers. These alcohols also have low taste thresholds and are readily apparent as "sharp" notes. Fatty acids, although they take part in the chemical reactions that produce the desired compounds, also tend to oxidize in old beers and produce cardboardlike and soapy off-flavors.

Yeast Terminology

The following are some terms that are used to describe yeast behavior.

Attenuation. This term is usually given as a percentage to describe the percent of malt sugar that is converted by the yeast strain to ethanol and carbon dioxide. Most yeast strains attenuate in the range of 67 to 77%. More specifically, this range is the "apparent" attenuation. The apparent attenuation is determined by comparing the original and final gravities of the beer. A 1.040 OG that ferments to a 1.010 FG would have an apparent attenuation of 75%.

$$(\text{From FG} = \text{OG} - (\text{OG} \times \%) \rightarrow \% \text{ att.} = (\text{OG-FG}) / \text{OG})$$

The "real" attenuation is less. Pure ethanol has a gravity of about 0.800. If you had a 1.040 OG beer and got 100% real attenuation, the resulting specific gravity would be about 0.991 (corresponding to about 5% alcohol by weight). The apparent attenuation of this beer would be 122%. The apparent attenuation of a yeast strain will vary depending on the types of sugars in the wort that the yeast is fermenting. Thus the number quoted for a particular yeast is an average. For purposes of discussion, apparent attenuation is ranked as low, medium, and high by the following percentages:

- 67-70% = Low
- 71-74% = Medium
- 75-78% = High

Attenuation is not entirely up to the yeast. The fermentability of the wort, as determined by the brewer, sets the limits to which a particular yeast may work.

Flocculation. This term describes how fast or how well a yeast clumps together and settles to the bottom of the fermenter after fermentation is complete. Different yeast strains clump differently and will settle faster or slower. Some yeasts practically "paint" themselves to the bottom of the fermenter, while others are ready to swirl up if you so much as sneeze. Highly flocculant yeasts can sometimes settle out before the fermentation is finished, leaving higher than normal levels of diacetyl or even leftover fermentable sugars. Pitching an adequate amount of healthy yeast with adequate aeration is the best solution to this potential problem.

Lag time. This term refers to the amount of time that passes from when the yeast is pitched to when the airlock starts bubbling vigorously on the fermenter. A long lag time (more than 24 hours) may indicate that the wort was poorly aerated, not enough yeast was pitched, and/or that the yeast was initially in poor shape.

Pitching rate. This term indicates the number of yeast cells to add per volume of wort. The most often cited pitching rate is 1 billion cells per liter of wort per 1 degree Plato, which equates to about 0.95 billion cells per 1 gallon of wort per 1 point (1.001) of gravity. This rate is for the repitching of used yeast. For fresh yeast, i.e., from a starter, the pitching rate is about half that. For lagers, the rate needs to be higher. See Tables 8 and 9 for more details on pitching rates and starter quantities.

Yeast Types

There are two main types of yeast: ale and lager. Ale yeasts are referred to as top-fermenting, because much of the fermentation action takes place at the top of the fermenter, while lager yeasts would seem to prefer the bottom. While many of today's strains like to confound this generalization, there is one important difference, and that is temperature. Ale yeasts like warmer temperatures, going dormant below about 55° F (13° C), while lager yeasts will happily work at

40° F (4° C). Using certain lager yeasts at ale temperatures 60 to 70° F (18 to 20° C) produces a style of beer that is now termed California common beer. Anchor Steam Beer revived this unique nineteenth century style.

Yeast Forms

Yeast come in two main product forms, dry and liquid. (There is also another form, available as pure cultures on petri dishes or slants, which is basically liquid yeast with a low cell count.) Dry yeasts are select, hardy strains that have been dehydrated for storability.

Dry yeast is convenient because the packets provide a lot of viable yeast cells, they can be stored for extended periods of time, and they can be prepared quickly on brewing day. It is common to use one or two packets (11 to 22 grams) of dried yeast for a typical 5-gallon batch. This amount of yeast, when properly rehydrated, provides enough active yeast cells to ensure a strong fermentation. Dry yeast can be stored for up to two years (preferably in the refrigerator), but the packets do degrade with time. This is one of the pitfalls with brewing from a no-name yeast packet taped to the top of a can of malt extract. Don't use it. They are probably more than a year old and may not be very viable. It is better to buy another packet or three of a reputable brewer's yeast that has been kept in the refrigerator at the brewshop. Some leading and reliable brands of dry yeast are Fermentis Yeast, Coopers, Danstar (produced by Lallemand), Muntons, and Edme.

Dry ale yeasts make good beer, but the rigor of the dehydration process limits the number of different strains that are available, and in the case of dry lager yeast, eliminates them almost entirely. A few dry lager yeasts do exist, but popular opinion is that they behave more like ale yeasts than lager. The only thing missing with dry yeast is more variety, which is where liquid yeasts come in. There are more strains of yeast available in liquid form than in dry.

Liquid yeast comes in either 125-milliliter pouches (Wyeast Laboratories) or tubes (White Labs). These pitchable quantities do not require a starter and are the most popular forms of liquid yeast packaging. The same yeast strains are sold to commercial breweries in larger quantities.

Yeast Strains

There are many different strains of brewer's yeast available nowadays, and each strain produces a different flavor profile. Some Belgian strains produce fruity esters that smell like bananas and cherries, some German strains produce phenols that smell strongly of cloves. Those two examples are rather special; most yeasts are not that dominating. But it illustrates how much the choice of yeast can determine the taste of the beer. In fact, one of the main differences between different beer styles is the strain of yeast that is used.

Many major breweries have their own strain of yeast. These yeast strains have evolved with the style of beer being made, particularly if that brewery was a founder of a style, such as Anchor Steam. In fact, yeast readily adapts and evolves to specific brewery conditions, so two breweries producing the same style of beer with the same yeast strain will actually have different yeast cultivars that produce unique beers. Yeast companies have collected these different yeasts from around the world and package them for homebrewers.

Dry Yeast Strains

As I mentioned earlier, the dry ale yeast strains tend to be fairly similar, attenuative and clean tasting, performing well for most ale styles. To illustrate with a very broad brush, there are Australian, British, and Canadian strains, each producing what can be considered that country's style of pale ale. The Australian type is more woody, the British more fruity, and the Canadian a bit more malty. Fortunately, with international interest in homebrewing growing as it is, dry yeast strains and variety are improving. Some of my favorites are Nottingham (Danstar), London Ale (Danstar), and Coopers Ale.

Here is an incomplete list of popular dry yeast strains and their general characteristics:

Coopers Ale (Coopers). All-purpose dry ale yeast. It produces a complex, woody, citrus-fruity beer at warm temperatures. More heat tolerant than other strains, 65 to 75° F (18 to 24° C); recommended for summer brewing. Medium attenuation and flocculation.

Edme Ale (Edme Ltd.). One of the original dry yeast strains, this produces a soft, bready finish. Medium flocculation and medium attenuation. Fermentation range of 62 to 70° F (17 to 21° C).

Muntons. An all-purpose ale yeast selected for a long shelf life. A vigorous starter with estery flavors. Medium attenuation and high flocculation. Fermentation range of 64 to 70° F (18 to 21° C).

Muntons Gold. An all-purpose ale yeast that has higher attenuation than regular Muntons. A vigorous starter with a clean malt profile. High attenuation, high flocculation. Fermentation range of 64 to 70° F (18 to 21° C).

Nottingham Ale (Danstar). A more neutral ale yeast with lower levels of esters and a crisp, malty finish. Can be used for lagerlike beers at lower temperatures at very high pitching rates. High attenuation and medium-high flocculation. Fermentation range of 58 to 70° F (14 to 21° C).

Windsor Ale (Danstar). Produces a full-bodied, fruity English ale, but suitable for wheat beers also, including *hefeweizen*. Attenuation and flocculation are medium low. Fermentation range of 59 to 70° F (15 to 21° C).

Safale S-04 (Fermentis). A well-known commercial English ale yeast selected for its vigorous character and high flocculation. This yeast is recommended for a large range of ale and is especially well adapted to cask-conditioned ales. Recommended temperature range of 59 to 75° F (15 to 24° C).

Safale US-56 (Fermentis). A dry form of the well-known American ale yeast strain, this yeast produces fewer esters and low diacetyl compared to S-04, for a maltier-tasting beer. Medium attenuation, medium flocculation. Recommended temperature range of 59 to 75° F (15 to 24° C).

Safbrew S-33 (Fermentis). A general-purpose yeast that is used in Europe for many beer styles. This yeast produces an estery profile that is greater than S-04 but less than T-58. Used for many Belgian styles, including *wit* and abbey. Can ferment to 7.5% ABV. Low attenuation, medium flocculation. Recommended temperature range of 59 to 75° F (15 to 24° C).

Safbrew T-58 (Fermentis). A specialty yeast selected for it estery and spicy flavor development, this yeast can tolerate high alcohol levels up to 8.5% ABV. Low attenuation, medium flocculation. Recommended temperature range of 59 to 75° F (15 to 24° C).

Saflager S-23 (Fermentis). This lager strain is used by several European commercial breweries and originates from the Institute of Brewing in Berlin. This yeast develops soft, estery notes at the recommended temperature range of 48 to 59° F (9 to 15° C) and more alelike characteristics at warmer temperatures. The suggested optimum temperature is 54° F (12° C), and homebrewers have reported good results with this yeast. Given the recommended fermentation temperature range, this yeast should not be lagered any lower that 45° F (7° C). Medium attenuation, high flocculation.

Diamond Lager Yeast (White Labs). This lager strain also originates from a German brewery and is used by several breweries worldwide. The recommended temperature range is 50 to 59° F (10 to 15° C). The suggested optimum temperature is 54° F (12° C). Given the recommended fermentation temperature range, this yeast should not be lagered any lower that 45° F (7° C). High attenuation, high flocculation.

Liquid Yeast Strains

There are a lot of liquid yeasts to choose from, and in order to keep this simple, I will just describe them by general strain. This is not to say that all of the cultivars of a type are the same; within a strain there will be several cultivars that have different characteristics from what is listed here. You will find that each company's offering will be subtly different due to the conditions under which it was sampled, stored, and grown. You may find that you prefer one company's cultivar over another. Detailed descriptions of each company's cultivar will be available at your brewshop or on the company's website. This is an incomplete list, because new strains are being added to the market all the time.

General Purpose Ale Yeasts

American, Californian, or Chico Ale. A very "clean" tasting yeast, producing fewer esters than other types of ale yeast. Good for just about any type of ale. This strain is usually associated with Sierra Nevada Pale Ale. High attenuation, medium flocculation. Suggested fermentation temperature range is 60 to 72° F (15 to 22° C).

Australian Ale. This all-purpose strain typically comes from Thos. Cooper & Sons of Adelaide, and produces a very complex, woody, and fruity beer. Medium attenuation, medium flocculation. Great for pale ales, brown ales, and porters. Suggested fermentation temperature range is 65 to 75° F (18 to 24° C).

British Ale. This strain typically comes from Whitbread Brewing Company, and ferments crisp, slightly tart, and fruity. More maltiness is evident than with the American ale yeast. Medium attenuation, medium flocculation. Suggested fermentation temperature range is 64 to 72° F (18 to 22° C).

Irish Ale. The slight residual diacetyl is great for stouts. It is clean, smooth, soft, and full bodied. Very nice for any cold-weather ale, at its best in stouts and Scotch ales. Medium flocculation, medium attenuation. Suggested fermentation temperature range is 62 to 72° F (16 to 22° C).

Specialty Ale Yeasts

Belgian Ale. Lots of fruity esters (banana, spice), and can be tart. Very good for Belgian ales, *dubbels*, and *tripels*. This is actually a group of strains, and each particular strain will have its own personality. In general, medium flocculation, high attenuation. Suggested fermentation temperature ranges are 65 to 75° F (18 to 24° C).

European Ale. This ale yeast typically comes from Wissenschaftliche in Munich. A full-bodied, complex strain that finishes very malty. Produces a dense rocky head during fermentation. It's clean and malty, especially well suited to altbier. Reportedly a slow starter (longer lag times). High flocculation, low attenuation. Suggested fermentation temperature range is 62 to 72° F (17 to 22° C).

German Altbier. Ferments dry and crisp, leaving a good balance of sweetness and tartness. Produces an extremely rocky head and ferments well down to 55° F (13° C). A good choice for alt-style beers. Low flocculation, high attenuation. Suggested fermentation temperature range is 55 to 68° F (13 to 20° C).

Kölsch Ale. An old German style of beer that is more lagerlike in character. Nice maltiness without as much fruit character as other ales. Some sulfur notes that disappear with aging. Low flocculation, high attenuation. Suggested fermentation temperature range is 56 to 70° F (13 to 21° C).

London Ale. Complex, woody, tart, with strong mineral notes. Could be from one of the several renowned London breweries. Slight diacetyl. Medium flocculation, medium attenuation. Suggested fermentation temperature range is 62 to 72° F (17 to 22° C).

Wheat Beer Yeasts

Belgian Wit (White) Beer. Mild phenolic character for the classic Belgian wit beer style. Tart and fruity. Low flocculation, medium attenuation. Suggested fermentation temperature range is 65 to 75° F (18 to 24° C).

Weizen. Produces the distinctive clove and spice character of wheat beers. The low flocculation of this yeast leaves the beer cloudy (hefeweizen), but its smooth flavor makes it an integral part of a true unfiltered wheat beer. Low flocculation, high attenuation. Suggested fermentation temperature range is 65 to 75° F (18 to 24° C).

German Wheat. A tart/sour, fruity, and phenolic multi-strain with earthy undertones. Medium flocculation, high attenuation. May contain *Lactobacillus*. Suggested fermentation temperature range is 63 to 75° F (17 to 24° C).

Lager Yeast

American Lager. Very versatile for most lager styles. Gives a clean malt flavor. Some cultivars have an almost green-apple tartness. Medium flocculation, high attenuation. Suggested primary fermentation temperature range is 48 to 56° F (9 to 12° C).

Bavarian Lager. Lager yeast strain used by many German breweries. Rich flavor, full bodied, malty, and clean. This is an excellent general-purpose yeast for lager brewing. Medium flocculation, high attenuation. Suggested primary fermentation temperature range is 46 to 58° F (8 to 14° C).

Bohemian Lager. Ferments clean and malty, giving a rich residual maltiness in high-gravity Pilseners. Very suitable for Vienna and Oktoberfest styles. Probably the most popular lager yeast strain. Medium flocculation, medium attenuation. Suggested primary fermentation temperature range is 48 to 58° F (9 to 14° C).

California Lager. Warm-fermenting, bottom-cropping strain, ferments well to 62° F (17° C), having some of the fruitiness of an ale while keeping lager characteristics. Malty profile, high flocculation, medium attenuation. This is the yeast that is used for steam-type beers. Suggested primary fermentation temperature range is 58 to 68° F (14 to 20° C).

Czech Pils Yeast. Classic dry finish with rich maltiness. Good choice for Pilseners and bock beers. Sulfur produced during fermentation dissipates with conditioning. Medium flocculation, medium attenuation. Suggested primary fermentation temperature range is 50 to 58° F (11 to 14° C).

Danish Lager Yeast. Rich, yet crisp and dry. Soft, light profile that accentuates hop characteristics. Low flocculation, high attenuation. Suggested primary fermentation temperature range is 46 to 57° F (8 to 13° C).

Munich Lager Yeast. A classic lager yeast that is smooth, malty, well rounded, and accentuates hop flavor. It is reported to be prone to producing diacetyl, so use a diacetyl rest. Medium flocculation, high attenuation. Suggested primary fermentation temperature range is 48 to 56° F (9 to 12° C).

Determining Your Pitching Rate

There are many factors that combine to determine just how much yeast you should pitch to your wort to produce a good fermentation, and thus a good beer. The most obvious factors are wort gravity and fermentation temperature. If you intend to brew a low-gravity mild ale, you don't need a lot of yeast to do the job. With typical levels of nutrients and aeration, a relatively low number of yeast will easily reproduce enough cells to ferment that wort very well. On the other hand, if you are going to brew a high-gravity doppelbock lager, then you are going to need to pitch a lot more

Pitching Rates vs. Esters

The pitching rate also affects the aroma/flavor character of the beer. Lower pitching rates tend to produce more aromatics and esters than higher pitching rates. A lower pitching rate will encourage more yeast reproduction due to the perceived abundance of resources. The yeast will reproduce until the total yeast mass reaches the limit for what the wort resources can support. More reproduction generally means more synthesis of new cell membrane and increased production of an intracellular enzyme called alcohol acetyl transferase (AAT), which regulates the fluidity of the membrane and is believed to play a major role in the esterification of fatty acids (e.g., acetyl CoA) by the yeast. The production of AAT is also encouraged by environmental stresses on the yeast, such as temperature, pH, and nutrient levels. At higher pitching rates, less reproduction will occur to bring the total yeast mass up to the wort's resource limit, and less cell membrane and AAT synthesis occurs. The production of esters by the yeast is complicated, and the role of AAT is still a theory, but it is consistent with empirical observations and measurements. The bottom line is that lower pitching rates seem to produce more aromatics and esters than higher pitching rates.

yeast, because the cooler fermentation temperature will decrease the activity level and reproduction rate, and more total yeast mass will be needed to adequately ferment the higher-gravity wort. As a general rule, you need to pitch more yeast for higher-gravity worts, and you need to pitch more yeast for cooler fermentation temperatures. Recommended pitching rates for lager beers will be given in Chapter 10. Recommended ale pitching rate ranges for different wort gravities are given in Table 8.

The number of active yeast cells in yeast packages can be found on the manufacturers' websites. Most dry yeast packets have a cell density of about 6 billion per gram, so you will get 50 to 70 billion cells in a single packet, which is good for five gallons of most of the common beer styles. The White Labs pitchable tubes and the 125-milliliter Wyeast Activator pouches deliver about 100 billion. Wyeast also markets a 50-milliliter propagation pouch with 35 billion cells, which is designed to be pitched to a starter. So, look at the recipe and plan your pitching rates accordingly. You may want to pitch two packets of yeast or use a yeast starter to build up the cell count more. Yeast starter procedures are discussed later in this chapter.

Table 9 gives final yeast cell counts as a function of initial yeast cell count and volume of starter wort. In other words, if you pitch 60 billion cells from a dry yeast packet to 2 quarts of starter wort of 1.040 gravity, you can conservatively expect to produce 173 billion cells. These growth estimates were calculated from a general model developed by Wyeast Laboratories based on several growth experiments conducted across several yeast strains.

TABLE 8
Recommended Pitching Rates for Ale Yeast Strains As a Function of Wort Gravity

Wort Gravity	Cells per 20 Liters	Cells per 5 Gallons
Less than 1.055	60—120 billion	50—110 billion
1.055—1.065	120—180 billion	110—170 billion
1.065—1.075	180—240 billion	170—225 billion
1.075—1.085	240—300 billion	225—285 billion
1.085—1.095	300—360 billion	285—340 billion
Greater than 1.095	360—420+ billion	340—400+ billion

Yeast Nutritional Needs

Yeast cannot live on sugar alone. In Chapter 3 I described the types of sugars that make up a typical beer wort, and how yeast typically utilize them. Yeast also need minerals, nitrogen, and amino and fatty acids to enable them to live and grow. The primary sources for these building blocks are minerals in the water and the Free Amino Nitrogen (FAN), lipids, and minerals from the malted barley. Refined sugars like table sugar, corn sugar, and honey do not contain any of these nutrients. An all-malt extract should have all the nutrition that the yeast will need for a good fermentation. But if you are brewing a single can-type kit that instructs you to add 2 pounds of table sugar, you will probably want to add some yeast nutrients to assure a good fermentation.

From a yeast cell's point of view, its purpose in life is to grow, eat, and reproduce. Yeast can do all this with or without oxygen, but using oxygen makes the processes easier for the cell. Yeast use oxygen in the biosynthesis of the compounds that make up their cell membranes, which allow them to process sugars for food and grow. Without oxygen, yeast cannot synthesize sterols very well, which means that they can't grow more cell membrane, which means that they can't bud, and reproduction diminishes. Therefore, to ensure a good fermentation, we need to provide the yeast with sufficient oxygen to allow them to grow quickly and reproduce when they are first pitched to the fermenter. Once they have reproduced to sufficient numbers, we can let them get on with turning our wort into beer. The importance of oxygen in yeast growth will be emphasized again in Chapter 8.

TABLE 9
Estimated Final Yeast Cell Count (Billions)
Based on Initial Count and Starter Size

(The starter wort is assumed to be 1.040 with 8 ppm of dissolved oxygen. The final count is given per quart and (per liter) of wort.)

Initial Cell Count (Billions)	1 Quart (Liter)	2 Quarts (Liters)	3 Quarts (Liters)	4 Quarts (Liters)
35	92 (95)	125 (128)	149 (152)	168 (172)
50	113 (116)	153 (156)	182 (186)	206 (211)
60	125 (128)	169 (173)	202 (207)	229 (234)
70	137 (140)	185 (189)	220 (226)	250 (256)
80	148 (151)	199 (204)	238 (243)	269 (276)
90	158 (162)	213 (218)	254 (260)	288 (295)
100	168 (172)	226 (232)	270 (276)	305 (313)
110	177 (181)	239 (245)	285 (292)	322 (330)
120	186 (190)	251 (257)	299 (306)	339 (347)
130	195 (199)	263 (269)	313 (321)	354 (363)
140	203 (208)	274 (280)	326 (334)	370 (379)
150	211 (216)	285 (292)	339 (348)	384 (394)

If you use ion-exchanged softened water for brewing, the water may not have adequate calcium, magnesium, and zinc for some of the yeast's metabolic paths. Magnesium plays a vital role in cellular metabolism, and its function can be inhibited by a preponderance of calcium in the wort. Brewers adding calcium salts for water chemistry adjustment may want to include magnesium salts as part of the addition if they experience fermentation problems. Usually, the wort supplies all the necessary mineral requirements of the yeast, except for zinc, which is often deficient or in a non-assimilable form. Additions of zinc can greatly improve the cell count and vigor of the starter, but adding too much will cause the yeast to produce excessive by-products and cause off-flavors. Zinc acts as a catalyst and tends to carry over into the succeeding generation; therefore, it is probably better to add it to either the starter or the main wort, but not both. The nutrient pouches in the Wyeast smack-packs already contain zinc in addition to other nutrients. For best performance, zinc levels should be between 0.1 to 0.3 milligrams per liter, with 0.5 milligrams per liter being maximum. If you experience stuck fermentations or low attenuation, and you have eliminated other variables such as temperature, low pitching rate, poor aeration, poor FAN, age, etc., then lack of necessary minerals may be a significant factor.

Nutritional Supplements

You will see four types of yeast nutrients on the market that can supplement a wort that is high in refined sugars or adjuncts.

Diammonium phosphate. This is strictly a nitrogen supplement that can take the place of a lack of FAN.

Yeast hulls. This is essentially dead yeast, the carcasses of which act as agglomeration sites and contain some useful residual lipids.

Yeast nutrient or energizer. The name can vary, but the intent is a mixture of diammonium phosphate, yeast hulls, biotin, vitamins, and minerals (zinc, manganese, magnesium). These mixtures are a more complete dietary supplement for the yeast, and I recommend them.

Servomyces. This product from Lallemand is similar to yeast hulls but differs by having a useful amount of rapidly assimilable zinc, which is an essential enzyme co-factor for yeast health. This product falls within the provisions of the Reinheitsgebot.

Oxygen

Yeast need 8 to 16 ppm of oxygen (depending on the strain) to synthesize sterols and unsaturated fatty acids for cell membrane biosynthesis. Without aeration, fermentations tend to be underattenuated, because oxygen availability is a limiting factor for yeast growth—the yeast stop budding when sterol levels for cell membrane growth become depleted. Higher-gravity worts need more yeast for proper fermentation, and thus need more oxygen, but the higher gravity makes it more difficult to dissolve oxygen in the first place. Boiling the wort drives out the dissolved oxygen normally present, so aeration of some sort is needed prior to fermentation. Proper aeration of the wort can be accomplished several ways:

• shaking the container, e.g., the starter jar (about 8 ppm)
• pouring the cooled wort back and forth from the boiling pot into the fermenter (about 8 ppm)

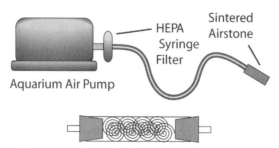

Alternative filter of tube with moist cotton.

Figure 40 Here is an example of an aquarium air pump with an airstone and microbial filter. The filter is a HEPA (medical) syringe filter. An alternative is to make an in-line filter from a plastic tube, cotton, and rubber stoppers. The premoistened cotton provides the filtering action and should be discarded after each use.

- using a bronze or stainless steel airstone with an aquarium air pump to bubble air into the fermenter for a half-hour (about 8 ppm, sustained)
- using an airstone with an oxygen tank and bubbling for about 5 minutes (about 25 ppm).

For the beginning brewer using rehydrated dry yeast, I recommend the simplest methods of shaking the starter and pouring the wort. Pouring is also effective if you are doing a partial boil and adding water to the fermenter to make up the total volume. Instead of pouring the wort, you can just pour the water back and forth to another sanitized pot prior to adding the wort.

Using an air pump and airstone to bubble air into the fermenter is effective and saves you from lifting a heavy fermenter. The saturation point of oxygen from the air in wort is 8 ppm. Most yeast strains require 8 to 16 ppm of oxygen for adequate growth and activity, but that requirement also depends on the pitching rate and the size of the wort. The yeast will process the oxygen quickly, generally in less than an hour. An air pump and airstone will reach 8 ppm for 5 gallons in about 5 minutes, but I recommend aerating for a half-hour, to make sure that the yeast get all that they need. The only precaution you need to take, other than sanitizing the airstone and hose, is to be sure that the air going into the fermenter is not carrying any mold spores or dust-borne bacteria. An inline filter is recommended to prevent airborne contamination from reaching the wort. One type is a sterile medical syringe filter, and these can be purchased at hospital pharmacies or at your local brewshop. An alternative, build-it-yourself bacterial filter is a tube filled with moist cotton balls. See Figure 40. The cotton should be changed after each use.

You can also buy small oxygen tanks that will deliver more oxygen faster to the wort. Pure oxygen has a wort saturation point of 40 ppm, so only a relatively short time is needed, as compared to ordinary air. I have had better fermentations using air rather than using pure oxygen.

Interestingly enough, that also seems to be the consensus of Ron Cooper and The Strand Brewers club of Redondo Beach, California, in the "For Geeks Only" section of the March/April 2004 issue of *Zymurgy* magazine. In the article "Oxygen and Hydrogen Peroxide in Beer," they brewed twenty-three batches of various beers, using shaking/pouring, air pumps, oxygen tank, and hydrogen peroxide. While they could not make any definitive conclusions, competition results for the various beers indicated that the oxygen tank beers "seemed thinner or washed out, like smaller beers." Malt and hop flavors seemed reduced. This perception was even greater in the hydrogen peroxide-treated batch (5 milliliters per 5 gallons), where a 47 IBU IPA was judged "thin and estery," "not much hop," "sweet and insipid." All of the beers had fermented well with good attenuation; the shortcomings may be due to an oxidized wort, as opposed to an aerated one.[1]

On the other hand, some commercial breweries use pure oxygen that is injected into the line as the wort is pumped from the whirlpool to the fermenter. Obviously, there is room for further experimentation and discussion in this area.

Aeration Is Good, Oxidation Is Bad

The yeast is the most significant factor in determining the quality of a fermentation, and oxygen can be the most significant factor in determining the quality of the yeast. Oxygen is both your friend and your enemy. It is important to understand when which is which.

You should not aerate when the wort is hot, or even warm. Aeration of hot wort will cause the oxygen to bind chemically to various wort compounds. Over time, these compounds will break down, freeing atomic oxygen back into the beer, where it can oxidize the fatty acids and alcohols, producing off-flavors and aromas like wet cardboard or sherry. The generally accepted temperature cutoff for preventing hot wort oxidation is 80° F (27° C).

Oxidation of your wort can happen in several ways. The first is by splashing or aerating the wort while it is hot. This problem is called hot-side aeration, or HSA. Older brewing books have advocated pouring the boiling-hot wort into cold water in the fermenter to cool it and add oxygen for the yeast. Unfortunately, the wort is still hot enough to be oxidized instead of aerated. Pouring it down the side of the bucket to minimize splashing doesn't really help either, since this increases the surface area of the wort exposed to the air. Therefore, you must cool the wort first to below 80° F (27° C) to prevent oxidation, and *then* aerate it to provide the dissolved oxygen that the yeast need. Cooling rapidly between 90 and 140° F (32 and 60° C) is important, because this temperature range is ideal for bacterial growth.

In addition, if oxygen is introduced after primary fermentation has started, it may cause the yeast to produce more of the early fermentation by-products, like acetohydroxy acids. However, some strains of yeast respond very well to "open" fermentations (where the fermenter is open to the air) without producing off-flavors. But even for those yeast strains, aeration after fermentation is complete can lead to staling. When you rack to a secondary fermenter or to the bottling bucket, it is very important to prevent gurgling or splashing. Keep the siphon flowing smoothly by placing the outlet of the siphon hose below the surface of the rising beer. Decrease the difference in height between the two containers when you begin. This will slow the siphon rate at first, and prevent turbulence and aeration until the outlet is beneath the surface.

To summarize, you want to pitch a sufficient amount of healthy yeast, preferably grown in a starter that matches your intended fermentation conditions. You want to cool the wort to fermentation temperature, and then aerate the wort to provide the oxygen that the yeast need to grow and reproduce. Then you want to protect the beer from oxygen after fermentation to prevent oxidation and staling.

Preparing Yeast and Yeast Starters

Preparing Dry Yeast
Dry yeast should be rehydrated in de-aerated water before pitching. Do not just sprinkle it onto the wort, as the manufacturer's instructions often suggest. Usually, the concentration of sugars in wort is so high that the yeast cannot draw enough water across the cell membranes to restart their metabolism. For best results, rehydrate the yeast in warm, preboiled water (95 to 105° F, 35 to 40° C). You want to

limit the yeast's exposure to dissolved oxygen until you pitch it to your wort, to maintain maximum vitality.

Rehydrating Dry Yeast
1. Put 1 cup (237 milliliters) of warm (95 to 105° F, 35 to 40° C), boiled water into a sanitized jar, and sprinkle the yeast on top. Do not stir it in. Cover with plastic wrap or aluminum foil, and wait 15 minutes.
2. Gently stir the yeast into the water to suspend it completely.
3. Re-cover the jar, and let it sit for 15 minutes to complete rehydration. The yeast will form a creamy layer on the

Figures 42 and 43 Dry yeast that has been rehydrated, and the same yeast after proofing

bottom of the jar. It should be pitched within a half-hour for best results. Swirl the jar to resuspend the yeast immediately before pitching.

Note: I used to recommend that the yeast be "proofed" by adding a spoonful of sugar after rehydration to check the viability. The yeast manufacturers do not recommend proofing after rehydration, because modern manufacturing procedures have optimized the yeast's nutritional reserves (e.g., glycogen and trehelose) for quick adaptation and starting in the main wort. Proofing expends some of those reserves and can make the yeast less able to adapt to the main wort, if that wort is lacking in nutrients or aeration (which can often be the case with a new brewer's first beer kit). If the main wort is nutritionally complete and well aerated, then proofing will not affect the yeast's ability to adapt and ferment.

Preparing Liquid Yeast

Liquid yeast is generally regarded as being superior to dry yeast. Liquid yeast allows for greater tailoring of the beer to a particular style. There are two kinds of liquid yeast packaging. One is the pitchable tube that you just pour in, and the other is the smack-pack, which contains an inner bubble of yeast nutrient. You smack the pouch to burst the inner bubble and release the nutrients to the yeast. The yeast ferment these nutrients and swell the pouch, acting as a built-in viability test.

Making a Yeast Starter

Step 1. Boil a pint (470 milliliters) of water and stir in ½ cup (120 milliliters) of dry malt extract. This will produce a starter of about 1.040 OG. Boil this for 10 minutes, adding a little bit of hops if you want to. Put the lid on the pan for the last couple of minutes, turn off the stove, and let it sit while you prepare for the next step. Adding a quarter-teaspoon of yeast nutrient (vitamins, minerals, biotin, and dead yeast cells) to the starter wort is always advisable to ensure good growth. It is available from your brewshop.

Step 2. Cool the starter wort. Fill the kitchen sink with a couple of inches of cold water. Take the covered pot and set it in the water, moving it around to speed the cooling. When the pot feels cool, about 80° F (27° C) or less, pour the wort into a sanitized glass jar or something similar. Pour all of the wort in, even the sediment. This sediment consists of proteins and lipids, which are actually beneficial for yeast growth at this stage.

Step 3. Pour the starter wort into the starter jar. Ideally, the starter wort temperature should be the same as what you plan the fermentation temperature to be. This allows the yeast to get acclimated to working at that temperature. If the yeast is started warmer and then pitched to a cooler fermentation environment, it may be shocked or stunned by the change in temperature and may take a couple of days to regain normal activity.

Step 4. Sanitize the pouch, and pour the yeast into the jar. Two-quart juice or cider bottles work well, and the opening is often the right size to accept an airlock and rubber stopper. Cover the top of the jar or bottle with plastic wrap and the lid.

Shake the starter vigorously to aerate it. Remove and discard the plastic wrap, insert an airlock, and put it somewhere out of direct sunlight. If you don't have an airlock that will fit, don't worry. Instead, put a clean piece of plastic wrap over the jar or bottle, and secure it loosely with a rubber band. This way, the escaping carbon dioxide will be able to vent without exposing the starter to airborne bacteria.

Step 5. This starter has been built up twice, and a substantial yeast layer can be seen on the bottom. Most any type of jar can be used for starters: mayonnaise, juice, or cider all work well. The top can be covered with plastic wrap, aluminum foil, or an airlock. Good sanitation is paramount!

During the next day or two some foaming or an increase in the white yeast layer on the bottom should be evident. These small wort starters can ferment quickly, so don't be surprised if you missed the activity. When the starter has cleared and the yeast have settled to the bottom, it is ready to pitch to the fermenter, although it will keep for two to three days without any problems.

The starter process may be repeated several times to provide more yeast to ensure an even stronger fermentation. In fact, a general rule is that the stronger the beer (more fermentables/higher gravity), the more yeast you should pitch. For strong beers and barley wines, at least 1 cup of yeast slurry or 1 gallon of yeast starter should be pitched to ensure that there will be enough active yeast to finish the fermentation before they are overwhelmed by the rising alcohol level. For more moderate strength beers (1.060 gravity) a 1 quart starter is sufficient. One recommendation when pitching a large starter is to chill the starter overnight in the refrigerator to settle all the yeast. Then the unpleasant-tasting starter beer can be poured off, so only the yeast slurry will be pitched. This helps prevent the taste of the starter from influencing the taste of the final beer if the starter volume was large, i.e., a half-gallon.

You don't need to warm up the starter before pitching to your fermenter. Many homebrewers report excellent performance and short lag times from pitching the starter right from the refrigerator.

When Is My Yeast Starter Ready to Pitch?

A yeast starter is ready to pitch when it has attained high kraeusen (full activity), or after it has settled out, and for about a day or two after, depending on the temperature. You should wait about 18 hours after activity has peaked, while the starter builds up its trehalose and glycogen reserves, before pitching it to your wort. Once it has built up those reserves and gone dormant, you have a couple of days of grace while its vitality is still near optimum. Colder conditions allow the yeast to be stored longer before pitching. Yeast starters that have settled out and sat at room temperature for more than a couple of days should be fed fresh wort and allowed to attain high kraeusen before pitching.

A key condition to this recommendation is that the composition of the starter wort and the main wort must be very similar if the starter is pitched at or near peak activity. Why? Because the yeast in the starter wort have produced a specific set of enzymes for that wort's sugar profile. If those yeast are then pitched to a different wort, with a different relative percentage of sugars, the yeast will be impaired and the fermentation may be affected—kind of like trying to change boats in mid-stream. This is especially true for starter worts made from extract that includes refined sugars, such as from a beer kit that is tailored to a light-bodied style like blonde ale. Yeast that have been eating a lot of sucrose, glucose, and fructose will quit making the enzyme that allows it to eat maltose—the main sugar of brewer's wort.

If you make your starter using a malt extract that includes refined sugar, it is better to wait until the yeast have finished fermenting and settled out before pitching to the main wort. Why? Because toward the end of fermentation, yeast build up their glycogen and trehalose reserves, kind of like a bear storing fat for the winter. Glycogen and trehalose are two carbohydrates that act as food reserves for the yeast cell. Yeast slowly feed off these reserves when other food is not present and use this food extensively to fuel the synthesis of essential lipids, sterols, and unsaturated fatty acids when pitched to an oxygenated wort. (Yeast will rapidly deplete their glycogen reserves when exposed to oxygen.) While glycogen can be likened to the fat that a bear stores for winter, the other component, trehalose, acts more like the bear's heavy fur coat. Trehalose seems to get built up on both the inside and outside of the cell membrane and is generally believed to make the membrane structure more robust and more resistant to environmental stresses. By allowing the yeast starter fermentation to go to completion, these reserves are built up, and upon pitching, the yeast starts out with a ready fuel supply and a clean slate to better adapt it to the new wort. As noted earlier, though, these same reserves are used by the yeast while in hibernation, so if the yeast are left too long before pitching, the reserves may be depleted and should be replenished with a fresh starter wort fermentation before use.

Using Yeast From Commercial Beers

There are many quality microbrewed beers on the market that are bottle conditioned, i.e., naturally carbonated and unfiltered, much the same as homebrewed beers are. The yeast layer from a bottle-conditioned beer can be harvested and grown just like the yeast from a liquid yeast packet. This is a common practice among homebrewers, because it allows for the use of some special yeast strains in homebrew that would not otherwise be available. This method can be used for cloning some of the specialty styles, such as Belgian wit, Trappist ales, or saison.

Harvesting yeast from a bottle-conditioned beer is quite simple.

1. After opening the bottle, thoroughly clean the bottleneck and opening with sanitizer to prevent bacterial contamination.
2. Pour the beer into a glass as you normally would, leaving the yeast layer on the bottom intact.
3. Swirl up the sediment with the beer remaining in the bottle, and pour the yeast sediment into a prepared starter solution as described in "Preparing a Liquid Yeast Starter."

For best results, add the sediment from two or three bottles, and be sure to use the freshest beer you can find. The starter should behave in the same way as any other liquid yeast pack starter, although it may take longer to build due to the smaller amount of yeast that you start out with. In fact, you may not notice any activity in the starter for the first couple of wort additions until the amount of yeast builds to higher levels. Add more wort as necessary to build the yeast slurry to pitching level. Be sure to taste, or at least sniff, the starter beer to check for contamination. It should be beerlike and not funky.

Note: Some beers (weissbiers, especially) are packaged with a different yeast than the one used for primary fermentation. Beers that have a high alcohol content are not good candidates, because the yeast is severely weakened and has probably mutated by the time you try to culture it.

Support Your Local Micro

In addition, if you have a quality brewpub or microbrewery nearby, the brewers are often happy to provide yeast to homebrewers. A good brewery produces a lot more yeast than it can use, and it is usually free of contamination. I keep a spare, sanitized, plastic pint container in the car in case I am visiting a micro and am able to talk to the brewers. (I know what you are thinking, "What are the odds that I will be at a brewpub when they are brewing?" Sometimes it requires several visits a week to even those odds, but that's life.) If they don't have any yeast available at the moment, they will usually suggest you come back the next day or week when they are transferring, and will give you some then. The advantage to obtaining yeast this way is that you usually get a cup or more of slurry, which is more than enough to ferment a 5-gallon batch. You are virtually assured of a vigorous, healthy fermentation without the fuss of preparing a yeast starter a few days beforehand. The yeast will stay viable for a couple of weeks if kept in the refrigerator. But remember, you may want to replenish the yeast's glycogen and trehalose reserves, as described in "When Is My Starter Ready to Pitch?" if the yeast is stored for a long time.

Simple Yeast Ranching

Each batch of beer you brew is a good source of yeast for a future batch. The best way to obtain yeast is to skim it from the kraeusen of a currently fermenting beer. To do this, you will need to be using a bucket-type fermenter and first skim off the green/brown hop and protein compounds with a sanitized spoon early in the primary phase. As the creamy white kraeusen builds up, you can skim this fresh yeast off with a sanitized spoon and transfer it to a sanitized jar. Fill the jar with cooled, boiled water and place it in the refrigerator. The lack of nutrients in the water will cause the yeast to kind of "hibernate," and it will keep for up to a couple of months. You should pitch this yeast to a starter after storage to revitalize it.

The only drawback to the above harvesting method is the contamination risk for the current batch. Experienced brewers with good sanitation practices can harvest yeast that way without much risk, but for newer brewers, it is probably better to collect the yeast after the fermentation is complete. You can collect yeast from the bottom of either the primary or secondary fermenter. The yeast from the primary is healthier but usually has a lot of trub mixed in. If you obtain yeast from the secondary, it will have smaller amounts of trub mixed in and will be easier to separate. However, you need to be aware that if you repitch yeast harvested from the secondary several times in succession, you will tend to select the less flocculent cells of the population, and future beers will be slow to clarify. But if you only re-pitch once or twice, it is not a big deal. I myself usually harvest yeast from the secondary.

If you harvest yeast from the primary fermenter, you will need to separate the yeast from all the trub that is mixed in. Professional brewers most often do this by "acid washing" the yeast—using acid to lower the pH to about 2.5 so that bacteria is inhibited, and using whirlpool methods to separate the heavier trub from the lighter yeast. But acid washing tends to inhibit the yeast, too, and is not strictly necessary. You can simply use chilled, boiled* water and two sanitized jars to separate the healthy yeast (white) away from the majority of the trub.

1. After racking the beer, swirl up the yeast layer on the bottom and pour some into a large sanitized jar (such as a mayonnaise jar).

2. Gently pour in some cold, boiled water, and swirl it up to get all the yeast and trub in suspension.

3. Let the jar sit for a minute or three to allow most of the trub to settle to the bottom. Gently pour the cloudy water, containing suspended yeast, into another sanitized jar. Discard the dark trub.

4. Add more water, and repeat this procedure until you are left with a substantially light-colored yeast suspension and only a thin brown layer of dead yeast and trub on the bottom of the jar. When the yeast finally settles, you will have a white yeast layer on top of a thin trub layer.

5. Store the jar in the refrigerator for up to a couple of months. The yeast will turn brown as it ages. Discard it once it turns the color of peanut butter. Eventually the yeast will autolyze and die, as its nutritional reserves are used up.

Pitch the yeast to a starter before using, to restore its vitality. If the starter smells wrong—rancid, rubbery, etc.—the yeast may be contaminated. The dominant smell of a starter should be a yeasty smell, but sulfur smells are not necessarily bad, especially with lager yeast strains.

* You want to use boiled water for two reasons: for sanitation, and to avoid exposing the yeast to dissolved oxygen, which would cause the yeast to deplete their glycogen reserves before storage.

[1] Cooper, Ron, "Oxygen and Hydrogen Peroxide in Beer," *Zymurgy* 27: 2 (March/April 2004), 45.

BOILING AND COOLING

Some Thoughts on Boil Gravity

Homebrewers have been using malt extract in the same way for the last thirty years, if not longer. The standard extract-brewing procedure has been to boil all of the extract at a high gravity and dilute that wort in the fermenter. The benefits of this technique were sanitization of all the extract and a very thorough hot break (coagulation) of any remaining protein from the extract manufacturing process. But high-gravity boils also result in reduced hop isomerization, poorer foam stability, and flavor changes from Maillard reactions. Reduced hop isomerization is well known at high gravities but probably not economically significant for homebrewers. Poorer foam stability may come as a surprise, but it is a result of the greater concentration of protein in a high-gravity wort causing a more efficacious coagulation and removal of foam-positive proteins from the wort. After dilution in the fermenter, there is less protein per volume to sustain the foam. Finally, many brewers talk about generating more complex malt flavors due to caramelization of wort sugars during high-gravity boils. The flavor changes are real, but they are actually due to Maillard reactions, not caramelization. True caramelization requires that the sugars be highly concentrated with little water, and temperatures in excess of 300° F (150° C). Maillard reactions occur at a wide range of temperature between a sugar and an amino acid, and the flavor produced depends on the temperature and the specific amino acid involved.

In Chapter 3, I mentioned a group of off-flavors known as extract twang. Some of these flavors are due to oxidation of fatty acids (i.e., staling), but others are due to Maillard reactions and can include molasses, licorice, and phenolic odors like ink. The potential flavor changes depend on many factors, and I am not saying that high-gravity boils always produce inky-tasting beers. In dark beers, the Maillard flavors may readily blend with the malt flavors, but in lighter beers, the flavors may stick out like a sore thumb. It will depend on the wort composition and on the conditions at the time. Maillard reactions also cause wort darkening, which can be frustrating for an extract brewer trying to brew a Munich helles or Pilsener to style. One partial solution to all these issues is to reduce the gravity of the boil by saving some of the extract until the end of the boil. This last extract can be boiled for just a few minutes for pasteurization and then cooled and diluted in the fermenter as before. The result is less wort darkening, better foam stability, and a reduction of potential off-flavors. I have made very good extract beers with this method; your mileage may vary.

First Recipe

OK, are you ready to take the plunge? For your first beer, let's make an American pale ale.

> ### RECIPE
> ### Cincinnati Pale Ale
>
> OG = 1.045 (11.2 °P), 30 IBUs
>
> Ingredients for a 5-gallon (19-liter) batch
>
> - 3.3 lbs. (1.5kg) pale malt extract syrup, unhopped
>
> - 2.5 lbs. (1.1kg) amber dry malt extract
>
> - 6 AAUs of bittering hops (any variety) For example, 0.5 oz. (14g) of 12% AA Nugget, or 0.75 oz. (21g) of 8% AA Northern Brewer
>
> - 5 AAUs of finishing hops (Cascade or other) For example, 1 oz. (28g) of 5% Cascade or 1.25 oz. (36g) of 4% Liberty
>
> - 2 new packets of dry ale yeast

> ### Working With Extract
>
> Dry malt extract is easiest to dissolve in cold water. In hot water it tends to clump and takes a lot of stirring to dissolve the clumps. On the other hand, liquid malt extract is easier to dissolve in hot water. It also will pour more easily if you warm the can beforehand and use a spatula to get every drop. Turn the heat off while you are dissolving liquid extract, so that it doesn't sit at the bottom of the pot and scorch.

American pale ale is an adaptation of the classic British pale ale. With the resurgence of interest in ales in the United States, pale ale evolved to reflect a renewed interest in American hop varieties and a higher level of bitterness, as microbreweries experimented with traditional styles.

American pale ale has a cleaner, less fruity taste than its British counterparts, because American ale yeast strains are less fruity than comparable English ale yeast. Pale ales vary in color from gold to dark amber and typically have a hint of sweet caramel (from the use of caramel malts) that does not mask the hop finish. We will use amber malt extract for part of our recipe, which contains caramel malt, to achieve this.

The Cascade hop has become a staple of American microbrewing. It has a distinct citrus aroma, as compared to the European hops, and has helped American pale ale stand shoulder-to-shoulder with other classic beer styles of the world. Prime examples of this style are Anchor Liberty Ale and Sierra Nevada Pale Ale. The finishing hops are usually Cascade, although other American hop varieties like Amarillo, Liberty, or Willamette work as well. American pale ale is also commonly dry-hopped. For more hop aroma, an additional half-ounce can be added to the primary fermenter after the bubbling starts to taper off. Dry-hopping does not increase the bitterness of the ale, but it adds a wonderful aroma and some flavor.

Beginning the Boil

1. **Prepare the brew water.** In the brewpot, bring about 3 gallons (11.4 liters) of water to a boil. Pour this water into the bucket fermenter, and leave it to cool. Actually, it helps to do this step the night before. (Don't pour hot water into a glass carboy.)

Figure 48 The brewing water is boiling in the pot, and the malt extract and hops are ready to be added. Warm water for rehydrating the yeast (p. 72-73) is ready, also. Have a large towel handy to soak up any spills that might occur. Four out of five spouses surveyed did not like sticky floors.

Note: If your tap water is clean and fresh tasting, you probably don't need to boil it before adding it to the fermenter. But if you have any doubts, boil it to be sure.

2. Add malt extract. Dissolve the 2.5 pounds (1.1kg) of dry malt extract into 3 gallons (11.4 liters) of cold water in the brewpot. You will be boiling the hops in this wort. Some water will evaporate during the boil, and some will be lost to the trub. Starting out with 6 gallons total between the brewpot and the fermenter will help ensure that you hit your 5-gallon recipe volume.

3. Boil it. Bring the wort to a boil, stirring regularly to be sure that it doesn't scorch.

The Hot Break

4. Watch the pot for boilovers. This next stage is critical. The pot needs to be watched constantly. As the wort boils, a foam will start to rise and form a smooth surface. This is good. If the foam suddenly billows over the side, this is a boilover (bad). If it looks like it is going to boil over, either lower the heat or spray the surface with water from a spray bottle. Putting a few copper pennies into the pot to act as boil initiators will also help prevent boilovers.

The foam is caused by the coagulation of proteins in the wort during the boil. The wort will continue to foam until the protein clumps get heavy enough to sink back into the pot. You will see particles floating around in the wort. It may look like egg drop soup. This is called the hot break, and may take 5 to 20 minutes to occur, depending on the amount of protein in your extract. The extract has already been boiled once when it was made, so usually there is not very much at this

stage. Often the first hop addition triggers a great deal of foaming, especially if hop pellets are used. I recommend waiting until the hot break occurs before doing your first hop addition and timing the hour. The extra boiling time won't hurt.

Covering the pot with the lid can help with heat retention and help you achieve your boil, but it can also lead to trouble. Murphy's Law has its own brewing corollary: "If it can boil over, it will boil over." Covering the pot and turning your back on it is the quickest way to achieve a boilover. If you cover the pot, watch it like a hawk . . . a hawk and ten buzzards, even.

Once you achieve a boil, only partially cover the pot, if at all. Why? Because there are sulfur compounds in wort that evolve and boil off. If they aren't removed during the boil, they will later form dimethyl sulfide, which contributes a cooked cabbage or cornlike flavor to the beer. If the cover is left on the pot, or left on in such a way that the condensate from the lid can drip back in, then these flavors will have a much greater chance of showing up in the beer.

Hop Additions

5. Add hops (T = 60 minutes). Once the hot break has occurred, add all of the bittering hops. Stir them in, so that they are all wetted. Be careful that the wort doesn't boil over when you add them. These should be boiled for about an hour to isomerize the alpha acids for bittering. See Chapter 5 for details on how the hop additions affect the beer's flavor.

6. Add more hops (T = 30 minutes). Continue the rolling boil for the remainder of the hour. Stir occasionally to prevent scorching. There will probably be a change in color and aroma, and there will be clumps of stuff floating in the wort. This is not a concern—it's the hot break material, i.e., coagulated/precipitated protein. Add half of the finishing hops at 30 minutes before the end of the boil.

7. Rehydrate the dried yeast. Although many people skip this step with fair results, rehydrating it assures the best performance. While you are waiting for the next hop addition, rehydrate one packet of Nottingham dried ale yeast. Put 1 cup (237 milliliters) of warm (95 to 105° F, 35 to 40° C), pre-boiled water into your sanitized jar, and sprinkle in the yeast. Cover with plastic wrap, and wait 15 minutes. Then gently stir the yeast to make sure it is fully wetted and suspended. Let it sit until you are ready to pitch. (The other packet was just in case you spilled the first.)

Another useful method for rehydration that I have been using is to pour that cup of preboiled water into a plastic self-sealing storage bag. I pour in my dry yeast, then carefully close the zipper most of the way and expel all of the air from the bag before finally sealing it. This way, I can squish and squeeze the bag to rehydrate the yeast without worrying about oxygen exposure. And it is very easy to open this bag and pitch it to the wort when I am ready. See Chapter 6 for more info.

8. Add more hops (T = 15 minutes). Add the last half of the finishing hops at 15 minutes before the end of the boil. These late additions allow less time for the volatile oils to boil away, increasing hop flavor and aroma. You can add a little more at knockout (after the heat is off and the wort is starting to cool) if still more hop aroma is desired. Refer to Chapter 5 for more information.

9. Add the rest of the extract (T = 5 minutes). OK, you are almost done brewing. It is time to add the rest of your malt extract (the pale liquid malt extract) to the boil to pasteurize it before we cool the wort and dilute it in the fermenter.

Cooling the Wort

At the end of the boil, it is important to cool the wort quickly, for several reasons. It is still susceptible to oxidation damage as it cools. If the wort is cooled slowly, the dimethyl sulfide precursors will continue to be produced in the hot wort. Without the boil to drive them off, DMS off-flavors will be generated in the beer. The objective is to rapidly cool the wort to below 80° F (27° C) before oxidation or contamination can occur. For your first batch, I recommend using a cold water bath to chill the wort, but alternative methods are presented on the next page.

Rapid cooling also forms the "cold break." This is composed of another group of proteins that need to be thermally shocked into precipitating out of the wort. Slow cooling will not affect them. Cold break, or rather the lack of it, is the cause of "chill haze." When a beer is chilled for drinking, these proteins partially precipitate, forming a haze. As the beer warms up, the proteins redissolve. Only by rapid chilling from near-boiling to room temperature will the cold break proteins permanently precipitate and not cause chill haze. Chill haze is usually regarded as a cosmetic problem—you cannot taste it. However, chill haze indicates that there is an appreciable level of cold-break-type protein in the beer, which has been linked to long-term stability problems. Hazy beer tends to become stale sooner than non-hazy beer.

Water Bath

10. Cool it. Place the pot in a sink or tub filled with cold/ice water that can be circulated around the hot pot. As mentioned in the previous chapter, it is best to keep the pot lid on, but if you are careful, you can speed up the cooling by stirring. Gently stir the wort in a circular manner, so the maximum amount of wort is moving against the sides of the pot. Aim for minimize splashing to avoid oxidation. Don't let water from your hands drip inside the pot; this could be a source of contamination. If the cooling water gets warm, replace with colder water. The wort should cool to 70° F (21° C) in about 30 minutes. The closer you can get it to your fermentation temperature, the better.

11. Ferment the wort. See the next chapter for a discussion of what fermentation is, and Chapter 9 for the rest of the instructions for your first batch.

Ice

People often wonder about adding ice directly to the cooling wort. This idea works well if you remember a couple of key points:
- Never use commercial ice. It can harbor dormant bacteria that could spoil your beer.
- Always boil the water before freezing it in an airtight plastic food container. It must be airtight, because most freezers also harbor dormant bacteria.
- If the ice will not be in direct contact with the wort (e.g., you are using a frozen plastic soda bottle or other container in the wort), make sure you sanitize the outside of the bottle first before you put it in the wort.

Copper Wort Chillers

Figure 55

A wort chiller is a coil of copper tubing that is used as a heat exchanger to cool the wort in place. Wort chillers are not necessary for your first batch of beer, when you are only boiling two to three gallons, but this is a good time to make you aware of them. Wort chillers are useful for cooling full-volume boils, because you can leave the wort on the stove instead of carrying it to a sink or bathtub. Five gallons of boiling hot wort weighs almost 45 pounds and is hazardous to carry.

There are two basic types of wort chillers: immersion and counterflow. Immersion chillers are the simplest and work by running cold water through the coil. The chiller is immersed in the wort, and the water carries the heat away. Counterflow chillers work in an opposite manner. The hot wort is drained from the pot through the copper tubing, while cold water flows around the outside of the chiller. Immersion chillers are often sold in homebrew supply shops or can be easily made at home. Instructions for building both types of chiller are given in Appendix D.

Murphy's Laws of Brewing

- If it can boil over, it will boil over.

- No good beer goes unfinished.

- Nature always hides in the hidden flaw.

- If you keep messing with it, you will probably screw it up.

- If you don't have time to do it right, you will probably end up doing it over.

- The race is not always to the swift, nor the battle to the strong, but that's the way to bet. (In other words, the most conscientious brewer may not win all the ribbons, but he will probably win most of them.)

Did you ever wonder where Murphy's Law came from? Well, back at work there was a photocopy of a short article from one of the aerospace trade journals on the wall of my friend's cubicle. It went something like this:

Captain Murphy was part of an engineering team out at Edwards Air Force Base in California. Their team was investigating the effects of high-gravity decelerations on jet pilots back in the 1950s. One of their tests involved strapping a test pilot into a rocket chair equipped with strain gauges and other sensors to help them quantify the effects of high-G stopping. The responsibility for the placement of the various sensors was Murphy's. Well, the test was run (subjecting the pilot to something like 100 G's of deceleration), and he got pretty banged up.

Only after it was over did the team realize that of all the possible combinations of placing those sensors, Murphy had done it in the one configuration that resulted in useless data. They would have to run the test again. Upon realizing this, Murphy stated, "If there are two or more ways of doing something, and one of them can result in catastrophe, someone will do it that way." Upon hearing this the team leader said, "That's Murphy's Law." The next day at the test debriefing the team leader shortened it to the now famous, "If anything can go wrong, it will."

Murphy still likes his version better.

FERMENTATION

In this chapter, we will discuss fermentation—how the yeast turns wort into beer. As important as the yeast process is to achieving a good batch, it is also the one step that is most often taken for granted by beginning brewers. A lot of thought will be given to the recipe: which malts, which hops, but often the yeast choice will be whatever was taped to the top of the kit. *Sigh*. Even if some consideration is given to the brand of yeast and the strain, very often the pitching conditions are not planned or controlled. The brewer cools the wort, aerates it a bit, and then sprinkles the yeast on the wort and waits for it to do its thing.

It has been common for brewing texts to overemphasize a short "lag time"—the period of time after pitching the yeast before the foamy head appeared in the fermenter. This lag time was the benchmark that everyone would use to gauge the health of their yeast and the vigor of the fermentation—the shorter the better.

While it is a notable indicator, a short lag time does not guarantee an exemplary fermentation and an outstanding beer. A short lag time only means that initial conditions were favorable for growth and metabolism. It says nothing about the total amount of nutrients in the wort or how the rest of the fermentation will progress.

The fermentation may also appear to finish quickly, when in fact it was not superefficient but rather incomplete. The point is that speed does not necessarily correlate with quality. You need to understand the fermentation process, and how it is affected by conditions, before you can judge it solely on time.

Factors for a Good Fermentation

There are three principal factors that determine fermentation activity and results: yeast, wort nutrients, and temperature.

Yeast Factors

The first step to achieving a good fermentation is to pitch enough yeast. Plan on pitching at least ⅓ cup (75 ml) of yeast slurry into a typical 5-gallon batch of ale, or ⅔ cup (150 ml) of slurry for lagers. For stronger beers, with an OG of more than 1.055, more yeast should be pitched to ensure optimal fermentations. For very strong beers like *doppelbocks* and barley wines, at least 2 cups of slurry should be pitched. See Chapter 6 for recommended pitching rates.

The yeast can be grown via yeast starters, or it can be harvested from previous fermentations. When yeast is harvested from a previous fermentation, it should be skimmed from the kraeusen, or taken from the upper layer of the primary yeast cake. This yeast will have the optimum characteristics for repitching. The yeast from the secondary typically has low sterols and should be pitched to a well-aerated starter before brewing.

Healthy yeast that is obtained from a starter or recently from a prior fermentation will have good vitality and will readily adapt to the new wort. With good levels of aeration and nutrients, the yeast will quickly multiply to the numbers necessary for an exemplary fermentation.

Yeast consume sugars methodically, starting with the monosaccharides (and the disaccharide sucrose), before fermenting the main wort constituent maltose, and finally finishing up with the trisaccharide maltotriose.

Wort Factors

Two considerations are needed to ensure that the wort has been properly prepared to support a good fermentation. The first is oxygen supplied via aeration. The role of oxygen in yeast growth and methods for aerating the wort were covered in Chapter 6.

The second consideration is the level of amino acid nutrients in the wort, specifically referred to as Free Amino Nitrogen or FAN. Malted barley normally supplies all of the FAN and nutrients that the yeast need to grow and adapt to the fermentation environment. So, for a typical all-malt brew, this is not a problem. However, if the recipe incorporates large amounts of adjuncts (e.g., corn, rice, unmalted wheat, unmalted barley), honey, or refined sugars, then the wort may not have the minimum levels of nutrients necessary for the yeast to build strong cells.

Extracts from light beer kits are sometimes thinned with corn sugar, so it's a good idea to add some yeast nutrient powder to worts that are made exclusively from them.

In addition to the lack of nutrients, wort with a high percentage of refined sugar (about 30%) may cause the yeast to lose the ability to secrete the enzymes that allow them to ferment maltose, resulting in a stuck fermentation.

Temperature Factors

The third factor for a good fermentation is temperature. Yeast are greatly affected by temperature—too cold, and they go dormant, too hot (more than 10° F above the nominal range), and they indulge in an orgy of fermentation, creating excessive by-products that often ruin the flavor of the beer. High temperatures can lead to excessive levels of diacetyl.

A common mistake that homebrewers make is pitching the yeast when the wort has not been chilled enough and is still warm (higher than 80° F [27° C]). If the wort is warm when the yeast is pitched and slowly cools to room temperature during primary fermentation, more metabolites (by-products) will be produced in the early stages than the yeast can reabsorb during the secondary stage.

Furthermore, primary fermentation is an exothermic process. The internal temperature of the fermenter can be as much as 10° F above ambient conditions, just due to yeast activity. This is one good reason to keep the fermenter environment in the proper temperature range, so that with a normal vigorous fermentation, the beer turns out as intended, even if it was warmer than the surroundings. So, if it's midsummer and you don't have a way to keep the fermenter cool, then the beer will probably not be very good.

Green apple flavors from acetaldehyde, and buttery flavors from diacetyl, can be cleaned up by conditioning, but others cannot. High temperatures encourage the production of fusel alcohols— heavier alcohols that can have harsh, solventlike flavors. High temperature fermentation can also create an excess of esters, resulting in banana- or bubble-gum-flavored beers. Once created, these flavors cannot be reduced by conditioning. See Chapter 10 for more discussion on how to prevent and control these off-flavors during fermentation.

Redefining Fermentation

The fermentation of malt sugars into beer is a complicated biochemical process. It is more than just the conversion of sugar to alcohol, although that can be considered the primary activity. Total fermentation is better defined as three phases—the adaptation or lag time phase, the attenuative or primary phase, and a conditioning or secondary phase. The yeast do not end primary before beginning secondary— the processes occur in parallel—but the conditioning processes occur more slowly. As the

The Three Phases of Fermentation

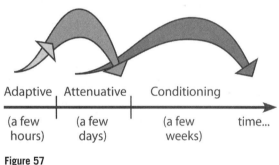

Figure 57

majority of simple sugars are consumed, more and more of the yeast will transition to eating the larger, more complex sugars and early yeast by-products. This is why beer and wine improve with age, to a degree, as long as they are on the yeast. Beer that has been filtered or pasteurized will not benefit from aging.

Lag Time or Adaptation Phase

Immediately after pitching, the yeast start adjusting to the wort conditions and undergo a period of high growth. The yeast use any available oxygen in the wort to facilitate their growth processes. They can use other methods to adapt and grow in the absence of oxygen, but they can do it much more efficiently with oxygen. Under normal conditions, the yeast should work through the adaptation phase and begin primary fermentation within 24 hours. If 48 hours pass without apparent activity, then a new batch of yeast should probably be pitched.

At the beginning of the adaptation phase, the yeast take stock of the sugars, FAN, and other nutrients present and figure out which enzymes and other attributes they need to adapt to the environment. The yeast use their own glycogen reserves, oxygen, and wort lipids to synthesize sterols to build up their cell membranes. The sterols are known to be critical for enabling the cell membrane to be permeable to wort sugars and other wort nutrients. Sterols can also be produced by the yeast under poor oxygen conditions from lipids found in wort trub, but that pathway is much less efficient.

Once the cell walls are permeable, the yeast can start metabolizing the amino nitrogen and sugars in the wort for food. Like every animal, the goal in life for the yeast cell is to reproduce. Yeast reproduce asexually by "budding." Daughter cells split off from the parent cell. The reproduction process takes a lot of energy, and aerobic metabolic processes are more efficient than anaerobic. Thus, an oxygen-rich wort shortens the adaptation phase, and allows the yeast to quickly reproduce to levels that will ensure a good fermentation. When the oxygen is used up, the yeast switch metabolic pathways and begin what we consider to be fermentation—the anaerobic metabolism of sugar to alcohol. This pathway is less energy efficient, so the yeast cannot reproduce as proficiently as during the adaptation phase.

The key to a good fermentation is lots of strong, healthy yeast—yeast that can get the job done before going dormant due to depleted resources, rising alcohol levels, and old age. As noted, the rate of reproduction is slower in the absence of oxygen. At some point in the fermentation cycle of the beer, the rate of yeast reproduction is going to fall off toward zero. By planning the initial pitching rate and providing optimum conditions for yeast reproduction and growth in the wort initially, we can ensure that there is enough yeast to attenuate and condition the beer fully.

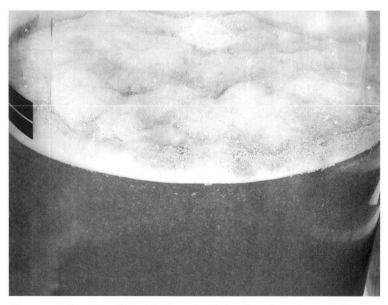

Figure 58 A healthy, creamy, kraeusen of yeast floats on top during the primary fermentation stage. This is a good time to skim off some yeast to save for a future batch.

Primary or Attenuative Phase

The primary or attenuative phase is marked by a time of vigorous fermentation and can last anywhere from two to six days for ales or four to ten days for lagers, depending on conditions. The majority of the attenuation occurs during the primary phase, when the gravity of the beer drops by two-thirds to three-fourths of the original gravity.

A head of foamy kraeusen will form on top of the beer. The foam consists of yeast and wort proteins and is a light creamy color, with islands of green-brown gunk that collect and tend to adhere to the sides of the fermenter. The gunk is composed of extraneous wort protein, hop resins, and dead yeast. These compounds are very bitter, and if stirred back into the wort would result in harsh aftertastes. Fortunately, these compounds are relatively insoluble and are typically removed by adhering to the sides of the fermenter as the kraeusen subsides. It is not necessary to use a blowoff hose or to skim the gunk from the kraeusen, unless you want to harvest some of the yeast.

As the primary phase winds down, most of the yeast start settling out, and the kraeusen starts to subside. If you are going to transfer the beer off of the trub and primary yeast cake, this is the proper time to do so. Take care to avoid aerating the beer during the transfer. At this point in the fermentation process, any exposure to oxygen will only contribute to staling reactions in the beer, or worse, expose it to contamination.

Many canned kits will advise bottling the beer after one week or after the kraeusen has subsided. This is not a good idea, because the beer has not yet completed the conditioning phase. At this time the beer would taste a bit rough around the edges (e.g., yeasty flavors, buttery tones, green apple flavors), but that will disappear after a few days or weeks of conditioning, depending on the yeast strain and the fermentation environment.

Figure 59 As the primary stage winds down and the secondary stage takes over, the yeast start to flocculate, and the kraeusen settles back into the beer.

Secondary or Conditioning Phase

The reactions that take place during the conditioning phase are primarily a function of the yeast. The vigorous primary stage is over, the majority of the wort sugars have been converted to alcohol, and a lot of the yeast cells are going dormant, but some are still active.

The secondary phase allows for the slow reduction of the remaining fermentables and early by-products. The yeast have eaten most of the easily fermentable sugars and now start to work on the heavier sugars like maltotriose. Diacetyl and acetaldehyde continue to be reduced as well.

There has been a lot of controversy within the homebrewing community on the value of racking beers, particularly ales, to secondary fermenters. Many seasoned homebrewers have declared that there is no real taste benefit, and that the dangers of contamination and the cost in additional time are not worth what little benefit there may be. There is a risk tradeoff between letting the yeast finish the job and getting the beer off the trub.

The dormant yeast on the bottom of the fermenter will excrete undesirable amino and fatty acids. Leaving the post-primary beer on the trub and yeast cake for too long (more than a month, for example) can result in soapy flavors in the beer due to oxidation and other chemical reactions. Further, after very long times, the yeast may begin to die and break down—autolysis, which produces meaty, sulfuric tastes and smells. Depending on the yeast strain, wort composition, fermentation conditions, and phase of the moon, it may be necessary to get the beer off the trub and dormant yeast during the conditioning phase. However, now that you have been duly warned, I will say that I routinely leave my beer in the primary for three to four weeks, due to lack of time, clean bottles, and a sanitized siphon, without any problems.

Leaving an ale beer in the primary fermenter for a total of two to three weeks, instead of just one, will provide time for the conditioning reactions and improve the beer. The extra time will also let more sediment settle out before bottling, resulting in a clearer beer and easier pouring.

Conditioning Processes

After the vigorous primary stage is over, the majority of the wort sugars have been converted to alcohol, and a lot of the yeast are going dormant, but there is still yeast activity. During the earlier phases, the yeast produced many different compounds in addition to ethanol and CO_2, (e.g., acetaldehyde, esters, amino acids, ketones, dimethyl sulfide, etc.). Once the easy food is gone, the yeast start reprocessing some of these by-products.

Diacetyl and pentanedione are two diketones that have buttery and honeylike flavors. These compounds are considered flaws when present in large amounts and can cause flavor stability problems during storage. Acetaldehyde is an aldehyde that has a pronounced green apple smell and taste. It is an intermediate compound in the production of ethanol. The yeast reduce these compounds during the latter stages of fermentation.

The yeast also produce an array of fusel alcohols during primary fermentation in addition to ethanol. Fusels are higher molecular weight alcohols that often give harsh solventlike tastes to beer. During secondary fermentation, the yeast will convert some of these alcohols to more pleasant, fruity-tasting esters. Warmer temperatures encourage ester production.

Toward the end of secondary fermentation, the suspended yeast flocculates (settles out), and the beer clears. This is your indicator for when it is time to bottle. High molecular weight proteins also settle out during this stage. Tannin/phenol compounds will bind with the proteins and also settle out, greatly smoothing the taste of the beer.

This process can be helped by chilling or lagering the beer. In the case of ales, this process is referred to as cold conditioning and is a popular practice at most brewpubs and microbreweries. Cold conditioning for a week helps clear the beer with or without the use of finings. Fining agents, such as isinglass (made from fish bladders), Polyclar® (plastic dust), or gelatin, can be added to the fermenter to help speed the flocculation process and promote the settling of haze-forming proteins and tannins. While much of the emphasis on using finings is to combat aesthetic chill haze, the real benefit of dropping those compounds is to improve the taste and long-term stability of the beer. See Appendix C for more info.

Using Secondary Fermenters

Using a two-stage fermentation is usually only necessary for lagers and high OG ales, and requires a good understanding of the fermentation process. At any time, racking the beer can adversely affect it because of potential oxygen exposure and contamination risk. It is important to minimize the amount of head space in the secondary fermenter to minimize the exposure to oxygen until the head space can be purged by the still-fermenting beer. For this reason, plus the fact that they're permeable to oxygen, plastic buckets do not make good secondary fermenters. Five-gallon glass carboys make the best secondary fermenters.

The following is a general procedure for using a secondary fermenter.

1. Allow the primary fermentation stage to wind down. This will be two to six days (four to ten days for lagers) after pitching, when the bubbling rate drops off dramatically to about one to five per minute. The kraeusen will have started to settle back into the beer, and the surface will begin to clear.

2. Using a sanitized siphon (no sucking or splashing!), rack the beer off the trub into another clean fermenter, and affix an airlock. The beer should still be fairly cloudy with suspended yeast.

Racking from the primary may be done at any time after primary fermentation has more or less been completed. Most brewers will notice a brief increase in activity after racking, but then all activity may cease. This is very normal; it is not additional primary fermentation per se, but just dissolved carbon dioxide coming out of solution due to the disturbance. Fermentation (conditioning) is still taking place, so just leave it alone.

Different beer styles benefit from different lengths of conditioning. Generally, the higher the original gravity, the longer the conditioning time to reach peak flavor. Small beers like 1.035 pale ales will reach peak flavor within a couple of weeks of bottling. Stronger, more complex ales, like stouts, may require a month or more. Very strong beers like doppelbocks and barley wines will require six months to a year before they condition to their peak flavor. (If oxidation doesn't take its toll first; I have had some pretty awful year-old barley wines.)

Especially long times in secondary (for light ales, more than eight weeks) may require the addition of fresh yeast at bottling time for good carbonation. This situation is usually not a problem, however. See Chapter 10 for related information on lager brewing.

When bottling your first few batches, it is always a good idea to set aside a six-pack in the corner of the basement and leave it for a time. It is enlightening to taste a homebrewed beer that has had two months to bottle condition and compare it to what the batch initially tasted like.

Secondary Fermenter vs. Bottle Conditioning

Conditioning can be done in either the secondary fermenter or the bottle, but the two methods do produce different results. It is up to you to determine how long to give each phase to produce your intended beer.

Yeast activity is responsible for conditioning, so it is logical that the greater yeast mass in the fermenter is more effective at conditioning than the smaller amount of suspended yeast in the bottle. This is why I recommend that you give your beer more time in the fermenter before bottling. When you add the priming sugar and bottle your beer, the yeast go through the same three stages of fermentation as the main batch, including the production of by-products. If the beer is bottled early, e.g., one week old, then the small amount of yeast in the bottle has to do the double task of conditioning the priming by-products as well as those from the main fermentation. You could very well end up with an off-flavored batch.

Studies have shown that priming and bottle conditioning is a very unique form of fermentation due to the oxygen present in the head space of the bottle, only about 30% of which is used. The other 70% can contribute to staling reactions. Additional fermentables have been added to the beer to produce the carbonation, and this results in very different ester profiles than those that are normally produced in the main fermenter. In some styles, like Belgian-style strong ale, bottle conditioning and the resultant flavors are the hallmark of the style. These styles cannot be produced with the same flavors via kegging.

For the best results, the beer should be given time to condition before priming and bottling. And to minimize the risk of off-flavors from sitting on the trub, extended conditioning should be done in a secondary fermenter. There will still be sufficient yeast in suspension to ferment the priming sugar and carbonate the beer, even if the yeast have flocculated and the beer has cleared.

Summary

I hope this chapter has helped you understand what fermentation is and how it works. You need to have sufficient yeast and the right conditions for them to work under to achieve the best possible beer. The next chapter will use this information to walk you through fermenting your first batch.

FERMENTING YOUR FIRST BATCH

So now you have the fruit of your labors cooled in the boiling pot, and you feel like celebrating. But don't call in your friends, because it's not beer yet. It won't be beer until you have pitched your yeast, and the beer won't be finished until it has completed fermenting, which is probably a couple of weeks away at least. And then you will still need to bottle it. . . . But have no fear, the hard part is over. What we need to do now is transfer it to your fermenter, make sure the wort has been aerated, pitch the yeast, and find a cool, quiet place to put the fermenter for the next couple of weeks.

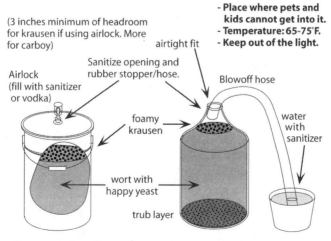

(3 inches minimum of headroom for krausen if using airlock. More for carboy)

- **Place where pets and kids cannot get into it.**
- **Temperature: 65-75°F.**
- **Keep out of the light.**

airtight fit

Sanitize opening and rubber stopper/hose.

Airlock (fill with sanitizer or vodka)

Blowoff hose

foamy krausen

water with sanitizer

wort with happy yeast

trub layer

Figure 60 Fermenter diagrams during primary phase

Choosing Your Fermenter

Buckets vs. Carboys

There are two types of fermenter commonly available: food-grade plastic buckets (bins) and glass carboys. Each type has its own merits. The plastic buckets are less expensive than the glass and much safer to handle. The buckets have the outstanding option of being fitted with spigots, which makes siphoning unnecessary—a real plus. The buckets are typically six gallons, leaving one gallon of head space for the fermentation, which is usually sufficient.

The spigot option eliminates siphoning between fermenters if you are racking to a secondary and simplifies bottle filling. A bucket with a spigot can be used as a bottling bucket, which provides better distribution of the priming sugar for bulk priming and greater control of the fill level. Priming and bottling will be discussed in Chapter 11.

Although you will need a siphon, a glass carboy has the advantage of letting you see your beer and being able to gauge the activity of the fermentation. There are two sizes commonly available, a 6.5-gallon size that is perfect for primary fermentations and a 5-gallon size, which is ideal for secondary fermentation. The large size typically has enough head space to contain the kraeusen, while the 5-gallon size almost completely eliminates the head space above the beer, preventing oxidation during the conditioning phase. You will need to shield the carboys from the light, but you can easily tell when fermentation is over and the yeast is settling out.

Airlocks vs. Blowoffs

The decision to use an airlock or blowoff hose is determined by head space. Usually the buckets and large carboys have enough head space (at least 3 inches), so that the foam does not enter the airlock. If the fermentation is so vigorous that the foam pops the airlock out of the lid, just rinse it out with sanitizer solution and wipe off the lid before replacing it. Contamination is not a big problem during the primary phase. With so much coming out of the fermenter, not much gets in. If the fermentation keeps filling the airlock with crud and popping it out, there is an alternative.

The alternative is called a blowoff hose/tube, and it allows foam and hop remnants to be carried out of the fermenter. A blowoff is a necessity if you are using a 5-gallon carboy as your main fermenter, but it will likely result in the loss of a couple of quarts of beer. Get a 1-inch diameter plastic hose and fit this snugly inside the mouth of the carboy or enlarge the hole in the bucket lid, if necessary. Run the hose down the side and submerge the end in a bucket of sanitizer/water.

Always use a large diameter hose to prevent clogging. If the tube gets clogged, the fermenter can get pressurized and blow goo all over the ceiling—or worse, burst. Blowoffs are sometimes necessary for 6.5-gallon carboys, too, but there won't be any beer loss; only the foam will be carried out.

Transferring the Wort

Your wort should be cool before you pour it into the fermenter. If it is not, refer to Chapter 7 for suggested cooling methods. But before you transfer the wort to the fermenter, you may be wondering what to do about all the hops and gunk in the bottom of the pot.

There will be a considerable amount of hot break, cold break, and hops in the bottom of the boiling pot after cooling. It is a good idea to remove the hot break (or the break in general) from the wort before fermenting. The hot break consists of various proteins and fatty acids that can cause off-flavors, although a moderate amount of hot break can go unnoticed in most beers. The cold break is not considered to be as much of a problem; in fact, a small amount of cold break in the fermenter is good, because it can provide the yeast with needed nutrients. The hops do not matter at all, except that they are pretty well mixed up with the break.

In general however, removal of the break is necessary to achieve the cleanest tasting beer. If you are trying to make a very pale beer, such as a Pilsener-style lager, the removal of most of the hot and cold break will make a significant difference.

The most common method for separating the wort from the break is to carefully decant the wort off into the fermenter, leaving the break behind. Pouring the wort through a stainless steel strainer can also help with this approach. If you are siphoning the cooled wort from the pot, then attaching a copper or stainless scrubby pad to the end of the siphon will help.

Whirlpooling will also help. Whirlpooling is a means of gathering most of the break and hops into the center of the pot to better enable the siphon to draw off clear wort from the side. Rapidly stir the wort in a circular manner. Continue stirring until all the liquid is moving and a whirlpool forms. Stop stirring, and let the whirlpool slow down and settle for 10 minutes or so. The hops and trub will form a pile in the center of the pot, leaving the edge relatively clear. The siphon won't clog as quickly now if it draws from the side of the pot.

But let's get back to the job at hand, pouring the wort into the fermenter.

1. Pour the water. Pour the reserved 2 to 3 gallons of water into the sanitized fermenter. Aeration of the water in the fermenter before adding the cooled wort is a good way to provide enough dissolved oxygen for the yeast. It is much easier to aerate this smaller volume of water first, rather than the entire volume later.

2. Pour the wort. Pour the cooled wort into the fermenter, allowing vigorous churning and splashing. This provides additional dissolved oxygen that the yeast need. Try to prevent the majority of the hot and cold break from getting into the fermenter. Whole hops help to provide a filter. If some hops and break make it into the fermenter, it is not a big deal.

Figure 61 Pouring the wort into the fermenter. Aeration works best if it is poured back and forth a few times.

Figure 62 Having poured most of the wort into the fermenter, I am now attempting to keep most of the trub out. After I throw the trub away, I will pour the wort back and forth to aerate it more.

HOW TO BREW

Using a Secondary Fermenter to Reduce Trub in the Fermenter

You can use a 5-gallon carboy to reduce the trub in a couple of ways:

Siphon first, pitch later. You can siphon the wort into the first vessel, let it sit for a few hours to let the trub settle, rack to your main fermenter, and then pitch.

Pitch first, siphon later. The alternative is to pitch your yeast and let it ferment for several days as it undergoes its primary/attenuation phase. (This is the way I do it.) Wait until the bubbling of the fermenter slows way down, and then rack to a secondary fermenter. Off-flavors associated with sitting on the trub typically take a couple of weeks to develop. Although removal of the trub from the fermentation is not critical, keep it in mind as a brewing variable that can be utilized in your quest for the perfect batch.

3. Pour it back. Discard the hops and trub from the brewpot, and pour some wort from the fermenter back and forth to the brewpot several times. This will help ensure you have enough dissolved oxygen for the yeast. Short of using an airstone and air pump, this is the best way to aerate your wort.

Conducting Your Fermentation

Pitching the Yeast

4. Pitch. No, this doesn't mean to throw the yeast away. It means to throw it in. Pitch (pour) the yeast into the fermenter, making sure to add it all. It is best (for the yeast) if the yeast temperature is same or colder than the wort temperature you are pitching to, and it is best for the beer if the wort temperature when you pitch is the same or a couple of degrees cooler than the intended fermentation temperature. For ale yeasts, the fermentation temperature range is typically 65 to 75° F (18 to 24° C). Starting out warmer than your intended fermentation temperature will cause more off-flavors due to fermentation by-products and in extreme cases may cause the yeast to stall out.

5. Seal. Put the fermenter lid in place, and seal it. But don't put the airlock in quite yet; if you didn't pour it back and forth earlier, we'll want to shake this up. Place a piece of clean plastic wrap over the hole in the lid and insert the stopper.

6. Shake. With the fermenter lid tightly sealed, place it on the floor and rock it back and forth for several minutes to churn it up. This distributes the yeast into the wort and provides more dissolved oxygen for the yeast. If any wort leaks out, wipe it off with a paper towel that is wet with your sanitizer solution. Place the sanitized airlock and rubber stopper in the lid. The airlock should be filled to the line with sanitizer solution. Many people use vodka or plain boiled water as alternatives. You want something that will not grow mold or contaminate the batch, in case it inadvertently gets sucked inside the fermenter.

Note: If the fermenter starts out warm and then cools, you run the risk of the pressure difference sucking the sanitizer solution out of the airlock and into the fermenter. This will generally not be enough to kill the yeast, but it can cause off-flavors if you use bleach water.

Fermentation Location

Place the fermenter in a protected area that has a stable temperature between 65 and 75° F (18 and 24° C). Good places are closets, basements, or a spare bathroom. You will probably want to set the fermenter inside a shallow pan or put a towel under it, in case any foam escapes through the airlock. Place it in an area that is not exposed to direct sunlight, for two reasons: first, to keep it from getting too warm, and second, if you are using glass, sunlight will cause a photochemical reaction with the hop compounds and skunk your beer.

Maintain a consistent temperature if possible, because fluctuating temperature stresses the yeast and can impair the fermentation. If the temperature drops overnight and the bubbling stops, don't worry—simply move it to a warmer room, and it should pick up again. Temperatures below 55 to 60° F (13 to 16° C) will cause ale yeast to go into hibernation and slow or stop the fermentation process.

Animals and small children are fascinated by the smell and noises from the airlock, so keep them away. Dogs tend to like beer and will try to sneak samples before it's done. Cats hate being left out of the decision-making during brewing and will attempt to get a paw in later. I also remember an acquaintance that was surprised when his fermentation started bubbling again after it had previously quieted. When he later opened the fermenter to bottle, he discovered his three-year-old son had been dropping crayons and pencils in through the airlock hole.

Figure 66 Decision time: To rack or not to rack . . .

Primary Fermentation

Active fermentation should start within 12 hours, but it can be longer due to lower pitching rates—about 24 hours. The airlock will bubble regularly. The fermentation activity can be vigorous or slow; either is fine. The three important factors for a successful fermentation are pitching enough yeast, good wort nutrients, and maintaining a consistent temperature in the correct range. If you do these right, it is not unheard of for an ale's primary fermentation to be completed in 48 hours. Three days at 65 to 70° F (18 to 24° C) for primary fermentation is typical for the simple pale ale being described here. Once the bubbling slows down, however, do not open the lid to peek. The beer is still susceptible to bacterial infections, particularly anaerobic ones like *Pediococcus* and *Lactobacillus* found in your mouth. If you really want to look, peek in through the airlock hole, but keep the lid on.

Secondary Fermentation

Here is where you will need to make a decision. Are you going to use single-stage or two-stage fermentation for your beer? If you are going to use single stage, i.e., just this one fermenter, then you have nothing further to do but to leave the beer where it is for a total of two to three weeks. The conditioning processes will proceed, and the beer will clear.

If you are going to rack to a secondary fermenter, I strongly recommend that you use a 5-gallon glass carboy to minimize the head space and oxygen exposure during conditioning.

Racking

Racking is the term for the process of transferring the beer without disturbing the sediments or exposing it to air. Usually this is done by siphoning. If you have a bucket fermenter with a spigot, then transfer becomes simple. It is imperative not to aerate the wort during transfer after primary fermentation. Any oxygen in the beer at this time will cause staling reactions that will become evident in the flavor of the beer within a couple of weeks. Always transfer the beer slowly and keep the outlet tube beneath the surface of the beer as you fill the secondary. Don't let the stream guzzle or spray as you fill.

The only way to combat aeration damage is to introduce young beer to the fermenter at bottling time. This process is called "kraeusening," and is a time-honored method of carbonating beer, but it is an advanced technique that I do not cover.

Estimating the Alcohol Content

How much alcohol will there be? This is a common question. While there are various laboratory techniques that can be employed to determine it precisely, there is a simple way to estimate it. The easiest is to use a "triple scale hydrometer," which has a "percent alcohol by volume" scale right on it. Subtract the respective percentages that correspond to your OG and FG, and there you have it.

If you don't have this type of hydrometer, the following table based on the work of Balling should satisfy your curiosity. Find the intersection of your OG and FG to read your estimated percentage of alcohol by volume.

In the next chapter, we will discuss how the brewing and fermenting of lager beer differs from ales. Then in Chapter 11 we will prepare to prime, bottle, and ultimately consume our beer.

TABLE 10
Percent Alcohol By Volume (ABV) From OG and FG

	1.030	1.035	1.040	1.045	1.050	1.055	1.060	1.065	1.070	1.075
0.998	4.1	4.8	5.4	6.1	6.8	7.4	8.1	8.7	9.4	10.1
1.000	3.9	4.5	5.2	5.8	6.5	7.1	7.8	8.5	9.1	9.8
1.002	3.6	4.2	4.9	5.6	6.2	6.9	7.5	8.2	8.9	9.5
1.004	3.3	4.0	4.6	5.3	5.9	6.6	7.3	7.9	8.6	9.3
1.006	3.1	3.7	4.4	5.0	5.7	6.3	7.0	7.7	8.3	9.0
1.008	2.8	3.5	4.1	4.8	5.4	6.1	6.7	7.4	8.0	8.7
1.010	2.6	3.2	3.8	4.5	5.1	5.8	6.5	7.1	7.8	8.4
1.012	2.3	2.9	3.6	4.2	4.9	5.5	6.2	6.8	7.5	8.2
1.014	2.0	2.7	3.3	4.0	4.6	5.3	5.9	6.6	7.2	7.9
1.016	1.8	2.4	3.1	3.7	4.4	5.0	5.7	6.3	7.0	7.6
1.018	1.5	2.2	2.8	3.4	4.1	4.7	5.4	6.0	6.7	7.3
1.020	1.3	1.9	2.5	3.2	3.8	4.5	5.1	5.8	6.4	7.1
1.022	1.0	1.6	2.3	2.9	3.6	4.2	4.9	5.5	6.2	6.8
1.024	0.8	1.4	2.0	2.7	3.3	4.0	4.6	5.2	5.9	6.5

WHAT IS DIFFERENT ABOUT BREWING LAGER BEER?

What makes lager beer different from ale beer, you ask?

Well, the main difference is temperature. Make that temperature and time. No, there's three: temperature, time, and yeast. Let's start with yeast.

Yeast Differences

As discussed in Chapter 6, lager yeasts like lower fermentation temperatures. Lager yeasts produce fewer fruity esters than ale yeasts and have an enzyme that can ferment a sugar called raffinose that ale yeast strains can't. Raffinose is a trisaccharide of sucrose and galactose, but it doesn't actually occur in beer wort, so don't expect an increase in attenuation; the ability of lager yeast to ferment raffinose is purely academic.

Lager yeast also produce more sulfur compounds during primary fermentation than ale yeast. Many first-time lager brewers are astonished by the rotten egg smell coming from their fermenters, sometimes letting it convince them that the batch is infected and causing them to dump it. Don't do it! Fortunately, these compounds continue to vent during the conditioning (lagering) phase, and the chemical precursors of other odious compounds are gradually eaten up by the yeast. A previously rank-smelling beer that is properly lagered will be sulfur-free and delicious at bottling time.

Speaking of Time . . .

Additional Time

The lower fermentation temperature decreases the rate at which the yeast work and lengthens both the primary and secondary fermentation times. The primary phase for ales is often two to five days, but one to three weeks is normal for a lager. As mentioned in the previous chapter, the primary and conditioning phases of fermentation happen concurrently, but the conditioning phase takes longer. This is especially true with lager yeasts. The defining character of a lager beer is a clean, malty taste without ale fruitiness. Obviously those rotten egg odors don't belong, either. The time that it takes for these compounds to be processed by the yeast can be several weeks to a few months. It depends on the malts used, the yeast strain, and the temperature at which conditioning occurs.

Lower Temperatures

Lager comes from the German word *lagern*, which means "to store." A lager beer is in cold storage while it ages in the conditioning phase. Temperature influences lagers in two ways: flavor and clarity. During primary fermentation, the cooler temperature (45 to 55° F, 7 to 13° C) inhibits the formation of fruity esters by the yeast. The cooler temperatures result in a longer conditioning phase to finish residual sugars and metabolize other off-flavors and aromas like diacetyl and acetaldehyde. The other main effect of lagering at cold temperatures is brilliant beer clarity. The traditional near-freezing lagering temperatures cause almost all of the haze-forming proteins and tannins to settle out. See Appendix C for more info.

Unfortunately, this long time with the beer in contact with the yeast can potentially cause a problem. The problem is autolysis, i.e., yeast breakdown, which can produce terrible off-flavors in the beer.

Autolysis

When a yeast cell dies, it ruptures, releasing several off-flavors (sulfur, rubber, etc.) into the beer. When you have a large yeast mass on the bottom of the fermenter, you have a high potential for off-flavors due to autolysis. A lightly autolyzed beer will have a yeasty or brothy aroma or flavor. Smelling a jar of Vegemite is a good comparison. A moderately autolyzed beer will have a meaty aroma/flavor that is very similar to the smell of a bottle of B vitamins. A heavily autolyzed beer will have a rubbery aroma/flavor and will be virtually undrinkable.

Luckily, the propensity of yeast to autolyze is decreased by a decrease in activity and a decrease in total yeast mass. What this means to a brewer is that racking to a secondary fermenter to get the beer off the dead yeast and lowering the temperature for the long cold storage allows the beer to condition without much risk of autolysis.

As a final note on this subject, I should state that by brewing with healthy yeast in a well-prepared wort, many experienced brewers, myself included, have been able to leave a beer in the primary fermenter for several months without any evidence of autolysis. In fact, I didn't even rack the last Vienna lager I made; I just let it lager in the primary for four weeks, and it turned out fine. Autolysis is not inevitable, but it is lurking.

Lager Yeast Fermentation

It is easier to brew a bad lager than it is to brew a bad ale, because the expectations are higher for lagers. Brewers and beer drinkers are more forgiving about off-flavors in ale, calling it "complexity," but lagers should be "clean." A good lager should have a clean malt character with minimal off-flavors due to esters, diacetyl, acetaldehyde, or fusels. Lager brewing is best described in a book of its own, and fortunately Greg Noonan has done so with *New Brewing Lager Beer* from Brewers Publications (Boulder, Colo., 2003). I strongly suggest you read that book if you want to get serious about lagers, but meanwhile, I will try to get you off on the right foot.

In my opinion, the most important step for brewing good lagers is understanding how the three factors mentioned above combine to determine the fermentation performance. A lager yeast fermentation is less active due to the cooler temperatures, so all the fermentation processes occur more slowly. In other words, it will take more yeast to ferment a wort at a lower temperature in the same amount of time that it would take to ferment the same wort at a higher temperature.

In the past, it was common practice for homebrewers to cool their wort to room temperature, pitch the yeast, and place the fermenter in a cool cellar or refrigerator at the intended primary fermentation temperature of 45 to 55° F (7 to 13° C), depending on yeast strain. The fermentation would start right up with a short lag time, and the activity would slowly decrease over the next few days as the beer cooled.

This sequence is not ideal, because it can take a couple of days for the wort to get down to the proper fermentation temperature. Many fermentation by-products are produced in the first couple of days of fermentation, as the yeast go through their exponential growth phase. The amount of by-products produced is proportional to the level of yeast activity (i.e., vigor), which is proportional to temperature. So, the warmer the wort is in the first days of fermentation, the more total by-products there are for the yeast to clean up during conditioning. And as the wort cools down after all of this initial activity, the yeast are less efficacious at cleaning up the by-products.

The best way to ensure a strong, healthy lager fermentation is to pitch more yeast than you would for an ale. You should use 150 billion cells for a 1.050 OG lager, where you would have pitched 100 billion cells for a 1.050 ale. This is the equivalent of about ½ to ¾ cup of yeast slurry. Recommended pitching rates for lager beers are given in Table 11. When you need to pitch a large starter, I recommend that you ferment that yeast starter at no more than 5°

TABLE 11
Recommended Lager Yeast Pitching Rates

Wort Gravity	Cells per 20 Liters	Cells per 5 Gallons
Less than 1.055	120—180 billion	110—170 billion
1.055—1.065	180—240 billion	170—225 billion
1.065—1.075	240—300 billion	225—285 billion
1.075—1.085	300—360 billion	285—340 billion
Greater than 1.085	360—420+ billion	340—400+ billion

F (3° C) above the primary fermentation temperature. After the starter fermentation finishes (about two days), I recommend chilling the starter in the refrigerator overnight to settle all the yeast.

On brewing day, when you are ready to pitch your yeast, take the starter out of the fridge and pour off most of the starter beer. Swirl up the remaining beer and yeast, and pitch this to your wort *while the yeast is still cold*. Experience among homebrewers has shown that pitching yeast to a relatively warmer wort shortens the acclimation period of the yeast. Also, pitching only the slurry avoids some off-flavors from the starter beer.

Pitching Rate

The pitching rate can have a great effect on the character of the beer, and this is especially true with lagers. In the first few days of the fermentation cycle, when the yeast are rapidly reproducing, more diacetyl precursor (acetohydroxy acids), acetaldehyde, and fusel alcohols are being produced than at any other time. Low pitching rates mean more total cell growth, more amino acid synthesis, and therefore more by-products. High pitching rates mean less total cell growth and fewer by-products.

TABLE 12
Estimated Final Cell Counts Based on Initial Cell Count and Starter Size

Initial Cell Count (Billions)	1 Quart (Liter)	2 Quarts (Liters)	3 Quarts (Liters)	4 Quarts (Liters)
50	113 (116)	153 (156)	182 (186)	206 (211)
60	125 (128)	169 (173)	202 (207)	229 (234)
70	137 (140)	185 (189)	220 (226)	250 (256)
80	148 (151)	199 (204)	238 (243)	269 (276)
90	158 (162)	213 (218)	254 (260)	288 (295)
100	168 (172)	226 (232)	270 (276)	305 (313)
110	177 (181)	239 (245)	285 (292)	322 (330)
120	186 (190)	251 (257)	299 (306)	339 (347)
130	195 (199)	263 (269)	313 (321)	354 (363)
140	203 (208)	274 (280)	326 (334)	370 (379)
150	211 (216)	285 (292)	339 (348)	384 (394)

Wort Nutrients

The other aspect to consider is yeast nutritional supplements, namely oxygen and amino acids. Either of these will encourage yeast growth. The oxygen can come from aeration with an aquarium pump and airstone or from an oxygen tank. With the aquarium pump, you will never get above 8 ppm of dissolved oxygen, which is the average requirement for most yeast strains, and even a couple of ppm low for a few. If you use an oxygen tank, you can hit 40 ppm after a half-hour, which is too much and can cause excessive cell growth and a corresponding increase in diacetyl and fusel alcohols. See Chapter 6 for more info on recommended oxygen levels.

Diacetyl

Diacetyl is not actually produced by the yeast. The vicinal diketones diacetyl and pentanedione are created chemically by oxidative decarboxylation, (i.e., removal of hydrogen and carbon dioxide) of the acetohydroxy acids. Warm temperatures and the presence of oxygen promote this reaction. The ability of the yeast to remove diacetyl is about ten times the creation rate, but as the wort temperature finally gets to the primary fermentation temperature, the yeast activity decreases, and they biochemically reduce it more slowly. The result is a buttery/butterscotch flavor in the lager, which is considered an off-flavor. Some amount of diacetyl is considered good in other styles such as dark ales and stouts but is considered a flaw in most lager styles. To remove any diacetyl that may be present after primary fermentation, a diacetyl rest may be used. This rest at the end of primary fermentation consists of raising the temperature of the beer to 55 to 60° F (13 to 16° C) for 24 to 48 hours before cooling it down for the lagering period. This makes the yeast more active and allows them to eat up the diacetyl before downshifting into lagering mode. Be careful to minimize oxygen contact during racking, because this will generate still more diacetyl. Some yeast strains produce less diacetyl than others; a diacetyl rest is needed only if the pitching or fermentation conditions warrant it.

Acetaldehyde

Acetaldehyde production is often at odds to the other by-products. It is produced early in the fermentation cycle as part of the ethanol production process and is reduced later. It is typically caused by rapid fermentation due to warm temperatures (greater than 60° F, 16° C) or by over-pitching and underaeration. It is reduced by conditions that favor the conditioning processes, such as warmer lagering temperatures (40 to 45° F, 4 to 7° C), keeping the beer on the yeast longer, and keeping the yeast suspended. In addition, a less flocculant yeast strain will allow more time for acetaldehyde reduction.

Fusel Alcohols

The fusel alcohols are not reduced by the yeast and will affect the final flavor of the beer. While a few fusel alcohols can be esterified, it is a minor path and not a viable means of fusel reduction. Fusel alcohol levels are increased by warmer temperatures, excessive aeration, excessive amino acids, and underaeration and a lack of amino acids. Nice, eh? To control fusel alcohols:
- increase the pitching rate
- pitch when the wort is cool
- ferment at the lower temperatures in the suggested range
- don't add sucrose or other refined sugars to the wort.

Esters

An ester is a compound formed by an alcohol and a fatty acid. Most esters in beer are produced by esterification of ethanol with acetyl-CoA and other long-chain fatty acids. The enzyme alcohol acetyl transferase (AAT) plays an important role in this process. Fusel alcohols can also esterify with fatty acids, but usually the concentrations of these esters are very low. Ester formation is encouraged by:
- underaeration
- underpitching
- pitching warm
- warm fermentation temperatures
- high-gravity worts
- worts with a significant proportion of refined sugar.

To summarize, a bad lager beer could have some or all of the following flaws:
- a sweetish, buttery aroma/flavor due to diacetyl
- a green apple aroma/flavor due to acetaldehyde
- sharp, solventlike aromas/flavors due to fusel alcohols
- fruity aromas/flavors due to esters.

The recommended way to produce a clean lager beer is to:
- Cool the wort to primary fermentation temperature *before* pitching the yeast
- Pitch a relatively high quantity of yeast to limit cell growth
- Aerate sufficiently but not excessively
- Don't chill/lager too soon; give the yeast time to finish the job.

What Is Different About Brewing Lager Beer?

When to Lager

It takes experience for a brewer to know when primary fermentation is winding down and the beer is ready to be transferred. If you insist on brewing a lager for your very first beer, you are going to be flying blind. You can play it safe by waiting several weeks for the primary phase to finish completely (no more bubbling) and rack then, but you will have missed your opportunity for a diacetyl rest. As discussed in the previous chapter, you should rack to a secondary when the kraeusen has started to fall back in. The bubbling in the airlock will have slowed dramatically to one or four bubbles per minute, and a hydrometer reading should indicate that the beer is three-quarters of the way to the terminal gravity. Knowing when to rack takes experience; it's as simple as that.

I like to ferment and lager in glass carboys, because the glass allows me to see the activity in the beer. During primary fermentation, there are clumps of yeast and trub rising and falling in the beer and it's bubbling like crazy—it literally looks like there is someone stirring it with a stick. When you see that kind of activity slow down, and things start settling towards the bottom, you know the primary phase is over and it's safe to rack.

The lagering temperature and duration are affected by both the primary fermentation temperature and the yeast strain. These are the four main factors that determine the final character of a lager beer. Some general guidelines for lager fermentation times and temperatures are listed below:

- Check the yeast package information for recommended fermentation temperature(s).
- The temperature difference between the primary phase and the lager phase should be 10 to 15° F (5 to 8° C).
- Suggested lagering times are three to four weeks at 45° F (7° C), five to six weeks at 40° F (4° C), or seven to eight weeks at 35° F (2° C).
- Stronger beers need to be lagered longer.
- Nothing is absolute. Brewing is as much art as it is science.

A common question is, "If the beer will condition faster at higher temperatures, why would anyone lager at the low temperature?" Two reasons. First, in the days before refrigeration when lager beers were developed, icehouses were the common storage method—it's tradition. Second, the colder lagering temperatures work better than the warmer lagering temperatures for precipitating extraneous proteins (like chill haze) and tannins, which produces a smoother beer.

Aagh!! It Froze!!

By the way, what if your beer freezes during lagering?? Horrors!!

Well, it happened to me. Let me tell you about my first lager. . . .

'Twas a few weeks before Christmas and all around the house, not an airlock was bubbling in spite of myself. My Vienna was lagering in the refrigerator out there, with hopes that a truly fine beer I soon could share.

The Airstat* was useless, 32° F couldn't be set, so I turned the fridge to Low to see what I would get. On Monday it was 40°, on Tuesday lower yet, on Wednesday morning I tweaked it, seemed like a good bet.

Later that day when I walked out to the shed, my nose gave me pause, it filled me with dread. In through the door I hurried and dashed, when I tripped on the stoop and fell with a crash.

Everything looked ordinary, well what do you know, but just in case, I opened the fridge slow.

When what to my wondering eyes should appear, my carboy was FROZEN, I had made Ice beer! My first thought was tragic, I was worried a bit, I sat there and pondered, then muttered, "Aw Sh##!"

More rapid than eagles, my curses they came, and I gestured and shouted and called the fridge bad names. "You bastard! How could you! You are surely to blame! You're worthless, you're scrap metal, not worth the electric bills I'm paying! To the end of the driveway, with one little call, they will haul you away, haul away, haul away all!"

Unlike dry leaves that before the hurricane fly, when brewers meet adversity, they'll give it another try. So back to the house, wondering just what to do, five gallons of frozen beer, a frozen airlock, too. And then in a twinkling I felt like a goof, the carboy wasn't broken, the beer would probably pull through.

I returned to the shed after hurrying 'round, gathering cleaning supplies, towels, whatever could be found. I'd changed my clothes, having come home from work, I knew if I stained them, my wife would go berserk. I was loaded with paper towels, I knew just what to do, I had iodophor-ed water and a heating pad, too.

The carboy, how it twinkled! I knew to be wary, the bottom wasn't frozen but the ice on top was scary! That darn refridge, it had laid me low, trying to kill my beer under a layer of snow. I cleaned off the top and washed off the sides, picked up a block of ice and threw it outside. I couldn't find the airlock, it was under the shelf, and I laughed when I saw it, in spite of myself.

The work of a half-hour out there in the shed, soon gave me to know I had nothing to dread. The heating pad was working, the ice fell back in, I resanitized the airlock, I knew where it had been. Not an eisbock but a Vienna I chose, it was the end of the crisis of the lager that froze.

I sprang to my feet, to my wife gave a whistle, and we went off to bed under the down comforter to wrestle. But the 'fridge heard me exclaim as I walked out of sight, "Try that again, you bastard, and you'll be recycled all right!"

* The now-discontinued Hunter Airstat was a temperature controller used to regulate the refrigerator more precisely than the normal controls.

Should I Add More Yeast?

When your lager freezes, chances are the yeast has been impaired. If you are toward the beginning of the lagering cycle, then there may not be enough yeast activity after it thaws to properly complete the attenuation and condition the beer. You should probably add new yeast. If you are at the end of the lagering cycle and were planning on priming and bottle conditioning it, then you should probably add more yeast also. If you are planning on kegging it and force carbonating (like I was), then you don't have to worry about it. I say "probably" because some yeast will survive. Even if the beer freezes completely for a short time, typically 20% of cells will remain active. The questions are: 20% of how many, and just how active? Therefore, you should probably add new yeast.

The yeast you add to the fermenter should be of the same strain as the original yeast. If you are using yeast from a ready-to-pitch package, then that quantity is probably sufficient, and you can pour it right in and swirl it around to mix it evenly. Because you are not trying to conduct a primary fermentation and are not concerned about a fast start, you do not need to build up the count any further, nor do you need to acclimate it to the lagering temperature first. The yeast will acclimate over several days and finish the fermentation cycle.

If your yeast came from a small smack-pack or slant, then you may want to build up the cell count by pitching to a starter wort first. And you may want to conduct that starter at your primary fermentation temperature to help the yeast acclimate to the lagering cycle. As noted above, these steps are probably not necessary, but it never hurts to stack the odds in your favor. You can either pitch the starter at full kraeusen or wait for it to ferment out before adding it. The small amount of primary fermentation by-products that you add to the beer by pitching at full kraeusen will not affect the flavor significantly.

Maintaining Lager Temperature

Temperature controllers, from Johnson Controls and Ranco, are very handy for maintaining a constant brewing temperature in a spare refrigerator. A controller plugs into the wall outlet, and you then plug the fridge into it. A temperature probe is run inside the fridge, and it governs the on/off cycling of the compressor to maintain a narrow temperature range. Here in Southern California, I use it to maintain 65° F (18° C) in the summertime for brewing ales. Check your local homebrew supply shop or some of the larger mail order suppliers for one of the newer controllers. Some controllers will also operate a separate heating circuit (usually in conjunction with a heat lamp) for cold weather brewing conditions.

In my case, my frozen Vienna lagered for six weeks at 34° F (1° C). I placed blocks of ice next to the carboy instead of relying on the refrigerator for temperature control. In fact, insulated ice boxes are a good way to control temperature for lagering. The blocks of ice will last about three or four days. Because of the alcohol present, the beer actually freezes at several degrees below normal. Depending on the time of year and your ambient temperature, an insulated box (like a large picnic cooler) is a very convenient way to lager. My Cold But Not Baroque Vienna lager went on to take first place in two separate contests in the Vienna/Oktoberfest category.

Bottling

See the next chapter for information on how the bottling and carbonating of lager beers can differ from ale beers.

Brewing American Lager Beer

A lot of people want to know how to brew their favorite American light lager beer, like Budweiser, Miller, or Coors. First thing I will tell you is that it is difficult to do. Why? Because these beers are brewed using all-grain methods that incorporate rice or corn (maize) as about 30% of the fermentables. The rice or corn must be cooked to fully solubilize the starch and then added to the mash, so that the enzymes can convert the starches to fermentable sugars. See Chapters 12 and 14 for more info.

Second, there is no room in the light body of these beers for any off-flavors to hide. Your sanitation, yeast handling, and fermentation control must be rigorous for this type of beer to turn out right. The professional brewers at Bud, Miller, and Coors are very good at what they do—turning out a light beer, decade after decade, that tastes exactly the same. Though come to think of it, bottled water companies do that, too. . . .

You can brew either rice or corn-type lagers. Rice extract is available in both syrup and powder form, and will produce a beer similar to Heineken or Budweiser. Refined corn syrups and corn sugar have had most of their corn character stripped away but will still produce a beer similar to Miller or Coors. To brew these American lager styles most accurately, you need to find syrup that is high in maltose. It can be hard to find, so if you buy ordinary corn syrup at the grocery store, check the ingredients to avoid additives like vanilla. Also, look at the ratio of sugars to total carbohydrates on the nutrition label to get an idea of the fermentability. The grocery store corn syrups are typically high in dextrins for body.

To brew a corn-type lager, substitute corn syrup for the rice syrup below. If you want to brew a classic American Pilsner (CAP), with a richer corn character, refer to the recipe in Chapter 20 "Your Father's Mustache," for appropriate OG and IBU levels. The cereal mash procedure using flaked corn or corn grits described in the "YFM" recipe will produce more corn character than extract methods using corn syrup.

Typical American Lager Style Guidelines

Style	OG	FG	IBUs	Color
American Lager	1.035-50	0.098-1.012	8-22	2-8

Commercial Examples

American Lager	Budweiser

Typical American Lager Beer

Malts	Gravity Points
3.5 lbs. (1.6kg) pale DME	49
1.5 lbs. (0.7kg) dry rice solids (powder)	21
BG for 3 gallons (11.4 liters)	1.049 (12.1 °P)
OG for 5 gallons (19 liters)	1.042 (10.5 °P)

Hops	Boil Time	IBUs
1 oz. (28g) Tettnang (5%)	60	17
½ oz. (14g) Tettnang (5%)	10	3
Total IBUs		20

Yeast	Fermentation Schedule
American Lager (liquid)	2 weeks at 50° F (10° C) in primary fermenter, rack and lager at 40° F (4° C) for 4 weeks. Prime and store bottles at room temperature.

PRIMING AND BOTTLING

In this chapter we will focus on getting your hard-won beer into a bottle and ready for drinking. To bottle your beer, you will need: clean bottles, bottle caps, a bottle capper, and (I heartily recommend) a bottling bucket. You will also need some sugar to use for priming—that extra bit of fermentable sugar that is added to the beer at bottling time to provide the carbonation.

Many homebrewers get used bottles from restaurants and bars or buy them new from homebrew shops. Every once in a while you will hear about a guy whose dad or uncle has given him a couple of cases of empty swing-top Grolsch bottles. He may ask you if he can use them for brewing or something. . . . If this happens, just look him straight in the eye and tell him, "No, those can be quite dangerous, let me dispose of them for you." Be sure to keep a straight face and do your best to sound grim. If you don't think you are up to it, give me a call and I will take care of it. Swing-top bottles are great; grab any you can. New rubber gaskets for the stoppers can be purchased at most homebrew shops.

When to Bottle

Ales are usually ready to bottle in two to three weeks, when fermentation has completely finished. There should be few, if any, bubbles coming through the airlock. If you are fermenting in glass, you

will see the beer darken and clear as the yeast flocculates. Although two to three weeks may seem like a long time to wait, the flavor won't improve by bottling any earlier. Some older books recommend bottling after the bubbling stops, or in about one week, but this is usually bad advice. It is not uncommon for fermentation to stop after three to four days and begin again a few days later due to a temperature change. If the beer is bottled before fermentation is complete, the beer will become overcarbonated, and the pressure may exceed the bottle strength. Exploding bottles are a disaster (and messy to boot).

Bottle Cleaning

As discussed in Chapter 2, used bottles need to be cleaned thoroughly before sanitizing. The first time a bottle is used, it should be soaked in a cleaning solution (like bleach water) and scrubbed inside and out with a nylon bottle brush. A heavy-duty cleaning is needed to ensure that there are no deposits in which bacteria or mold spores can hide. This way, the sanitizing solution can reach all areas, and you can be assured of sanitized bottles. If you are diligent in rinsing your bottles promptly and thoroughly after each use with your homebrew, only the sanitizing treatment will be necessary before each use in the future. By maintaining clean equipment, you will save yourself a lot of work.

After the bottles have been cleaned with a brush, soak them in sanitizing solution, or use the dishwasher with the heat cycle on to sanitize them. If you use bleach solution to sanitize, allow the bottles to drain upside down on a rack, or rinse them. Also sanitize the priming container, siphon unit, stirring spoon, and bottle caps. But don't boil or bake the bottle caps, as this may ruin the gaskets.

Which Sugar Should I Prime With?

You can prime your beer with any fermentable that you want. Any sugar—white cane sugar, brown sugar, honey, molasses, even maple syrup—can be used for priming. The darker sugars can contribute a subtle aftertaste (sometimes desired) and are more appropriate for heavier, darker beers. Simple sugars, like corn or cane sugar, are used most often, although many brewers use dry malt extract, too. Ounce for ounce, cane sugar generates a bit more carbon dioxide than corn sugar, and both pure sugars carbonate more than malt extract, so you will need to take that into account. For all priming in general, you want to add two to three gravity points of sugar per gallon of beer.

As mentioned earlier, you can choose either of two paths when deciding on a priming sugar: Do you want keep the priming sugar hiding in the wings, or do you want to bring it on stage? The monosaccharides and plain sucrose allow you to carbonate the beer without changing the existing flavor profile. The other sucrose-based sugars—invert sugar syrups, honey, and maple syrup—will add some degree of flavor accent to the beer. The next big question is, how much to use?

The most commonly quoted answer to this question is ¾ cup (about 4 ounces by weight) of corn sugar for a 5-gallon batch. This will produce about 2.5 volumes of carbon dioxide in the beer, which is pretty typical of most American and European pale ales. Three ounces (weight) will produce a little lower carbonation level of about 2.0 volumes, and 5 ounces will produce about 3.0 volumes. The point is that 4 ounces of glucose is typically used to carbonate 5 gallons, and this is the basis for calculating amounts of other priming sugars.

For example, let's calculate how much honey to use to equal 4 ounces (115 grams) of corn sugar. Honey is about 18% water and is quoted as being 95% fermentable.

The equation is:

(Weight of A)(Percent Solids of A)(Fermentability of A) =
  (Weight of B)(Percent Solids of B)(Fermentability of B)
(4 oz.)(92%)(100%) = (X)(82%)(95%)
X = 4.72 oz. of honey
Using the extract yield numbers from Table 13 below, the equation becomes:
(4 oz.)(42)(100%) = (X)(38)(95%)
    X = 4.65 oz. of honey (which rounds to 4.7)

The calculation for malt extract is similar, because it can have a significant proportion of unfermentable sugars, varying from 15 to 40%, depending on the extract brand and yeast strain. A typical fermentability for malt extract is probably about 75%. The calculation for other sucrose products are more straightforward, because the sugars are usually 100% fermentable, except in the case of partially refined sugars like molasses, where there is a lot of material present other than sugar.

Be aware that malt extract will generate break material when boiled, and that the fermentation of malt extract for priming purposes will sometimes (though rarely) generate a krauesen/protein ring around

TABLE 13
Priming Sugar Information for 5 U.S. Gallons

Priming Sugar	Percent Solids (i.e., moisture)	Extract Yield (ppg)	Fermentability	Equivalent Weight for 5 U.S. Gallons ounces (grams)
Corn sugar	92%	42	100%	4 (114)
Cane sugar	100%	46	100%	3.7 (104)
Brown sugar	~95%	44	~97%	4.0 (113)
Molasses/treacle	80%	36	50-70%	7.8 (222)
Candi sugar	100%	46	100%	3.7 (104)
Lyle's Golden Syrup	82%	38	100%	4.5 (126)
Maple syrup	67%	31	100%	5.5 (155)
Honey	80%	38	95%	4.7 (133)
Dry malt extract	90%	42	~75%	5.4 (152)

the water line in the bottle, just like it does in your fermenter. Simple sugars don't have this cosmetic problem, and the small amount used for priming will not affect the flavor of the beer.

Making the Priming Solution

The best way to prime your beer is to mix your priming sugar into the whole batch prior to bottling. This ensures that all the bottles will be carbonated the same. Older books used to recommend adding 1 teaspoon of sugar directly to the bottle for priming. This is not a good idea, because it is time consuming and imprecise. Bottles may carbonate unevenly and explode. However, there are some commercial priming agents for individual bottle carbonation that avoid these problems. See p. 112.

Here's how to make and add priming solutions:

1. Boil ¾ cup of corn sugar (4 ounces [113 grams] by weight), or ⅔ cup of white sugar, or 1¼ cups of dry malt extract in 2 cups (473 milliliters) of water, and let it cool. Use the nomograph in

Figure 71—Racking to the bottling bucket

Figure 72 to determine a more precise amount of priming sugar, if you wish. You can add the priming solution in either of two ways, depending on your equipment; I prefer the first (2a).

2a. If you have a bottling bucket (see Figure 71), gently pour the priming solution into it. Using a sanitized siphon, transfer the beer into the sanitized bottling bucket. Place the outlet beneath the surface of the priming solution. Do not allow the beer to splash, because you don't want to add oxygen to your beer at this point. Keep the intake end of the racking tube an inch off the bottom of the fermenter (most racking canes have an end cap that does this for you), to leave the yeast and sediment behind.

2b. If you don't have a bottling bucket, open the fermenter and gently pour the priming solution into the beer. Stir the beer gently with a sanitized spoon, trying to mix it in evenly while being careful not to stir up the sediment too much. Wait a half-hour for the sediment to settle back down and to allow more diffusion of the priming solution to take place. Use a bottle filler attachment with the siphon to make the filling easier.

Commercial Priming Agents

There are several brands of off-the-shelf priming agents available that can take some of the preparation out of the priming and bottling process. Bulk priming by adding a solution of glucose to the entire batch has the advantage of achieving a consistent carbonation across all the bottles, as compared to pouring a spoonful of sugar into each one. However, making the solution is considered a hassle by some folks, so Forbis Homebrew Inc., markets a ready-made solution called Forbis' Original Corn Sugar Primer. Coopers Brewery markets bags of sucrose/glucose Carbonation Drops (like an unflavored cough drop) that enable you to simply put one drop in each bottle, fill, and cap. PrimeTabs (manufactured by Venezia & Company) also markets corn sugar tablets for adding directly to your bottles. However, the tablets are sized in such a way that you can adjust the level of carbonation in your bottles depending on the style and your tastes. For a low carbonation level, typical of a British draft ale, use two tablets per 12-ounce bottle. Use three for a more average carbonation level, and use four or five for a higher carbonation level like that of an American lager.

Bottle Filling

The next step is filling the bottles. Place the fill tube of the bottling bucket or bottle filler at the bottom of the bottle. Fill slowly at first to prevent gurgling and keep the fill tube below the water line

Nomograph For Determining Amount Of Priming Sugar (by Wt.) For 5 US Gallons

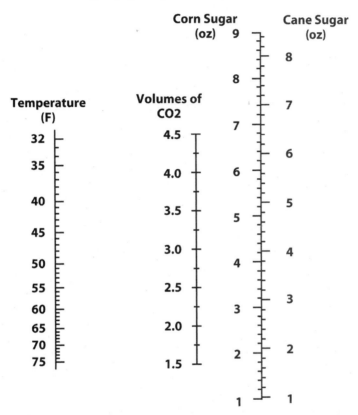

Figure 72 Nomograph for determining more precise amounts of priming sugar. To use the nomograph, draw a line from the temperature of your beer through the volumes of carbon dioxide that you want, to the scale for sugar. The intersection of your line and the sugar scale gives the weight in ounces (either glucose or sucrose) to be added to 5 gallons of beer to achieve the desired carbonation level. If you are priming more (e.g., 6 gallons), then the amount of priming sugar can be determined by ratio (e.g., 6:5) to the 5-gallon amount. Here is a list of typical volumes of carbon dioxide for various beer styles:

British ales	1.5-2.0
Porter, stout	1.7-2.3
Belgian ales	1.9-2.4
American ales	2.2-2.7
European lagers	2.2-2.7
Belgian lambic	2.4-2.8
American wheat	2.7-3.3
German wheat	3.3-4.5

Figure 73 Bottling using a bottling bucket with a filling tube

Figure 74 Bottling using a siphon with a bottle filler attachment

---

Check Your Carbonation

When you are bottling your beer, use a screw-top 16-ounce or half-liter plastic soda bottle for one of the bottles. Leave a normal amount of head space when you fill it, but squeeze out the excess air, leaving the bottle partially collapsed. Then, as the beer carbonates, it will pop the bottle back into normal shape and become increasingly hard. It will never get as hard as a bottle of soda, which is really highly carbonated, but it's easy to monitor.

–Submitted by J. Renner

---

to prevent aeration. Fill to about ¾ inch from the top of the bottles. Place a sanitized cap on the bottle, and cap. Many people will place the caps on the bottles and then wait to cap several at the same time. After capping, inspect every bottle to make sure the cap is secure.

Age the capped bottles at room temperature for two weeks, out of the light. Aging up to two months can improve the flavor considerably, but one week will often do the job of carbonation for the impatient; it depends on the type and vitality of the yeast.

Priming and Bottling of Lager Beer

Ninety-five percent of the time, there is no difference between priming lager beer and priming ale. But once in a while you will need to add fresh yeast for priming and carbonation purposes. This is most common when the beer is cold lagered for more than two months. If the beer is very clear at bottling time, then the majority of the yeast may have settled out, and there may not be enough left to carbonate the beer in the bottle. Prepare some fresh yeast of the same strain, and mix it with the priming solution when you rack the beer to the bottling bucket. You will not need as much as you originally pitched to the wort—either one ready-to-pitch package of liquid yeast or about ¼ cup of slurry for 5 gallons.

Since the yeast is being added for carbonation after the lagering phase, there are a couple of procedural differences from those used to ferment the original wort. Grow the yeast at the temperature at which you will be carbonating and storing the beer (usually room temperature) instead of the original pitching temperature. This will produce higher esters than the yeast normally would, but the percentage of sugar that is being fermented for carbonation at this stage is so small that the added difference in taste is unnoticeable. The reason for doing it this way is to avoid thermally shocking the yeast and to speed up the carbonation time. It is not necessary to store the beer cold after lagering. The beer can be stored at room temperature without affecting the taste of the beer.

Storage

Two common questions are, "How long will a homebrewed beer keep?" and "Will it spoil?" The answer is that homebrewed beer has a fairly long storage life. Depending on the style and original gravity, the beer will keep for more than a year. I occasionally come across a year-old six-pack of pale ale that I had forgotten about, and it tastes great! Of course, there are other cases when that year-old six-pack has gotten very oxidized in that time, tasting of cardboard or cooking sherry. It really depends on how careful you were with the bottling. Quality in, quality out.

When cooled before serving, some batches will exhibit chill haze, which is caused by proteins left over from those taken out by the cold break. The proteins responsible for chill haze need to be thermally shocked into precipitating out of the wort. Slow cooling will not affect them. When a beer is chilled for drinking, these proteins partially precipitate, forming a haze. As the beer warms up, the proteins redissolve.

Chill haze is usually regarded as a cosmetic problem. You cannot taste it. However, chill haze indicates that there is an appreciable level of cold-break-type protein in the beer, which has been linked to long-term stability problems. Hazy beer tends to become stale sooner than non-hazy beer. See Appendix C for more info.

Finally, it is important to keep the beer out of direct sunlight, especially if you use clear or green bottles. Exposure to sunlight or fluorescent light will cause beer to develop a skunky character, which is the result of a photochemical reaction with hop compounds and sulfur compounds. Contrary to popular belief, this is not a character that Heineken, Grolsch, and Molson strive for in their beer. It is simply a result of poor handling by retailers, and storing them under fluorescent lighting. Other beers, like Miller High Life, don't boil hops with the wort but instead use a specially processed hop extract for bittering that lacks the compounds that cause skunking (and flavor). Brown bottles are best, unless you make a point of keeping your beer in the dark.

Drinking Your First Homebrew

One final item that nobody ever remembers to tell new brewers until it's too late is: "Don't drink the yeast layer on the bottom of the bottle."

People will say, "My first homebrew was pretty good, but that last swallow was terrible!" or "His homebrew really gave me gas," or "It must have been spoiled, I had to go to the bathroom right away after I drank it."

Welcome to the laxative effect of live yeast!

When you pour your beer from the bottle, pour it slowly, so you don't disturb the yeast layer. With a little practice, you will be able to pour out all but the last quarter-inch of beer. The yeast layer can really harbor a lot of bitter flavors. It's where the word "dregs" came from. I remember one time my homebrew club was at a popular watering hole for a Belgian beer tasting. The proprietor prided himself on being a connoisseur of all the different beers he sold there. But our entire club just cringed when he poured for us. The whole evening was a battle for the bottle so we could pour our own. Chimay Grande Réserve, Orval, Duvel; all were poured glugging from the bottle, the last glass-worth inevitably being swirled to get all the yeast from the bottom. It was a real crime—not every beer is a hefeweizen. At least I know what their yeast strains taste like now. . . .

Figure 75 Keep the yeast layer in the bottle! Pour it slowly to avoid disturbing the yeast layer on the bottom. With practice, you will leave no more than a quarter-inch of beer behind in the bottle.

SECTION 2

BREWING WITH EXTRACT AND SPECIALTY GRAIN

In this section of the book, I will start to teach you how to produce some of the wort from the malted grain itself. We will use an intermediate step on the path to all-grain brewing, known as "steeping," to add some fresh malt character and complexity to an extract-based wort. However, I am going to make you jump into the deep end of the pool and swim to the ladder before I turn you loose to play. The steeping process is not difficult, but it helps to have an understanding of the characteristics and attributes of the different malts—those that can be steeped versus those that need to be mashed. Once you understand the differences, steeping will make perfect sense, and you won't make the mistake of trying to steep the wrong kind of malt.

In Chapter 12, I will explain what malt really is and how it is produced. Then, I will describe some of the most common malts and their different uses.

Chapter 13 will describe how to improve your extract brewing by using small amounts of specialty grains in an example recipe for a porter. This method does not require any extra equipment (except a sock or grain bag) and gives you a lot more flexibility in producing the wort for your intended style of beer. This chapter will guide you step-by-step through the additions to the brewing process. The additional work is so small, and the results are so gratifying, that you will probably never brew solely with extract again!

UNDERSTANDING MALTED BARLEY AND ADJUNCTS

What Is Barley, and Why Do We Malt It?

Barley is a member of the grass family and the fifth-largest cultivated cereal crop in the world. It was domesticated about the same time as wheat and has been cultivated for about 8,000 years. There are three varieties of barley: two-row, four-row, and six-row—referring to the arrangement of the kernels around the shaft. Only two- and six-row are used for brewing. The kernels of six-row are physically smaller than those of two-row but higher in protein. Two-row is considered to be superior to six-row for malting and brewing, but modern malting varieties of six-row still make excellent beer.

Barley is harvested in the field, sorted, dried, cleaned, and stored. The malting process begins when the highest-grade barley, brewing grade, is steeped in water until it has absorbed almost 50% of its initial weight in water. The barley is then drained and moved to a germination room, where the actual malting process occurs. The barley is held at controlled humidity and periodically turned/moved

Figure 76 The barley is steeped for a total of 38 to 46 hours. (*Photo courtesy of Briess Malt & Ingredients Company*)

Figure 77 The end of steeping is signaled by the emergence of the rootlets, or "chits." Once the barley is chitted, it must be moved to the germination tank, where it will have more oxygen. *(Photo courtesy of Briess Malt & Ingredients Company)*

Figure 78 After steeping, the malt is moved to a germination tank, where it is aerated and moved over several days to obtain uniform growth. The malt spends about four days in the germination tank before it is dried in a kiln room. *(Photo courtesy of Briess Malt & Ingredients Company)*

to keep the temperature in the grain bed uniform. At this stage it is referred to as *green malt*. After germination, the green malt is moved to a kiln, where it is carefully dried at low temperatures of 122 to 158° F (50 to 70° C) to about 4% moisture. This malt is typically referred to as base malts or lager malt.

The malting process allows the grain to germinate partially, making the seed's resources available to the brewer. During germination, enzymes in the aleurone layer (see Figure 79) are released, and new enzymes are created that break down the endosperm's protein/carbohydrate matrix into smaller carbohydrates, amino acids, and lipids, and open up the seed's starch reserves.

The endosperm is composed of large and small starch granules that are packed like bags of jellybeans in a box. The cell walls (bags) within the matrix holding the starch granules (jellybeans) are primarily composed of beta-glucans (a type of cellulose), some pentosans (gummy polysaccharide), and some protein. The box in this metaphor is the outer husk.

The degree to which the enzymes tear open the bags and start unpacking the starch granules (i.e., break down the endosperm) for use by the growing plant (or brewers, in our case) is referred to as the "modification." One visual indicator that a maltster uses to judge the degree of modification is the length of the acrospire (plant shoot), which grows underneath the husk. The length of the acrospire in a fully modified malt will typically be 75 to 100% of the seed length.

If germination continued, a plant would grow, and all of the starches that the brewer hoped to use would be used by the plant. So, the maltster gauges the germination carefully and stops the process by drying, when he judges he has the proper balance between resources converted by the acrospire and resources consumed by the acrospire.

The purpose of malting is to create these enzymes, break down the matrix surrounding the starch granules, prepare the starches for conversion, and then stop this action until the brewer is ready to utilize the grain. After modification, the grain is dried, and the rootlets are knocked off by tumbling. The kiln drying of the new malt denatures (destroys) a lot of the different enzymes, but several types remain, including the ones necessary for starch conversion. The amount of enzymatic starch conversion potential that a malt has is referred to as its "diastatic power."

Malted barley is the principal source of the sugars (principally maltose) that are fermented into beer. From a brewer's point of view, there are basically two kinds of malts—those that need to be mashed, and those that don't. Mashing is the hot water soaking process that provides the right conditions for the enzymes to convert the grain starches into fermentable sugars. The basic light-colored malts, such as pale ale malt, Pilsener malt and malted wheat, need to be mashed to convert the starches into fermentable sugars. These malts make up the bulk of the wort's fermentable sugars. Some of these light malts are kilned or toasted at higher temperatures to lend different tastes, e.g., biscuit, Vienna, Munich, brown. The toasting destroys some of their diastatic power.

The diastatic power of a particular malt will vary with the type of barley from which it is made. Two-row barley is the preferred variety for all-malt beers, having a bit higher yield per pound, lower protein levels, and claiming a more refined flavor than six-row. However, six-row has a little higher diastatic power than two-row. Historically, the higher protein level of six-row barley (which can produce a very heavy-bodied beer) led brewers to thin the wort with low-protein grains such as corn and rice. Brewers were able to take advantage of six-row barley's higher diastatic power to achieve full conversion of the mash in spite of the non-enzymatic starch sources (adjuncts).

Besides the lighter-colored base and

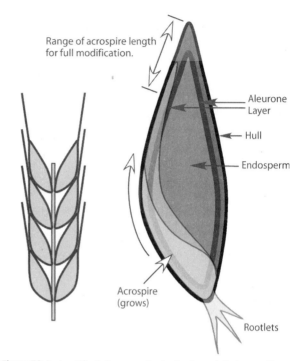

Figure 79 A simplified diagram of a barley kernel during malting, showing a progressive picture of how the acrospire (the plant shoot) grows along one side of the kernel. As it grows, pre-existing enzymes are released, and new enzymes are created in the aleurone layer, which "modify" the endosperm (the protein/carbohydrate matrix starch reserve) for the acrospire's use.

toasted malts, there is a group of malts that don't need to be mashed. These are often referred to as "specialty malts." They are used for flavoring and have no diastatic power whatsoever. Some of these malts have undergone special heating processes in which the starches are converted to sugars by heat and moisture right inside the hull. As a result, they contain more complex sugars, some of which do not ferment, leaving a pleasant, caramellike sweetness. These preconverted malts (called caramel or crystal malts) are available in different roasts or colors (denoted by the color unit Lovibond), each having a different degree of fermentability and characteristic sweetness (e.g., crystal 40 °L, crystal 60 °L).

Also within the specialty malt group are the roasted malts. These malts are produced by roasting at high temperatures, giving them a deep red/brown or black color (e.g., chocolate malt 350 °L). None of the specialty malts need to be mashed; they can simply be steeped in hot water to release their character. These grains are very useful to the extract brewer, making it easy to increase the complexity of the wort without much effort.

Lastly, there are fermentables not derived from malted barley that are called "adjuncts." Adjuncts include refined sugars, corn, rice, unmalted rye and wheat, and unmalted barley. They are not to be scorned; some adjuncts like wheat and unmalted roasted barley are essential to certain beer styles. Whole brewing traditions like Belgian-style *lambic*, American lager, and Irish stout depend on the use of adjuncts. Adjuncts made from unmalted grains must be mashed with enzymatic malts to convert

Figure 80 Notice the difference in color between the base malt 2 °L (top), the crystal 60 °L malt (below right), and the roasted barley 550 °L.

TABLE 14
Caramelization Temperatures

Sugar	Temperature
Fructose	110° C, 230° F
Galactose	160° C, 320° F
Glucose	160° C, 320° F
Maltose	180° C, 356° F
Sucrose	160° C; 320° F

their starches to fermentable sugars. Roasted barley is an exception to this rule, because its starches have been converted by high roasting, and it can be steeped.

Malt Flavor Development

Maltsters usually divide the malt world into four types: base malts, kilned malts (including highly kilned), roasted, and kilned and roasted. Varying the moisture level, time, and temperature develops the characteristic flavors and colors of each specialty malt. Caramelization and Maillard reactions both play a role in the development of the wide variety of flavors in these malts and the beers made from them.

Caramelization is the thermal decomposition of sugar, and it occurs at high temperatures (see sidebar). It is a sugar-to-sugar reaction and depends on low moisture to occur. Maillard reactions can occur at a range of temperatures, starting as low as 120° F up through 450° F (48 to 230° C). Maillard reactions occur between an amino acid and a sugar, producing volatile low molecular weight flavor compounds and higher molecular weight compounds like reductones and melanoidins. Reductones can oxidize and bind oxygen to improve flavor stability. Melanoidins are the browning aspect of the Maillard reaction.

Both types of reactions can generate some of the same flavors, like toffee, molasses, and raisin, but generally caramelization reactions are responsible for the toffee sweet caramel flavors in malt, while Maillard reactions are responsible for the malty, toasty, biscuity flavors associated with baking. The low-temperature, high-moisture Maillard reactions produce malty and fresh bread flavors, and the high-temperature, low-moisture Maillard reactions produce the toasty and biscuit flavors.

Figure 81 After kilning, specialty malts like caramel and chocolate are roasted at high temperatures to produce caramelization and Maillard reactions for distinctive flavors. *(Photo courtesy of Briess Malt & Ingredients Company)*

The kilned malts, such as pale ale malt and Vienna malt, are heated dry (3 to 10% moisture) at low temperatures (120 to 160° F/50 to 70° C) to retain their diastatic enzymes. The flavors expressed are lightly grainy with hints of toast and warmth. Aromatic and Munich malt are kilned at higher temperatures (195 to 220° F/90 to 105° C) to produce rich malty and bready flavors. Only Maillard reactions are involved.

The caramel malts like caramel 60 °L and caramel 120 °L are produced by roasting green malt, i.e., malt that was not dried by kilning after germination. These malts are put into a roaster and heated to the starch conversion range of 150 to 158° F (65 to 70° C). The converted sugars are in a semi-liquid state inside the kernel. After conversion, these malts are roasted at higher temperatures of 220 to 320° F (105 to 160° C), depending on the degree of color wanted. Roasting at these temperatures causes the sugars inside the kernels to caramelize, breaking them down and recombining them into less-fermentable forms. Maillard reactions are also occurring and cause darkening of the sugars. The lighter caramel malts have a light honey to caramel flavor, while the darker caramel malts have a richer caramel and toffee flavor with hints of burnt sugar and raisin at the darkest roasts.

The kilned-and-roasted malts are amber, brown, chocolate, and black malt. These malts start out green like the caramel malts above but are kilned to a lower percentage of moisture (5 to 15%) before roasting. Amber malts are produced by roasting fully kilned pale ale malt at temperatures up to 335° F (170° C). These temperatures give the malt the characteristic toasty, biscuity, and nutty flavors. Brown malts are roasted longer than amber malts and achieve a very dry dark toast flavor, with color equal to that of the caramel malts.

Chocolate malt starts out with more moisture than brown malt does but less than caramel malt as it goes to roasting. The roasting process begins at about 165° F (75° C) and is steadily increased to above 325° F (160° C). At this point the malt begins fuming, and as the temperature is raised to 420° F (215° C), the fumes turn blue and the malt develops chocolaty flavors. Some degree of caramelization occurs, but the majority of the flavors are from Maillard reactions. Black (patent) malts are roasted to slightly higher temperatures of 428 to 437° F (220 to 225° C), producing coffeelike flavors. The malt will actually burn at temperatures exceeding 480° F (250° C), so the trick is to spray the roasted malt with water at the critical point in time, and this was the basis of the invention of black patent malt. Roasted barley is produced in a similar manner, but the difference is that it is never malted to begin with.

To summarize, kilning produces breadlike flavors from the low-temperature, low-moisture Maillard reactions. Roasting dry malts increases the Maillard reactions and accentuates the malt flavors of biscuit and toast. Roasting green malt causes both Maillard and caramelization reactions that produce sweet toffee flavors. Kilning and roasting of green malt at high temperatures produces the chocolate and coffeelike flavors.

Common Malt Types and Usages

Note: There are a few trademarked products in the following list. I have listed them because they best represent a particular style of malt that is commonly used for a particular flavor or purpose. But this is an incomplete list; every malting house has its own specialties, and I don't come close to listing every malt. Typical Lovibond color values are listed as °L.

Base Malts

(need to be mashed)

Lager/Pilsener malt 2 °L. The name comes from the fact that pale lagers are the most common style of beer, and this is the type of malt used to produce them. Lager malt can be used for brewing nearly every other style as well. More lager malt is produced than all other types combined; it is the base malt for the world of beer.

The barley can be either two-row or six-row, although the label "Pilsener malt" is usually reserved for two-row varieties. "Pilsener" may also indicate a malt with lower modification as compared to other base malt products from the same maltster.

After germination, lager malt is carefully heated in a kiln to 90° F (32° C) for the first day, withered at 120 to 140° F (49 to 60° C) for 12 to 20 hours, and then cured at 175 to 185° F (79 to 85°

C) for 4 to 48 hours, depending on the maltster. This produces a malt with fine mild flavor and excellent enzyme potential.

Pale ale malt 3 °L. This malt type is kilned at higher temperatures than lager malt, giving a slightly toastier malt flavor well suited to pale ales, and will produce a golden to pale amber beer.

Wheat malt 3 °L. Wheat has been used for brewing beer for nearly as long as barley and has equal diastatic power. Malted wheat is used for 5 to 70% of the mash, depending on the style. Wheat has no outer husk and therefore has fewer tannins than barley. It is generally smaller than barley and contributes more protein to the beer, aiding in head retention. But it is much stickier than barley due to the higher protein content and may cause lautering problems if not given a protein rest during the mash. Rice hulls are commonly added to the mash to help with lautering.

Rye malt 3 °L. Malted rye is not common but is gaining in popularity. It can be used as 5 to 10% of the grain bill for a rye "spicy" note. It is even stickier in the mash than wheat and should be handled accordingly.

Kilned Malts

(need to be mashed)

These malts are commonly produced by increasing the curing temperatures used for base malt production, but they can also be made at home by toasting base malt in the oven. Suggested times and temperatures are given in Chapter 21.

Vienna malt 4 °L. This malt is lighter and sweeter than Munich malt and is a principal ingredient of light amber beers. It retains enough enzymatic power to convert itself but is often used with a base malt in the mash. Typically used as 10 to 40% of the grain bill, depending on beer style.

Munich malt 10 °L. This malt has an amber color and gives a very malty flavor. It has just enough diastatic power to convert itself but is usually used in conjunction with a base malt in the mash. This malt is used as 10 to 60% of the grain bill for Oktoberfests, bocks, and many others, including pale ales.

Aromatic malt 20 °L (a.k.a. melanoidin malt). This malt is similar to a dark Munich 20 °L, and in some cases probably is literally that. Very low diastatic power, but wonderful rich malt flavor and aromas. It contributes a deep amber or walnut brown color to beer. Use as 5 to 10% of the grain bill for accent.

Amber malt 25 °L (e.g., Biscuit™, Victory™). This fully toasted, lightly roasted malt is used to give the beer a bread-and-biscuits flavor. It is typically used as 10% of the grain bill. Gives a deep amber color to the beer.

Brown malt 60 °L. This malt is getting hard to find, because it's only used in a couple of styles like old ale, porter, and stout. It has a very dry, roasted character that is between amber and chocolate malt, but it is not sweet. Kind of like pure bread crust. Use as 5 to 10%, depending on style.

Caramel Malts

(may be steeped or mashed)

Caramel malts (a.k.a. crystal malts) have undergone a special heat "stewing" process after the malting, which converts the starches and liquefies the sugar inside the kernels. These malts are roasted at various temperatures to caramelize the sugars to different degrees and yield a range of flavors, from honey sweet, to toffee, to dark caramel. The same color rating from different maltsters can have different flavors due to individual techniques; malting is as much of an art as brewing. Caramel malts are used to some degree in most beer styles. They are ideal for adding aroma and body to extract beers by steeping, but it is possible to overdo it and make the beer cloyingly sweet. Caramel malts are typically added in half-pound amounts to a total of 5 to 15% of the grain bill for a 5-gallon batch.

CaraPils malt 3 °L (Briess). Also known as dextrin malt. This malt is used at 1 to 5% of the grain bill and enhances the body, mouthfeel, and foam stability of the beer without affecting the color or flavor. A common amount for a 5-gallon batch is a half-pound. CaraPils is very hard and difficult to crush. Consequently, it does not give a good yield from steeping, even though it is fully converted like other caramel malts.

Caramel 10 10 °L. This malt adds a light honeylike sweetness and some body to the finished beer.

Honey malt 25 °L. Also known as Brumalt, this malt has a rich honey flavor that is very versatile.

Caramel 40 40 °L. The additional color and light caramel sweetness of this malt is perfect for pale ales and amber lagers.

Caramel 60 60 °L. This is the most commonly used caramel malt, also known as medium crystal. It is well suited for pale ales, English-style bitters, porters, and stouts. It adds a full caramel taste and body to the beer.

Caramel 80 80 °L. This malt is used for making reddish-colored beers and gives a lightly bittersweet caramel flavor.

Caramel 120 120 °L. This malt adds a lot of color. It has a toasted, bittersweet caramel flavor, with hints of burnt sugar and raisin. Useful in small amounts to add complexity or in greater amounts for old ales, barley wines, and doppelbocks.

Special "B" 150 °L (Cargill). This unique Belgian malt has a definite roasty/toasty flavor consisting of dark caramel and raisin. Used in moderation ($\frac{1}{4}$ to $\frac{1}{2}$ pound), it is very good in brown ales, porters, and doppelbocks. Larger amounts, i.e., more than a half-pound in a 5-gallon batch, will lend a plumlike flavor to abbey ale styles like dubbel.

Kilned and Roasted Malts
(may be steeped or mashed)

These highly roasted malts contribute a bitter chocolate, coffee, or burnt toast flavor to brown ales, porters, and stouts. Obviously, these malts should be used in moderation. Some brewers recommend that they be added toward the end of the mash to reduce the acrid bite that they can contribute. This practice will produce a smoother beer for people brewing with naturally "soft" or low bicarbonate water. These malts are typically used in small amounts and may be ground finely to achieve a better color contribution with a smaller addition.

Rostmalz 300 to 500 °L. These German roasted malts are generally smoother in roast character than their North American counterparts. The malts range from a light chocolate-type malt to a black malt suitable for Munich *dunkel* and *schwarzbier*.

Chocolate malt 300 to 400 °L. Used in small amounts ($\frac{1}{2}$ pound for 5 gallons) for brown ale and extensively (1 pound) in porters and stouts, this malt has a bittersweet chocolate flavor, pleasant roast character, and contributes a deep ruby black color. Using too much will dominate the character of the beer.

Debittered black malt 500 °L. This special roast malt has had 60% of the husk removed prior to malting, creating a much smoother roasted character in the beer.

Roasted barley 500 °L. This is not actually a malt but highly roasted plain barley. It has a dry,

Figure 82 Some of the common flaked adjuncts: (clockwise from upper left): flaked barley, flaked corn, malted wheat (for comparison), flaked wheat, and flaked oats in the center.

distinct coffee taste and is the signature flavor of Irish/dry stouts. It has less of a charcoal bite to it than does black patent. Use about ½ to 1 pound per 5 gallons for stout.

Black (patent) malt 500 to 600 °L. This is the blackest of the black. It should be used sparingly, generally less than ½ pound per 5 gallons. It contributes a highly roasted flavor that can actually be quite unpleasant if used in excess. It is useful for contributing color and/or setting a "limit" on the sweetness of other beer styles using a lot of caramel malt; 1 or 2 ounces is useful for this purpose.

Other Grains and Adjuncts

Note: If you intend to use more than 10% of any of these adjuncts in your recipe, you may want to conduct a cereal mash to better utilize them and achieve better flavors. See Chapter 16 for more information.

Oatmeal. Oats are wonderful in a porter or stout. Oatmeal lends stout a smooth, silky mouthfeel and a creaminess that must be tasted to be understood. Oats are available whole, steel-cut (e.g., grits), rolled, and flaked. Rolled and flaked oats have had their starches gelatinized (made soluble) by heat and pressure and are most readily available as "instant oatmeal" in the grocery store. Whole oats and "old-fashioned rolled oats" have not had the degree of gelatinization that instant have had and must be cooked before adding to the mash. "Quick" oatmeal has had a degree of gelatinization but does benefit from being cooked before adding to the mash. Cook according to the directions on the box (but add more water) to ensure that the starches will be fully utilized. Use ½ to 1½ pounds per 5-gallon batch. Oats need to be mashed with barley malt (and its enzymes) for conversion.

Flaked corn (maize). Flaked corn is a common adjunct in British bitters and milds and used to be used extensively in American light lager (although today, corn grits are more common). Properly used, corn will lighten the color and body of the beer without overpowering the flavor. Use ½ to 2 pounds per 5-gallon batch. Corn must be mashed with base malt.

Flaked barley. Flaked unmalted barley is often used in stouts to provide protein for head retention and body. It can also be used in other strong ale styles. Use ½ to 1 pound per 5-gallon batch. Flaked barley must be mashed with base malt.

Flaked wheat. Unmalted wheat is a common ingredient in wheat beers and is essential to styles like Belgian-style lambic and wit. It can add starch haze and higher levels of protein than malted wheat. Flaked wheat also imparts more wheat flavor "sharpness" and a thicker mouthfeel than malted wheat. Use ½ to 2 pounds per 5-gallon batch or up to 50% in classic witbier or lambic recipes. Must be mashed with base malt.

Flaked rice. Rice is the other principal adjunct used in American and Japanese light lagers. Rice has very little flavor and makes for a drier-tasting beer than corn. Use ½ to 2 pounds per 5-gallon batch. It must be mashed with base malt. Whole rice needs to be cooked in a cereal mash to effectively utilize it in the mash.

Oat and rice hulls. Not an adjunct *per se*, the hulls of oats and rice are not fermentable, but they can be useful in the mash. The hulls provide bulk and help prevent the mash from settling and becoming stuck during the sparge. This can be very helpful when making wheat or rye beers with a low percentage of barley malt and barley husks. Use 2 to 4 quarts of oat or rice hulls for 6 to 10 pounds of wheat if making an all-wheat beer. The barley hull is 5% of the kernel's weight, so 5% of the adjunct weight is a good place to start. Do not exceed 3% by weight of the total grainbill, or you will start tasting them as astringency in the beer.

How to Read a Malt Analysis Sheet

Every batch of malt is unique, so every lot is tested, sometimes multiple times, to check the consistency of large batches. The requirements differ across the various types of malt, depending on the primary usage and individual customer needs. At a minimum, each lot is tested for percent moisture, yield, and color. There are two ways of measuring the yield: percent extract and hot water extract.

The other malt testing parameters are typically size characterization, protein levels, modification, diastatic power, and color. Example values for various malt types are given in Table 15 (p. 130) for comparison.

Extract—Fine Grind, Dry Basis

A malt analysis sheet does not give the malt's yield in points per pound per gallon. Instead, what you will most likely see for North American and European malts is a weight percentage called %Extract—Fine Grind, Dry Basis (FGDB). This percentage is the maximum soluble extract that the malt will yield when mashed, and is typically 80% for base malt. This soluble extract percentage equates to 37 ppg.

When a malting house analyzes a malt sample to determine its extract yield, it conducts a "Congress mash" (named for the Congress of the European Brewing Convention [EBC] of 1975, which standardized the procedure). A Congress mash consists of a multi-infusion mash using a standard weight of finely ground malt (i.e., flour). The mash is continually stirred over a two-hour period and then drained for another hour. These times may not seem remarkable until you consider that the malt test sample is only 50 grams! This procedure yields the maximum soluble extract as a weight percentage of the original sample.

This yield is known as the %Extract–Fine Grind, As-Is (FGAI). It is called "As-Is" because properly kilned malt contains about 4% moisture by weight. To compare different lots of malt with different moisture levels, this weight needs to be accounted for in the extract calculation. Therefore the basis of comparison, and the number you will most consistently see on an analysis, is the Fine Grind, Dry Basis (FGDB)—corresponding to a malt that has been oven-dried to zero moisture. Extract yield will be discussed further in Chapter 18.

The moisture content for the lot should be listed on the certificate of analysis, and should be 2 to 4% for base and kilned malts. Caramel and roasted malts typically have more moisture, at 5 to 6%, but it should always be less than 6%.

Extract—Coarse Grind, As-Is, and Dry Basis

Coarse Grind represents a mill setting that is closer to what many professional breweries would use. The same Congress

> **Determining Percent Extract with a Congress Mash**
>
> In a Congress mash, 50 grams of finely ground malt is infused with 200 milliliters of warm distilled water to reach a temperature of 45° C (113° F). The beaker is placed in a warm water bath to maintain that temperature for 30 minutes. The mash beaker is then heated at a rate of 1° C per minute to 70° C (158° F) and infused with 100 milliliters of 70° C water. The mash is held at 70° C for 60 minutes, and then gradually cooled to room temperature by the addition of cold water. The total weight of the mash is adjusted to 450 grams with more distilled water, and drained through filter paper. The wort is measured for specific gravity to an accuracy of 0.00001 and then converted to %Extract As-Is (FGAI) by means of the ASBC Reference Tables for "Extract Determination of Malt and Cereals." The percent moisture is determined from another sample of malt from the same lot, and that measurement is used to calculate the %Extract—Fine Grind, Dry Basis (FGDB).

mash method is used to determine the %Extract–Coarse Grind, As-Is (CGAI), and the moisture is measured to calculate the Dry Basis value. The CGAI is a slightly more realistic number for gauging the extract potential of a malt, but it's still a maximum that very few professional breweries would attain.

Extract–Coarse Grind is not measured for most specialty malts due to the extra time and effort it takes. Professional brewers are not as concerned about the yield of specialty malts, because they usually only represent a small percentage of the grain bill. Thus, the standard parameter of FGDB is the only value that is determined for specialty malts like caramel, chocolate, and roasted.

Fine/Coarse Difference

The F/C Difference value is simply the percent difference between the fine and coarse grind numbers (both As-Is and Dry Basis—same difference). This value allows the brewer to convert quickly between the two parameters. For example, looking at the numbers for Munich malt in Table 15 (p. 130), the %Extract for Coarse Grind, Dry Basis, is 2% less than the %Extract Fine Grind, Dry Basis, as indicated by F/C. The F/C Difference also serves as an indicator of malt modification, although the soluble/total protein ratio is most often used.

Hot Water Extract (HWE)

This parameter may be seen on malt analyses from the United Kingdom and Australia, where they utilize a single-temperature infusion mash method that differs from the American Society of Brewing Chemists and Congress mash methods. The main difference is that the malt sample is mashed at 65° C/149° F for one hour. HWE (As-Is) is measured as Liter •Degrees/Kilogram, and as a unit, it is equivalent to ppg when the metric conversion factors for volume and weight are applied. (Note: points/pound/gallon=gallon•degrees/pound). The conversion factor is HWE=8.345 x ppg. However, the grind/mash procedures for HWE and % Extract differ enough that the measurements are not actually equivalent, even though they are close. The best analogy I can think of is the trying to compare the power ratings of a racecar to a farm tractor—power is power, but the way it is expressed and utilized is different. That being said, if you get a malt sheet for pale ale malt with an HWE (As-Is) of 308 Liter°/kilogram, the conversion of that number by 8.345 to 37 ppg is close enough for homebrewing purposes.

Color

Historically, the color of beer and brewing malts has been rated as degrees Lovibond (°L). This system was created in 1883 by J.W. Lovibond and consisted of glass slides of various shades that could be combined to produce a range of colors. In 1950 the ASBC adopted the utilization of optical spectrophotometers to measure the absorptance of a specific wavelength of light (430 nanometers) through a standard-sized sample, and the Standard Reference Method (°SRM) for determining color was born. The SRM method was originally set up to approximate the Lovibond scale, and the two scales can be considered to be nearly identical for most of their range. However, the resolution of a spectrophotometer diminishes greatly as the worts darken and very little light can penetrate the sample to reach the detector.

The human eye is better than a spectrophotometer at distinguishing very narrow differences in color when provided with consistent, precise references. More information is conveyed from the variety of wavelengths of visible light coming from a sample than can be conveyed by a single wavelength. There is less variation in a single wavelength measurement, but there is also a corresponding loss in range. For this reason, the Lovibond scale is still in use today, in the form of precision visual comparators. The use of the comparator is most prevalent in the malting industry, and thus the color of malts is discussed as °L, while beer color is discussed as °SRM, although the basis (absorptance at 430nm) is the same. See Figure 80 and the °SRM color samples on the inside of the front cover.

Prior to 1990, the European Brewing Congress used a different wavelength for measuring absorptance, and conversion between the two methods was an approximation. Today, the EBC scale uses the same wavelength for measurement but uses a smaller sample glass. The current EBC scale for rating beer color is about twice (1.97 times) the °SRM rating. See Appendix B for more information on beer color.

Size

The average size of the kernels and the distribution is important to the brewer, because it affects how well the malt is crushed by the roller mills. If a significant proportion of the kernels are small, then those kernels will not be crushed well, and the extract from the mash and lauter will decrease. Kernel size and distribution are measured by sieving. The ASBC method uses standard sieves with mesh sizes of $7/64$ inch, $6/64$ inch, and $5/64$ inch. Kernels that pass through the $5/64$-inch sieve are caught in a pan and classified as "thru." The sum of the percentages captured by the $7/64$ and $6/64$ sieves is often described on the malt analysis sheet as "% Plump." Typically, malt is required to have 80 or 90% of the batch be Plump. The percentage that passes thru the $5/64$ is often labeled "% Thin," and the requirement is typically 2% maximum.

In Europe and the United Kingdom, the sieve sizes are very slightly larger: 2.8 millimeters, 2.5 millimeters, and 2.2 millimeters.

Protein

The protein measurement in malt is actually an approximation based on chemical analysis of the total amount of nitrogen in a malt sample. Every 1% of nitrogen is assumed to represent 6.25% of protein. You may see Total Nitrogen on an analysis instead of Total Protein.

American barley varieties are usually higher in protein than European varieties. The range of protein for two-row varieties is 11 to 13% for North American varieties; European and Australian are 9.5 to 12%. Six-row averages a little higher at 12 to 13.5%. Barley with total protein measuring more than 13.5% is not used for malting.

S/T Ratio

The Soluble-to-Total-Protein Ratio (S/T ratio), also known as the Kolbach Index, is the most commonly used indicator of malt modification. During the malting process, the proteolytic enzymes in barley cleave the large insoluble proteins into smaller soluble proteins. About 38 to 45% of the malt protein (as measured by nitrogen as total protein above) is converted to soluble protein, including enzymes, foam-positive proteins and amino acids. The ratio of soluble nitrogen to total nitrogen for the malt describes the extent of unlocking of the endosperm. To generalize, a ratio of 36 to 40% is a less modified malt, 40 to 44% is a well-modified malt, and 44 to 48% is a highly modified malt. Soluble protein levels below 35% can result in low extraction due to inaccessibility of the starch matrix and difficulty in lautering due to higher beta-glucan levels. Soluble protein levels exceeding

55% will lead to excessive darkening during wort boiling, beer haze, and loss of body in the beer. See Chapter 14 for more explanation of malt modification.

Diastatic Power

The diastatic power of a malt is a measure of the starch conversion capability in degrees Lintner (°L)*. Diastatic power is measured by evaluating the effects of all the diastatic enzymes in the malt. The diastatic enzymes in malt are degraded by kilning, and thus the diastatic power of highly kilned malts like Munich and Vienna is less than that of lager malt. Malts with DP of 40 or greater are able to convert themselves. Munich typically has a DP of 40 to 50; pale ale malt is about 80. Lager malt generally has a DP of 100 to 140, and wheat malt and six-row brewers malt can have a DP as high as 165 °L. High diastatic power is most useful when brewing with starch adjuncts. You can determine the conversion potential of an adjunct mash by calculating the dilution of the enzymatic malts and their diastatic power. In other words, a six-row brewers malt could support a dilution ratio of two-thirds adjuncts and still have an equivalent DP of 55 for the mash. The only caveat is that low DP mashes will take longer to convert, and there is the risk that all of the beta-amylase will be denatured by the mashing temperature before conversion is finished. See Chapter 14 for more information on starch conversion.

* An extensive search of both printed references and the Internet did not reveal just what a Lintner is. Perhaps named after Carl Lintner, 1828-1900, director of the brewing school at Weihenstephan.

TABLE 15
Example Malt Analysis Numbers

Malt	Two-Row Lager Malt	Six-Row Brewers Malt	Pale Ale Malt	Munich Malt	Amber Malt	Caramel 60	Chocolate Malt	Black Malt	Roasted Barley
Mealy/Half/ Glassy	98/2/0	95/5/0	98/2/0	95/5/0	95/5/0	0/5/95	—	—	—
Size									
7/64	60	45	60	55	55	40	—	—	—
6/64	20	30	20	25	25	40	—	—	—
5/64	—		—	—	—	—	—	—	—
thru	2	3	2	2	5	2	—	—	—
% Moisture	4	4.5	4	3.3	2.5	5.5	6	6	5.5
FGDB	80.5	78	80	78	73	73	73	70	72
CGDB	79.5	76.5	78.5	76	—	—	—	—	—
F/C	1	1.5	1.5	2	—	—	—	—	—
Protein	12	13	11.7	11.7	—	—	—	—	—
S/T	42	40	42	38	—	—	—	—	—
DP	140	160	85	40	30	—	—	—	—
Color	1.8	1.8	3.5	10	28	60	350	500	300

Summary

The malting process allows the grain to partially germinate, making the seed's resources available to the brewer. Malted barley is the principal source of the sugars that are fermented into beer. From a homebrewer's point of view, there are basically two kinds of malts: those that need to be mashed, and those that don't. Mashing is the hot water soaking process that provides the right conditions for the enzymes to convert the grain starches into fermentable sugars. The basic light-colored malts, such as Pilsener malt, pale ale malt, and Munich, have sufficient diastatic power to convert their starches into fermentable sugars. Highly kilned malts, like amber and brown malt, do not have significant diastatic power and need to be mashed with base malts.

Specialty malts are non-enzymatic malts that can be divided into two groups and are used for flavor and coloring. Caramel malts have had their starches converted to sugars by heat and moisture right inside the hull and can be steeped or mashed. The sugars in caramel malts have a pleasant, caramellike sweetness. The sugars in kilned and roasted malts have bitter chocolate and coffee-like flavors. These malts can also be steeped or mashed.

Lastly, there are nonenzymatic fermentables that are not derived from malted barley, called "adjuncts." Adjuncts include refined sugars, corn, rice, unmalted rye and wheat, and unmalted barley. Adjuncts made from unmalted grains must be mashed with enzymatic malts to convert their starches to fermentable sugars.

In the next chapter, we will steep some specialty malts to make porter.

13

STEEPING SPECIALTY GRAINS

One of the best things that a new brewer can do to get a feel for using grain is to steep specialty grains in hot water and use this wort for an extract-based recipe. Using specialty grain allows the brewer to increase the complexity of the wort as compared to what's usually available from plain extract.

Historically, brewers had to settle for light, amber, or dark extract, so steeping specialty grain was practically a necessity. Nowadays, there is a lot more variety in brewing kits, and many extract producers make top-quality kits for particular styles that incorporate several malts and real individuality. But if a brewer wants to create his own recipe, then steeping specialty grain offers more flexibility.

Almost every beer style can be made by using pale malt extract and steeping specialty grains; brown ale, bitter, India pale ale, stout, weizen, and Pilsener can all be made using this method. And the resulting beer flavor will be superior to what can be made using extracts alone. Award-winning beers can be made solely from extract, but freshness of the extract can be an issue, and using grain can make the difference between a good beer and an outstanding one.

Often the extract kit you buy may be more than a year old, and the resulting beer may have a dull, soapy character due to oxidation. Stay away from dusty cans! Look for a brand that the shop sells a lot of, so that the extract is always fresh. Shops that sell their own extract kits will often go through a 55-gallon drum of extract every couple of weeks. Dry malt extract has a much longer shelf life (years), so look for dry if you aren't sure of the liquid. Creating some new wort by steeping crushed grain adds back some of the fresh malt character that is often missing from purely extract recipes.

And it's fun to experiment, right?

The Grain

As was discussed in the previous chapter, there are basically two kinds of malts: those that need to be mashed, and those that don't. Mashing is the hot water soaking process that provides the right conditions for the enzymes to convert the grain starches into fermentable sugars. Specialty malts like caramel and roasted malts do not need to be mashed. Caramel malts have their starches converted to sugars by heat right inside the hull. These malts contain some unfermentable sugars, leaving a pleasant, caramellike sweetness. Caramel malts are available in different Lovibond ratings (color), each having a different degree of fermentability and characteristic sweetness. Roasted malts have had their sugars charred by roasting at high temperatures, giving them a deep red/brown or black color and bittersweet, dark chocolate, or coffeelike flavors.

Mechanics of Steeping

To use the caramel and roasted specialty malts, the grain must be crushed to expose the sugars to the water. While the grain is soaking, the hot water is leaching the sugars out of the grain and dissolving them into the wort. The factors that influence how well the sugars are extracted are the steeping time, temperature, and particle size. Obviously, the more finely you crush the malt, the more completely you can extract the sugars. However, most supply shops have their mills adjusted for mashing and lautering purposes, and if the particle size were much smaller, it would be difficult to contain within the grain bag.

Steeping specialty grain is like making tea. The crushed grain is soaked in hot water (150 to 170° F, 66 to 77° C) for 30 minutes. Even though a color change will be noticeable early on, steep for the entire 30 minutes to get as much of the available sugar dissolved into the wort as possible. The grain is removed from the water, and that water (now a wort) is then used to dissolve the extract for the boil.

The one sticky part is the phrase, "The grain is removed from the water. . . ." How? Well, the best way is to buy a grain bag. These bags are made of nylon or muslin and have a drawstring closure. They will hold about a pound of crushed specialty grain, making in essence a giant teabag. Many homebrew supply shops have prepackaged specialty grains in ½- to 1-pound amounts for just this purpose. Don't try to put all of the grain into one bag; use two or more bags if necessary. If you put too much in, the grain will swell and compact, and the extraction will decrease.

The analogy to a teabag is a good one, in that if the grain is steeped too long (hours), astringent tannin compounds (a.k.a. polyphenols) can be extracted from the grain husks. The compounds give the wort a dry, puckering taste, just like a black teabag that has been steeped too long. The extraction of tannins is especially prevalent if the water is too hot (above 170° F [77° C]). Previous practices for steeping specialty grains had the brewer putting the grain in the pot and bringing it to a boil before removal. That method often resulted in tannin extraction.

Water chemistry also plays a role in tannin extraction. Steeping the heavily roasted malts in low alkalinity water (i.e., low bicarbonate levels) will produce conditions that are too acidic, and harsh flavors will result. Likewise, steeping the lightest crystal malts in highly alkaline water could produce conditions that are too alkaline, and tannin extraction would be a problem again. For best results, the ratio of steeping water to grain should be less than one gallon per pound. For more information on water chemistry for steeping and mashing, see Chapter 15.

Steeping differs from mashing in that there is no enzyme activity taking place to convert grain or adjunct starches to sugars. Steeping specialty grains is entirely a leaching and dissolution process, the addition of existing sugars to the wort. If grain with enzyme diastatic potential is steeped, that's a mash. You can "steep" the enzymatic malts, but as the following chapters in Section 3 will explain, if you don't steep them under the right conditions, you won't get good conversion of the sugars. Meanwhile, let's use steeping to make a batch of porter.

Example Batch

As an example, I will describe the steeping procedure using a porter recipe (one of my favorite styles). A porter is an ale with a dark color, very malty flavor, and a bit of a roasted finish. A porter differs from a brown ale by being more assertive, darker, and more full bodied, but with less of a roasted malt flavor than a stout.

TABLE 16	
Typical Malt Steeping Yields in Points/Pound/Gallon	
Malt Type	**PPG Steep**
Two-row base malt	-
Six-row base malt	-
Two-row British pale malt	-
Amber malt	-
Vienna malt	-
Munich malt	-
Brown malt	8
CaraPils malt	8*
Light crystal (10-15 °L)	14
Pale crystal (25-40 °L)	22
Medium crystal (60-75 °L)	18
Dark crystal (120 °L)	16
Special "B"	16
Chocolate malt	15
Roasted barley	21
Black malt	21
Wheat malt	-
Rye malt	-

Steeping data is experimental and was obtained by steeping 1 pound in 1 gallon at 160° F (71° C) for 30 minutes. All malts were crushed in a two-roller mill at the same setting. Your results may differ.

* Difficult to crush

Port O' Palmer Porter

Malts	Gravity Points	
6.6 lbs. (3kg) pale malt extract (liquid)	40	
0.5 lb. (227g) crystal 60 °L malt	3	
0.5 lb. (227kg) chocolate malt	3	
0.25 lb. (113g) black patent malt	1	
Boil gravity for 3 Gallons	1.047 (13.3 °P)	
OG for 5 Gallons	1.054 (11.7 °P)	

Hops	Boil Time	IBUs
0.5 oz. (14g) Horizon (12%)	60	21
0.75 oz. (21g) Willamette (5%)	40	12
0.5 oz. (14g) Willamette (5%)	20	5
Total IBUs		38

Yeast	Fermentation Schedule
London Ale (liquid)	Primary fermentation at 65° F (18° C) for 2 weeks

---

Procedure. The only change from your regular extract brewing procedure is that you will be steeping the grain in the brewpot before you add the malt extract. For best flavor results, the ratio of steeping water to grain should be less than 1 gallon per pound.

1. Heat 1 gallon of water in the brewpot until it reaches 160° F ± 10°.
2. Immerse the grain bag in the pot for 30 minutes. The grain bag may be dunked and swirled like a teabag during this time to make sure that all of the grain is wetted. Moving it around will help to improve the yield, but don't splash. Maintaining the temperature during the steep is not vital.
3. After 30 minutes, remove the grain bag from the pot, and let it drain to avoid dripping on the stove.
4. Now you have a preliminary wort to which the malt extract is added. Stir in one can (3.3 lbs., 1.5kg) of pale malt extract. Add more water to the pot to bring the wort volume up to 3 gallons (11.4 liters).
5. Bring the wort to a boil, and add hop additions as listed in the recipe.
6. When the wort is finished boiling, add the remaining can of pale malt extract to the brewpot. Stir it in to make sure it is fully dissolved. After 10 minutes total time has elapsed, the additional extract is pasteurized, and you can proceed to cooling the wort, pouring it into the fermenter, pitching the yeast, etc.

Figure 86 Joe Brewer checks the temperature of the water for steeping the specialty grain. The temperature should be between 150 and 170° F (66 and 77° C).

Figure 87 The grain bag is being dunked up and down to fully wet the grain and improve extraction.

Figure 88 Ok, the specialty grains have steeped for 30 minutes and are ready to come out. The bag is drained, and the grain is discarded.

Figure 89 Joe Brewer stirs in the malt extract, and the boil is off and running. Brewing proceeds exactly as described in Chapter 7.

SECTION 3

ALL-GRAIN BREWING

Welcome to the third section of *How to Brew*. Here is where we remove the training wheels and do everything from scratch. All of the world's classic beers are produced using malted grain and the methods that I am now going to teach you. The all-grain brewing method allows you the most flexibility in designing and producing an individual wort. Once you have mastered these basic techniques, you will be able to walk into any beer store or pub, select any beer, and say with confidence, "I can brew this." The fundamental techniques and related science will be explained in the following chapters.

Using all-grain brewing can be like driving a car. You can get in, turn the key, and off you go, using it to go from point A to point B without much thought about it. Or you can know what's under the hood—knowing that by checking the oil, changing the spark plugs, and listening for clanking noises you can make that car work more efficiently for you. Without getting into internal combustion theory, I am going to teach you what is under the hood of your mash. You may not use all of this information (Lord knows, I haven't changed my oil in more than a year), but at least you will have a good understanding of what is available to you.

To make an all-grain beer, you can simply crush the grain, soak the grain in hot water for an hour, drain the grain, rinse the grain, and be done. It really is that simple. This section will make it seem really technical, but that is only because I am trying to give you all the tools. People have been doing this for thousands of years; it works at any level of technology. Feel free to skip directly to Chapter 19 and just do it. You will make beer.

In Chapter 14—How the Mash Works, I will explain how different temperatures activate different malt enzymes, and how these enzymes convert the malt starches into fermentable sugars.

Each temperature rest and its related enzyme groups will be described with respect to the effects on the composition of the wort.

The difference between a good brewer and a great brewer is his or her ability to control the brewing process. The pH of the mash affects enzyme activity as well as the flavor of the wort. In Chapter 15—Understanding the Mash pH, we will discuss how the malts and the brewing water combine to determine the pH of the mash. Water chemistry will be explained by showing you how to use the information in a city water report to customize your mash. The chemistry of the brewing water can be adjusted through the use of brewing salts to ensure proper mash conditions for best performance of the enzymes discussed in the preceding chapter.

In Chapter 16—The Methods of Mashing, I describe how to actually do the mash. There are two principal methods—infusion and decoction. Infusion is the simpler, and I will discuss how to use it to brew your first all-grain beer. Equations for both infusion and decoction temperature rests are discussed, with examples.

In Chapter 17—Getting the Wort Out, I discuss the fluid mechanics of lautering, so that you will have a better idea of how to conduct the lauter for the best extraction. I will also describe several commonly used lautering techniques.

Chapter 18—What to Expect When You Are Extracting, brings the malt types, mashing parameters, and lautering techniques together to show you how much wort you can expect from your efforts. The concept of brewing efficiency is presented to enable you to adapt any recipe to your equipment and methods.

Finally, in Chapter 19—Your First All-Grain Batch, we do it, step-by-step. Sounds interesting? Let's go!

HOW THE MASH WORKS

The technology behind malting and brewing is, quite literally, one of the oldest in the history of mankind. Brewing scientists helped develop the microscope, pH, pasteurization, and a whole host of other technologies. And yet, it could be argued that we know more about flying than we do about the biochemistry of beer. Why? Well, to borrow a line from President John F. Kennedy, " . . . not because they are easy, but because they are hard. . . ." Making beer is so easy that people have been just *doing* it for thousands of years. They didn't need to know how it worked, it just worked.

If it works, what more is there to know? The short answer to that question is given below. The long answer takes up the rest of the chapter. If you want, you can just read the "nutshell," and skip to Chapter 19 to brew your first all-grain batch. The purpose of the rest of this chapter and the chapters to follow is to teach you how to control and manipulate the mashing process to fine-tune your beer's character, adapting the process to your recipe (or vice versa), and to optimize your yield. But don't get bogged down in the details. Skim and move on if you want to; it will all make more sense after you have done it a couple times.

Mashing: In a Nutshell

Mashing is the term for the hot water steeping process that hydrates the malt, gelatinizes its starches, releases its natural enzymes, and converts the starches into fermentable sugars. The malt is crushed to facilitate hydration and infused with 160 to 165° F (70 to 74° C) water at a water-to-grist ratio of 2 quarts per pound (4 liters per kilogram) to achieve a mash temperature of 150 to 155° F (65 to 68° C). The mash is typically held at that temperature for an hour, although a half-hour is usually sufficient for conversion. After mashing for an hour, the mash is drained of wort and infused with an equal volume of sparge water. The mash is stirred, allowed to settle, and drained again. Done.

The temperatures cited above are important but not critical. To generalize, warmer temperatures will produce a more dextrinous wort, lower temperatures will make the wort more fermentable. However, if the mash temperature exceeds 158° F (70° C), the starch conversion is inhibited, and fermentability will decrease significantly. The temperature can drift downward during the hour, but as long as it doesn't get below 140° F (60° C), it's fine. The starches will be converted to fermentable sugars, and you will have made wort.

An Allegory

Cast of Characters:
You: Amylase, the starch converter
Brother: Beta-Glucanase, the gum chewer
Sisters: Proteinase and Peptidase, they share the work
Dad: Limit Dextrinase
Mom: Gelatinization Temperature

Our Story:

There has been a big windstorm that has blown down a big tree and a lot of other branches in the backyard. Your parents decide that some yard work will build character—yours. Your task is to cut as much of it as you can into two-inch lengths and haul it out to the road. You have two tools with which to do this: a hedge trimmer and a pair of handheld clippers. The hedge trimmer is in the garage, but the last time anyone saw the clippers, they had been left outside in the grass, which has since grown knee high. Plus, there are a lot of brambles growing around the tree that will make access difficult. Fortunately, your dad has decided that your older brother and sisters should take part in this, too, and will send them out there with the lawn mower and weed whacker right now. Likewise, Dad will gas up the chainsaw and be ready to cut through the big limbs at the joints as you work. This will ensure that you will be able to keep working and not leave any big pieces behind. As soon as the grass and brambles are cut, you can find your clippers and get to work.

Your tools are rather limited for the amount of work you have to do. The hedge trimmer will be really useful for cutting all the end twigs off but will quit working once you get back towards the branches. The clippers will be useful then—they will be able to cut the middles of all the branches but aren't strong enough to cut through the joints. When you are done, there will be a lot of odd branched pieces left over, in addition to your little pieces. Your success will be measured by how many little pieces make it out to the road. A large part of your success is going to depend on how well your family does in making the tree accessible to you. If you leave a lot of the tree behind, and if the stuff you get out to the road consists of a lot of big pieces instead of the small pieces your dad wanted, then you won't have done the job correctly. You had better plan your activity carefully.

Ok, your brother and sisters have done their work, and your dad is ready and waiting, but just as you are ready to get started, your mom says that you have to wait until it warms up to 60 degrees

TABLE 17
Major Enzyme Groups and Functions

Enzyme	Active Temperature Range	Preferred Temperature Range	Active pH Range	Preferred pH Range	Function
Phytase	86-126° F 30-52° C	Unknown	5.0-5.5	Unknown	Lowers the mash pH No longer utilized
Beta-glucanase	68-122° F 20-50° C	95-113° F 35-45° C	4.5-6.0	4.5-5.5	Best gum breaking rest for unmalted adjuncts
Proteases	68-149° F 20-65° C	113-131° F 45-55° C	4.5-6.0	5.0-5.5	Solubilize insoluble barley storage proteins
Peptidases	68-152° F 20-67° C	113-131° F 45-55° C	4.5-6.0	5.0-5.5	Produce Free Amino Nitrogen (FAN) from soluble proteins
Alpha-glucosidase	140-158° F 60-70° C	Unknown	4.5-6	5.0-5.5	Cleaves maltose and larger sugars into glucose Negligible effect on total yield
Limit dextrinase	140-153° F 60-67° C	140-150° F 60-65° C	4.8-5.8	4.8-5.4	Cleavage of limit dextrins
Beta-amylase	140-150° F 60-65° C	140° F 60° C	5.0-6.0	5.2-5.8	Produces maltose
Alpha-amylase	140-167° F 60-75° C	140-158° F 60-70° C	4.0-6.0	4.5-5.5	Produces a variety of sugars and dextrins including maltose

Note: The pH ranges are quoted at 25° C. The active temperature range for each enzyme indicates substantial measured enzyme activity under laboratory conditions. In the case of the diastatic enzymes, the preferred range begins where the starch becomes soluble (gelatinized), so that it is most accessible for efficient enzyme action without being inactivated. The enzymes will be active outside the indicated ranges but will be denatured as the temperature increases above each range.

outside, because she doesn't want you to catch a cold. It's more likely to get too hot to finish the job later on, but you still have to wait until it warms up before you can get started.

Defining the Mash

The allegory above attempted to illustrate all the activity that combines to convert the malt starches into fermentable sugars. There are several key enzyme groups that take part in the conversion of the grain starches to sugars. During malting, beta-glucanase (lawn mower) and proteolytic (weed whacker) enzymes do their modification work, opening the starch matrix for easy access and conversion to sugars. A small amount of further modification can occur during the mash, but the main event is the conversion of starch molecules into fermentable sugars and non-fermentable dextrins by the diastatic enzymes (clippers, hedge trimmer, and chainsaw).

Each of these enzyme groups can be influenced by different temperature and pH conditions. However, enzyme activity is usually more dependent on temperature than on pH. You can adjust the mash temperature to favor each successive enzyme's function and thereby customize the wort to your taste and purpose.

Both malted and unmalted grains have their starch reserves locked in a tightly packed protein/carbohydrate matrix that prevents the enzymes from being able to physically access the starches for conversion. The starches must be gelatinized and liquefied before they can be efficiently converted to sugars. Crushing or rolling the grain helps to expose the starch granules to hydration during the mash. Once hydrated, the starches will begin to gelatinize (i.e., swell with increased hydration) from a combination of heat and enzyme action.

Alpha-amylase is able to work on the surface of ungelatinized starch, but it is not very effective. It's like trying to trim the tree branches without a ladder.

Gelatinized starch is much more accessible to diastatic enzyme action. The average temperature for barley starch gelatinization is between 140° F (60° C) and 149° F (65° C). However, this is a gradual process, with a portion of starch being gelatinized below these temperatures and a portion above. In addition, some cereal starch adjuncts like oats and corn contain small amounts of polar lipids that are associated with the amylose, making the starch more resistant to degradation. The best way to assure accessibility is to pre-gelatinize the starch by rolling and/or cooking before adding it to the mash.

After gelatinization, alpha-amylase is able to more efficiently break up the long starch chains into smaller starch chains (dextrins), which greatly reduces the mash viscosity. This stage is called liquefaction. These shorter starch chains are now fully accessible to the other diastatic enzymes (beta-amylase, limit dextrinase, and alpha-glucosidase), and conversion of these shorter gelatinized starches to fermentable sugars begins.

TABLE 18
Starch Gelatinization Temperatures

Barley	140-150° F	60-65° C
Wheat	136-147° F	58-64° C
Rye	135-158° F	57-70° C
Oats	127-138° F	53-59° C
Corn (Maize)	143-165° F	62-74° C
Rice	154-172° F	68-78° C

Barley, wheat, oats, and rye can be gelatinized in the mash, because their temperature range is below or mostly below the saccharification temperature range. Corn and rice need to be pre-gelatinized by cooking or hot rolling into flakes, before they can be utilized in the mash. The degree of gelatinization depends on how hot the starch gets during the rolling/flaking process. The gelatinization temperature of a starch does not change significantly with malting.

The Acid Rest

Before the turn of the twentieth century, when the interaction of malt and water chemistry was not well understood, brewers in Pilsen used the temperature range of 86 to 126° F (30 to 52° C) to help the enzyme phytase acidify their mash when using only pale malts. The water in the area is so pure and devoid of minerals that the mash would not reach the proper pH range without this acid rest. Most other brewing areas of the world did not have this problem.

Malted barley is rich in phytin, an organic phosphate containing calcium and magnesium. Phytase breaks down phytin into insoluble calcium and magnesium phosphates and myo-inositol—a vitamin. The process lowers the pH by removing the phosphate ion buffers and producing weak acids. The acid rest is not used nowadays, because it can take several hours for this enzyme to lower the mash pH to the desired 5.4 to 5.8 range (at room temperature). Today, proper mash pH ranges can be achieved from the outset through knowledge of water chemistry and appropriate mineral additions, without needing an acid rest.

Doughing-In

To the best of my knowledge, the temperature rest (holding period) for phytase is no longer used for lowering the mash pH by any commercial brewery. However, this regime (95 to 113° F/ 35 to 45° C) is sometimes used by brewers for "doughing-in"— mixing the grist with the water to allow time for the enzymes to be distributed. The use of a 20-minute rest at temperatures near 104° F (40° C) has been shown to be beneficial to improving the yield from all enzymatic malts. This step is considered optional but can improve the total yield by a couple of points.

One caveat for doughing-in is the issue of hot-side aeration. When you mix the grist with the water, long-chain fatty acids can be oxidized through the action of the enzyme lipoxygenase. Once oxidized, these compounds can cause the formation of oxidized flavors in the beer later on. For example, 2-trans-nonenal is an oxidation product that has the taste and aroma of old paper. You can use boiled and cooled water for doughing-in to reduce the oxygen incorporated into the mash and minimize the oxidation effects due to lipoxygenase. Alternatively, you can skip the dough-in and mash-in at 140° F (60° C) or greater, because lipoxygenase is denatured around that temperature, and its effects will be greatly reduced. Just remember to minimize aeration of the mash while stirring.

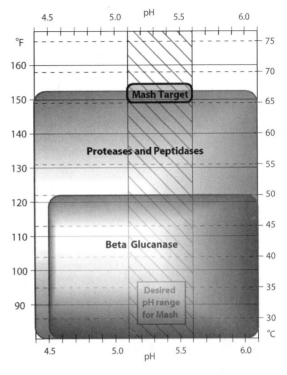

Figure 91 A graphical representation of the activity ranges for the proteolytic enzymes and beta-glucanase. The lighter areas within each range indicate a preferred or higher activity region.

Beta-Glucanase

The other enzymes in this temperature regime are the beta-glucanases/cytases—part of the cellulose enzyme family, which are used to break up the beta-glucans (non-starch polysaccharides) in unmalted barley, rye, oatmeal, and wheat. These glucan hemi-celluloses (i.e., allegorical brambles) are partly responsible for the stiffness of the mash and if not broken down will cause lautering difficulties. Most of the beta-glucan in barley is degraded during malting (from 4 to 6% by weight to less than 0.5%), so it is usually not a problem for well-modified malts. The same applies to malted wheat, oats, and rye. Oats and rye typically have 2 to 3% beta-glucan by weight, and wheat typically has 1 to 2% by weight. Corn and rice do not contain significant levels of beta-glucan compared to the other cereal grains.

Resting the mash at 95 to 113° F (35 to 45° C) for 20 minutes will break down these gums. The use of this rest is recommended to improve the lauterability of mashes using more than 20% of unmalted or flaked barley, oatmeal, rye, or wheat. Usage amounts of 10 to 20% is a gray area, and amounts less than 10% can usually be handled by increasing the temperature at lautering time (mash-out). In addition, beta-glucan in the wort acts as a non-Newtonian fluid—the viscosity decreases as you stir it, just like ketchup. So if your mash is not lautering well, give it a few stirs to thin it.

The Protein Rest and Modification

Barley contains a lot of amino acid chains that are used to form the proteins needed by the germinating plant. During malting and mashing, amino acids are enzymatically cleaved from these chains, and the amino acids are utilized by the yeast for their own growth and development during fermentation. The two main proteolytic enzyme groups responsible are the proteases and peptidases.

Proteases work by cleaving the large, generally insoluble protein chains into smaller soluble proteins, which can enhance the head retention of beer but are also involved in haze formation. Peptidase works by cleaving amino acids from the ends of the chains to produce small peptides and amino acids, which are the wort nutrients that can be used by the yeast. In well-modified malts, these enzymes have done the majority of their work during the malting process.

Most base malt in use in the world today is well modified. Modification is the term that describes the degree of breakdown during malting of the cell walls and protein-starch matrix of the endosperm. Moderately modified malts benefit from a protein rest to break down any remnant large proteins into smaller proteins and amino acids, as well as to further release the starches from the endosperm.

Well-modified malts have already made use of these enzymes and do not benefit from more time spent in the protein rest regime. In fact, using a long (more than 30-minute) protein rest on well-modified malts tends to remove some of the body of a beer and reduce its foam stability, but this warning tends to be overstated, making a mountain out of a molehill.

Moderately modified malts are becoming harder to find, but one example (Pilsen malt) is available from Briess Malting, and others may be available from German or Czech maltsters. Moderately modified malts work better with decoction mashing, and brewers claim this method produces fuller, maltier flavors than infusion mashing with well-modified malt.

The active temperature and pH ranges for the protease and peptidase enzymes overlap. Both types of enzymes are active enough between 113 and 152° F (35 to 65° C) that talking about an optimum range for each is not relevant. At one time it was thought that protein rests at higher temperatures favored proteases, and lower temperatures favored peptidases, but more recent studies have shown that is not true. You cannot favor one enzyme over another by controlling the mash temperature.

There are several kinds within each group, and different kinds are active across a wide range of temperature and pH (2 to 8.5). The total activity of the proteolytic enzymes is highest at lower pH (3.8 to 4.5), but the difference is only about 15% more than the activity at a typical mash pH of 5.8.[1]

Historically, the optimum pH and temperature ranges for proteolytic activity were thought to be lower, between 4 to 5 pH, and less than 140° F (60° C), but recent work by Jones, et al.,[2] has shown that the isolation and measurement techniques of the time had influenced the results, and the activity ranges in an actual mash are wider. The recommended temperature and time for a protein rest is 120 to 131° F (45 to 55° C) for 15 to 30 minutes, but the enzymes will still be active for some time at single-rest mash temperatures of 140 to 155° F (60 to 67° C).

The main purpose of a protein rest is to provide FAN to the wort. Less-modified and moderately modified malts have less soluble protein than well-modified malts, and unmalted starches contain only a small amount. Thus, worts made from a large proportion of unmalted grains like barley, or particularly corn (maize) and rice, can be deficient in FAN, due to lack of soluble protein for peptidase to act on. Generally speaking, the raw barley contains about 30% of the total soluble protein, about 50% of

---

Malt Modification in a Nutshell

One topic that new all-grain brewers will often hear about, and one that even experienced all-grainers may not have a clear understanding of, is malt modification.

To explain it in brief:

The starches that a brewer wants to convert to sugars by mashing are locked within the seed in a protein-carbohydrate matrix called the *endosperm*. During malting, the grain germinates, and enzymes in the seed begin unlocking the endosperm to make the nutrients available for growth of the new plant. The purpose of malting is to allow germination to proceed just far enough to unlock the endosperm but stop the process by drying before the plant can use those starches, and save them for the brewer. The degree to which the endosperm is unlocked is called the *modification*. The more the endosperm is modified, the easier it is for the amylase enzymes to access and convert the starches to sugars.

The most commonly used indicator of malt modification is the Soluble-to-Total-Protein ratio (S/T ratio), also known as the Kolbach Index. During malting, the proteolytic enzymes break up the large proteins in the endosperm, exposing the starch granules and creating soluble proteins, peptides and amino acids. The ratio of soluble protein to total protein for the malt describes the extent of unlocking of the endosperm. To generalize, a ratio of 36 to 40% is a moderately modified malt, 40 to 44% is a well-modified malt, and 44 to 48% is a highly modified malt. Historically, some of the German malts of a hundred years ago had ratio of 30 to 35% and can be considered less modified.

The yield from moderately modified malts can be improved by decoction mashing—where the boiling of portions of the mash and multiple temperature rests help to fully solubilize and convert the starches. The yield from well-modified malts can benefit marginally from multiple temperature rests during mashing, but most of the extract can be obtained using a single temperature rest at 150 to 155° F (65 to 68° C). Highly modified malts do not benefit significantly from multiple temperature rests during the mash and can be easily converted using a single temperature rest at 150 to 155° F (65 to 68° C).

---

the total is solubilized during malting, and 20% (or less) is solubilized during the mash. Also, only about 3% of the total soluble protein will be converted to FAN by the end of malting and mashing.

A secondary purpose of a protein rest is to break down large proteins that might otherwise cause lautering problems due to excessive top-dough (a proteinaceous mat that forms on top of the grain bed during lautering) and clarification problems due to haze-active proteins. While the foam retention of beer can be improved to some degree by a protein rest, the necessity of a protein rest to improve head retention has been overstated. A protein rest need only be used for moderately modified malts, or when using well-modified malts with more than 20% of malted wheat, rye, or oats. Malted wheat contains twice as much high molecular weight protein as barley malt. A beta-glucanase rest can be combined with a protein rest by resting 113 to 122° F (45 to 50° C) for 15 to 30 minutes.

Starch Conversion/Saccharification Rest

Finally we come to the main event: converting the starch reserves into sugars (also known as saccharification). There are a grand total of four types of diastatic enzymes that hydrolyze starches into sugars: alpha- and beta-amylase, limit dextrinase, and alpha-glucosidase. A single, straight-chain starch molecule is called an amylose. A large, branched-chain starch molecule (which can be considered as being built from multiple amylose chains) is called an amylopectin. Shorter chains are called branched dextrins to differentiate. The amylase enzymes work by hydrolyzing the straight chain bonds between the individual glucose molecules that make up

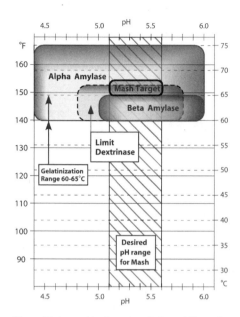

Figure 92 A graphical representation of the activity ranges of the diastatic enzymes. The lighter areas within each range indicate a preferred or higher activity region.

the amylose and amylopectin starch chains. These starches are polar molecules and have chemically different ends. (Think of a line of batteries.) Amylopectin differs from amylose by having a different type of molecular bond at the branch point that is not affected by the alpha- and beta-amylase enzymes. However, this branched bond is hydrolyzed by the limit dextrinase enzyme, which allows the amylases to convert these dextrins to fermentable sugars. The other diastatic enzyme, alpha-glucosidase, makes glucose out of both starches and dextrins. It is a bit of a "dog"—it appears to have a negligible effect on starch conversion in the mash. In all likelihood, it's probably very useful to a growing barley plant, but it doesn't seem to help us make beer.

Let's go back to our yardwork allegory for a second. You have three tools to make sugars with: a pair of clippers (alpha-amylase), a hedge trimmer (beta-amylase), and a chainsaw (limit dextrinase). While beta-amylase and some limit dextrinase are pre-existing, alpha-amylase (and more limit dextrinase) are synthesized in the aleurone layer during malting. In other words, the hedge trimmer and chainsaw are in the garage, but the clippers are out in the grass and brambles somewhere.

Beta-amylase works by hydrolyzing the straight chain bonds, but it can only work on "twig" ends of the chain, not the "root" end. It can only remove one maltose sugar unit at a time, so it works sequentially down the amylose molecule. On an amylopectin, there are many ends available, and it can remove a lot of maltose very efficaciously (like a hedge trimmer). However, beta cannot get close to the branch joints, probably due to its size/structure. It will stop working about three glucoses away from a branch joint, leaving behind a "beta-amylase limit dextrin," unless it is assisted by limit dextrinase. But there appears to be much less limit dextrinase in the mash than beta-amylase, so the assistance is limited, especially at higher mash temperatures (more than 150° F/65° C).

Alpha-amylase also works by hydrolyzing the straight chain bonds, but it can attack them randomly, much as you can with a pair of clippers. Alpha-amylase is instrumental in breaking up large amylopectins into smaller amylopectins and amyloses, creating more ends for beta-amylase to work on. Alpha is able to get within one glucose unit of an amylopectin branch, and it leaves behind an "alpha-amylase limit dextrin," unless it is assisted by limit dextrinase.

The temperature most often quoted for mashing is about 153° F (67° C). This is a compromise between starch gelatinization completion and beta-amylase and limit dextrinase inactivation. Collectively, the diastatic enzymes work best from 130 to 150° F (55 to 65° C), but remember, the starch is not accessible until the mash temperature is 140 to 150° F (60 to 65° C). Alpha works best at 150 to 158° F (60 to 70° C), while beta is denatured at 150° F/65° C, working best between 131 and 150° F (55 and 65° C). While the rate of denaturing will depend on the particular malt and mashing conditions, one study by Stenholm, et al., showed that in typical brewery mashing conditions beta-amylase was reduced to 75% of its initial activity after 30 minutes at 150° F (65° C) and to 10% of its original activity after 60 minutes.[3]

As a general rule, the thermostability and thermal optimal numbers cited in textbooks and most scientific papers are made using purified enzymes acting on a suitably buffered substrate and not in an actual mash. The information I have presented above comes from work published in the last ten years using actual barley starches. This helps explain the discrepancy between what past laboratory data told us shouldn't work, versus what we have been able to do for the past 5,000 years.

So, how can we use this information? The practical application of this knowledge allows us to customize the wort in terms of its fermentability. A lower mash temperature, of 140 to 150° F (60 to 65° C), yields a lighter-bodied, more attenuable beer. A higher mash temperature, of 150 to 160° F (65 to 71° C), yields a more dextrinous, less attenuable beer. This is where a brewer can really fine-tune a wort to best produce a particular style of beer.

As a practical example, see Figure 93. In the study, "Assessing the Impact of the Level of Diastatic Power Enzymes and Their Thermostability on the Hydrolysis of Starch During Wort Production to Predict Malt Fermentability," Evans, et al., looked at the fermentable sugars profiles produced by conducting two-step mashes, where the primary temperature rest was conducted at temperatures ranging from 131 to 169° F (55 to 76° C) for 50 minutes, and the second rest was at 158° F (70° C) for 15 minutes, followed by forced cooling. The sugar profiles were compared to that of an ASBC Congress mash (see Chapter 12), which is a standard malt test for determining the maximum percentage of extract by weight. While the mash profile of the Congress mash has a basis in actual lager brewing practice, it was originally designed for less well-modified malts, and utilizes a 30-minute long rest at 45° C (113° F) between the beta-glucanase and proteinase enzyme regions. But the Congress mash schedule is the reference standard for total soluble extract, and thus its fermentable sugar profile is included for comparison.

The chart shows that the percentage of maltose and degree of attenuation is highest at 149° F (65° C) and that it falls as the primary mash temperature increases. The presence of maltose for primary mash temperatures below the gelatinization temperature is best explained by the action of alpha-amylase and limit dextrinase, because beta-amylase is rapidly denatured at the second temperature rest of 158° F (70° C). The degree of fermentability or apparent attenuation limit (AAL) was determined by measuring the OG and FG of the worts using an agitated fermentation with a high pitching rate, according to industry standards. It is interesting to note how fast the AAL falls when mash temperatures are above 150° F (65° C), and beta-amylase is denatured. It doesn't take a large shift in mash temperature to produce a big change in wort fermentability. Mashing-in at 158° F (70° C) instead of 150° F (65° C) would raise the FG of a 1.050 wort from 1.005 to 1.011, based on this data (which is definitely in the ballpark, based on my experience).

Other Factors for Starch Conversion

There are three other factors besides temperature that affect the amylase enzyme activity to a lesser extent. These are the time, mash pH, and the grist/water ratio. Enzyme activity is highest during the first 20 minutes of the mash and tapers off thereafter, with a steep drop after 60 minutes (typically). Depending on the mash pH, water ratio and temperature, the time required to completely convert the mash can vary from under 30 minutes to more than 60. There is a lot of talk on the homebrewing forums about mashes that are finished in 20 minutes, as verified by an iodine/starch test. But the iodine test only tells you that you have degraded the starches, it does not tell you to what extent, nor the resulting fermentability, which will depend upon which sugars have been released. Generally, more time is needed to achieve the highest degree of

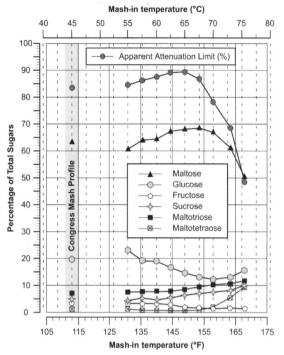

Figure 93 These curves plot the fermentable sugar profiles of four different base malt samples of similar diastatic power tested under the same procedure. Test mashes were conducted at nine different mash-in temperatures and compared to the fermentable sugar profile and apparent attenuation limit (AAL) of a Congress mash for the same malts.

Each data point is the mean of four different base malts.

The Congress mash consists of mashing-in at 45° C (113° F) for 30 minutes, ramping at 1°/minute to 70° C (158° F), and holding for 60 minutes before cooling.

The mashes for mash-in temperatures less than 70° C (158° F) were held at the noted temperature for 50 minutes and then raised to 70° C for 10 minutes before cooling.

The samples mashed-in at temperatures higher than 70° C were held isothermally for 60 minutes.

(Data extracted from Evans, et al., *Journal of the American Society of Brewing Chemists* 63:4 [2005]).

extract from the grist and good fermentability, and I recommend mashing for an hour to be sure.

Beta-amylase is favored by a wort pH of about 5.5, while alpha is favored by a lower pH of about 5.0. However, total diastatic enzyme activity is robust for mash pH values ranging from 4.5 to 6, and manipulation of mash pH within that range to promote beta over alpha is probably not going to have a significant effect on fermentability.

Problems due to mash pH occur when the pH is less than 4.5 or greater than 6. When the pH is less than 4.5, the beta-amylase activity is severely impacted, and wort clarity is a real problem as well. When the mash pH is greater than 6, silicates and tannin extraction from the malt husks increases substantially, affecting beer flavor.

Brewing salts can be used to raise or lower the mash pH, but these salts should only be used to a limited extent, because they can also affect the flavor. Water treatment is an involved topic and will be discussed in more detail in the next chapter. For the beginning masher, it is often best to let the pH do what it will and work the other variables around it, as long as your water is not extremely soft or hard. Malt selection can do as much or more to influence the pH as using salts, in most situations. The pH of the mash or wort runnings can be checked with the pH test strips that are sold at brewshops and swimming pool supply stores, although a pH meter is recommended for better accuracy.

The grist/water ratio is the least significant factor influencing the performance of the mash. A thinner mash of more than 2 quarts of water per pound (more than 4 liters per kilogram) dilutes the relative concentration of the enzymes, slowing the conversion, and leads to quicker denaturing, but could ultimately lead to a more fermentable mash, because the enzymes are not inhibited by a high concentration of sugars. A stiff mash of less than 1.25 quarts of water per pound (less than 2.5 liters per kilogram) is better for protein breakdown and results in a faster overall starch conversion, but the resultant sugars may be less fermentable and could result in a sweeter, maltier beer.

There is so much interaction of the various factors in the mash that it is difficult to generalize, especially with such a weak variable as mash ratio. When it comes to the mechanics of mashing, however, a thicker mash is better for multi-rest mashes, because it is gentler to the enzymes and easier to step up from rest to rest due to the lower heat capacity of grain compared to water (0.4:1).

Summary

A compromise of all factors yields the standard mash conditions for most homebrewers: a mash ratio of about 1.5 to 2 quarts of water per pound grain (3 to 4 liters per kilogram), pH of 5.4 to 5.8 (at 25° C), temperature of 150 to 155° F (65 to 68° C), and a time of about 1 hour. These conditions yield a wort with a nice maltiness and good fermentability.

[1] B. Jones and A. Budde, "How Various Malt Endoproteinase Classes Affect Wort Soluble Protein Levels," *Journal of Cereal Science* 41(2005), 95-106.

[2] B.L. Jones, A.D. Budde, "Effect of Reducing and Oxidizing Agents and pH on Malt Endoproteolytic Activities and Brewing Mashes," *Journal of Agricultural Food Chemistry* 51(2003), 7504-7512.

[3] K. Stenholm, S. Home, K. Pietila, L.H. Macri, A.W. MacGregor, "Starch Hydrolysis in Mashing," *Proceedings of the Congress of the European Brewing Convention* 26(1997), 142-145.

UNDERSTANDING THE MASH PH

What Kind of Water Do I Need?

Usually, the water should be of moderate hardness and low-to-moderate alkalinity, but it depends. . . .

This chapter is all about answering those questions. The answers will depend on what type of beer you want to brew and the mineral character of the water that you have to start with. The term "hardness" refers to the amount of calcium and magnesium ions in the water. Hard water commonly causes scale on pipes. Water hardness is often overmatched by water alkalinity. Alkaline water is high in bicarbonates. Water that has high alkalinity causes the mash pH to be higher than it would be normally. Using dark roasted malts in the mash can neutralize alkaline water to achieve the proper mash pH, and this concept will be explored throughout this chapter.

But remember, enzyme activity in the mash is most dependent on temperature, not pH. We are concerned with mash pH to make sure we are in the right ballpark, not to specify how close we are playing to the bag. Our goal is to prevent tannin extraction and enzyme impairment due to being in the wrong ballpark. And this goal is fairly easy to achieve.

Reading a Water Report

To understand your water, you need to get a copy of your area's annual water analysis. Call the Public Works department at City Hall and ask for a copy; they will usually send you one free of charge. An example for Los Angeles is shown in Table 19. Water quality reports are primarily oriented to the safe drinking water laws regarding contaminants like pesticides, bacteria, and toxic metals. As brewers, we are interested in the Secondary or Aesthetic Standards that have to do with taste and pH. In some states, particularly in the West, the source of the water supply can change seasonally, which can result in a big difference in brewing character.

<table>
<tr><td>

What Is an Ion?

An ion is an atom or group of atoms that has a net positive or negative charge, due to the loss or gain of an electron. In our discussion of brewing water, the ions are the anion (negative) and cation (positive) components of the minerals dissolved in the water.

</td></tr>
</table>

There are several important ions to consider when evaluating brewing water. The principal ions are calcium (Ca^{+2}), magnesium (Mg^{+2}), bicarbonate (HCO_3^{-1}), and sulfate (SO_4^{-2}). Sodium (Na^{+1}), chloride (Cl^{-1}), and sulfate (SO_4^{-2}) can influence the taste of the water and beer but do not affect the mash pH like the others. Ion concentrations in water are usually discussed as parts per million (ppm), which is equivalent to a milligram of a substance per liter of water (mg/L). Descriptions of these ions follow.

Calcium (Ca^{+2})

Atomic weight	40.0
Equivalent weight	20.0
Brewing range	50-150 ppm

Calcium is the principal ion that determines water hardness and has a +2 charge. As it is in our own bodies, calcium is instrumental to many yeast, enzyme, and protein reactions, both in the mash and in the boil. It promotes clarity, flavor, and stability in the finished beer. Calcium additions may be necessary to assure sufficient enzyme activity for some mashes in water that is low in calcium. Calcium that is matched by bicarbonates in water is referred to as "temporary hardness." Temporary hardness can be removed by boiling (see Bicarbonate). Calcium that is left behind after the temporary hardness has been removed is called "permanent hardness."

Magnesium (Mg^{+2})

Atomic weight	24.3
Equivalent weight	12.1
Brewing range	10-30 ppm

This ion behaves very similarly to calcium in water but is less efficacious. It also contributes to water hardness. Magnesium is an important yeast nutrient in small amounts (10 to 30 parts per million), but amounts greater than 50 ppm tend to give a sour-bitter taste to the beer. Levels higher than 125 ppm have a laxative and diuretic affect.

Bicarbonate (HCO_3^{-1})

Molecular weight	61.0
Equivalent weight	61.0
Brewing range	0-50 ppm for pale, base malt-only beers
	50-150 ppm for amber-colored, toasted malt beers
	150-250 ppm for dark, roasted malt beers

The carbonate family of ions is the big player in determining brewing water chemistry. Carbonate (CO_3^{-2}), is an alkaline ion, raising the pH and neutralizing dark malt acidity. Its cousin, bicarbonate (HCO_3^{-1}), has half the buffering capability but actually dominates the chemistry of most brewing water supplies, because it is the principal form for carbonates in water with a pH less than 8.4. Carbonate itself typically exists as less than 1% of the total carbonate/bicarbonate/carbonic acid species until the pH exceeds 8.4.

There are two methods the homebrewer can use to bring the bicarbonate level down to the nominal 50 to 150 ppm range for most pale ales, or even lower for light lagers such as Pilsener. These methods are boiling and dilution.

TABLE 19
Los Angeles Metropolitan Water District Quality Report (1996 data)

Parameter	State Maximum Level (mg/L)	Delivered Average (mg/L)
Primary Standards		
Clarity	0.5	0.08
Microbiological		
Total Coliform	5%	0.12%
Fecal Coliform	(detection)	0
Organic Chemicals		
Pesticides/PCBs	(various-JP)	ND
Semi-Volatile Organics	(various-JP)	ND
Volatile Organics	(various-JP)	ND
Inorganic Chemicals (list edited-JP)		
Arsenic	0.05	0.002
Cadmium	0.005	ND
Copper	(zero goal)	ND
Fluoride	1.4-2.4	0.22
Lead	(zero goal)	ND
Mercury	0.002	ND
Nitrate	10	0.21
Nitrite	1	ND
Secondary Standards—Aesthetic		
Chloride	*250	91
Color	15	3
Foaming Agents	0.5	ND
Iron	0.3	ND
Manganese	0.05	ND
pH	NS	8.04
Silver	0.1	ND
Sulfate	*250	244
Total Dissolved Solids	*500	611
Zinc	5	ND
Additional Parameters		
Alkalinity as $CaCO_3$	NS	114
Calcium	NS	68
Hardness as $CaCO_3$	NS	283
Magnesium	NS	27.5
Potassium	NS	4.5
Sodium	NS	96

* = Recommended Level
NS = No Standard   ND = Not Detected

Carbonate can be precipitated (ppt) out as calcium carbonate ($CaCO_3$) by aeration and boiling, as described in Chapter 4, according to the following reaction:

$$2HCO_3^{-1} + Ca^{+2} \leftrightarrow CaCO_3 \text{ (ppt)} + H_2O + CO_2 \text{ gas}$$

where oxygen from aeration can act as a catalyst and the heat of boiling prevents the carbon dioxide from dissolving back into the water to create carbonic acid. The limitation of this method is that only the temporary hardness will be removed, and not even all of that. About one milliequivalent (50 ppm) of dissolved calcium carbonate will remain in solution, due to its solubility constant.

Temporary hardness is the lesser of either the total alkalinity as $CaCO_3$ or the total hardness as $CaCO_3$, because the "temporary" aspect is actually the neutralization and precipitation of the calcium and bicarbonate. If the total hardness exceeds the total alkalinity, then nearly all of the alkalinity can be removed, down to the 50 ppm limit. If the total alkalinity as $CaCO_3$ exceeds the total hardness (as it often does), then only part of the alkalinity and nearly all of the calcium will be precipitated, which is not a good situation. You will probably want to add more calcium to the water to equalize the alkalinity.

However, dark beer styles depend on having more alkaline water to achieve the right mash pH. This will be discussed in the sections to follow.

Lime treatment is another way to reduce alkalinity, and it does not require boiling. Look for food-grade "slaked lime" or "pickling lime" in the grocery store. Each gram of slaked lime will treat 1.35 grams of alkalinity as $CaCO_3$ according to the equation:

$$Ca^{+2} + Ca(OH)_2 + 2HCO_3^{-1} \leftrightarrow 2CaCO_3 + 2H_2O$$

The problem with this method is that the amount of lime to add needs to be calculated and added gradually while monitoring the pH, in order to avoid creating very alkaline water due to excess hydroxide.

Here is a lime treatment procedure recommended by A.J. deLange in his paper, "Understanding Alkalinity and Hardness—Part II":[1]

1. Add 1 teaspoon of chalk for each 5 gallons of water to be treated to the water.

2. Multiply the temporary hardness of the water by 0.74 to get a rough idea of the amount of lime required (in milligrams) to treat 1 liter. Then multiply by the number of liters to be treated, and divide by 1,000 to get the number of grams required for the entire volume.

3. Increase the result from Step 2 by 20 to 30%, and place this in a small beaker or flask. Add enough water to get this into suspension.

4. Add the slurry from Step 3 to the water in initially large and then smaller increments. Stir thoroughly, and check pH after each addition.

5. Continue additions fairly rapidly until a pH between 9.5 and 10 is reached.

6. Monitor pH. As precipitation takes place, the pH will fall back.

7. At this point, add only small amounts of additional slurry to maintain the pH in the 9.5 to 10 region.

8. pH will continue to drop as CO_2 from the air is dissolved, but the rate of drop will slow. When it does, stop addition of lime, and let the water sit while the precipitate settles.

9. Decant the water from the precipitate, and measure hardness and alkalinity.

Dilution is the easiest method of producing low-carbonate water. Use distilled water from the grocery store (often referred to as purified water for use in steam irons) in a 1:1 ratio, and you will effectively cut your bicarbonate levels in half, although there will be a minor difference due to buffering reactions. Bottom line: If you want to make soft water from hard water (e.g., to brew a Pilsener), dilution with distilled water is the easiest route.

Sulfate (SO_4^{-2})

Molecular weight	96.0
Equivalent weight	48.0
Brewing range	50-150 ppm for normally bitter beers
	150-350 ppm for very bitter beers

The sulfate ion also combines with Ca and Mg to contribute to permanent hardness. It accentuates hop bitterness, making the bitterness seem drier and crisper. At concentrations higher than 400 ppm, however, the resulting bitterness can become astringent and unpleasant, and at concentrations above 750 ppm, it can cause diarrhea. Sulfate is only weakly alkaline and does not contribute to the overall alkalinity of water.

Sodium (Na^{+1})

Atomic weight	22.9
Equivalent weight	22.9
Brewing range	0-150 ppm

Sodium can occur in very high levels, particularly if you use a salt-based (i.e., ion exchange) water softener at home. In general, you should never use softened water for mashing. You probably needed the calcium it replaced, and you definitely don't need the high sodium levels. At levels of 70 to 150 ppm it rounds out the beer flavors, accentuating the sweetness of the malt. But above 200 ppm the beer will start to taste salty. The combination of sodium with a high concentration of sulfate ions will generate a very harsh bitterness. Therefore, keep at least one or the other as low as possible, preferably the sodium.

Chloride (Cl^{-1})

Atomic weight	35.4
Equivalent weight	35.4
Brewing range	0-250 ppm

The chloride ion also accentuates the flavor and fullness of beer. Chloride does not have the same effect as chlorine. However, concentrations above 300 ppm (from heavily chlorinated water or residual bleach sanitizer) can lead to mediciney flavors due to chlorophenol compounds. See Chapter 4 for information on reducing chlorine and chloramine from your brewing water.

Water Hardness, Alkalinity, and Milliequivalents

Hardness and alkalinity of water are often expressed "as $CaCO_3$"—hardness-as referring to the cation concentration, and alkalinity-as referring to the anions, i.e., bicarbonate. If your local water analysis does not list the bicarbonate ion concentration (ppm), nor "Alkalinity as $CaCO_3$," to give the water's buffering power to the mash pH, then you will need to call the water department and ask to speak to one of the engineers. They will have that information.

Calcium, and to a lesser extent magnesium, combine with bicarbonate to form chalk, which is only slightly soluble in neutral pH (7.0) water. The total concentration of these two ions in water is termed "hardness" and is most noticeable as carbonate scale on plumbing. Water hardness is often listed on municipal water data sheets as "Hardness as $CaCO_3$" and is equal to the sum of the Ca and Mg concentrations in milliequivalents per liter (mEq/L) multiplied by 50 (the "equivalent weight" of $CaCO_3$). An "equivalent" is a mole of an ion with a charge, + or -, of 1. The equivalent weight of

Ca^{+2} is half of its atomic weight of 40, i.e., 20. Therefore, if you divide the concentration in ppm or mg/L of Ca^{+2} by 20, you have the number of milliequivalents per liter of Ca^{+2}. Adding the number of milliequivalents of calcium and magnesium together and multiplying by 50 gives the hardness as milliequivalents per liter of $CaCO_3$.

$$(Ca\ (ppm)\ /\ 20 + Mg\ (ppm)\ /\ 12.1) \times 50 = \text{Total Hardness as } CaCO_3$$

These operations are summarized in Table 20.

TABLE 20
Conversion Factors for Ion Concentrations

To Get	From	Do This
Ca (mEq/L)	Ca (ppm)	Divide by 20
Mg (mEq/L)	Mg (ppm)	Divide by 12.1
HCO_3 (mEq/L)	HCO_3 (ppm)	Divide by 61
$CaCO_3$ (mEq/L)	$CaCO_3$ (ppm)	Divide by 50
Ca (ppm)	Ca (mEq/L)	Multiply by 20
Ca (ppm)	Total Hardness as $CaCO_3$	You can't
Ca (ppm)	Ca Hardness as $CaCO_3$	Divide by 50 and multiply by 20
Mg (ppm)	Mg (mEq/L)	Multiply by 12.1
Mg (ppm)	Total Hardness as $CaCO_3$	You can't
Mg (ppm)	Mg Hardness as $CaCO_3$	Divide by 50 and multiply by 12.1
HCO_3 (ppm)	Alkalinity as $CaCO_3$	Divide by 50 and multiply by 61
Ca Hardness as $CaCO_3$	Ca (ppm)	Divide by 20 and multiply by 50
Mg Hardness as $CaCO_3$	Mg (ppm)	Divide by 12.1 and multiply by 50
Total Hardness as $CaCO_3$	Ca as $CaCO_3$ and Mg as $CaCO_3$	Add them
Alkalinity as $CaCO_3$	HCO_3 (ppm)	Divide by 61 and multiply by 50

Water pH

You would think that the pH of the water is important, but actually it is not. It is the pH of the mash that is important, and that number is dependent on all of the ions we have been discussing. In fact, the ion concentrations are not relevant by themselves, and it is not until the water is combined with a specific grain bill that the mash pH is determined. It is that pH which affects the activity of the mash enzymes and the propensity for the extraction of astringent tannins from the grain husks.

Many brewers have made the mistake of trying to change the pH of their water with salts or acids to bring it to the mash pH range before adding the malts. You can do it that way if you have enough experience with a particular recipe to know what the mash pH will turn out to be, but it is like putting the cart before the horse. It is better to start the mash, check the pH with test paper, and then make any additions you feel are necessary to bring the pH to the proper range. Most of the time adjustment won't be needed due to the natural acidity of the malts.

However, most people don't like to trust to luck or go through the trial and error of testing the mash pH with pH paper and adding salts to get the right pH. There is a way to estimate your mash pH before you start, and this method is discussed in a section to follow. But first, let's look at how the grain bill affects the mash pH.

Balancing the Malts and Minerals

Let me state the goal right up front: for best results, the mash pH should be 5.1 to 5.5 when measured at mash temperature, and 5.4 to 5.8 when measured at room temperature. (At mash temperature the pH will measure about 0.3 lower due to greater dissociation of the hydrogen ions.) When you mash 100% base malt grist with distilled water, you will usually get a mash pH between 5.7 to 5.8

(measured at room temperature). The natural acidity of roasted specialty malt additions (e.g., caramel, chocolate, black) to the mash can have a great effect on the pH. Using a dark crystal or roasted malt as 20% of the grain bill will often bring the pH down by half a unit (0.5 pH). In distilled water, 100% caramel malt would typically yield a mash pH of 4.5 to 4.8, chocolate malt 4.3 to 4.5, and black malt 4.0 to 4.2. The chemistry of the water determines how much of an effect each malt addition has.

The best way to explain this is to describe two of the world's most famous beers and their brewing waters. See Table 21 (p. 160). The Pilsen region of the Czech Republic was the birthplace of the Pilsener style of beer. A Pils is a soft, golden, clear lager with a very clean, hoppy taste. The water of Pilsen is very soft, free of most minerals, and very low in bicarbonates. The Pilsen brewers use an acid rest with this water to bring the pH down to the target mash range of 5.1 to 5.5 using only the pale lager malts.

The other beer to consider is Guinness, the famous stout from Ireland. The water of Ireland is high in bicarbonates (HCO_3^{-1}) and has a fair amount of calcium but not enough to balance the bicarbonate. This results in hard, alkaline water with a lot of buffering power. The high alkalinity of the water makes it difficult to produce light pale beers that are not harsh tasting. The water does not allow the pH of a 100% base malt mash to hit the target range—it remains higher (above pH 6), and this extracts phenolic and tannin compounds from the grain husks. The lower pH of an optimum mash (5.1 to 5.5) normally prevents these compounds from appearing in the beer. But why is this region of the world renowned for producing outstanding dark beers? The reason is the dark malt itself. The highly roasted black malts used in making Guinness Stout add acidity to the mash. The natural acidity of these malts counteracts the alkalinity of the carbonates in the water, lowering the mash pH into the target range.

The fact of the matter is that dark beer cannot be brewed in Pilsen, and light lagers can't be brewed in Dublin, without adding or removing the proper type and amount of buffering salts. Before you brew your first all-grain beer, you should get a water analysis from your local water utility and look at the mineral profile to establish which styles of beer you can best produce. Roasted malts such as caramel, chocolate, black patent, and the toasted malts such as Munich and Vienna can be used successfully in areas where the water is alkaline (i.e., a pH greater than 7.5 and a carbonate level of more than 200 parts per million) to produce good mash conditions. If you live in an area where the water is very soft (like Pilsen), then you can add brewing salts to the mash and sparge water to help achieve the target pH. Two sections of this chapter, Residual Alkalinity and Mash pH, and Salts for Brewing Water Adjustment, discuss how to do this.

Table 21 lists examples of classic beer styles and the mineral profile of the city that developed them. By looking at the city and its resulting style of beer, you will gain an appreciation for how malt chemistry and water chemistry interrelate. Descriptions of the region's beer styles follow.

Pilsen. The very low hardness and alkalinity allow the proper mash pH to be reached with only base malts, achieving the soft rich flavor of fresh bread. The lack of sulfate provides for a mellow hop bitterness that does not overpower the soft maltiness; noble hop aroma is emphasized.

Dublin. Famous for its stout, Dublin has the highest bicarbonate concentration of the cities of the British Isles, and Ireland embraces it with the darkest, maltiest beer in the world. The low levels of sodium, chloride and sulfate create an unobtrusive hop bitterness to balance all of the malt properly.

Dortmund. Another city famous for pale lagers, Dortmund export has less hop character than a Pilsener, with a more assertive malt character due to the higher levels of all minerals. The balance of the minerals is very similar to Vienna, but the beer is bolder, drier, and lighter in color. The sodium and chloride bring out a rich roundness in the malt character.

TABLE 21
Water Profiles From Notable Brewing Cities

City/Style	Ca^{+2}	Mg^{+2}	HCO_3^{-1}	SO_4^{-2}	Na^{+1}	Cl^{-1}
Pilsen Pilsener	10	3	3	4	3	4
Dublin Dry stout	118	4	319	54	12	19
Dortmund Export lager	225	40	220	120	60	60
Vienna Vienna lager	200	60	120	125	8	12
Munich Oktoberfest	76	18	152	10	?	2
London British bitter	52	32	104	32	86	34
Edinburgh Scottish ale	125	25	225	140	55	65
Burton India pale ale	352	24	320	820	54	16

Numbers are given in parts per million (ppm).[2]

Vienna. The water of this city is similar to Dortmund but lacks the level of calcium to balance the carbonates, as well as the sodium and chloride for flavor. Attempts to imitate Dortmund export failed miserably until a percentage of toasted malt was added to balance the mash, and Vienna's famous red-amber lagers were born.

Munich. Although moderate in most minerals, alkalinity from carbonates is high. The smooth flavors of the dunkels, bocks, and Oktoberfests of the region show the success of using dark malts to balance the carbonates and acidify the mash. The relatively low sulfate content provides for a mellow hop bitterness that lets the malt flavor dominate.

London. The higher carbonate level dictated the use of toasted and dark malts to balance the mash, but the chloride and high sodium content also smoothed the flavors out, resulting in the well-known ruby-dark porters and copper-colored pale ales.

Edinburgh. Think of misty Scottish evenings, and you think of strong Scotch ale—dark ruby highlights, a sweet, malty beer with a mellow hop finish. The water is similar to London's but with a bit more bicarbonate and sulfate, making a beer that can embrace a heavier malt body while using fewer hops to achieve balance.

Burton-on-Trent. Compared to London, the calcium and sulfate are remarkably high, but the hardness and alkalinity are balanced to nearly the degree of Pilsen. The high level of sulfate and low level of sodium produce an assertive, clean hop bitterness. Compared to the ales of London, Burton ales are paler but much more bitter, although the bitterness is balanced by the higher alcohol and body of these ales.

Residual Alkalinity and Mash pH

Before you conduct your first mash, you probably want to be assured that it will probably work. Many people want to brew a dark stout or a light Pilsener for their first all-grain beer, but these very dark and very light styles need the proper brewing water to achieve the desired mash pH. While there is not any sure-fire way to predict the exact pH, there are empirical methods and calculations that can put you in the ballpark, just as with hop IBU calculations. To estimate your probable mash pH, you will need the calcium, magnesium, and alkalinity ion concentrations from your local water utility report.

Background:

In 1953, German brewing scientist Paulas Kohlbach determined that 3.5 equivalents (Eq) of calcium reacts with malt phytin to release 1 equivalent of hydrogen ions, which can "neutralize" 1 equivalent of water alkalinity. Magnesium, the other water hardness ion, also works but to a lesser extent, needing 7 equivalents to neutralize 1 equivalent of alkalinity. This chemical reaction does not require enzyme activity or an acid rest. Alkalinity that is not neutralized is termed "residual alkalinity" (abbreviated RA).

On a per volume basis, this can be expressed as:

$$mEq/L \; RA = mEq/L \; Alkalinity - [(mEq/L \; Ca) / 3.5 + (mEq/L \; Mg) / 7]$$

where mEq/L is defined as milliequivalents per liter.

This residual alkalinity will cause an all-base malt mash to have a higher pH than is desirable, resulting in tannin extraction, etc. To counteract the RA, brewers in alkaline water areas like Dublin added dark roasted malts that have a natural acidity that brings the mash pH back into the right range. To help you determine what your RA is and what your mash pH will probably be for a 100% base malt mash, I have put together a nomograph (Figure 207, on the inside back cover) that allows you to read the pH after marking off your water's calcium, magnesium, and alkalinity levels. To use the chart, you mark off the calcium and magnesium levels to determine an "effective" hardness (EH), then draw a line from that value through your alkalinity value to point to the RA and the approximate pH.

After determining your probable pH, the chart offers you two options:

1. You can plan to brew a style of beer that approximately matches the color guide above the pH scale.

2. You can estimate an amount of calcium, magnesium, or bicarbonate to add to the brewing water to hit a targeted pH. I will show you how this works in the following examples.

Determining the Beer Styles That Best Suit Your Water

1. A water report for Los Angeles states that the three ion concentrations are:

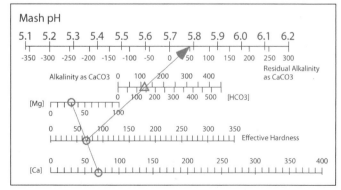

Figure 94 Estimating the mash pH for Los Angeles

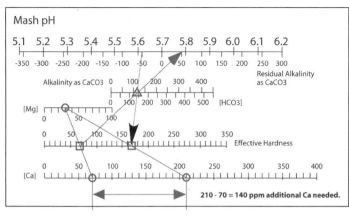

Ca (ppm) = 70
Mg (ppm) = 30
Alkalinity = 120 ppm as $CaCO_3$

2. Mark these values on the appropriate scales (indicated by circles and triangle on Figure 94).

3. Draw a line between the Ca and Mg values to determine the Effective Hardness (middle circle).

4. From the value for EH, draw a line through the Alkalinity value to intersect the RA/pH scale. This is your estimated mash pH (5.8).

Figure 95 Using nomograph to determine calcium addition

5. Looking directly above the pH scale (Figure 207, inside back cover), the color guide shows a medium-light shade, which corresponds to most amber, red, and brown ales and lagers. Most pale ale, brown ale, and porter recipes can be brewed with confidence.

Determining Calcium Additions to Lower the Mash pH

But what if you want to brew a much paler beer, like a Pilsener or a helles? Then you will need to add more calcium to balance the alkalinity that your malt selection cannot. (See Figure 95)

1. Go back to the nomograph and pick a point on the RA scale that is within the desired color range. In this example, I picked an RA value of -50.
2. Draw a line from this RA value back through your Alkalinity value (from the water report), and determine your new EH value.
3. From the original Mg value from the report, draw a line through the new EH value and determine the new Ca value needed to produce this effective hardness.
4. Subtract the original Ca value from the new Ca value to determine how much calcium (per unit volume) needs to be added. In this example, 140 ppm of additional calcium is needed.
5. The source for the calcium can be either calcium chloride or calcium sulfate (gypsum). (Calcium chloride is more appropriate than gypsum for lagers.) See the following section for guidelines on just how much of these salts to add.

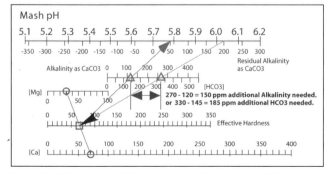

Figure 96 Using nomograph to determine bicarbonate addition

Determining Bicarbonate Additions to Raise the Mash pH

Likewise, you can determine how much additional alkalinity (HCO_3) is needed to brew a dark stout if you have water with low alkalinity. (See Figure 96)

1. You determine your residual alkalinity from your water report (e.g., about 50), and then determine your desired RA based on the color of the

style you want to brew. In this example, I have selected an RA of 200, which corresponds to a dark beer on the color guideline.

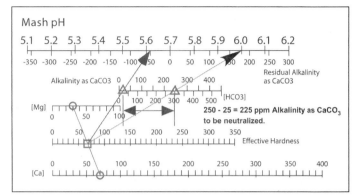

2. The difference is that this time, you draw a line from the desired RA to the original EH, passing through a new alkalinity.

3. Subtract the original alkalinity from the new alkalinity to determine the additional

Figure 97 Using nomograph to determine milliequivalents of acid to lower RA

bicarbonate needed (185 ppm HCO₃ or 150 ppm Alkalinity as CaCO₃). The additional bicarbonate can be added by using either sodium bicarbonate (baking soda) or calcium carbonate. Using calcium carbonate additions would also affect the EH, causing you to re-evaluate the whole system, while using baking soda would also contribute high levels of sodium, which can contribute harsh flavors at high levels. You will probably want to add some of each to achieve the right bicarbonate level without adding too much sodium or calcium.

Acids for Brewing Water Adjustment

Acid additions are another way to lower mash pH to brew pale beers in high alkalinity areas.

Determining Acid Additions to Lower the Mash pH

1. In this example, your local water report (Ca = 70, Mg = 30, Alk. = 250) indicates a base malt mash pH of 6.0, which means that the water is only suitable for brewing dark beers (if untreated). See Figure 97.

2. Pick a point on the RA scale that is within the desired beer color range. For this example, I picked an RA value of -50.

3. Draw a line from this RA value back through the Alkalinity as CaCO₃ scale to the Effective Hardness value as shown.

4. The difference in alkalinity is the amount of acid you need to add per liter of the mash. Divide the Alkalinity as CaCO₃ difference by 50 to get mEq/L of Alkalinity.

225 mg/L ÷ 50 = 4.5 mEq/L of Alkalinity as CaCO₃

5. Let's assume the volume of your mash is 4 gallons or 15 liters. To neutralize 4.5 mEq/L of alkalinity, we will need 4.5 x 15L = 67.5 mEq of acid.

6. There are several acids you can choose from to affect your mash pH. (See Table 22.) The most readily available are lactic acid and hydrochloric (muriatic) acid.

TABLE 22
Acids for Mash pH Adjustment

Acid	Standard Concentration	Milliequivalents/ Liter
Lactic	88%	11.8 mEq/L
Hydrochloric (muriatic)	37%	15 mEq/L

Understanding the Mash pH

Phosphoric acid is not recommended, because it reacts chemically with calcium in the mash and changes the whole playing field, rather than simply adjusting the pH.

If the mash water volume is 15 liters (4 gallons), then 4.5 x 15L = 67.5 mEq of acid are needed to neutralize the alkalinity and bring the mash pH near 5.6.

Using hydrochloric acid: 67.5 ÷ 15 mEq/L = 4.5 milliliters

Using lactic acid: 67.5 ÷ 11.8 mEq/L = 5.7 milliliters

If you are using common muriatic acid (e.g., used for swimming pool pH correction), the concentration may be different. If so, then you simply need to ratio the concentrations to arrive at the final volume. If the muriatic acid is a 32% solution rather than the laboratory standard 37%, the volume required is 37 / 32 x 4.5ml = 5.2 milliliters.

A dosing syringe like those used for measuring medicine for babies works well here.

Sparge Water Adjustment With Acid

Lowering the pH of your sparge water is usually unnecessary. The malts in the mash have a lot of buffering power that will last until the gravity falls below 1.012. Batch sparge and no-sparge techniques typically have second runnings that are 1.016 or greater, so tannin and silicate extraction are inhibited. If you live in an area of very high alkalinity and know from experience that you need to lower the pH of your sparge water, then add the same concentration that you used for the mash. This will maintain the pH equilibrium in your mash as you sparge.

Likewise, brewing salt additions of calcium can be added to the sparge water to help maintain pH during the sparge. The salts used must be readily soluble, like calcium chloride or calcium sulfate.

Salts for Brewing Water Adjustment

Brewing water can be adjusted by the addition of brewing salts. Unfortunately, the addition of salts to water is not a matter of 2 + 2 = 4; it tends to be 3.9 or 4.1, depending. Water chemistry can be complicated; the rules contain exceptions and thresholds where other rules and exceptions take over.

Fortunately, for most practical applications you do not have to be that rigorous. You can add needed ions to your water with easily obtainable salts. To calculate how much to add, use the nomograph or another water chart to figure out what concentration is desired, and then subtract your water's ion concentration to determine the difference. Next, consult Table 23—Brewing Salts (p. 166) to see how much of an ion a particular salt can be expected to add. Don't forget to multiply the difference in concentration by the total volume of water you are working with.

Let's look back at the nomograph example, where we determined that we needed 145 ppm of additional calcium ion. Let's say that 4 gallons of water are used in the mash.

1. Choose a salt to use to add the needed calcium. Let's use gypsum.
2. From Table 23, gypsum adds 61.5 ppm of Ca per gram of gypsum added to 1 gallon of water.
3. Divide the 145 ppm by 61.5 to determine the number of grams of gypsum needed per gallon to make the desired concentration. 145 / 61.5 = 2.4 grams
4. Next, multiply the number of grams per gallon by the number of gallons in the mash (4). 2.4 x 4 = 9.6 grams, which can be rounded to 10 grams.
5. Unless you have a gram scale handy, you will want to convert that to teaspoons, which is more convenient. There are about 4 grams of gypsum per teaspoon,

which gives us 10 / 4 = 2.5 teaspoons of gypsum to be added to the mash.

6.   Lastly, you need to realize how much sulfate this addition has made. 2.5 grams per gallon equals 368 ppm of sulfate added to the mash, which is a lot. In this case, it would probably be a good idea to use calcium chloride for half of the addition.

Table 23 provides information on the use and results of each salt's addition. Brewing salts should be used sparingly to make up for gross deficiencies or overabundance of ions. The concentrations given are for 1 gram dissolved in 1 gallon of distilled water. Dissolution of 1 gram of a salt in your water will probably result in a slightly different value due to your water's specific mineral content and pH. However, the results should be reasonably close.

There are several brewing software programs that are very handy for these types of water calculations, as well as all types of mashing and recipe calculations. Two examples are Promash at www.promash.com and Strangebrew at www.strangebrew.ca. The functionality of these brewing applications has been thoroughly reviewed, and I can assure you that they are comprehensive and easy to use.

My final advice on water treatment is that if you want to brew a pale beer and have water that is very high in carbonates and low in calcium, then your best bet is to use bottled water* from the store or to dilute your water with distilled water and add gypsum or calcium chloride to make up the calcium deficit. Watch your sulfate and chloride counts, though. Mineral dilution with water is not as straightforward as it is with wort dilution, due to the various ion buffering effects, but it will be reasonably close.

Good luck!

* You should be able to get an analysis of the bottled water by calling the manufacturer. I have done this with a couple of different brands.

TABLE 23
Brewing Salts for Water Adjustment

Brewing Salts for Raising Mash pH

Brewing Salt (formula) Common Name	Conc. at 1 gram/gal.	Grams per level teaspoon	Comments
Calcium Carbonate (CaCO₃) a.k.a. chalk Formula weight 100g	105 ppm Ca^{+2} 158 ppm CO_3^{-2}	1.8	Because of its limited solubility, it is only effective when added directly to the mash. Use for making dark beers in areas of soft water. Use nomograph and monitor the mash pH with pH test papers to determine how much to add.
Sodium Bicarbonate (NaHCO₃) a.k.a. baking soda Formula weight 84g	75 ppm Na^{+1} 191 ppm HCO_3^{-1}	4.4	Raises pH by adding alkalinity. If your mash pH is too low or your water has low residual alkalinity, then you can use this in the same way as calcium carbonate.

Brewing Salts for Lowering Mash pH

Brewing Salt (formula) Common Name	Conc. at 1 gram/gal.	Grams per level teaspoon	Comments
Calcium Sulfate (CaSO₄ *2 H₂O) a.k.a. gypsum Formula weight 172.2g	61.5 ppm Ca^{+2} 147.4 ppm SO_4^{-2}	4.0	Useful for adding calcium if the water is low in sulfate. Can be used to add sulfate "crispness" to the hop bitterness.
Calcium Chloride (CaCl2 *2 H₂O) Formula weight 147g	72 ppm Ca^{+2} 127 ppm Cl^{-1}	3.4	Useful for adding calcium if the water is low in chlorides
Magnesium Sulfate (MgSO₄ *7 H₂O) a.k.a. Epsom salt Formula weight 246.5g	26 ppm Mg^{+2} 103 ppm SO_4^{-2}	4.5	Lowers pH by a small amount. Used to add sulfate "crispness" to the hop bitterness

[1] DeLange, A.J., *Understanding Alkalinity and Hardness – Part II*, unpublished, 2001.

[2] Draper, D. "Brewing Waters of the World." Available at www.unm.edu/~draper/beer/waterpro.html.

THE METHODS OF MASHING

In Chapters 14 and 15, you learned about the chemistry in the mash tun. In this chapter, we will discuss how to physically manipulate the mash to create a desired character in the wort and the beer. There are two basic schemes for mashing: single-temperature, a compromise temperature for all the mash enzymes, and multi-rest, where two or more temperatures are used to favor different enzyme groups. You can heat the mash in two ways, also, by the addition of hot water (infusion) or by heating the mash tun directly. There is also a combination method, called decoction mashing, where part of the mash is heated on the stove and added back to the main mash to raise the temperature. All of these mashing schemes are designed to achieve saccharification (convert starches to fermentable sugars). But the route taken to that goal can have a considerable influence on the overall wort character. Certain beer styles need a particular mash scheme to arrive at the right wort for the style.

Single-Temperature Infusion

This method is the simplest and does the job for most beer styles. All of the crushed malt is mixed (infused) with hot water to achieve a mash temperature of 150 to 155° F (65 to 68° C), depending on the style of beer being made. The infusion water temperature varies with the water-to-grain ratio being used for the mash, but generally the initial "strike water" temperature is 10 to 15° F (5 to 8° C) above the target mash temperature. The equation is listed below in the section "Calculations for Infusions." The mash should be held at the saccharification temperature for about an hour, ideally losing no more than a couple of degrees. The goal is to achieve a steady temperature.

The best way to maintain the mash temperature is to use an ice chest or picnic cooler as the mash tun. This is the method I recommend for the rest of the book. Instructions for building a picnic cooler mash/lauter tun are given in Appendix E.

Generally I recommend a water-to-grist ratio of 1.5 to 2 quarts per pound (3 to 4 liters per kilogram), and a strike water temperature of 160 to 165° F (70 to 74° C). It may help to start out with a lower grist ratio of 1.5 quarts/pound (3 liters/kilogram) in case you undershoot the target temperature. If at first you don't succeed, you can add more hot water according to the infusion calculations to make up the difference. It is always a good idea to heat more water than you think you'll need, in case your mash temperature comes out lower than expected. Preheating the mash tun with hot water will help you achieve your predicted temperatures more consistently.

Multi-Rest Mashing

A popular multi-rest mash schedule is the 104 to 140 to 158° F (40 to 60 to 70° C) mash, using a half-hour rest at each temperature, first advocated for homebrewers by George Fix. This mash schedule produces high yields and good fermentability. The time at 104° F (40° C) improves the hydration of the mash and promotes enzyme activity.

As can be seen in Figures 91 and 92 (pp. 145 and 148), several types of enzymes are at work, liquefying the mash and gelatinizing the starches in the endosperm. Varying the times spent at the 140° F (60° C) and 158° F (70° C) rests allows you to adjust the fermentable sugar profiles. For example, a 20-minute rest at 60° C, combined with a 40-minute rest at 70° C, produces a sweeter, more dextrinous beer, while switching the times at those temperatures would produce a drier, more attenuated beer from the same grain bill. You can also change the rest temperatures to change the profiles. For instance, you could rest at 145° F (63° C) and 155° F (68° C) to improve gelatinization and beta-amylase activity to make a more attenuable wort.

If you use a moderately modified malt, such as Briess Pilsen malt, a multi-rest mash will produce a better yield than a single infusion. These malts often need a protein rest to fully realize their potential. The mash schedule suggested by Fix in this case is 122 to 140 to 158° F (50 to 60 to 70° C), again with half-hour rests. The rest at 122° F (50° C) takes the place of the hydration rest at 40° C and provides the necessary protein rest. This schedule is well suited for producing continental lager beers from moderately modified malts. These schedules are provided as guidelines. You, as the brewer, have complete control over what you can choose to do. Play with the times and temperatures, and have fun.

Multi-rest mashes require you to add heat to the mash to achieve the various temperature rests. You can add the heat in

To Rest or Not to Rest, That Is the Question . . . .

When should you do a protein rest?

A protein rest is done for two reasons: to improve the breakdown of the endosperm in less-modified malts, and to increase the FAN in high-adjunct worts. Malts with an S/T ratio or Kolbach Index of 36 to 40% benefit from a protein rest to further degrade the protein matrix around the starches of the endosperm. If the S/T ratio is less than 36%, then a longer protein rest and the boiling action of a decoction mash will probably be necessary to fully release the malt starches into the mash.

You can also do a protein rest in mashes with a high proportion adjunct (more than 40%) of unmalted wheat, oats, or rye in the mash. Unmalted starch adjuncts like wheat, oats, and rye contain little soluble protein that can be converted to FAN. Corn (maize) and rice contain very little protein at all. A protein rest helps provide more soluble protein and FAN to the wort, which will actually improve head retention and promote a healthy fermentation.

If you do a protein rest on a well-modified, all-malt beer, you will not ruin it. Protein rests are common practice in well-modified, high-adjunct commercial brewing. A really long protein rest, for more than an hour, could potentially degrade too much of the foam-positive soluble protein into amino acids to have the best head retention, but it will not be "ruined." Relax. Don't worry.

a couple of ways, either by infusions or by direct heat. If you are using a kettle as a mash tun, you can heat it directly using the stove or a stand-alone hotplate. (See Figure 98.)

The first temperature rest is achieved by infusion using the single-temperature mash method described above. The subsequent rest(s) are achieved by carefully adding heat from the stove and constantly stirring to avoid scorching and heat the mash uniformly. After the conversion, the mash is carefully poured or ladled from the mash tun into the lauter tun and lautered. The hot mash and wort is susceptible to oxidation from hot-side aeration (HSA) due to splashing at this stage, which can lead to long-term flavor stability problems.

Note: A good way to prevent hot spots and scorching with enamelware and stainless steel pots is to use a "flame tamer" under the pot. A flame tamer is a ⅛-inch-thick aluminum or copper plate that spreads the heat more uniformly across the bottom of the pot due to its high heat conductivity.

If you are using a picnic cooler for your mash tun, multi-rest mashes are a bit trickier. You need to

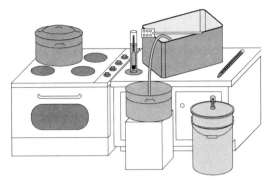

Figure 98 Mashing in the kitchen: The grist is added to the cooler and infused with the strike water to bring the mash temperature to the desired rest temperature. Additional boiling water can be added to raise the temperature to a second rest, if desired. During the mash, sparge water is heated on the stove. After mashing, additional water is added (if necessary) to bring the wort volume to half of the intended boiling volume, and the first runnings are drained to the boiling pot. The sparge water is then added to the mash tun, stirred thoroughly, and allowed to steep for 15 minutes before recirculation and draining. The full wort is then placed on the stove and boiled with the hops.

start out with a stiff mash (e.g., 0.75 to 1 quart per pound of grain, or 1.5 to 2 liters per kilogram), to leave yourself enough room in the tun for the additional water. Usually only two temperature rests are possible with this method, because the amount of heat necessary to change the temperature of the mash increases with each addition. Reaching a third rest is possible if the change in temperature is only a few degrees. For example, raising the mash temperature for 8 pounds of grain from 150° F to 158° F at a mash ratio of 2 quarts per pound would require approximately 2.7 quarts of boiling water.

Infusion Calculations

These calculations allow you to estimate the amount of heat provided by a volume of hot water, so you can predict how much that heat will change the temperature of the mash. This method makes a few simplifications, one of which is the assumption that no heat will be lost to the surroundings, but we can minimize this error by preheating the tun with some boiling hot water. Pour a gallon or two of boiling water into your cooler (before you add the grist), swirl it around and let it sit for a few minutes with the lid on, and then dump it. By preheating the cooler just before you add your grist and strike water, most of the infusion heat will go to the grist rather than the cooler, and your infusion calculations will be more accurate.

Most of the thermodynamic constants used in the following equations have been rounded to single digits to make the math easier. The difference in the results is at most a cup of hot water and less than 1° F. Experience has shown the equation to be fairly reliable and consistent batch to batch, as long as you preheat the tun.

The calculation for the initial infusion only depends on your initial grain temperature, the target mash temperature, and the ratio (R) of water-to-grain in quarts per pound. The amount of grain is taken into account in the ratio. These equations also work for liters, kilograms, and degrees Celsius. The only change you need to make is to change the thermodynamic constant in the equations from 0.2 to 0.41.

Initial Infusion Equation

Strike Water Temperature Tw = (0.2 / R)(T2 - T1) + T2

Mash Infusion Equation

Wa = (T2 - T1)(0.2G + Wm) / (Tw - T2)

where:

R = The ratio of water to grain in quarts per pound (or liters/kilogram)
Wa = The amount of boiling water added (in quarts or liters)
Wm = The total amount of water in the mash (in quarts or liters)
T1 = The initial temperature (° F or ° C) of the mash
T2 = The target temperature (° F or ° C) of the mash
Tw = The actual temperature (° F or ° C) of the infusion water
G = The amount of grain in the mash (in pounds or kilograms)

The infusion water does not have to be boiling; a common choice is to use the sparge water at 170° F (77° C). Then Tw becomes 170° F, and more water (Wa) will be needed to make up the additional quantity of heat.

Multi-Rest Infusion Example:

This example will push the envelope with three rests. We are going to mash 8 pounds of grain through a 104° F, 140° F, and 158° F (40, 60, and 70° C) multi-rest mash schedule. For the purposes of this example, we will assume that the temperature of the dry grain is 70° F (21° C). The first infusion will need to take the temperature of the mash from 70° F to 104° F.

1. We will start with an initial water ratio of 1 quart per pound. Using the initial infusion equation, the strike water temperature is:

Tw = (0.2 / R)(T2 - T1) + T2
= (0.2 / 1)(104 - 70) +104 = 110.8 or 111° F

2. For the second infusion, to bring the temperature to 140° F, we need to use the mash infusion equation. At 1 quart/pound, Wm is 8 quarts. We will assume that our boiling water for the infusions has cooled somewhat to 210° F.

Wa = (T2 - T1) x (0.2G + Wm) ÷ (Tw - T2)
Wa = (140 - 104) x (1.6 + 8) ÷ (210 - 140)
Wa = 36 x 9.6 ÷ 70 = 4.9 qts.

3. For the third infusion, the total water volume is now 8 + 4.9 = 12.9 quarts.

Wa = (158 - 140) x (1.6 + 12.9) ÷ (210 - 158)

Wa = 18 x 14.5 ÷ 52 = 5.02 qts.
The total volume of water required to perform this schedule is:
8 + 4.9 + 5.0 = 17.9 qts, or 4.5 gals.
The final water-to-grain ratio has increased to 2.25 quarts/pound (18 ÷ 8).

Decoction Mashing
Equipment needed:
    Cooler mash tun
    4-gallon heavy stockpot (aluminum preferred)
    1-quart glass measuring cup
    Thermometer

ZWEIMAISCHVERFAHREN

Decoction mashing was developed to get the best extraction from the old-time Northern European barley strains that depended on overwintering to germinate and were more difficult to malt and modify. Decoction mashing provided for better breakdown and solubilization of the starches and better extraction from those less-modified malts. Beer connoisseurs claim better malt flavor and aroma from decoction mashing of those malts. These days, less-modified malts are hard to find, but decoction mashing is still useful for extracting that extra bit of malt character for bock and Oktoberfest-style lagers. In addition, the decoction mashing provides for increased hot break and clarity in the wort. The pH from decoction mashes has been shown to be 0.1 to 0.15 pH units lower than the same wort from an infusion mash.

Decoction mashing is a good way to conduct multi-step mashes without adding additional water or applying heat to the mash tun. It involves removing a portion of the mash to another pot, heating it to the conversion rest on the stove, then boiling it, and returning it to the mash to raise the rest of the mash to the next temperature rest. The portion removed should be pretty stiff—no free water should be showing above the top of the grain. The decoction should be held at conversion rest temperatures (150 to 155° F, 65 to 68° C) for 10 to 15 minutes before being boiled. Stir constantly!

You can use a decoction to move to any temperature rest you want, but it was traditionally used to move the main mash from a dough-in rest to the beta-glucanase/protein rest, to the conversion rest, to mash-out. This three-step decoction process is called *Dreimaischverfahren*. As lager malts became more modified, the dough-in stage was dropped, and the main mash was initially infused to the protein rest temperature. This two-step decoction for taking the mash from protein rest to conversion rest and then to mash-out is called *Zweimaischverfahren*. You can also do a single decoction from conversion to mash-out. According to *The Seven Barrel Brewery Brewers' Handbook* (Noonan, et al., Ann Arbor: G.W. Kent, 1996), the important thing when brewing for extra malt character is not the number of decoctions, but the time spent boiling (one of the decoctions) to develop the Maillard reactions and flavors. It recommends boiling for 20 to 45 minutes. What this means to me is that you can use triple decoctions with less-modified malts, double decoction with moderately modified malts, and single decoctions with well-modified malts to achieve the same degree of extract, and (it is hoped) the same sorts of malt flavors by adjusting the boiling time of the main decoction. Maillard reactions are complex, though; you would probably have to experiment a bit to find the flavors you are looking for. See Figure 100 for a diagram of the decoction process, and keep your thermometer handy.

For recipes and more insight on when to use decoction mashing, I encourage you to read books like the previously mentioned *New Brewing Lager Beer* by Greg Noonan and *Designing Great Beers* by Ray Daniels, along with *Radical Brewing* by Randy Mosher (Boulder, Colo.: Brewers Publications, 2004) and some of the *Classic Beer Styles* books by Darryl Richman, Eric Warner, and George Fix (Brewers Publications).

Decoction Calculations

The key difference with decoction mashing is in the way heat is added to the system. With infusion mashing, heat is always being added to the system, which makes the calculations straightforward. Decoction differs in that a volume of mash is removed from the tun, heated to boiling on the stove,

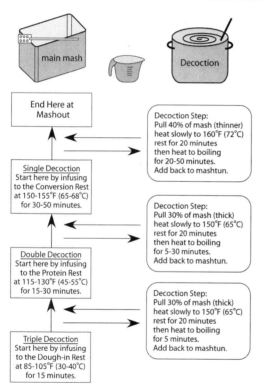

Single Decoction
Start here by infusing to the Conversion Rest at 150-155°F (65-68°C) for 30-50 minutes.

Double Decoction
Start here by infusing to the Protein Rest at 115-130°F (45-55°C) for 15-30 minutes.

Triple Decoction
Start here by infusing to the Dough-in Rest at 85-105°F (30-40°C) for 15 minutes.

End Here at Mashout

Decoction Step:
Pull 40% of mash (thinner) heat slowly to 160°F (72°C) rest for 20 minutes then heat to boiling for 20-50 minutes. Add back to mashtun.

Decoction Step:
Pull 30% of mash (thick) heat slowly to 150°F (65°C) rest for 20 minutes then heat to boiling for 5-30 minutes. Add back to mashtun.

Decoction Step:
Pull 30% of mash (thick) heat slowly to 150°F (65°C) rest for 20 minutes then heat to boiling for 5 minutes. Add back to mashtun.

Figure 100 Use this diagram to help you plan your decoction mash. If you are going to do a Zweimaischverfahren, start at the Double Decoction box and infuse your mash with hot water to achieve a protein rest. Next, pull your first decoction according to the decoction step description, and add it back to your mash to achieve the conversion rest. Then pull your second decoction according to its description to achieve mash-out. Use the measuring cup or a saucepan to transfer the decoctions. You can use the decoction calculations presented on the next pages, or just wing it and watch your thermometer. Good Brewing!

and returned to the tun to raise the mash to the next temperature rest. You need to calculate how much heat is in the tun, how much is removed by the decoction volume, and how much heat that decoction volume is adding back to the tun. Infusion mashing is easy in this respect, because the amount of heat in water is easily calculated. The difficulty in decoction mashing is estimating what the water-to-grain ratio in the pulled volume is, so that its heat value can be calculated.

The key to making these calculations is knowing what the minimum ratio of fully wetted grain is, and from there, determining the respective weights of grain and water that a volume may contain. The equation for the volume of a quantity of mash is given by:

$$V = G (R + 0.32)$$
where:
V = total volume (quarts)
G = (dry) weight of grain (pounds)
R = water-to-grain ratio (quarts/pound)

With this equation, by measuring V and estimating R, we can solve for the amount of grain in a pulled volume and calculate the heat of that volume. However, the equation is only valid for fully wetted grain. The minimum ratio was experimentally determined to be 0.6 quarts per pound; grist ratios above this number only add water volume. The experiments were conducted on two separate occasions using laboratory graduated cylinders and scales. The minimum ratio for fully wetted grain was determined to be between 0.5 and 0.6 quarts per pound, and the statistical mean unit volume of a ratio of 1 quart per pound was determined to be 1.32 quarts. In metric units, this would be equivalent to a ratio of 2 liters per kilogram having a unit volume of 2.667 liters, and the minimum fully wetted ratio would be 1.25 liters per kilogram. For liters and kilograms, $V = G (R + 0.667)$

The following equation calculates the quarts of mash that need to be removed and boiled to provide the heat to reach the next temperature rest.

V_d (quarts) = $[(T2 - T1)(0.4G + 2W)] / [(T_d - T1)(0.4g_d + w_d)]$
where:

V_d = decoction volume
T1 = initial mash temperature
T2 = target mash temperature
T_d = decoction temperature (212° F, 100° C)
G = grain bill weight
W = volume of water in the mash (i.e., initial infusion volume) See note below.
g_d = pounds of grain per quart of decoction = $1 / (R_d + 0.32)$
g_d = kilograms of grain per liter of decoction = $1 / (R_d + 0.667)$
w_d = quarts of water per quart of decoction = $gd \cdot R_d \cdot$ water density = $2g_dR_d$
w_d = liters of water per liter of decoction = $g_d \cdot R_d$
R_d = ratio of grain to water in the decoction volume (range of 0.6 to 1 quart/pound). Thick decoctions will have a ratio of 0.6 to 0.7, thinner decoctions will have a ratio of 0.8 to 0.9 quarts/pound. You need to choose an R_d based on how thick you think your pulled decoction is.

For metric, the equivalent ratios are:

quarts/pound	liters/kilogram
0.6	1.25
0.7	1.46
0.8	1.67
0.9	1.88
1	2.0864 (unit conversion factor)
1.5	3.13
2.0	4.17
2.5	5.22

Note: this equation assumes that an initial dough-in infusion has been done and that the starting water volume is W. For example, let's say that your grain bill was 10 pounds, and you dough-in at a ratio (R) of 1 quart/pound. The initial infusion would be 10 quarts, and W in the decoction equation is 10.

Cereal Mashing Procedure

I wanted to open this section with the Monty Python line: "And now for something completely differ-ent. . . ." But that's wrong. It's actually something completely the same, being just a combination of some of the methods we have already discussed. To brew with starch adjuncts, you need to hydrolyze and gelatinize the starches, so the amylase enzymes can break them into fermentable sugars.

Brewing Tip: Use Decoctions to Fix Infusions

Let's suppose your infusions didn't quite work—the mash temperature is too low. If you have added all the hot water the mash tun can take, and/or you have a ratio of more than 3 quarts per pound, you can use a small decoction to add heat without adding any more water!

Calculate the necessary decoction volume from the equations above. Use a saucepan to pull out a thick portion (mostly grain), and heat it to the conversion temperature of 155° F (67° C), hold it there for about 10 minutes, and then boil it for about 5 minutes. Return this hot decoction to the mash tun, and stir it in evenly to raise the mash temperature without creating hotspots. Check your mash temperature. If it is still low, the decoction process can be repeated.

Accessibility is the key. You can gelatinize the starches by just boiling them, but you can do it more effectively by using a combination of enzymes and heat.

What about flaked adjuncts like corn (maize) and oats? Aren't they already pre-gelatinized? Yes, to a degree. Gelatinization is not like being pregnant, it's like cooking. Actually it is cooking. Instant oats are more gelatinized than old-fashioned rolled oats. Also, just because an adjunct is flaked and pre-gelatinized does not mean that it is fully accessible to the mash enzymes. It helps to grind the rolled flakes, too, especially the big flakes like barley, oats, rye, and wheat.

Rice and corn (maize) contain very little beta-glucan and protein. There is no need to do a beta-glucanase rest when mashing these grains. Unmalted barley has a lot of beta-glucan, as do unmalted rye, oats, and wheat, and a beta-glucanase rest is necessary for good lauterability. If you are using malted wheat, oats, or rye, you don't need a beta-glucan rest, but you will probably want to include a protein rest to break up the higher levels of higher molecular weight proteins these malts contribute if you are using more than 20% in your grain bill.

And lastly, you may want to include rice hulls in the mash to help with lautering. The husk of malted barley constitutes about 5% of the weight, so if you have 20% malted wheat (which has no husk) in your brew, you would want to add at least 1% of the total grain bill weight in rice hulls to make up for it. Rice hulls are probably going to be necessary with wheat beers, rye beers, and high-adjunct beers like American lager. The corn and rice don't have the beta-glucan that makes lautering difficult, but the high proportion of no-hulls will affect the lauterability all the same. I have not needed rice hulls for oatmeal stouts.

To conduct a cereal mash, I recommend that you use a heavy aluminum stockpot that can hold at least 4 gallons. The high conductivity of aluminum will help prevent scorching.

To conduct a cereal adjunct mash:

1. If the adjunct is not flaked, then grind it a few times in your roller mill, or use small coffee grinder or a hammer. You need to break it down for the best results.

2. Combine your cereal grist with 0.5 to 1 pound of barley malt, and infuse it at a ratio of 2 to 3 quarts per pound (4 to 6 liters per kilogram) to an appropriate starting temperature. The higher dilution will help prevent scorching. Try not to exceed a 4:1 ratio of adjunct to malt to avoid diluting the enzymes too much. Barley, oats, rye, and wheat should be started at 113° F (45° C) for a combined beta-glucan and protein rest. (You can cover all your bases that way.) You can start corn and rice at the beta-amylase rest of 145° F (63° C).

3. Hold the mash at the beta-glucanase rest for about 15 minutes, and then heat it slowly, stirring constantly to get to the conversion rest. Barley, wheat, oats, and rye can be fully converted at 150 to 155° F (65 to 67° C). Corn and rice will need higher temperatures to assure gelatinization, 165 to 172°

F (74 to 78° C), but the barley enzymes will convert the pre-gelatinized starch due to rolling.

4. Next, bring the mash to a gentle boil for about 10 to 15 minutes.
5. Now, add this boiling hot mash back to your main mash, using the decoction equations to determine how much heat you are adding. Or, just wing it and watch the thermometer. The main mash can be infused and waiting at whatever temperature rest is appropriate for your recipe. Depending on the amount and type of adjunct, you may be at the protein rest stage to generate sufficient FAN, or somewhere in the saccharification rest region.
6. You can conduct further decoctions as necessary to finish the mash and then add rice hulls as necessary to help lautering. Good Brewing!

Summary

There you have it: the two or three methods of mashing and the calculations to take out the guesswork. Most brewers keep it simple and use single-rest infusion in a picnic cooler. It is the easiest method for producing an all-grain wort. Decoction mashing used to be the hallowed domain of expert all-grain brewers, but it is just another tool that any brewer can use to gain an extra malty edge on a pale wort. The most common homebrewing mash schedule consists of a water-to-grain ratio of 1.5 quarts per pound, and holding the mash between 150 to 155° F (65 to 67° C) for 1 hour.

Probably 90% of the beer styles in the world today can be produced with this method. The next chapter describes the different methods for conducing the lauter, i.e., getting the wort out of the grain.

GETTING THE WORT OUT (LAUTERING)

Ok, let's see where we are: We have discussed the different types of grain and how they can be used, we have talked about the mash enzymes and how they are affected by temperature and pH, and we have learned how the brewing water and grain bill combine to determine the mash pH and how we can manipulate it. In the last chapter, we moved from the chemical aspects of the mash to the physical. We learned about the basic methods of conducting a mash and producing the wort. In this chapter, we are going to discuss how we separate the malt sugars from the grain.

A Good Crush Means Good Lautering

There is a tradeoff between particle size and extraction efficiency when mashing crushed grain. Fine particles are more readily converted by the enzymes and achieve the anticipated yield sooner. However, if all the grain were finely ground, you would end up with porridge that could not be lautered. Coarse particles allow for good fluid flow and lautering but are not converted as well by the enzymes. A good crush has a range of particle sizes that allows for a compromise between extraction and lautering.

If you look back at the discussion of malt analysis sheets in Chapter 12, we discussed how the extract of a malt is gauged according to two conditions: fine grind

Figure 101 A well-crushed grist with a good mix of large and small particles and unshredded husk.

Figure 102 Here is a picture of fine grind and coarse grind of the same malt sample, according to the ASBC Methods of Analysis, Malt-4. Note that the fine grind has the consistency and particle size of cornmeal or flour. The barley husks have been ground up, as well. The coarse grind sample below has much larger particles than the fine grind, but is still smaller than the home grind picture in Figure 101. Also note that the husks in the coarse grind sample have been broken up and even shredded to some extent.

and coarse grind. The degree to which a malt is ground does have an effect on the speed of starch conversion by the enzymes but only a small effect on the total amount of extract. Usually, there is only a 1% difference between the ASBC Congress mash values for fine grind and coarse grind.

A good crush is essential for getting the best mash efficiency and extraction. You need to thoroughly crush the endosperm while leaving the husks as intact as possible. You can get the grain crushed at the brew shop or buy a mill to crush it at home. There are two basic kinds of grain mills commercially available today. The first is a Corona corn mill that uses two counter-rotating disks to grind the malt. It is actually intended to grind corn into cornmeal, not for crushing malt for brewing. Setting the gap between the plates too close together will result in barley flour and shredded husks, which is not good for lautering purposes, often leading to a stuck sparge. This type of grain mill can produce a reasonable crush without too much husk damage if the spacing is set properly (0.035 to 0.042 inch). It is the least expensive kind of mill, but I really don't recommend getting one except for grinding adjuncts.

The other type of grain mill crushes the malt between two rollers (or a roller and flat plate) like a clothes wringer. There is much less damage to the husks this way, which helps keep the wort flowing easily during the sparge. Roller mills are available in several configurations, with either fixed or adjustable gap settings, and will give a better, more consistent crush than a Corona-type mill.

The insoluble grain husks are very important for a good lauter. The grain bed forms its own filter from the husk and grain material. The husks allow water to flow through the bed, extracting the sugar, and prevent the grain bed from compacting. The wort is drawn out through the bottom of the bed by means of a false bottom or manifold, which has openings that allow the wort to be drawn off but prevent the grain from being sucked in as well. Usually these openings are narrow slots, or holes up to an eighth of an inch in diameter. Let me repeat: The grain bed is the filter; the false bottom or manifold underneath only serves to distribute the wort collection points and keep the grain in the grain bed. If you use too fine a screen or slots, the fine particles will actually collect there and block flow, something I learned the hard way.

Note: You may want to add rice hulls to the mash to help with lautering. The husk of malted barley constitutes about 5% of the weight, so if you are using 20% malted wheat (which has no husk) in your brew, you would want to add at least 1% of the total grain bill weight in rice hulls to make up for it. Rice hulls are probably going to be necessary with wheat beers, rye beers, and high-adjunct beers like American lager. The corn and rice don't have the beta-glucan that makes lautering difficult, but the high proportion of no-hulls will affect the lauterability all the same. I have not needed rice hulls for oatmeal stouts.

Yield Comparison

How does the degree of crushing affect the extraction? When new all-grain brewers complain on the forums that their yield from their mash was low, the experienced brewers often point to the crush. Did they buy the malt precrushed? Did they crush it themselves? Was it coarse? Was it crushed at all? (It happens.)

Increasing the degree of crush can significantly improve the yield from home mashing systems. It doesn't have much effect on the results from an ASBC Congress mash (fine/coarse difference typically about 1%). Why the difference in response? The ASBC method mashes a small sample of malt for two hours in a multi-rest mash. It is then lautered for another one to two hours! Homebrewers are diehards if they spend half that much time on 10 pounds of malt.

I conducted an experiment with the help of Briess Malting & Ingredients Company. We compared the maximum extract values for four different grinds of the same lot of malt using the Congress mash. I was hoping to show the difference in yield that homebrewers usually experience with their systems as compared to commercial brewers and the coarse grind numbers on malt analysis sheets. The extraction results and the particle size assay (sieve analysis) for fine grind, coarse grind, one pass, and two passes through a homebrewing two-roller mill are shown in Tables 24 and 25.

It's interesting that the values are all within 1% of each other. This level of variation is not significant. In other words, the difference in yield is not necessarily due to the difference in the particle size distribution, but may simply be due to normal measurement error. Statistically, all the values could be the same, but we don't have enough data here to prove it.

So how can we account for the difference in homebrewer yields with differences in crush? Based on what I have read in professional brewing journals and discussed with professional brewers, I think the difference is in the efficacy of the mashing and lautering process. There is a tradeoff between the crush size, the time required to achieve starch conversion, and the time required to lauter to get that extract out. Allow me to illustrate with two anecdotes.

Bob Hansen, the manager of technical service at Briess Malting, tells me:

> "I often tell craftbrewers that they should relax their grind, because the small difference they get by fine grinding can keep them lautering so long that there is no savings in terms of time. For craftbrewers, where labor/barrel is very high and most people are overworked, it's a no-brainer.

TABLE 24
Comparison of Particle Size Distribution (%) as a Function of Crush

Particle Size	1 Pass	2 Pass	Coarse Grind	Fine Grind
14	70.4	58.4	10.6	1.0
20	16.2	23.2	61.0	7.8
60	6.2	8.6	13.6	52.8
Pan	7.2	9.8	14.8	38.4

TABLE 25
Comparison of Yield As a Function of Crush

Congress mash	Pass 1	Pass 2	Coarse Grind	Fine Grind
Yield (dry basis)	79.4	80.1	79.7	80.9

"I'm not sure they believe the guy who works for the malting company, though, when I say, Grind coarser and use more malt, but go home a half an hour earlier; it will be cheaper in the long run."

Don Obenauer, designer of the Crankandstein two- and three-roller mills, tells me:

"... the best crushes might theoretically look like fine grinds. Yet in practice, and in ASBC recommendations, the sieve tests show that most brewers, especially hobbyists, prefer medium to coarse grinds that reduce the likelihood of stuck mashes and recirculations. This discrepancy is reflected in a funny story, though tragic to the all-too-experienced, multi-award-winning Homebrewer of the Year who sieve-tested a Crankandstein three-roller mill at his local microbrewery and came to the conclusion that running the grain through twice gave the ideal textbook result. He went home and ended up with a 45-pound stuck sparge, even after being warned not to blindly trust the screen results. His pipe-with-a-stainless-mesh-screen turned into a straw full of concrete, and the whole mess got dumped. Next time, the single pass at the factory setting worked just fine."

The Lautering Process

Lautering is the method of separating the sweet wort from the mash. A lauter tun consists of a large vessel to hold the mash and a false bottom or manifold to allow the wort to drain out while leaving the grain behind. Lautering can be conducted in several ways, but it usually consists of three steps: mash-out, recirculation, and sparging.

What Is Mash-out?

Before the sweet wort is drained from the mash and the grain is rinsed (sparged) of the residual sugars, many brewers perform a mash-out. Mash-out is the term for raising the temperature of the mash to 170° F (77° C) prior to lautering. This step stops all of the enzyme action (preserving your fermentable sugar profile) and makes the grain bed and wort more fluid. For most mashes with a ratio of 1.5 to 2 quarts of water per pound of grain, the mash-out is not needed. The grain bed will be loose enough to flow well. For a thicker mash, or a mash composed of more than 25% wheat or oats, a mash-out may be needed to prevent a set mash/stuck sparge. This is when the grain bed plugs up and no liquid will flow through it. A mash-out helps prevent this by making the sugars more fluid—like the difference between warm and cold honey. If your mash has lost a lot of heat during the mash and dropped below 140° F (60° C), beta-glucans, pentosans, and any unconverted starches will turn gummy and make lautering very difficult. The mash-out step can be done using external heat or by adding hot water according to the multi-rest infusion calculations. (See Chapter 16.) A lot of homebrewers tend to skip the mash-out step for most mashes with no consequences. (I usually don't do one, although if you are having lautering problems, it's the first thing to try.)

What Is Recirculation?

After the grain bed has settled and is ready to be lautered, the first few quarts of wort are drawn out through the drain of the lauter tun and poured back in on top of the grain bed. This is also known as the *vorlauf* step. The first few quarts are always cloudy with proteins and grain debris, and this step filters out the undesired material from getting into your boiling pot. The wort should clear fairly quickly. After the wort starts running clear (it will still be dark and a little bit cloudy, but chunk-free), you are ready to collect the wort and sparge the grain bed. Recirculation may be necessary any time the grain bed is disturbed and bits of grain and husk appear in the runoff, although if your grain bed has good depth, disturbing it is unlikely.

What Is Sparging?

Sparging is the rinsing of the grain bed to extract as much of the sugars from the grain as possible without extracting mouth-puckering tannins from the grain husks. Sparging means "to sprinkle," and you may have seen "sparge arms" or sprinklers in the lauter tuns of commercial breweries. In commercial breweries, the lauter tun is separate from the mash tun, and it is fitted with rakes and sprinkling systems to ensure that every useful gallon of extract is rinsed from the grain. On a home-brewing scale, we don't need to be that economical; in fact, the smaller scale makes it easier to rinse the grain bed of the wort. Typically, 1.5 times as much water is used for sparging as for mashing (e.g., 8 pounds malt at 2 quarts per pound equals 4 gallons of mash, so up to 6 gallons of sparge water). The temperature of the sparge water is important. The water should be no more than 170° F (77° C), as husk tannins become more soluble above this temperature, especially when the wort pH gets to 6 or above. This will lead to astringency in the beer. But it shouldn't be much less than 170° F, either (i.e., 165° F or 74° C). You want good fluidity.

There are several sparging methods practiced by homebrewers.

Continuous sparging. Also known as fly sparging, this method usually results in the best yield. The wort is recirculated and drained until about an inch of wort remains above the grain bed. The sparge water is slowly added as the wort is drained. Sparge time varies (½ to 2 hours), depending on the amount of grain and the type of collection system. The yield is highly dependent on the uniformity of fluid flow through the grain bed to ensure that every grist particle is fully rinsed. The sparge is stopped when the gravity from the runnings is less than or equal to 1.008, or when enough wort has been collected, whichever comes first. This method demands more attention by the brewer but can produce a higher yield per pound of malt.

Parti-gyle. This brewing method was common in England before the nineteenth century, and it allows you to make two beers from the same mash. A large mash is produced, and the first wort is drained completely before more water is added to the grist for a second mash and drained again. The first and second runnings are used to make separate beers. The first runnings typically had a gravity of about 1.080 and were used for making an "aging" beer. The second runnings were lighter in gravity and used for making a "running" or table beer, and the mash was often "capped" with some additional grain strewn onto the grain bed to produce a low-gravity small beer. Depending on the amount of grain in your mash, you can brew a barley wine and a pale ale, or a strong ale and a mild using this method. The first runnings is typically one-third of the total wort volume for the batch and twice the gravity of the second runnings.

Batch sparging. This method is a U.S. homebrewing practice in which large volumes of sparge water are added to the mash all at once, instead of gradually, and is most often used with large chest coolers. The grain bed is allowed to settle, recirculated for clarity, and then the wort is drained off. Usually two or sometimes three sparges are combined to create the wort. This method differs from the English method in that the different runnings are combined to produce a single beer. This method was originally developed from parti-gyle to make large quantities of porter and was known as "entire." It is less efficient than continuous sparging (you will use 10 to 15% more grain than with a continuous sparge recipe), but it is convenient.

No-sparge. This method is the least efficient in terms of points per pound, but it's easy and has the benefit of being immune to tannin extraction during the sparge. Like batch sparge, no-sparge is a draining rather than a rinsing method, and the beer is produced entirely from first runnings, resulting in a smoother, richer-tasting wort at the expense of efficiency.

Draining vs. Rinsing

Commercial breweries practice continuous sparging because it is the most efficient way to rinse the grain of all the fermentable sugars. Extraction efficiency matters to commercial brewers because they are trying to get the most beer for the buck from their processes. Homebrewers generally have a different priority: We are trying to get the best beer for the buck. The difference in scale is in our favor. We can spend an extra dollar on malt to make up for a lack of efficiency, whereas a brewery would have to spend an extra five hundred dollars and carry that cost through to the bottom line.

Continuous sparging is a rinsing process that depends on uniform flow through the grain bed to achieve the best yield. The first runnings are rich in sugar, and as the sparge water moves through the bed, this heavy wort is displaced by the less dense hot water, so the grain does not float as well. This causes the grain bed to compact, which can lead to a stuck sparge. You will also get a stuck sparge if the runoff rate is too fast; it will create a partial vacuum around the false bottom or manifold and compact the grain around it. The maximum recommended rate for continuous sparging is about one quart per minute. After the heavy first wort has been displaced, the remaining sugars in the grist particles will diffuse into the sparge water. This diffusion process takes time, and that is another reason to go slowly; otherwise, the boil pot will simply fill with sparge water.

The grain bed can be a few inches to a couple of feet deep, but the optimum depth depends on the overall tun geometry and the total amount of grain being mashed. If the grain bed is very shallow, from lautering too little grain in too large a tun, then the filter bed will be inadequate, the wort won't clear, and you will get hazy beer. A minimum useful depth is probably about 4 inches, but a depth of about 8 inches is preferable. In general, deeper is better, but if it is too deep, then the grain bed is more easily compacted and may not let any wort through, making lautering nearly impossible. Since fluids always follow the path of least resistance, compaction can lead to preferential flow, in which some regions of grain are completely rinsed while others are not rinsed at all. Non-uniform flow is a major cause of poor extraction.

But what if we didn't have to rinse? If we simply drain the grain bed of the wort that was there, then all of our concerns about uniform flow and rinsing go out the window! This is basically what the no-sparge method consists of—you get a very rich wort with little effort. The problem is that quite a bit of wort is left behind. This is where batch sparging steps in—we mix another batch of water into the mash tun, let it sit 15 minutes to allow diffusion of the sugars to occur, and then drain this second wort to the brewpot. The second wort typically has a gravity of 1.016 or greater, so tannin extraction due to rising mash pH is usually prevented. (See Chapter 15 for more info.)

Sparging Calculations

How do these different methods affect the beer recipe? Glad you asked, because it is a good way to illustrate the differences.

For example, here is a comparison of the standard 5-gallon recipe (continuous sparging) and the batch sparge and no-sparge recipes for a simple brown ale recipe:

Grain Bill	Standard	Batch	No-Sparge
Pale ale malt	7 lbs.	7.6 lbs.	8.5 lbs.
Crystal 60 malt	1 lb.	1.1 lbs.	1.25 lbs.
Chocolate malt	0.25 lb.	0.3 lb.	0.5 lb.
Total weight	**8.25 lbs.**	**9.0 lbs.**	**10.25 lbs.**
Brewing efficiency	80%	75%	65%
Total mash volume	**3.75 gal.**	**4.9 gal.**	**8 gal.**

Each method produces the same 6 gallons of 1.041 wort using progressively more grain. The other difference is the size of the mash: 4.9 for batch sparge and 8 gallons for no-sparge, versus 3.75 gallons for the continuous sparge. The numbers above were calculated using "the long way" method described below.

Batch Sparge Calculations—The Short Way

The easy way to do the batch sparge and no-sparge calculations is to use the brewing efficiency percentages above to determine your grain bill and just see what you get. Many people do it that way and are very satisfied with the results. The method is the same as calculating malt extract quantities, except that the typical yield in ppg for batch sparging is 28 points/pound/gallon instead of 36 or 42 for liquid or dry malt extract. The 28 ppg comes from 75% efficiency x 37 ppg, based on the maximum percent extract for lager base malt. (Extract efficiency is explained fully in the next chapter.)

Example: To brew 5 gallons of a 1.049 OG beer:

49 points x 5 gallons = 245 total points

245/28 ppg = 8.75 pounds of grain. This estimate includes your specialty malts, which typically have a little lower yield. To obtain a more accurate grain bill, use this estimate as a starting point to figure out how much of each malt you would like to use in your grain bill and add up the contributions for each malt as described in the next chapter.

As you probably noticed, the grain bill for the batch sparge recipe cited above was 9 pounds, while here it's only 8.75. The discrepancy is simply due to rounding up the individual malt weights in the "long way" example below. The difference between the continuous sparge and batch sparge grain bills is only a half-pound of malt, and you could simply add that difference solely as base malt and keep the specialty malts at their original amounts, instead of trying to weigh up 0.533 pounds of crystal malt. The difference to the recipe character will be negligible.

If you use a mash ratio of 2 quarts/pound (4.2 liters/kilogram), you will easily get half your intended boiling volume from draining the first runnings. Typically, you want to collect 1 to 1.5 gallons of wort more from your mash than the recipe volume to boil down to your intended OG.

Batch Sparge Calculations—The Long Way

Batch sparging works best when two sparge volumes of the same size are combined to create the wort. To keep the process simple, we want the first sparge volume to be what we get when we simply drain the mash. To do this, we need to calculate the batch sparge mash ratio that will give us that volume, including the water that will be absorbed by the grain. Then the batch sparge brewing process becomes as easy as conducting the mash, draining the first runnings to the boiling kettle, adding an equal volume of sparge water back to the mash, draining again, and boiling!

First, let's define the terms in the equations:

Inputs:
- OG: Standard recipe original gravity (just the points part, i.e., 1.049)
- Gr: Standard recipe grain bill (total pounds)
- Vr: Standard recipe batch size (e.g., 5 gallons)
- Vb: Standard recipe boil volume (e.g., 6 gallons)

Calculation Coefficients:
- k: Water-retention coefficient (0.5 quart per pound)

Outputs:
- W: Batch sparge water volume (quarts)
- Rb: Batch sparge mash ratio (quarts/pound)
- S: Scale-up factor for grain bill
- Gb: Batch sparge grain bill (total pounds)
- Vm: Volume of water for the mash (quarts)
- BG: Boil gravity (points)
- BG_1:   Gravity of the first runnings (points)
- BG_2:   Gravity of the second runnings (points)
- Vt: Total volume of the mash (quarts)

1. Decide how many gallons of wort you will boil to achieve your recipe volume and thus your sparge volume (e.g., Vb = 6 gallons).
   $$W = Vb/2 \quad \text{(3 gallons, i.e., 12 quarts)}$$
2. Calculate the batch sparge mash ratio.
   $$Rb = (Vb + (Vb2 + 2k \cdot Vb \cdot Gr)^5) / Gr \quad \text{(1.85 qts./lb.)}$$
3. Calculate the scale-up factor.
   $$S = 1/ (1 - k2/Rb2) \quad \text{(1.08)}$$
4. Calculate the batch sparge grain bill.
   $$Gb = S \cdot Gr \quad \text{(8.9 or ~9 lbs.)}$$

Grain Bill	Standard	Batch
Pale ale malt	7 lbs.	7.6 lbs.
Crystal 60 malt	1 lb.	1.1 lbs.
Chocolate malt	0.25 lb.	0.3 lb.
Total weight	8.25 lbs.	9.0 lbs.

5. Calculate the volume of water for the mash.
   $$Vm = Rb \cdot Gb = W + k \cdot Gb \quad \text{(16.6 quarts)}$$
6. Calculate the gravity of the first runnings.

$BG_1 = 4 \cdot S \cdot Vr \cdot OG/Vm$ (1.0$\underline{64}$)

7. Calculate the gravity of the second runnings.
   $BG_2 = 4 \cdot Vr \cdot OG \cdot (k/Rb) \cdot (1 - (k/Rb)) / (Gr \cdot (Rb - k))$ (1.017)

8. Verify the combined boil gravity and recipe gravity.
   $BG = (BG_1 + BG_2) / 2$ and $OG = BG \cdot Vb/Vr$ (1.0$\underline{40}$ and 1.0$\underline{49}$)

9. Calculate the total batch sparge mash volume (quarts). The volume of 1 pound of dry grain, when mashed at 1 quart per pound, is 42 fluid ounces (1.3125 quarts or 0.328 gallon). Higher ratios only add the additional water volume.
   $Vt = Gb \cdot (Rb + 0.32)$ (19.5 quarts, i.e., 4.9 gallons)

No-Sparge Calculations—The Short Way

The easy way to do the no-sparge calculations is to use the brewing efficiency percentages above to determine your grain bill and just see what you get. Many people do it that way and are very satisfied with the results. The method is the same as calculating malt extract quantities, except that the typical yield in ppg for no-sparge is 24 points/pound/gallon instead of 36 or 42 for liquid or dry malt extract. The 24 ppg comes from 65% typical efficiency x 37 ppg, based on the maximum percent extract for lager base malt. (Extract efficiency is explained fully in the next chapter.)

Example: To brew 5 gallons of a 1.049 OG beer:

1. 49 points x 5 gallons = 245 total points

2. 245/24 ppg = 10.2 pounds of grain. This estimate includes your specialty malts, which typically have a slightly lower yield. To obtain a more accurate grain bill, use this estimate as a starting point to figure out how much of each malt you would like to use in your grain bill, and add up the contributions for each malt as described in the next chapter.

3. As you probably noticed, the grain bill for the no-sparge recipe cited above was 10.25 pounds, while here it's only 10.2. The discrepancy is simply due to rounding up the individual malt weights in the "long way" example below. The difference here between the continuous sparge and no-sparge is 2 pounds, which is big enough that you will want to scale up your specialty malts, too, and not just the base malt. In this case, you will want to add at least a quarter-pound to each of the two specialty malts, and add the remainder to the base malt. Check the malt weight percentages to verify that your new recipe is still proportional to the original.

4. When you batch sparge, you don't want to add the full boil volume of water at mash-in, because this will be too dilute for good mash chemistry and conversion. Instead, use a normal mash ratio of 1.5 to 2 quarts/pound (3 to 4 liters/kilogram), then add the remaining water after the mash is complete (an hour). Stir in the additional water, let the grain bed settle, recirculate, and drain to your boiling pot.

5. To calculate how much water to add after the mash:
   The initial mash volume is 10.25 x R(2) = 20.5 quarts
   The mash will retain about 0.5 quart/pound = 5 quarts
   which leaves about 15 quarts of free wort. To collect 6 gallons (24 quarts) of wort total, you will need to add another 9 quarts of hot water to the mash.

No-Sparge Calculations—The Long Way

Here is how to calculate a no-sparge version from a standard recipe, such as those given in Chapter 20. These calculations combine the scaling-up of the grain bill with a three-step infusion mash method that makes the whole process more manageable.

Inputs:

OG: Standard recipe original gravity (just the points part, i.e., 1.049)

Gr: Standard recipe grain bill (total pounds)

Vr: Standard recipe batch size (e.g., 5 gallons)

Vb: Standard recipe boil volume (e.g., 6 gallons)

Calculation Coefficients:

k: Water-retention coefficient (0.5 quart per pound)

Rr: Standard recipe conversion rest mash ratio (e.g., 2 quarts/pound)

Outputs:

S: Scale-up factor for grain bill

Gn: No-sparge grain bill (total pounds)

BG: No-sparge boil gravity (points)

Rn: No-sparge final mash ratio (quarts/pound)

Wn: No-sparge total water volume (quarts)

Wmo: Mash-out water volume (quarts)

Vt: No-sparge total mash volume (quarts)

1. Decide how many gallons of wort you will boil to achieve your recipe volume (e.g., Vb = 6 gallons).

2. Calculate the scale-up factor.
    $$S = 4 \cdot Vb / (4 \cdot Vb - k \cdot Gr) \qquad (1.2)$$

3. Calculate the no-sparge grain bill.
    $$Gn = S \cdot Gr \quad (9.96 \text{ lbs.}^\dagger \text{ See below.})$$

4. Calculate the no-sparge boil gravity.
    $$BG = OG \cdot Vr/Vb \qquad (1.0\underline{41})$$

5. Calculate the no-sparge mash ratio.
    $$Rn = (4 \cdot Vb + k \cdot Gn) / Gn \qquad (2.84 \text{ (qts./lb.)})$$

6. Calculate the total no-sparge water volume (quarts).
    $$Wn = Gn \cdot Rn = 4 \cdot Vb + k \cdot Gn \quad (29.1 \text{ qts.})$$

7. Calculate the volume of water you will use for mash-out (quarts).
    $$Wmo = Gn(Rn-Rr) \text{ or } Wn - \text{infusions} \quad (8.6 \text{ qts.})$$

8. Calculate the total no-sparge mash volume (quarts).
    $$Vt = Gn \cdot (Rn + 0.32) \quad (32.3 \text{ qts., i.e., 8 gal.})$$

No-Sparge Multiple Infusion Mash Procedure

1. From the no-sparge recipe equations, we determined that the scale-up factor for the Oak Butt Brown Ale is 1.2. Applying the scale-up factor to each malt gives us:

Grain Bill	Standard	No-Sparge
Pale ale malt	7 lbs.	8.5 lbs.†
Crystal 60 malt	1 lb.	1.25 lbs.†
Chocolate malt	0.25 lb.	0.5 lb.†
Total weight	8.25 lbs.	10.25 lbs.
Total mash volume	3.75 gal.	8 gal.

†When scaling up the individual malts, you can round up to the nearest quarter-pound to make weighing easier.

2. From Chapter 16, we can calculate the infusions for dough-in and conversion, based on the new grain bill of 10.25 pounds.

Dough-in Infusion

Target temperature:	104° F
Dough-in infusion ratio:	1 quart/pound
Infusion water temperature:	111° F
Infusion volume:	10.25 quarts

Conversion Infusion

Water volume of mash is:	10.25 quarts
Target temperature:	154° F
Infusion water temperature:	210° F
Infusion volume:	10 quarts
Total water volume	20.25 quarts

3. At this point, we have a rather ordinary mash of 10.25 pounds in 20.25 quarts of water, i.e., a mash ratio of about 2 quarts/pound. The total volume of this mash is about 6 gallons. Now we will calculate how much water we need to add to make up the total no-sparge water volume (Wn) and use it for a mash-out infusion.

Wn = 4(Vb + kGn) = 29.125 quarts

Wmo = Wn − infusions = 29.125 − 20.25 = 8.875 or 9 quarts

4. At first glance, you might say, "just add 9 more quarts and call it good," but we really don't want to push the mash-out temperature above 170° F. So we want to calculate the infusion temperature that will give us a final mash temperature of 170° F (max). From Chapter 16, we can rearrange the infusion equation to find the infusion temperature.

Tw = (T2 − T1)(0.2G + Wm) / Wa + T2

Tw = (170 − 154)(0.2•10.25 + 20.25) / 9 + 170 = 209.6 or 210° F

In this case, using our usual infusion water temperature of 210° F, we don't need to worry about increasing the potential for tannin extraction. However, if we were going to collect 7 gallons instead of 6, which would mean infusing 13 quarts instead of 9, the temperature of the infusion would need to be reduced to 198° F.

5. Yes, there are a few calculations involved, and it's a much bigger mash, but it does simplify things to add all the water to the mash, recirculate, and drain it to start your boil. No worrying about the pH and gravity of the final runnings, no worrying about whether you will hit your target gravity—this process is robust. And if you want to simplify the calculations aspect, then putting the equations into a spreadsheet or using a brewing software program like Promash or Strangebrew will make it easy.

In the next chapter we will explore the concept of extraction efficiency more fully, and use it to plan all-grain recipes.

WHAT TO EXPECT WHEN YOU'RE EXTRACTING

Ok, now we are getting down to brass tacks. We have identified the different kinds of malts and adjuncts that can be used to make the wort. We have described how the enzymes in the malt are activated during the mash and convert the available starches to fermentable sugars. We have discussed the different methods of mashing and the different methods for separating the wort from the spent grains. Now it is time to put all of this information together and figure out how much wort we are going to get from our efforts. To brew the same beer recipe consistently, or to brew a new recipe right the first time, we need to know how much yield we can expect from each type of grain. Then, once we know the potential, we need to be able to measure how much extract we actually achieve from our mashing and lautering process and calculate our brewing efficiency. The first question is, how much is available?

The answer to this question is contained in a malt analysis sheet. These information sheets from the maltster describe the amount of extract that each lot of malt can yield. Typical analysis for the malt type should be available over the Internet from the maltster, and a lot-specific analysis may be available at your local brew shop where you buy the grain. (Usually you don't need to get lot-specific data.) Unfortunately, calculating your OG from several malt analysis sheets is not as straightforward as calculating it for malt extract. When you target an OG with malt extract, it's as simple as multiplying the weight of the extract in pounds by its yield (36 gravity points per pound per gallon for liquid malt extract, or 42 ppg for dry), and dividing by the recipe volume. For example, 6 pounds of liquid malt extract (36 ppg) for a 5-gallon batch equals an OG of 6 x 36/5 = 43.2 or 1.043. To calculate an OG from the yield information on a malt sheet, we will need to convert that information to potential gravity points (i.e., ppg) and learn how to calculate an efficiency factor that adjusts that yield to our brewery's processing capability. Once we understand malt yield and efficiency, we will be able to calculate a grain bill to hit any gravity.

Malt Analysis Sheet Review

Extract—Fine Grind, As-Is and Dry Basis

A malt analysis sheet does not give the malt's yield in points per pound per gallon. Instead, what you will most likely see for North American and European malts is a weight percentage called %Extract—Fine Grind, Dry Basis (FGDB). This percentage is the maximum soluble extract that the malt can yield when mashed.

When a malting house analyzes a malt sample to determine its extract yield, it conducts a laboratory mash, known as a "Congress mash." A Congress mash consists of a multi-infusion mash using a standard weight of finely ground malt. This procedure yields the maximum soluble extract as a weight percentage of the original sample. This yield is known as the %Extract—Fine Grind, As-Is (FGAI). It is called "As-Is" because properly kilned malt contains about 4% moisture by weight, although it can range from 2 to 10%. To compare different lots of malt with different moisture levels, this weight needs to be accounted for in the extract calculation. Therefore, the basis of comparison, and the number you will most consistently see on an analysis, is the Fine Grind, Dry Basis (FGDB)—corresponding to a malt that has been oven-dried to zero moisture.

Converting %Extract to Ppg

In a Congress mash, each grain will yield a maximum amount of fermentable and nonfermentable sugars that is referred to as its *percent extract or maximum yield*. This number typically ranges from 60 to 80% by weight, with some wheat malts hitting as high as 85%. For example, 80% Extract means that 80% of the malt's weight is soluble and extracted by the laboratory mash and lauter. (The other 20% represents the husk and insoluble proteins and starches.) In the real world, homebrewers will never hit this target, but it is a useful basis for comparison.

The reference for comparison is pure sugar (sucrose), because it yields 100% of its weight as soluble extract when dissolved in water and has no moisture of its own. One pound of sugar will yield a specific gravity of 1.046 when dissolved in water to form 1 gallon of solution. To calculate the maximum yield for different malts and adjuncts, the %Extract FGDB for each is multiplied by the reference number for sucrose—46 points/pound/gallon (ppg).

For example, let's consider two-row lager malt. This base malt has an FGDB of 81.7% by weight of soluble materials. So, if we know that sugar (sucrose) will yield 100% of its weight as soluble sugar and that it raises the gravity of the wort by 46 ppg, then the maximum increase in gravity we can expect from this malt, at 81.7% soluble extract, is 81.7% of 46 or 37 ppg.

Hot Water Extract (HWE)

This parameter may be seen on malt analyses from the United Kingdom, where the Institute of Brewing utilizes a single-temperature infusion mash that differs from the ASBC and EBC Congress mash methods. Method 2.3—Hot Water Extract of Ale, Lager, and Distilling Malts, uses an hourlong mash at 65° C (149° F) to measure the maximum extract. HWE (As-Is) is measured as Liter•Degrees/Kilogram, and as a unit, it is equivalent to ppg when the metric conversion factors for volume and weight are applied. (Note: points/pound/gallon = gallon•degrees/pound). The overall conversion factor is HWE = 8.345 x ppg. However, the grind/mash procedures for HWE and %Extract differ enough that the measurements are not actually equivalent, even though they are close. The best analogy I can think of is the trying to compare the power ratings of a racecar to a farm tractor—power is power, but the way it is expressed and utilized is different. That being said, if you get a malt sheet for pale ale malt with an HWE (As-Is) of 308 liter°/kilogram, the conversion of that number by 8.345 to 37 ppg is close enough for homebrewing purposes.

Extract Efficiency and Typical Yield

The maximum yield is just that, a value you might get if all the mash variables (e.g., pH, temperature, time, viscosity, grind, phase of the moon, etc.) lined up, and 100% of the starches were converted to sugars. But most brewers, even commercial brewers, don't get that value from their mashes. Most brewers will approach 70 to 80% of the maximum yield (i.e., 70% of a malt's FGDB of 81.7%). You may be wondering how useful the maximum yield number of a malt can be if you can never expect to hit it. The answer is to apply an efficiency factor to the maximum yield and derive a number we will usually achieve—a typical yield.

This factor is called the brewer's extract *efficiency*, and it's the ratio of the brewer's yield to the malt's maximum yield (FGAI). Every brewery is unique, and your extract efficiency is dependent on your methods and equipment. I will show you how to calculate your efficiency in the next section. The As-Is and Dry Basis ppg's at 75% efficiency are listed in the last two lines of Table 26. The As-Is

---

TABLE 26
Extract Analysis Sheet Data for Several Malts

The percentage of soluble extract by weight is given for several common malts with the equivalent value in points/pound/gallon (i.e., gallon•degrees/pound) given in parentheses.

Parameter	2-Row Lager Malt	2-Row Pale Ale (U.K.)	Munich Malt	Caramel 15	Caramel 75	Chocolate Malt	Roasted Barley
%Moisture	4.4	3.5	4.0	7.9	4.8	3.5	3.3
%Extract, Fine Grind, As-Is (ppg As-Is)	78.1 (36 ppg)	—	78.7 (36 ppg)	73.3 (34 ppg)	75.7 (35 ppg)	74.3 (34 ppg)	64.5 (30 ppg)
%Extract, Fine Grind, Dry Basis (ppg Dry)	81.7 (38 ppg)	310 HWE (37 ppg)	82 (38 ppg)	79.6 (37 ppg)	79.5 (37 ppg)	77 (35 ppg)	66.7 (31 ppg)
%Extract, Coarse Grind, As-Is	77.1 (35 ppg)	—	77.6 (35.5 ppg)	—	—	—	—
%Extract, Coarse Grind, Dry Basis	80.6 (37 ppg)	308 HWE (37 ppg)	80.9 (37 ppg)	—	—	—	—
F/C Difference	1.1	0.8	1.1	—	—	—	—
As-Is ppg at 75% efficiency	27	27	27	25	26	26	22
Dry Basis ppg at 75% efficiency	28	28	28	27	27	27	23

value, which accounts for moisture, is preferred for estimating your yield, but it may not always be listed on an analysis. You can estimate the As-Is value from the Dry Basis and %Moisture numbers. If your extract efficiency is high, (near 90%), then you can figure on losing 1 ppg for every 3% moisture; if your efficiency is lower (about 75%), then you will lose 1 ppg about every 4%.

In Table 26 (p. 193) below, we assume an extract efficiency of 75%, which is considered average for homebrewers using a batch sparge technique with current malts. A few points less yield (e.g., 70% extraction efficiency) is still considered to be good extraction. A large commercial brewery would see the 5% reduction as significant, because they are using thousands of pounds of grain a day. For a homebrewer, adding 5% more grain per batch to make up for the difference in extraction is a pittance.

Calculating Your Efficiency

There are two different gravities that matter to a brewer: one is the extraction or boil gravity (BG), and the other is the post-boil or original gravity (OG). Most of the time, people refer to the OG, because it determines the strength of the beer. When brewers plan recipes, they think in terms of the OG, which assumes that the wort volume is the final size of the batch, e.g., five gallons.

But when it comes to the extract efficiency, we want to think in terms of the boil gravity, because that volume of wort and its gravity is our actual yield. When all-grain homebrewers get together to brag about their brewing prowess or equipment and they say something like, "I got 30 (ppg) from my mash schedule," they are referring to their yield in terms of the amount of wort they collected.

It is important to realize that the total amount of sugar is constant, but the concentration (i.e., gravity) changes, depending on the volume. To understand this, let's look at the unit of points/pound/gallon. This is a unit of concentration, so the unit is always expressed in reference to 1 gallon ("per gallon"). Another way of writing this unit is gallon•degrees/pound. When mashing, you are collecting "x" gallons of wort that has a gravity of "1.0yy" that was produced from "z" pounds of malt. To calculate your mash extraction in terms of ppg, you need to multiply the number of gallons of wort you collected by its gravity and divide that by the amount of malt that was used. This will give you the gravity (gallon•degrees), per pound of malt used. Let's look at an example.

Grain Bill for Palmer's Short Stout
(Yield = 6 gallons of 1.038 wort)
6.5 lbs. 2-row
0.5 lb. caramel 15
0.5 lb. caramel 75
0.5 lb. chocolate malt
0.5 lb. roasted barley
(8.5 lbs. total)

For our example batch, we will assume that 8.5 pounds of malt was mashed to produce 6 gallons of wort that yielded a gravity of 1.038. The brewer's total sugar extraction (yield) for this batch would be 6 gallons multiplied by 38 points/gallon = 230 points. Dividing the total points by the pounds of malt gives us our mash extraction in points/pound, e.g., 230/8.5 = 27 ppg. Comparing these numbers to lager malt's maximum 36 ppg (As-Is) gives us a good approximation of our mash efficiency: 27/36 = 75%.

TABLE 27
Typical Malt Yields in Points/Pound/Gallon

Malt Type	FGDB (Max.% Yield)	Maximum Ppg	Typical Ppg (75%)	Ppg Steep
2-row lager malt	80%	37	28	—
6-row base malt	76%	35	26	—
2-row pale ale malt	81%	38	29	—
Biscuit malt	75%	35	26	—
Victory malt	75%	35	26	—
Vienna malt	75%	35	26	—
Munich malt	75%	35	26	—
Brown malt	70%	32	24	8*
CaraPils malt	70%	32	24	4*
Light crystal (10-15L)	75%	35	26	14*
Pale crystal (25-40L)	74%	34	25.5	22
Medium crystal (60-75L)	74%	34	25.5	18
Dark crystal (120L)	72%	33	25	16
Special "B"	68%	31	23	16
Chocolate malt	60%	28	21	15
Rostmalz	70%	32	24	21
Roasted barley	55%	25	19	21
Black patent malt	55%	25	19	21
Wheat malt	79%	37	28	—
Rye malt	63%	29	22	—
Oatmeal (flaked)	70%	32	24	—
Corn (flaked)	84%	39	29	—
Barley (flaked)	70%	32	24	—
Wheat (flaked)	77%	36	27	—
Rice (flaked)	82%	38	28.5	—
Maltodextrin powder	100%	40	(40)	(40)
Corn sugar	92%	42	(42)	(42)
Cane sugar	100%	46	(46)	(46)

Malt % Yield data obtained and averaged from several sources.

Steeping data is experimental and was obtained by steeping 1 pound in 1 gallon at 160° F (71° C) for 30 minutes. All malts were crushed in a two-roller mill at the same setting.

* The low extraction from steeping is attributed to unconverted starches as revealed by an iodine test.

If we look at the maximum ppg As-Is numbers from Table 27 for each of the recipe's malts, we can calculate our actual mash efficiency:

Malts	Max. Ppg As-Is
6.5 lbs. 2-row	36 x 6.5/6 = 39
0.5 lb. caramel 15	34 x 0.5/6 = 2.8
0.5 lb. caramel 75	35 x 0.5/6 = 2.9
0.5 lb. chocolate malt	34 x 0.5/6 = 2.8
0.5 lb. roasted barley	30 x 0.5/6 = 2.5
Maximum Yield (As-Is)	*50 points or 1.050*

In this case, our mash extraction of 1.038 means our actual efficiency was 38/50 = 76%.

Planning Malt Quantities for a Recipe

Using Ppg

We use the efficiency concept in reverse when designing a recipe to achieve a targeted OG.

How much malt do we need to produce 5 gallons of 1.050 wort?
Let's go back to our Short Stout example.

1. First, we need to assume an efficiency (e.g., 75%) for our primary malt (78% FGAI) and calculate an anticipated yield.

    78% x 75% x 46 (ppg/100% sucrose) = 27 ppg

2. Then we multiply the target gravity (50) by the recipe volume (5) to get the total amount of sugar. 5 x 50 = 250 pts.

3. Dividing the total points by our anticipated yield (27 ppg) gives the pounds of malt required.
    250/27 = 9.25 lbs. (I generally round up to the nearest half-pound, i.e., 9.5 lbs.)

4. So, 9.5 pounds of malt will give us our target OG in 5 gallons. Using the malt values for 75% Efficiency in Table 26, we can figure out how much of each malt to use to make up our recipe. You can build a grain bill "top-down" or "bottom-up," meaning that you can plan the bulk of your fermentables from the base malt first and adjust the specialty grains to make up the rest, or you can plan your specialty grain additions first and use the base malt to complete the OG. I generally use the bottom-up approach, and for this example, I am going to use a half-pound of each specialty malt, and then calculate how much base malt I need to hit my target gravity.

Specialty Malt OG Contributions Based on Ppg, As-Is at 75% Efficiency

Caramel 15	26 x 0.5/5 =	2.6
Caramel 75	25.5 x 0.5/5 = 2.6	
Chocolate malt	21 x 0.5/5 =	2.1
Roasted barley	19 x 0.5/5 =	1.9
	9.2 pts. out of 50	

To calculate how much base malt is required, subtract the specialty malt contribution from the total, multiply that amount by the recipe volume and divide that by the base malt's 75% ppg number (28).

(50 - 9.2) x 5 gal. ÷ 28 = 7.3 lbs. of base malt, which I would round up to the nearest half-pound for convenience's sake (7.5 lbs.)

Thus, the grain bill for Palmer's Short Stout, based on these particular lots of malt and 75% extract efficiency is:

2-row lager malt	7.5 lbs.
Caramel 15	0.5 lb.
Caramel 75	0.5 lb.
Chocolate malt	0.5 lb.
Roasted barley	0.5 lb.
	For a total of 9.5 lbs.

Remember, though, that this is the OG—the post-boil gravity. When you are collecting your wort and are wondering if you have enough, you need to ratio the measured gravity by the amount of wort you have collected to see if you will hit your target after the boil. For instance, to have 5 gallons of 1.050 wort after boiling, you would need (at least):

> 6 gallons of 1.042 (250 pts./6 gal.)
> or   7 gallons of 1.036 (250 pts./7 gal.)

Using Liter Degrees per Kilogram

The concepts work the same with Hot Water Extract and liter°/kilogram. The HWE value for pale ale malt in Table 26 is 310 L°/kg. To calculate the weight of pale ale malt for 20 liters of a 1.045 OG wort:

1. 20L x 45 = 900 gravity points
2. If we assume the same 75% brewer efficiency, 310 HWE for the pale ale malt becomes 232.5 L°/kg.
3. Dividing the gravity points by the HWE gives the weight of malt in kilograms. 900/232.5 = 3.87 kg.

To calculate your actual brewing efficiency for a batch, let's say we collected 28 liters of 1.042 wort from 5 kilograms of pale ale malt (310 HWE FGDB).

1. 28L x 42 pts. = 1,176 gravity points (or L°)
2. 1,176/5 kg = 235 L°/kg
3. 235/310 = 0.758 or 76% efficiency.

Using °Plato

You may have a hydrometer that measures in °Plato instead of specific gravity (SG). Refractometers are based on the Brix scale, which is functionally equivalent to °Plato. You have two options for calculating your brewing efficiency and malt quantities when measuring in °Plato:

1. Convert the °Plato to specific gravity (See Table 31 in Appendix A) and estimate your malt quantities and efficiency using the PPG and HWE methods described above.

2. Use the °Plato and the extract weight-percent method to calculate these quantities.

Degrees Plato measures the amount of extract in wort as a weight percentage (solute:solution). In other words, a wort that measures 10 °Plato has 10 grams of soluble extract (sugars, carbohydrates, proteins, and lipids) in 100 grams of wort. Commercial breweries use this unit more often than ppg or HWE to figure malt quantities, because it gives them better visibility to their malt usage, being malt weight-oriented rather than wort volume-oriented.

To calculate your brewing efficiency using °Plato, the equation is:

> Brewing Efficiency = wt. of actual extract/wt. of maximum extract
> Brewing Efficiency = (wort volume x wort density x wt. % extract in the wort) /
>   (malt wt. x maximum yield)

So what we are doing is calculating the actual weight of the extract in the wort, compared to the maximum extract we could have gotten from the grain bill. The weight of the actual extract is calculated by multiplying the volume of wort by its density to get the total weight of the wort, and then using the measured °Plato to say how much of that total weight is extract. The density of the wort is equal to the density of the water (1 kilogram/liter or 8.32 pounds/gallon) multiplied by the specific gravity of the wort. (Specific gravity is actually a ratio of the solution's density to the density of pure water.) To get the specific gravity value for the wort, you either have to measure it separately with another hydrometer or convert the °Plato reading to specific gravity using the ASBC tables in Appendix A. The conversion between °Plato and specific for worts less than 13 °P is simply the gravity points divided by 4, i.e., 1.040 = 10 °P, although the error increases at higher gravities.

The maximum yield weight is simply the weight of malt multiplied by the maximum yield, e.g., 80% Extract FGDB. Then the equation becomes:

> Brewing Efficiency = [(wort volume x water density x SG) x °Plato] /
>   (malt (kg) x %FGDB)

For example, let's say we used 4 kilograms of malt to brew 20 liters of wort that measures 12 °P. Using the rule of thumb for worts less than 13 °P, the specific gravity is 1.048. The brewing efficiency equation is:

> %Efficiency = [(20L x 1kg/L x 1.048) x 12%] / (4kg x 80%) = 78.6%

The equation can also be rearranged to calculate the grain bill necessary to brew 20 liters of a 12 °P wort. For this example, let's use our standard brewing efficiency of 75%. The equation becomes:

Malt (kg) = [(wort volume x wort density x SG) x °P] / (% FGDB x Efficiency)

Malt (kg) = [(20L x 1kg/L x 1.048) x 12%] / (80% x 75%)

Malt (kg) = [(21kg wort) x 12% extract by weight] / (60%) = 4.2 kilograms of malt

Notes:
1. The calculations can also be conducted in gallons and pounds by using the water density constant of 8.32 pounds per gallon.
2. I should mention that commercial brewers are most likely to use the coarse grind, as-is (CGAI) number from the malt lot analysis sheet, because that number takes the moisture loss into account and helps them more accurately plan their malt usage and maintain better process consistency. On a home-brewing scale, we can be less rigorous and base our efficiency on the more readily available FGDB number. To take moisture into account, multiply the dry basis number by the percentage of dry weight. For example, 80% FGDB at 4% moisture becomes:
80% x 96% = 76.8% FGAI

If the F/C difference of the malt is 1.2%, then the CGAI would be:
76.8% - 1.2% = 75.6%

Substituting this CGAI number for FGDB into the malt quantity calculation above gives 4.4 kilograms required versus 4.2 kilograms. (Although if you recalculate your brewing efficiency using 4.2 kilograms and 75.6% CGAI, your brewing efficiency jumps up to 79.2%. It depends on whether you want to take the moisture of each lot of malt into account outside of your brewing efficiency, or just assume that the moisture content is going to be fairly consistent across different lots of malt, and take it into account as part of a lower overall brewing efficiency.)

Summary
So there you have it, the key to understanding malt yield, extract efficiency, and determining your grain bill for all-grain brewing. A malt analysis sheet will list the maximum yield as %Extract, Fine Grind, and we can convert that weight percentage to specific gravity points via the 46 ppg of sucrose. By comparing the collected wort gravity with maximum calculated yield, we can determine our extract efficiency, and by knowing our efficiency, we can to calculate a grain bill for any wort we want to brew. Cheers!

YOUR FIRST ALL-GRAIN BATCH

One of the comments you will most often hear from first-time all-grainers is, "I didn't realize it would be so easy!" Making beer from scratch is really very easy; it just takes some preparation and some understanding of what needs to be done.

So far, you have seen the various steps and delved into the details in a few areas, but the best way to learn is by doing. Ideally, you have done several extract batches and a couple of extract-and-specialty grain batches by now. You should know to have your ingredients and brewing water ready, with everything clean and sanitized. Unless you have purchased a grain mill, have the grain crushed for you at the brewshop. Crushed grain will stay fresh for about two weeks if kept cool and dry.

Additional Equipment

Mash/lauter tun. The easiest way to brew all-grain beer is to use a picnic cooler mash/lauter tun. I described how they can aid mashing and lautering in Chapters 16 and 17, and instructions for building one are given in Appendix E. A 36- to 48-quart rectangular cooler or 10-gallon round beverage cooler is probably the best choice.

Sparge water pot. You will need a large pot to heat your mash water and your sparge water. You can use your old 5-gallon brewpot for this, or you can purchase a larger 8-gallon pot. You will probably use 3 to 4 gallons of water for a typical mash, and you will need another 3 to 4 gallons of water for the typical sparge, so be forewarned.

Wort boiling pot. You will need to get a new brewpot, because you are going to be boiling the whole batch. You need a pot that can comfortably hold 6 gallons without boiling over. An aluminum 8-gallon stockpot from a restaurant supply store is probably the best choice at about $80. A more economical alternative is an 8-gallon enamelware pot for about $40, although these are

more prone to chipping and scorching. Aluminum has the advantage of good heat conductivity, which helps prevent scorching and boilovers.

Hydrometer. You will want to purchase a hydrometer, if you don't have one already. A hydrometer allows you to monitor the extraction process, and its use is explained in Appendix A.

Suggested Recipe

For this beer, we will make a brown ale, using four malts and a single-temperature infusion mash. I will take you through the entire grain brewing procedure and then go back and discuss some options for various steps. Of course, if there is another beer style that you prefer, you are welcome

Figure 104 Kitchen Mashing Setup. This picture depicts what is probably the most common all-grain brewing setup. The mash/lauter tun sits on the counter near the stove, and two large pots are used: one to prepare the sparge water, and the other to receive and boil the wort.

to use one of the other recipes from Chapter 20. Be sure to adjust your hopping schedule to take the full volume boil and lower boil gravity into account.

Oak Butt Brown Ale

Malts	Gravity Points
7 lbs. (3.2kg) pale ale malt	30
2 lbs. (0.9kg) Victory malt	8
½ lb. (227g) crystal 60L malt	2
¼ lb. (113g) chocolate malt	1
BG for 6.5 gallons	1.041
OG for 5.5* gallons	1.049

Hops	Boil Time	IBUs
½ oz. (14g) Nugget (12%)	60	21
½ oz. (14g) Willamette (5%)	15	4
Total IBUs		25

Yeast	Fermentation Schedule
WLP013 London Ale	Primary ferment at 68° F (20° C) for 2 weeks

Options	
Partial mash	2 lbs. (0.9kg) pale ale malt
	2 lbs. (0.9kg) Victory malt
	½ lb. (227g) crystal 60L malt
	¼ lb. (113g) chocolate malt
(Add to boil)	4 lbs. (1.8kg) pale LME

Mash Schedule—Single-Temperature Infusion

Rest Type	Temperature	Duration
Conversion	152° F (67° C)	60 min.

Mash Schedule

- Single infusion of 160° F (71° C) strike water at a ratio of 2 quarts/pound grain (= 19.5 quarts or 18.5 liters)
- Target mash temperature of 152° F (67° C) Mash time of 1 hour. No mash-out
- Drain wort to collect 3 to 3.5 gallons. Batch sparge with 3.5 gallons to collect 6.5 gallons total.
- Target gravity of 1.041 for 6.5 gallons (or 1.049 for 5.5 gallons after boiling)
- Adjust the amount of chocolate malt (¼ to ½ pound) depending on how dark you want it.

* The extra half-gallon provides for wort soaked up by the hops and break material in the boiler, giving you 5 gallons of clean(er) wort in the fermenter.

Starting the Mash

1. Heat brewing water. Heat up enough water to conduct the mash. At a water-to-grain ratio of 2 quarts/pound (4 liters/kilogram), the amount would be 19.5 quarts (18.5 liters), or about 5 gallons. Always make more, you will often need it. Heat up 5 gallons (19 liters) in the larger of your two brewing pots. At a mash ratio of 2:1, the initial infusion temperature should be 160° F (71° C) to create a mash temperature of 152° F (67° C). Depending on the amount of heat lost to the tun, the strike water could be as hot as 165° F (74° C), but that would (theoretically) create a mash temperature of 156° F (69° C). That would make the wort more dextrinous than we intended, but it would still be a fermentable wort. (See Chapter 16 for the infusion calculations.)

2. Preheat the tun. Preheat the cooler with some boiling water, about a gallon. Swirl it around to heat up the cooler, and then pour it back to your sparge water pot. Preheating will prevent initial heat loss from the mash to the tun, which can throw off your infusion calculations.

3. Mash-in. You want to add the water to the grain, not the other way around. Use a saucepan or a plastic pitcher to pour in a gallon of your strike water at a time and stir between infusions. Don't try to pour 4 gallons of hot water into the mash tun all at once. You don't want to thermally shock the enzymes. Stir it thoroughly to make sure all the grain is fully wetted, but don't aerate it. Hot-side aeration is promoted by a malt enzyme called lipoxygenase at this stage, but it is denatured as the temperature reaches 140° F (60° C). Oxidation of

Partial Mash Option

Not everyone can jump right into full mashing. An option is to use a small mash to provide wort complexity and freshness, plus a can of extract to provide the bulk of the fermentables. This option is particularly attractive for brewers living in small apartments without room in the kitchen for a lot of equipment. Using a partial mash was how I first started using grain, and I was extremely pleased with the results.

A partial mash is carried out just like a full-scale mash, but the volume of wort collected is only the 3 to 4 gallons that you would normally boil when brewing with extract. The advantage over an extract and steeped specialty grain procedure is that you're actually mashing, which means you're not limited to just crystal and roasted grains. Typically, a can of extract is substituted for some of the base malt, and the specialty grains in the recipe are retained.

You can mash in either a pot on the stove or buy a smaller cooler (3 to 4 gallons) and build a small manifold. You probably have a small beverage cooler already that would work well with a drop-in manifold like those discussed in Appendix E. One advantage to using a manifold versus pouring the mash into a strainer is that you avoid aerating the wort while it is hot. As was discussed in previous chapters, oxidation of hot wort at any time will lead to flavor stability problems in the beer later.

wort compounds will not be affected by the subsequent boil and will cause off-flavors later. See Figure 105.

Note: If you needed to add any salts to the mash to adjust the mash pH per Chapter 15, add them now.

4. Check the temperature. Check the temperature of the mash to see if it has stabilized at the target temperature of 152° F (67° C) or at least in the range of 150 to 155° F (65 to 68° C). If the temperature is too low, e.g., 145° F (63° C), add some more hot water. If it is too high, e.g., 160° F (71° C), then add cold water to bring it down. 156° F (69° C) is the highest we would want for this recipe. It will yield a sweet, medium-bodied wort with good attenuation. See Figure 106.

5. Adjust the temperature. OK, the mash temperature came out a little low (148° F), so I added 1.5 quarts of boiling water to bring it up to 152° F. See Figure 107.

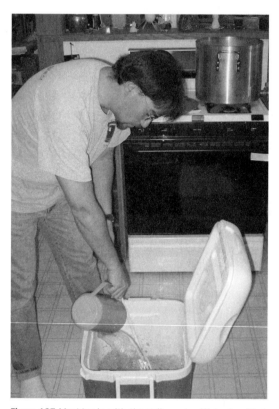

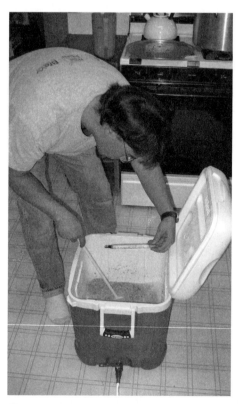

Figure 105 Mashing in with the strike water. Water is added slowly to the grist to avoid thermally shocking the enzymes. I am stirring between infusions. Once I have about half of the water in the mash and the grist is thoroughly wetted, I can pick up the pot and pour the rest of the water in.

Figure 106 Checking the temperature of the mash after the infusion

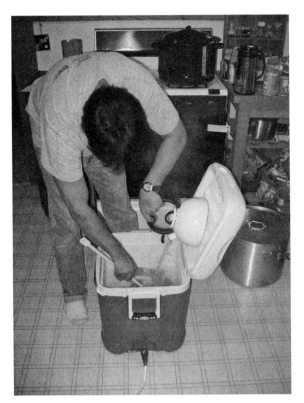

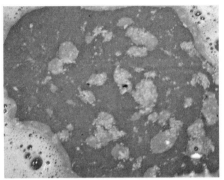

Figure 108 A picture of the mash at T = 0. The wort is cloudy with starch.

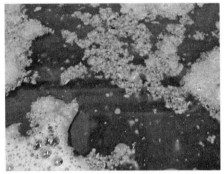

Figure 107 Adding 1.5 quarts of boiling hot water to raise the mash temperature another 4° F, to 152° F. You need to stir in this very hot water quickly to dissipate the heat quickly and minimize denaturing the enzymes.

Figure 109 A picture of the mash at T = 30 minutes. Some of the larger particles are floating around, as are some husks. Notice it has cleared; it is no longer cloudy with starch, and it smells great.

Conducting the Mash

6. Monitor. Stir the mash every 15 to 20 minutes to prevent cold spots and help ensure a uniform conversion. Monitor the temperature each time you stir. If the temperature drops by less than 5 degrees over the hour, nothing further needs to be done. Cover the mash tun with the cooler lid between stirrings, and let it sit for a total of 1 hour. If you notice that the temperature drops below 145° F (62° C) within a half-hour, you can add more water to bring the temperature back up. See Figure 109.

7. Heat the sparge water. Meanwhile, heat up your sparge water in the smaller of your two brewpots. You will need about 3.5 gallons (13 liters) for the batch sparge volume. The water temperature should be less than boiling, preferably 165 to 175° F (73 to 80° C). If the sparge water is too hot, the probability of tannin extraction from the grain husks increases substantially. See Figure 110.

Figure 110 I am heating the sparge water in my smaller brewpot while the mash is going on.

Figure 111 Drain about 2 quarts of the first runnings into a pitcher. The wort will be cloudy with bits of grain. Then, slowly pour the wort back into the grain bed, recirculating the wort. Repeat this procedure until the wort exiting the tun is pretty clear (like unfiltered apple cider). It will be dark amber, hazy, but not cloudy.

Figure 112 I have started draining the lauter tun of the first runnings.

Figure 113 I am adding the sparge water a pitcher at a time, until I can just dump in the rest of it, and then I will stir thoroughly to dissolve all the remaining extract into the wort.

Conducting the Lauter

Ok, the hour has gone by, and the mash should look a little bit different. It should be less viscous and smell great.

8. Recirculate. Open the valve slowly, and drain about 2 quarts/liters of the first runnings into a pitcher. The wort will be cloudy with bits of grain. Gently pour the wort back into the grain bed, recirculating the wort. Repeat this procedure until the wort exiting the tun is pretty clear (like unfiltered apple cider). It will be dark amber colored, hazy, but not cloudy. It should only take a couple of quarts. See Figure 111.

9. Lauter. Once the wort has cleared, drain the wort carefully into your boiling pot. If you open the valve wide at first, you will suck a lot of fine particles into your manifold or screen and can clog it. Only open it part way, until it starts running clear. Fill the pot slowly at first, and allow the level to cover the outlet tube. Be sure to have a long-enough tube, so that the wort enters below the surface and does not splash. The splashing of hot wort before the boil can cause long-term oxidation damage to the flavor of the beer. Once the outlet is submerged, you can open the valve more fully and drain the wort more quickly. But if you drain it too quickly, you can compact the grain bed and get a stuck sparge. See Figure 112.

10. Add the sparge. Close the valve, and add your sparge water to the mash tun with the pitcher, until there is a small enough volume to just dump in the rest. Stir the grist thoroughly to dissolve as much remaining sugar into the wort as possible. There is a chance of dissolving unconverted starch into the wort at this stage, so it doesn't hurt to let the mash sit for 15 minutes to allow residual alpha-amylase to convert it to sugars. Recirculate and drain to your brewpot. See Figure 113.

11. Stuck sparge? If the wort stops flowing, even with water above the grain bed, then you have a stuck sparge. There are two ways to fix it: (a) Blow back into the outlet hose to clear any obstruction of the manifold; and/or (b) Close the valve and add more hot water, stirring to resuspend the mash. You will need to recirculate again. Stuck sparges are an annoyance but usually not a major problem.

12. Calculate your efficiency. Measure the gravity in the boiling pot (stir it first), and multiply the points by the number of gallons you collected. Then divide by the number of pounds of grain you used. The result should be somewhere around 28. 27 is OK, 29 is better, and above 30 is great. If it is 25 or below, you are not getting good conversion in the mash, which could be caused by having too coarse a grist, the wrong temperature, not enough time, or a pH factor, etc. (In liters°/kilogram, these numbers are: 234 nominal, with a range of 225 to 250 liters°/kilogram.)

Ok, throw the spent grain on the compost pile, and you are done! You have produced your first all-grain wort! All-grain brewing produces more break material than extract brewing, so you will probably want to add Irish moss during the last 15 minutes of the boil to help with coagulation of the hot break and clarity. Rehydrate it in warm water before use for best results. Don't overboil, or its effects will be lost back into the wort.

Well, that was pretty easy, wasn't it? Not too much spillage, I hope. A little practice, and you will be able to do it in your sleep.

Figure 114 The brewpot is 6.5 gallons full and starting to boil. Oh, that smells good!

Figure 115 Now the boil is over, and it's time to chill the wort. Joe Brewer uses a large Binford immersion wort chiller made from 50 feet of ½-inch diameter soft copper tubing configured in a double coil (insert Tim Allen soundtrack).

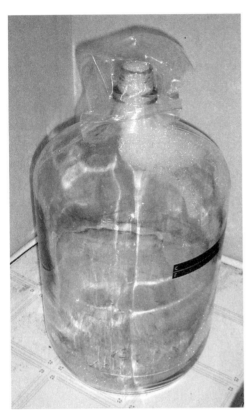

Figure 117 This picture shows the aquarium air pump aeration of the wort. Aeration is very important for a healthy fermentation.

Figure 116 The fermenter is sanitized and ready to receive the wort. Some StarSan foam is still visible in the neck of the carboy. It's fine; it won't affect the fermentation at all.

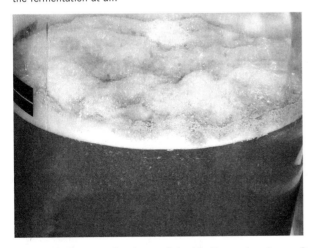

Figure 118 The yeast has been pitched to the wort and now, 8 hours later, a kraeusen has started to form on top. A blowoff tube is usually not needed for a 5-gallon (20-liter) batch fermenting in a 6.5-gallon (25-liter) carboy.

SECTION 4
RECIPES, EXPERIMENTATION, AND TROUBLESHOOTING

In this section, we learn how to design, improvise, experiment, and troubleshoot. In Chapter 20—Some of My Favorite Styles and Recipes, I present several of the most popular beer styles and my basic recipes for them. Unfortunately, I am one of those people who cook by adding a pinch of this and a handful of that, so I rarely brew the same beer twice. Recipes are presented from an extract and specialty grain basis, with options for all-extract and all-grain.

In the next chapter, Chapter 21—Developing Your Own Recipes, I attempt to convey how easy it is to develop your own recipe—it is just like making your own sandwich. I also present information on using brewing sugars, honey, and toasting your own malts. The intent of the chapter is to encourage you to try new things and tweak the things you are currently doing, without going overboard and fermenting everything in sight.

Naturally, it follows that the final chapter is titled Is My Beer Ruined? This is a frequent cry for help on the Internet brewing forums. In this chapter I will try to coach you through some of the most common problems by examining the symptoms and their possible causes. Hopefully this chapter will be very useful, but rarely needed. Right?

Good Brewing!

SOME OF MY FAVORITE BEER STYLES AND RECIPES

Style Descriptions

There are so many styles of beer, it's hard to know where to begin. There is a lot more to a style than just whether it's light or dark. Each beer style has a characteristic taste, imparted by either the yeast, the malts, the hops, the water, or all four. A style is best defined by naming all the ingredients and the fermentation particulars. Change any one item, and you have probably hopped into another style category (no pun intended). Each country, each geographic region, even each town can have its own style of beer. In fact, you may be starting to realize by now that many beer styles originate from local brewing conditions. Access to ingredients, the local water profile, the climate—all of these elements combine to dictate the character of the best beer that the brewer can produce. To a certain extent, your success and satisfaction as a homebrewer is going to depend on understanding what style(s) your local conditions will allow you to produce best.

The place to start when defining a style is the yeast. Is it an ale or a lager strain that is used? What is the temperature profile of the fermentation?

The next important aspect is the malt. Each of the malts and grains listed in Chapter 12 has a unique taste that it contributes to the beer. As an example, Irish-style stouts are defined in part by the flavor of roasted unmalted barley.

The hop variety plays a part, too. The difference between English pale ale and American pale ale is predominantly due to the differences in flavor between English and American hops. Even the same variety of hop grown in different regions will have a different character. Fuggles grown in the United States has an American character as compared to the original British variety.

Both ales and lagers are brewed in a wide variety of styles, from strong and rich (barley wine and doppelbock) to crisp and hoppy (India pale ale and Pilsener). The main difference between the two comes from the type of yeast used and the fermentation process. Ales are fermented at room temperature and typically have a noticeable amount of fruity-smelling esters due to this warm fermentation. The fruitiness can be subdued, as in a dry stout, or dominating, as in a barley wine.

Lagers, on the other hand, lack any fruity character and may be crisp and hoppy like a Pilsener, or sweet and malty like a doppelbock. Both ales and lagers are malty, but this character can vary from a minimal light toast/biscuit note to a thick and chewy symphony. Figure 119 visually illustrates the similarities and differences between beer styles based on the ratio of the hop bitterness to the original gravity.

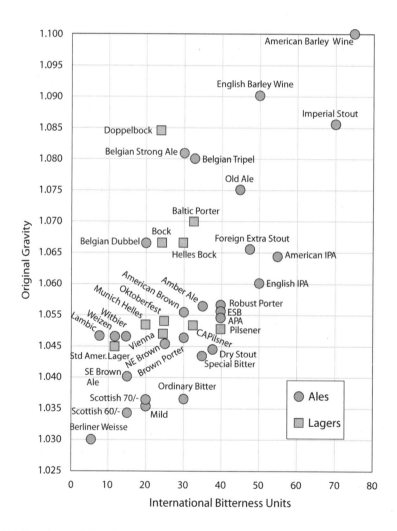

Figure 119 Relative Flavors of Beer Styles. This chart shows the mean IBUs versus the mean OG for the different styles, according to the 2004 BJCP style guidelines. A lot of styles are not shown on this chart, because so many of the styles overlap in the 20 to 40 IBU and 1.040 to 1.055 OG region. This chart can give you an idea of other beer styles to taste and brew for yourself.

Coming up with a common set of descriptors for beer styles is more difficult than it sounds since there are so many styles to compare, each with a different character. One way to do it is to describe ranges for physical attributes like original and final gravity, IBUs, and color, but this is really only half the story. To try and give you the other half, I illustrate each description with a commercial example and a baseline recipe. In each recipe, I identify the appropriate malt extracts and specialty grains, hop varieties, yeast strain, and fermentation conditions. I have grouped the styles by ale and lager according to the yeast, and sorted them on the basis of color and body to progress from lighter beers to heavier.

For each of the styles presented, I have listed the style/substyle guidelines from the Beer Judge Certification Program, a national organization that seeks to advance the appreciation of beer through common standards of evaluation and the education of its member judges (www.bjcp.org). Included in these style guidelines is the color range for the beer in °SRM. The unit is taken from the acronym for the Standard Reference Method used by the American Society of Brewing Chemists (ASBC). SRM units are equivalent to the older Lovibond units when comparing beer color. A discussion of how to use color in recipe design and calculations for estimating beer color are in Appendix B.

Notes on Recipes

The recipes in this chapter are presented in two or three versions depending on the brewing method: extract, extract with steeped grain, and all-grain brewing. The character of each version of a recipe is intended to be same, or nearly the same, but sometimes the defining ingredients do not work in another brewing method. Nonenzymatic kilned malts really don't work for steeping with extract; they require a mini-mash to convert their starches to fermentable sugars.

Boil gravity. The recipes in this chapter are built around two brewing methods: a) malt extract-based or extract-assisted brewing using a 3-gallon boil in a 5-gallon pot, or b) all-grain brewing using a full wort boil in an 8-gallon pot.

Extract-based recipes. All extract-based recipe calculations for the OG and the gravity of the boil (BG) assume the use of a 3-gallon partial boil for a 5-gallon batch. The basic procedure is to boil the hop additions with about half of the malt extract to create a normal gravity (1.040 to 1.050), 3-gallon boil. The rest of the malt extract is added afterwards (at knockout) when the heat is turned off, and the wort is allowed to pasteurize for 10 minutes before cooling.

Extract and steeping grain. The majority of the recipes present the extract and specialty grain version first, because this method offers the most flexibility and provides the greatest insight into the beer style for the beginning brewer. Steep the specialty grain in the boiling pot first, and then add your first extract addition and boil your hops. See Chapter 13 for a full discussion of the procedure.

If you do not have access to a particular specialty grain, you may be able to substitute an equivalent amount of an extract that contains that grain, although the results will not be identical. For example: amber malt extract instead of pale extract with crystal 60 malt, or dark malt extract instead of pale extract with chocolate malt.

All-grain. All-grain versions for the recipes assume an extract efficiency of 75% (see Table 26 in Chapter 18) and 6 gallons of wort being collected and boiled to produce the same 5-gallon batch. Depending on your equipment and brewing efficiency, you may want to adjust the recipe amounts to compensate.

Hop schedules. The hop utilization factor is a function of the boil gravity. I have attempted to keep the hop schedules the same across each version of a recipe by manipulating the quantity and form of malt extract (dry/liquid), so that the gravity of the boil is the same (within a couple points) whether you are using the 3-gallon boil (extract-based) or the 6-gallon boil (all-grain). I wanted to avoid confusion over the hop quantities for each recipe. However, you may want to verify the gravity of your boil, depending on the specific size of your pot, and recalculate the hop utilization factor accordingly. See the IBU nomographs in Chapter 5 for help in recalculating your hop quantities.

Batch size. In addition, it would probably be more realistic to formulate the recipes for an actual batch size of 5.5 gallons to account for wort lost to the trub and hops. Plus, you may need to collect more wort (e.g., 7 gallons) in order to have 5 gallons of beer at bottling time, depending on your extract efficiency and the vigor of your boil, etc. But those considerations depend on your own methods and equipment, so I have chosen to teach you how to do these calculations yourself and give you easy numbers to work with. Onward!

The Ale Styles

Wheat

You may not realize it, but wheat beer was one of the most popular styles in America a century ago. Wheat was abundant, and after a hot, hard day working in the fields, a light, tart wheat beer is very refreshing. The most popular style of wheat beer at the time was patterned after the acidic Berliner *weisse* beers of Germany. Berliner weisse is brewed using three parts wheat malt to one part barley malt and fermented with a combination of ale yeast and lactic acid bacteria. After fermentation, it is dosed with a substantial quantity of young, fermenting beer (kraeusened) and bot-

tled. American *weissbier* used similar yeast cultures, but the common practice was to use unmalted wheat in the form of grits; and only about 30% of the grist was wheat. The excess of proteins in wheat causes most wheat beers to be hazy, if not downright cloudy. Hefeweizens go a step further, with the beer being cloudy with suspended yeast. The thought of drinking that much yeast is appalling in a pale ale, but it really works with hefeweizens; they are quite tasty.

Hefeweizen is not tart like Berliner weisse, because it is not fermented with lactic acid cultures.

Wheat beer became extinct with Prohibition in the United States, and has only been revived in the last few decades. Today's American wheat beer is loosely modeled after weizen but is made with malted wheat and a standard, flocculent ale yeast and not the specialized German *weizenbier* yeasts with their spicy, clovelike character. The noble-type hops are most appropriate for the light body and spicy character of wheats. Wheat beers are usually light, but dunkel (dark), bock (strong), and *dunkel weizenbock* are common variations. Spices are often used with wheat beers; Belgian-style wit uses coriander and dried Curaçao orange peel with some lactic acid sourness to produce a truly unique beer.

Wheat Beer BJCP Style Guidelines

Substyle	OG	°P	FG	IBUs	Color
American Wheat	1.040-55	10-13.5	1.008-13	10-30	3-6
Bavarian Weizen	1.044-52	11-13	1.010-14	8-15	2-8
Bavarian Dunkelweizen	1.044-56	11-14	1.010-14	10-18	14-23

Berliner Weisse	1.026-36	6.5-9	1.006-09	3-8	2-4
Weizenbock	1.064-80+	16-19+	1.015-22	15-30	12-25
Belgian Wit	1.044-52	11-13	1.008-12	10-20	2-4

Commercial Examples

American Wheat ....Sierra Nevada Wheat
Bavarian Weizen...............Ayinger, Erdinger
Berliner Weisse.................Schultheiss Berliner Weisse
Belgian Wit ....Celis White

Three Weisse Guys—American Wheat Beer

Malts	Gravity Points
3.3 lbs. (1.5kg) wheat malt extract (LME) in boil	40
3.3 lbs. (1.5kg) wheat malt extract (LME) at knockout	(40)
(60% wheat, 40% barley)	

BG for 3 gallons (11.3L)	1.040	(10 °P)
OG for 5 gallons (19L)	1.047	(11.5 °P)

Hops	Boil Time	IBUs
0.5 oz. (14g) Sterling (7%)	60	13
0.75 oz. (21g) Liberty (4%)	30	9
1 oz. (28g) Liberty (4%)		105
Total IBUs		27

Yeast	Fermentation Schedule
Nottingham Dry Yeast	10 days at 65° F (18° C) in primary fermenter

Options

All-extract	(same)
All-grain	6 lbs. (2.72kg) 2-row base malt
	3 lbs. (1.4kg) flaked wheat*
	0.25 lb. (113g) rice hulls

Mash Schedule—Multi-Rest Infusion

Rest Type	Temperature	Duration
Beta-glucan	110° F (43° C)	15 min.
Protein rest	125° F (52° C)	15 min.
Conversion	150° F (65° C)	60 min.

* You could use malted wheat instead of flaked and raise the first rest temperature from 110° F (43° C) to 125° F (52° C) for a more effective protein rest at the same duration.

Some of My Favorite Beer Styles and Recipes

Pale Ales

There is a lot of variety in the pale ale family. Pale is a relative term and originally meant "pale as compared to stout." Pale ales can range from golden to deep amber, depending on the amount of crystal malts used. Crystal malts are the defining ingredient in the malt character of a pale ale, giving it a honeylike or caramel-like sweetness. The top-fermenting ale yeast and warm fermentation temperature give pale ales a subtle fruitiness. Pale ales are best served cool, about 55° F, to allow the fruit and caramel notes to emerge.

There are several varieties of pale ale—nearly every country has its own version—which is more than I will attempt to cover here. I will provide a description and recipe for my three favorite types: English, India, and American.

English Special Bitter

There are several substyles of British pale ale. These include the bitter, special bitter, and India pale ale. These beers usually have what is considered a low level of carbonation. Megabrew drinkers in the United States would probably describe them as flat. The beer is brewed to a low final gravity, yielding a dry finish with only a low level of residual sweetness that does not mask the hop finish.

In particular, English special bitter is a marvelous beer. The soft English hops, like East Kent Goldings, don't overpower the warm malt flavors and fruity overtones, but the hop bitterness is a distinguishing characteristic of the flavor and lingers in the finish. Bitters and special bitters often include corn (maize) to lighten the body and produce a more attenuable beer.

British Pale Ale BJCP Style Guidelines

Substyle	OG	°P	FG	IBUs	Color
Ordinary Bitter	1.032-40	8-10	1.007-11	25-35	4-14
Special Bitter	1.040-48	10-12	1.008-12	20-40	5-16
Burton Ale	1.048-60+	12-15+	1.010-16	30-50+	6-18

Commercial Examples

Ordinary Bitter	Fuller's Chiswick Bitter
Special Bitter	Young's Special Bitter
Burton Ale	Bass Worthington White Shield

Lord Crouchback's Special Bitter—English Pale Ale

Malts	Gravity Points
3.3 lbs. (1.5kg) pale malt extract (LME) in boil	40
3.3 lbs. (1.5kg) pale malt extract (LME) at knockout	(40)
0.5 lb. (227g) crystal 60 malt	3

BG for 3 gallons (11.3L)	1.040	(10 °P)
OG for 5 gallons (19L)	1.047	(11.5 °P)

Hops	Boil Time	IBUs
0.5 oz. (14g) Target (9%)	60	17
0.75 oz. (21g) EK Goldings (5%)	30	11
0.75 oz. (21g) EK Goldings (5%)	15	7
Total IBUs		35

Yeast
Wyeast 1099
Whitbread Ale

Fermentation Schedule
10 days at 65° F (18° C) in primary fermenter

Options

All-extract	4 lbs. (1.8kg) pale LME
	2 lbs. (0.9kg) amber DME
All-grain	7 lbs. (3.2kg) British pale ale malt
	0.5 lb. (227g) crystal 60L
	1 lb. (0.45kg) flaked corn (maize)

Mash Schedule—Single-Temperature Infusion

Rest Type	Temperature	Duration
Conversion	152° F (67° C)	60 min.

India Pale Ale

This ale was originally just a stronger version of the Burton pale ale, which was a high-sulfate brewing water ESB. According to popular mythos, the IPA style arose from the months-long sea journey to India, during which the beer conditioned with hops in the barrel. Extra hops were added to help prevent spoilage during the long voyage. This conditioning time mellowed the hop bitterness to a degree and imparted a wealth of hop aroma to the beer. Homebrewed IPA should also be given a long conditioning time, either in the bottle or in a secondary fermenter. If a secondary fermenter is used, the beer should be dry-hopped with a half-ounce of British aroma hops like East Kent Goldings. Conditioning time should be 3 to 5 weeks, depending on OG and IBU levels (stronger = longer). It is also worth noting that there are English and American versions of IPA, dictated by the hop varieties you use. I prefer the softer English hop varieties for this amount of hoppiness.

India Pale Ale Style Guidelines

Substyle	OG	°P	FG	IBUs	Color
English IPA	1.050-75	12.5-18	1.010-18	40-60	8-14
American IPA	1.056-75	13.5-18	1.010-18	40-60+	6-15
Imperial IPA	1.075-90+	18-22+	1.012-18	60-100+	8-15

Some of My Favorite Beer Styles and Recipes

Commercial Examples
India Pale Ale....................Anchor Liberty Ale, Victory Hop Devil

Victory and Chaos—India Pale Ale

Malts	Gravity Points
4 lbs. (1.8kg) pale malt extract (LME) in boil	48
4 lbs. (1.8kg) pale malt extract (LME) at knockout	(48)
0.5 lb. (227g) crystal 20L malt	7

BG for 3 gallons (11.3L)	1.055	(13.5 °P)
OG for 5 gallons (19L)	1.062	(15 °P)

Hops	Boil Time	IBUs
1 oz. (28g) Nugget (12%)	60	40
2 oz. (57g) EK Goldings (5%)	15	16
1 oz. (28g) EK Goldings (5%)	5	3
Total IBUs	59	

Yeast	Fermentation Schedule
White Labs P013	2 weeks at 65° F (18° C) in primary fermenter
London Ale	or 1 week primary and 3 weeks secondary
	with 1 ounce EKG dry-hopped instead of
	5-minute addition

Options

All-extract	4 lbs. (1.8kg) pale DME
	4 lbs. (1.8kg) amber LME
All-grain	10 lbs. (4.5kg) British pale ale malt
	0.5 lb. (227g) crystal 20L
	0.5 lb. (227g) Munich malt

Mash Schedule-Single-Temperature Infusion

Rest Type	Temperature	Duration
Conversion	152° F (67° C)	60 min.

American Pale Ale

American pale ale is an adaptation of classic British pale ale. The American ale yeast strain produces fewer esters than comparable British ale yeasts, thus, American pale ale has a less fruity taste than its British counterpart. American pale ales vary in color from gold to dark amber and typically have a hint of sweet caramel from the use of crystal malt that does not mask the crisp hop finish. With the resurgence of interest in ales in the United States, American

Lady Liberty Ale

pale ale evolved from a renewed interest in American hop varieties and a higher level of bitterness, as microbreweries experimented with traditional styles. The Cascade hop has become a staple of American microbrewing and is the signature hop for American pale ales. It has a distinctive citrusy aroma, as compared to European hops, and has enabled American pale ale to stand shoulder-to-shoulder with other classic beer styles.

American Pale Ale BJCP Style Guidelines

Style	OG	°P	FG	IBUs	Color
American Pale Ale	1.045-60	11-15	1.010-15	30-45+	5-14

Commercial Example

American Pale Ale ....Sierra Nevada Pale Ale

Lady Liberty Ale—American Pale Ale

Malts	Gravity Points
3.3 lbs. (1.5kg) pale malt extract (LME) in boil	40
3.3 lbs. (1.5kg) pale malt extract (LME) at knockout	(40)
0.5 lb. (227g) crystal 60 malt	3

BG for 3 gallons (11.3L)	1.040	(10 °P)
OG for 5 gallons (19L)	1.047	(11.5 °P)

Hops	Boil Time	IBUs
0.5 oz. (14g) Northern Brewer (11%)	60	21
0.5 oz. (14g) Cascade (6%)	30	9
1 oz. (28g) Cascade (6%)	15	11
Total IBUs		41

Yeast	Fermentation Schedule
White Labs WLP001	10 days at 65° F (18° C) in primary fermenter
American Ale	or 1 week primary and 2 weeks secondary
	with 0.5 oz. (14g) Cascade dry-hopped

Options

All-extract	3 lbs. (1.4kg) amber DME
	3 lbs. (1.4kg) pale LME

All-grain	7 lbs. (3.2kg) British pale ale malt
	0.5 lb. (227g) crystal 60L
	0.5 lb. (227g) amber malt
	0.5 lb. (227g) Munich malt

Mash Schedule—Single-Temperature Infusion

Rest Type	Temperature	Duration
Conversion	155° F (68° C)	60 min.

Amber Ale

Part of the American ale style spectrum that proceeds from pale to amber to brown to porter, amber ales bridge pale and brown ales by adding body and sweetness and shifting the beer's balance away from the hops to the malt. Amber ales are sweeter than brown ales but will have more hop flavor and aroma dancing on top than a brown. Amber ales have become one of my favorite beers. I like the balance of these beers—they are very hearty and satisfying. This is my clone of Red Nectar Ale.

American Ale BJCP Style Guidelines

Style	OG	°P	FG	IBUs	Color
American Amber Ale	1.045-60	11-15	1.010-15	25-40+	10-17

Commercial Examples

American Amber Ale ....Nectar Ales Red Nectar, Anderson Valley Boont Amber

Big Basin Amber Ale—American Amber Ale

Malts	Gravity Points
3.3 lbs. (1.5kg) pale malt extract (LME) in boil	40
3.3 lbs. (1.5kg) pale malt extract (LME) at knockout	(40)
2 lbs. (0.9kg) crystal 60 malt	12

BG for 3 gallons (11.3L)	1.052	(13 °P)
OG for 5 gallons (19L)	1.055	(13.5 °P)

Hop	Boil Time	IBUs
0.5 oz. (14g) Centennial (10%)	60	17
1 oz. (28g) Mt. Hood (7%)	30	18
1 oz. (28g) Willamette (5%)	15	8
Total IBUs		43

Yeast	Fermentation Schedule
Wyeast 1332	10 days at 65° F (18° C) in primary fermenter
Northwest Ale	

Options

All-extract	3.3 lbs. (1.5kg) amber LME
	4 lbs. (1.8kg) amber DME

All-grain   8 lbs. (3.6kg) British pale ale malt
             1 lb. (0.45kg) crystal 60L
             1 lb. (0.45kg) crystal 90L
             0.5 lb. (227g) flaked wheat

Mash Schedule—Single-Temperature Infusion

Rest Type	Temperature	Duration
Conversion	155° F (68° C)	60 min.

Brown Ale

There are several kinds of brown ale—mild, sweet, nutty, and hoppy. Low-gravity, low-bitterness brown ales are called milds. The sweet Southern brown ales of England are made with a lot of crystal malt and a low hopping rate. The Northern brown ales, also of England, are made with toasted (amber) malts (e.g., biscuit or victory) plus a small percentage of crystal malt and a low hopping rate. The hoppy brown ales, which can be nutty also, arose from the U.S. homebrew scene when hop-crazy homebrewers decided that most brown ales were just too wimpy. But American brown ales should not be brown IPAs! They should be malt-dominated beers with a toasted malt character, and the hops should be riding the crest of the wave of the beer's flavor. The hops should not be a tsunami.

Brown ales as a class have grown to bridge the gap between pale ales and porters. Contrary to popular myth, there are no nuts or nut extracts in classic brown ales; toasted malts give the beer a nutlike flavor and nut brown color. You can add some home-toasted base malt, victory malt, or biscuit malt to the recipe to give the beer a more nutty character. For the best results, this malt addition should be mashed with at least an equal amount of base malt. See Chapter 21 for a description of how to make your own toasted malt at home.

Brown Ale BJCP Style Guidelines

Substyle	OG	°P	FG	IBUs	Color
Mild	1.030-38	7.5-9.5	1.008-13	10-25	12-25
Northern Brown Ale	1.040-52	10-13	1.008-13	20-30	12-22
Southern Brown Ale	1.035-42	9-10.5	1.011-14	12-20	19-35
American Brown Ale	1.045-60	11.5-15	1.010-16	20-40	18-35

Commercial Examples

Mild ....Highgate Mild (U.K.)
Northern Brown Ale..........Samuel Smith's Nut Brown Ale
Southern Brown Ale..........Mann's Brown Ale
American Brown Ale ....Pete's Wicked Ale, Lost Coast Downtown Brown

Oak Butt Brown Ale

Malts	Gravity Points
7 lbs. (3.2kg) pale ale malt	30
2 lbs. (0.9kg) amber malt	8
0.5 lb. (227g) crystal 60L malt	2
0.25 lb. (113g) chocolate malt	1

BG for 6.5 gallons (24.5L)	1.041	(10 °P)
OG for 5.5* gallons (21L)	1.049	(12 °P)

Hops	Boil Time	IBUs
0.5 oz. (14g) Nugget (12%)	60	21
0.5 oz. (14g) Willamette (5%)	15	4
Total IBUs		25

Yeast	Fermentation Schedule
WLP013 London Ale	Primary ferment at 68° F (20° C) for 2 weeks

Options

Partial mash	2 lbs. (0.9kg) pale ale malt
	2 lbs. (0.9kg) amber malt
	0.5 lb. (227g) crystal 60L malt
	0.25 lb. (113g) chocolate malt
(Add to boil)	4 lbs. (1.8kg) pale LME

Mash Schedule—Single-Temperature Infusion

Rest Type	Temperature	Duration
Conversion	152° F (67° C)	60 min.

Mash Schedule:

- Single infusion 160° F (71° C) strike water at a ratio of 2 quarts/pound grain (= 19.5 quarts or 1.5 liters)
- Target mash temperature of 152° F (67° C). Mash time of 1 hour. No mashout.
- Drain wort to collect 3 to 3.5 gallons. Batch sparge with 3.5 gallons to collect 6.5 gallons total.
- Target gravity of 1.041 for 6.5 gallons (or 1.049 for 5.5 gallons after boiling).
- Adjust the amount of chocolate malt (0.25 to 0.5 lb.), depending on how dark you want it.
- * The extra half-gallon provides for wort soaked up by the hops and break material in the boiler, giving you 5 gallons of clean(er) wort in the fermenter.

Porter

Porter is a dark ale with a very malty flavor and a bit of a roasted finish. A porter differs from a brown ale by being darker, stronger, more full-bodied, and having a roastier malt finish than a brown but not as much as a stout. Porters should be fairly well attenuated (dry), although sweet ("brown") porters are popular, too. Compared to stout, a porter should be lighter in both body and color. When held up to the light, a porter should have a deep ruby-red glow.

Port O' Palmer

Historically, porters preceded stouts and had a much different character than they do today. At first, they were a blend of two or three other standard beers of the time. Eventually, someone hit on the idea of making porter (or "entire," as it was called) specifically. The first industrial beer was mass produced in swimming pool-sized wooden vats that harbored a yeast called *Brettanomyces*, which imparted a secondary fermentation characteristic commonly described as "horse sweat," barnyard, or leatherlike. The other dominant note was from the use of highly kilned brown malt, which was used as the base malt. The beer was then aged for about six months before serving. The aging time was necessary for the rough flavors of the brown malt to mellow. What starts out as harshly bitter malt beer turns into a sweeter, smooth elixir as the tannins settle out. Brown malt porter is a very good beer if you are careful not to oxidize it during brewing and let it age for several months before drinking.

For porters and stouts, British and Irish yeast strains are good choices for more of the tart character that is part of these styles. Any of the dry yeasts, like Nottingham or Safale US-56, would also be good. The Port 'O Palmer recipe uses American ale yeast, since it is intended to mimic Sierra Nevada Porter.

Porter Style Guidelines

Substyle	OG	°P	FG	IBUs	Color
Brown Porter	1.040-52	10-13	1.008-14	18-35	20-30
Robust Porter	1.048-65	14-16	1.012-16	25-50+	22-35+
Baltic Porter	1.060-90	15-21.5	1.016-24	20-40	17-30

Commercial Examples
Brown Porter ....Yuengling Porter
Robust Porter....................Sierra Nevada Porter

Port O' Palmer—Porter

Malts	Gravity Points
3.3 lbs. (1.5kg) pale malt extract (LME) in boil	40
3.3 lbs. (1.5kg) pale malt extract (LME) at knockout	(40)
0.5 lb. (227g) crystal 60L malt	3
0.5 lb. (227g) chocolate malt	3
0.25 lb. (113g) black patent malt	1

BG for 3 gallons (11.3L)	1.047	(11.5 °P)
OG for 5 gallons (19L)	1.054	(13.5 °P)

Hops	Boil Time	IBUs
0.5 oz. (14g) Horizon (12%)	60	21
0.75 oz. (21g) Willamette (5%)	40	12
0.5 oz. (14g) Willamette (5%)	20	5
Total IBUs	38	

Yeast	Fermentation Schedule
Wyeast 1056	2 weeks at 65° F (18° C) in primary ferment
American Ale	

Options

All-extract	4 lbs. (1.8kg) pale LME
	2 lbs. (0.9kg) amber DME
	1 lb. (0.45kg) dark DME

All-grain	8.5 lbs. (3.9kg) pale ale malt
	0.5 lb. (227g) chocolate malt
	0.5 lb. (227g) crystal 60L malt
	0.25 lb. (113g) black patent malt

Mash Schedule—Single-Temperature Infusion

Rest Type	Temperature	Duration
Conversion	156° F (69° C)	60 min.

Stout

Arguably one of the most popular styles among homebrewers, stouts vary a lot in flavor, degree of roastiness, and body. There are dry stouts, sweet stouts, export stouts, oatmeal stouts, coffee stouts, and more besides. The one defining characteristic of a stout is the use of highly roasted malts and/or unmalted roasted barley. The most popular, Guinness Extra Stout, is the defining example of Irish dry stout and uses only pale malt, unmalted roasted barley, and flaked barley; no crystal malt is used. English stouts tend to be of the sweet stout style and will include chocolate and crystal malts. Some English stouts do not use any black malt or roasted barley at all, getting their color from amber malt, dark crystal, and chocolate malt. Export stouts are brewed to a very high gravity, 1.075 to 1.100, with a

huge complexity of flavors: sweet and tarry, fruity, and quite bitter. Oatmeal stout is my favorite, being a sweet stout with the smooth silkiness of oatmeal added in. Coffee stouts are another homebrew favorite. The taste of coffee perfectly complements the roasted character of a stout.

Stout Style Guidelines

Substyle	OG	°P	FG	IBUs	Color
Dry Stout	1.036-50	9-12.5	1.007-11	30-45	25-40+
Sweet Stout	1.042-56	10.5-13.5	1.010-23	25-40	30-40+
Oatmeal Stout	1.048-65	12-16	1.010-18	25-40	22-40+
Foreign Extra Stout	1.056-75	13.5-18	1.010-18	30-70	30-40+
American Stout	1.050-75	12.5-18	1.010-22	35-75	30-40+
Russian Imperial Stout	1.075-95+	18-23+	1.018-30+	50-90+	20-40

Commercial Examples

Dry Stout ....Guinness Draught
Sweet Stout ....Mackeson Stout
Oatmeal Stout ....Anderson Valley Oatmeal Stout
Foreign Extra Stout ....Guinness Foreign Extra Stout
Russian Imperial Stout ......John Smith Imperial Russian Stout

Mill Run Stout

Malts	Gravity Points
3.3 lbs. (1.5kg) pale malt extract (DME) in boil	42
3.3 lbs. (1.5kg) pale malt extract (DME) at knockout	(42)
0.5 lb. (227g) crystal 60L malt	3
0.5 lb. (227g) roasted barley	3

BG for 3 gallons (11.3L)	1.048	(12 °P)
OG for 5 gallons (19L)	1.054	(13.5 °P)

Hops	Boil Time	IBUs
0.75 oz. (21g) Nugget (12%)	60	32
1 oz. (28g) Fuggles (5%)	30	13
Total IBUs	45	

Yeast

White Labs WLP004
Irish Ale

Fermentation Schedule

2 weeks at 68° F (20° C) in primary fermenter

Options

All-extract	6 lbs. (2.7kg) dark DME
All-grain	8 lbs. (3.6kg) pale ale malt
	1 lb. (0.45kg) crystal 60L
	0.5 lb. (227g) roasted barley
	0.5 lb. (227g) flaked barley

Mash Schedule—Single-Temperature Infusion

Rest Type	Temperature	Duration
Conversion	152° F (67° C)	60 min.

Grain option: Add a half-pound of chocolate malt in place of, or in addition to, the other grains.

Oatmeal stout: Oatmeal stout extract is now available from some of the larger mail-order homebrew suppliers. Use in place of the dark DME. The all-grain brewer can add a pound of instant oats to the mash with a 20-minute beta-glucan rest at 110° F to make lautering easier.

Coffee stout: This is an easy variation to any stout recipe. Simply steep 0.25 to 0.5 pound of freshly ground coffee in 1 to 2 quarts of water in the refrigerator for 24 hours. Pour that cold coffee through a paper coffee filter, and add it to your beer after fermentation is complete.

Barley Wine

Barley wine is the drink of the gods—the intellectual ones, anyway. Few beverages can equal the complexity of flavors that a properly aged barley wine has: malt, fruit, spice, and warmth from the high level of alcohol (9 to 14%). Barley wine as a style has been around for several hundred years, but the name was coined by Bass in 1903. It was known as strong ale in medieval times and was probably brewed long before the introduction of hops. Recipes for barley wines vary greatly but can be loosely organized into three categories. There are strong barley wines with more emphasis on the malt and sweetness than on the hop character. There are more balanced strong barley wines, which strive to keep the hop bitterness and flavor on equal footing with malt. Finally, there are the light-weights of the barley wine world, often the ones that are most available commercially in England, that make use of various brewing

BARLEYWINE

sugars to lighten the body while keeping the alcohol content high. The hop levels are usually balanced in these lighter barley wines.

Barley wines tend to require the use of malt extracts to help achieve the high gravities that are their hallmark. Barley wines usually consist primarily of pale and crystal malts to avoid masking the flavor with roasted malts. The color of barley wine ranges from deep gold to ruby red. Wheat and rye malts can be used for "accent," counterbalancing the heavy maltiness of the barley. A barley wine is meant to be sipped in front of the fire on a cold winter's night, providing the fuel for philosophical thoughts on science and the wonders of metallurgy.

Barley wines are consumed in small amounts, so it is best to use 12-ounce or smaller bottles. The amount of priming sugar should be reduced to 0.5 cup per 5 gallons, because the beer will continue to ferment for months in the bottle. The normal amount of priming sugar, plus this residual fermentation, would cause the bottles to overcarbonate.

My recipe is atypical in its high usage of wheat, but I liked the Rubicon's Winter Wheat Warmer in Sacramento. And yes, I read the books as a seventh-grader, long before the movie came out, and developed this recipe and the name in 1994. It seemed like a draught for the toughest orcs.

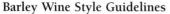
Barley Wine Style Guidelines

Substyle	OG	°P	FG	IBUs	Color
English Barley Wine	1.080-120+	19-28+	1.018-30+	35-70	8-22
American Barley Wine	1.080-120+	19-28+	1.016-30+	50-120+	10-19

Commercial Examples

English Barley Wine..........Young's Old Nick
American Barley Wine ......Anchor's Old Foghorn

Fightin' Urak-Hai Barley Wine

Malts	Gravity Points
5 lbs. (2.3kg) wheat malt extract (LME) in boil	60
8 lbs. (3.6kg) pale malt extract (DME) at knockout	(84)
0.5 lb. (227g) Special "B" malt	2
0.5 lb. (227g) chocolate malt	2

BG for 3 gallons (11.3L)	1.064	(16° P)
OG for 5 gallons (19L)	1.106	(25° P)

Hops	Boil Time	IBUs
1 oz. (28g) Magnum (13%)	60	40
1 oz. (28g) Horizon (12%)	30	28
1 oz. (28g) Sterling (8%)	30	19
1 oz. (28g) Sterling (8%)	15	12
Total IBUs		99

Yeast	Fermentation Schedule
Wyeast 1275 Thames Valley Ale	Pitch the entire yeast cake from a previous batch of beer, or use a 1-gallon starter to make 400+ billion cells. Be sure to use a blowoff tube in a 6.5-gallon fermenter—this will be messy. 2 to 3 weeks at 65° F (18° C) in the primary fermenter and 1 to 3 months in the secondary. Bottle and condition for an additional month before drinking.

Options

All-extract	Substitute 1.5 lbs. (0.7kg) dark DME for the specialty grains.
All-grain	5 lbs. (2.3kg) wheat malt
	12 lbs. (5.4kg) pale ale malt
	0.5 lb. (227g) Special "B"
	0.5 lb. (227g) chocolate malt

Mash Schedule—Multi-Rest Infusion

Rest Type	Temperature	Duration
Beta rest	145° F (63° C)	30 min.
Alpha rest	158° F (70° C)	30 min.

The Lager Styles

Pilsener

Beer as the world knew it changed dramatically in 1842, when the brewery in the town of Pilsen (today part of the Czech Republic) produced the first light golden lager. Until that time, beers had been rather dark, varying from amber ("pale"), to deep brown or black. Today Pilsner Urquell is that same beer, "the Original of Pilsen." The original Pilsener beer is a hoppy, dry beer of 1.045 OG. The Pilsener style is imitated more than any other, and interpretations run from the light flowery lagers of Germany to the maltier, more herbal versions of the Netherlands, to the increasingly tasteless varieties of light and dry from the United States and Japan. Most of these are broadly in the Pilsener style but lack the assertive noble hop bitterness and flavor of the original.

Plzenske Pivo

Brewing a true Pilsener can be fairly difficult, especially from an all-grain point of view. Pilsen has very soft water, the next closest thing to distilled water, and the malt flavors are very clean and fresh. There is no place for an off-flavor to hide. The sole usage of lightly kilned lager malt makes maintaining a proper mash pH difficult for brewers using moderately alkaline water, especially during lautering. Water that is high in carbonates has too much buffering capacity for the meager amount of acidity provided by the malt. When brewing an all-grain Pilsener, it is best to use a large proportion of distilled or de-ionized water to provide the right mash conditions and prevent tannin astringency.

Pilsener Style Guidelines

Substyle	OG	°P	FG	IBUs	Color
Northern German Pilsener	1.044-50	11-12.5	1.008-13	25-45	2-4
Bohemian Pilsener	1.044-56	11-14	1.013-17	35-45	3-6

Commercial Examples

Northern German Pilsener Bitburger Pils
Bohemian Pilsener .... Pilsner Urquell

Plzenske Pivo—Pilsener Lager

Malts	Gravity Points
3.3 lbs. (1.5kg) Briess Pilsen Light (LME) in boil	40
3.3 lbs. (1.5kg) Briess Pilsen Light (LME) at knockout	(40)

BG for 3 gallons (11.3L)	1.040	(10 °P)
OG for 5 gallons (19L)	1.048	(12 °P)

Hops	Boil Time	IBUs
1 oz. (28g) Perle (7%)	60	26
0.75 oz. (21g) Saaz (4%)	30	9
0.75 oz. (21g) Saaz (4%)	15	6
Total IBUs	41	

Yeast	Fermentation Schedule
Bohemian Lager	2 weeks at 50° F (10° C) in primary fermenter, rack and lager at 40° F (4° C) for 5 weeks. Prime and store bottles at room temperature.

Options

All-extract	(same)
All-grain	8.5 lbs. (3.9kg) 2-row base malt or Briess Pilsen malt*

Mash Schedule—Multi-Rest Infusion or Decoction*

Rest Type	Temperature	Duration
Protein*	125° F (52° C)	20 min.
Beta rest	140° F (60° C)	30 min.
Alpha rest	158° F (70° C)	30 min.

*If you use a less- or moderately modified malt, then decoction mashing and a protein rest are recommended. The protein rest is not advised for well-modified malt.

Classic American Pilsener

Around the turn of the century in the United States, the Pilsener style was very popular, but with a typically American difference. That difference was corn (maize). It's only natural that in the largest corn-growing region in the world some would wind up in beer as a fermentable. In addition, six-row barley was the most common variety available, but its higher protein levels made it difficult to brew with. Adding corn (with almost no protein) to the mash helped dilute the total protein levels and added some flavor complexity as well. Unfortunately, Prohibition and higher brewing costs afterward helped to increase the use of corn and rice in American Pilsener-style beers to the point of blandness.

Your Father's Mustache

Classic American Pilsner

The beer of our grandfathers was a delicious, malty, sweet beer with a balanced hoppiness. The brewing water should be low in sulfates. Today, there are only a few commercially produced examples that adequately represent this beer that started the lager revolution in the United States. The strength of this beer was typically between 1.045 and 1.050 with a hopping of 25 to 40 IBUs. The style had become lighter by the time of Prohibition and afterwards tended to have an average gravity in the low 40s with a correspondingly lower hopping rate of 20 to 30 IBUs. This beer is best brewed with a mash using flaked maize or using the cereal mash method in Chapter 16 with corn grits. I have also successfully brewed this style using pale malt extract and brewer's corn syrup, which has a high percentage of maltose (about 50%) and more closely mimics the sugar profile of barley wort. High-fructose corn syrup and refined corn sugar just don't have the same corn character. Corn grits are not hominy grits like you see in the grocery store. Brewers' corn grits most closely resembles cornmeal, although grocery store cornmeal is often vitamin- and mineral-fortified.

Classic American Pilsener Style Guidelines

Style	OG	°P	FG	IBUs	Color
Classic American Pilsener	1.044-60	11-14.5	1.010-15	25-40	3-6

Your Father's Mustache—Classic American Pilsener

Malts	Gravity Points
7 lbs. (3.2kg) 6-row (or 2-row) base malt	37
1.75 lbs. (0.8kg) flaked maize	10
or 2 lbs. (0.9kg) corn grits or polenta*	

BG for 6 gallons (23L)	1.047
OG for 5 gallons (19L)	1.056

Hops	Boil Time	IBUs
0.75 oz. (21g) Saaz (4%)	FWH (See pp. 42-43)	
1 oz. (28g) Cluster (7.5%)	60	27
0.5 oz. (14g) Tettnang (5%)	10	2
0.5 oz. (14g) Tettnang (5%)	0	0
Total IBUs	29	

Yeast	Fermentation Schedule
Bavarian Lager	2 weeks at 48° F (9° C) in primary fermenter,
(liquid)	rack and lager at 32° F (0° C) for 6 to 7 weeks. Prime and store bottles at room temperature.

Mash Schedule—Multi-Rest Infusion for Use With Grits

Rest Type	Temperature	Duration
Dough-in	122° F (50° C)	20 min.
Beta rest	145° F (63° C)	30 min.
Alpha rest	158° F (70° C)	30 min.
Mash-out	170° F (77° C)	10 min.

* If you are using corn grits or polenta, you need to cook this cereal first. Here's the whole show:

1. In a kitchen pot, combine the grits and about 10 ounces of crushed malt, and heat to 153° F. (67° C) Hold temperature in a warm (150° F) oven for 20 minutes.
2. Meanwhile, dough-in main mash at 122° F (50° C) for 20 minutes.
3. Bring cereal mash to a boil, and simmer for 30 minutes.
4. Raise the main mash to the 145° F (63° C) beta rest for 30 minutes.
5. Add the cereal mash to the main mash, and bring the temperature to the alpha rest and hold for 30 minutes.
6. Mash-out at 170° F (77° C), and hold for 10 minutes.
7. Lauter, and add FWH to brewpot.

(Recipe contributed by Jeff Renner)

California Common (Steam-type)

This is the most well-known historic American beer style; it was developed in the San Francisco Bay area in the mid-1800s. The "steam" name most likely refers to the high degree of carbonation that the beers were reportedly served with, as well as its then-high-tech sound. San Francisco has a moderate climate year-round, typically cool, cloudy, and about 60° F in the winter months. The new bottom-cropping (lager) yeasts did not behave like the ale yeasts brewers were used to working with. So, they hit on using wide, shallow vessels, normally used for cooling after boiling for fermentation, which allowed the wort to stay cooler during fermentation and provided for faster settling of the yeast after fermentation. Using lager yeast at these relatively high temperatures caused the beer to develop some of the fruity notes of ales while retaining the clean, crisp taste of lager beers.

No. 4 Shay Steam

The Coal Shoveler's Beer

American-grown hops, like Cluster, were used to the tune of 20 to 40 IBUs. The hop profile of steam-type beer is predominantly from higher alpha acid hops with a more herbal character. The present-day incarnation of California common beer, Anchor Steam, uses American-grown Northern Brewer exclusively. The beer should be highly carbonated with a medium body and a light caramel color.

California Common Beer Style Guidelines

Style	OG	°P	FG	IBUs	Color
California Common	1.048-54	12-13	1.011-14	30-45	10-14

Commercial Example

California Common ....Anchor Steam

(The name of this beer comes from a Shay Steam Locomotive (Engine No. 4) that I tended one summer at Cass Scenic Railroad in Cass, West Virginia.)

No. 4 Shay Steam—California Common Beer

Malts	Gravity Points
3.3 lbs. (1.5kg) pale malt extract (LME) in boil	40
3.3 lbs. (1.5kg) pale malt extract (LME) at knockout	(40)
0.75 lb. (340g) crystal 40L malt	5
0.25 lb. (113g) maltodextrin powder	3

BG for 3 gallons (11.3L)	1.048	(12 °P)
OG for 5 gallons (19L)	1.052	(13 °P)

Hops	Boil Time	IBUs
1 oz. (28g) Northern Brewer (7.5%)	60	27
1 oz. (28g) Northern Brewer (7.5%)	15	13
Total IBUs	40	

Yeast	Fermentation Schedule
California Lager (Liquid)	2 weeks at 60° F (15° C) in primary fermenter

Options

All-extract	3.3 lbs. (1.5kg) pale LME
	0.5 lb. (227g) amber DME
	0.25 lb. (113g) maltodextrin powder
	3.3 lbs. (1.5kg) pale LME
All-grain	8.5 lbs. (3.9kg) 2-row base malt
	0.75 lb. (340g) crystal 40L
	0.5 lb. (227g) dextrin malt

Mash Schedule—Single-Temperature Infusion

Rest Type	Temperature	Duration
Conversion	153° F (67° C)	60 min.

Bock

Bock beer is an old style, most likely introduced in Munich about 1638. The style grew out of the then-world-famous beer of Einbeck. It was a strong beer brewed from one-third wheat and two-thirds barley with a pale color, crisp taste, and a hint of acidity. (The acidity was a carryover from the sour wheat beers of the day.) It was brewed as an ale but was stored cold for extended periods. Einbecker beer was widely exported and was the envy of the region.

For years, the nobles of Munich tried to imitate the strong northern beer in their breweries, with limited success. Finally in 1612, the brewmaster of Einbeck was persuaded to go south and work on producing a strong beer for Munich. The beer was released in 1638, a strong beer interpretation of the Munich *braunbier*, a rich malty brown ale. The classic Munich bock beer is a lager with an assertive malt character, a warmth from the higher alcohol level, and only enough hop bitterness to balance the sweetness of the malt. Bock and its big monastic brother, doppelbock, should not have any fusel alcohol character nor any of the fruitiness of ales.

Doppelbock is a descendant of the heavy, rich beers of the Paulaner monks, who brewed this beer as liquid bread for their fasts at Lent and Advent. They named their beer "Salvator," and many breweries brewing in this style have appended -ator to their beer's names. Doppelbock has some roasted malt, yielding hints of chocolate or vanilla. These beers are fermented cold to force the yeast to take their time in consuming the high-gravity worts. The beer is lagered for a long period to encourage the yeast to reduce any off-flavors that would detract from the malt taste.

Bock BJCP Style Guidelines

Substyle	OG	°P	FG	IBUs	Color
Maibock/Helles Bock	1.064-72	16-17.5	1.011-18	23-35	6-11
Traditional Bock	1.064-72	16-17.5	1.013-20	20-27	14-22
Doppelbock	1.072-96+	17.5-23	1.016-24+	16-26+	6-25
Eisbock	1.078-120+	19-28+	1.020-35+	25-35+	18-30+

Commercial Examples

Traditional Bock ....Einbecker Mai Ur-Bock
Doppelbock ....Paulaner Salvator

Copper Country Bock—Bock

Malts	Gravity Points
3 lbs. (1.4kg) pale malt extract (DME) in boil	42
4 lbs. (1.8kg) pale malt extract (DME) at knockout	(42)
1.5 lbs. (0.7kg) crystal 15L malt	7
1.5 lbs. (0.7kg) Munich malt	7

BG for 3 gallons (11.3L)	1.056	(13.5 °P)
OG for 5 gallons (19L)	1.067	(16.5 °P)

Hops	Boil Time	IBUs
0.75 oz. (21g) Perle (9%)	60	22
0.75 oz. (21g) Tettnang (4%)	10	4
Total IBUs	26	

Yeast
Wyeast 2206

Fermentation Schedule
2 weeks at 50° F (10° C) in primary fermenter

Some of My Favorite Beer Styles and Recipes

Bavarian Lager   Lager for 6 weeks at 35° F (2° C)

Options

All-extract   8 lbs. (3.6kg) pale LME
                   2 lbs. (0.9kg) amber DME
                   0.25 lb. (113g) maltodextrin powder
All-grain   6 lbs. (2.7kg) Briess Pilsen malt
                   5 lbs. (2.3kg) Munich malt
                   1.5 lbs. (0.7kg) crystal 15L malt

Mash Schedule—Single-Temperature Infusion

Rest Type	Temperature	Duration
Dough-in	104° F (40° C)	20 min.
Beta rest	140° F (60° C)	30 min.
Alpha rest	158° F (70° C)	30 min.

Doppelbock option: Increase the extract to 9 pounds (4kg), and change the crystal malt from crystal 15 to crystal 80. Increase the hop amounts to maintain about 30 IBUs for the batch. Also, use a larger starter, about 1 gallon's worth, but only pitch the slurry.

Vienna

The Vienna style of lager was developed in the mid-1800s in the city of Vienna, Austria. It grew from the *Märzen*/Oktoberfest styles of Bavaria but was influenced by the rise of the Pilsener style of Bohemia, its political ally. Attempts to imitate the Pilsen style had resulted in harsh beers, due to the differences in brewing water between the two regions. The local water was higher in carbonates than that of Bohemia (Czech Republic). As discussed in Chapter 15, the use of pale malts in alkaline water results in too high a mash pH, which extracts tannins from the grain husks. Of course, they didn't know this back then. They did know that they could brew darker beers that didn't have the astringency problems. The sweet amber lager now known as Vienna was the result of their efforts to produce a lighter beer. It became immensely popular and was copied in other brewing countries.

Cold But Not Baroque

Vienna lager

There was a lot of immigration from Central Europe to Texas and Mexico at that time, and of course, the people brought their beer and brewing techniques with them. The hot climate was abysmal for lager brewing, however, and commercial offerings were poorly regarded. Fortunately, by the late 1800s, refrigeration became commercially viable, and variations of Old World-style lagers became very popular. The principle variation of the Vienna style in the New World is the Graf-style Vienna, named after the Mexican brewer (Santiago Graf) who developed it. It incorporated a small percentage of heavily roasted malt to compensate for the more alkaline water of the region, giving it a deep amber color with hints of red.

Vienna Style Guidelines

Style	OG	°P	FG	IBUs	Color
Vienna	1.046-52	11.5-13	1.010-14	18-30	8-12

Commercial Examples

Vienna ....Ambier, Negro Modelo

Cold But Not Baroque—Vienna

Malts	Gravity Points
3.3 lbs. (1.5kg) pale malt extract (LME) in boil	40
3.3 lbs. (1.5kg) pale malt extract (LME) at knockout	(40)
0.25 lb. (113g) crystal 30L malt	2
0.25 lb. (113g) crystal 80L malt	1
0.25 lb. (113g) crystal 120L malt	1
<0.25 lb. (113g) black patent malt	0

BG for 3 gallons (11.3L)	1.044	(11 °P)
OG for 5 gallons (19L)	1.050	(12.5 °P)

Hops	Boil Time	IBUs
1 oz. (28g) Liberty (4%)	40	13
1 oz. (28g) Liberty (4%)	20	9
1 oz. (28g) Liberty (4%)	10	5
Total IBUs	27	

Yeast	Fermentation Schedule
White Labs WLP820	2 weeks at 54° F (12° C) in primary fermenter
Oktoberfest Lager	Lager for 6 weeks at 35° F (2° C)

Options

All-extract	3.3 lbs. (1.5kg) pale LME
	1 lb. (0.45kg) amber DME
	3.3 lbs. (1.5kg) pale LME
	0.5 lb. (227g) dark DME
All-grain	5 lbs. (2.3kg) 2-row base malt
	4 lbs. (1.8kg) Vienna malt
	0.25 lb. (113g) crystal 80L malt
	<0.25 lb. (113g) debittered black malt

Mash Schedule—Multi-Rest Infusion

Rest Type	Temperature	Duration
Beta rest	140° F (60° C)	20 min.
Alpha rest	158° F (70° C)	40 min.

Oktoberfest

The Märzen and festival beers were part of the basis of the Vienna style. Whereas the Vienna was intended to be the everyday premium drinking beer, the Oktoberfest was made for festivals. The original festival was a royal wedding sometime around 1800, and they have been celebrating ever since. (Some beers are worth it.) This rich amber style incorporates quite a bit of variation, from being soft and malty, malty and dry, to malty and balanced, and malty/bitter. Be that as it may, the hallmark of the Oktoberfest/Märzen style is the maltiness and a drier finish to make it less filling. If you plan to polka for twelve hours straight, then this is your beer.

Denkenfreudenburgerbrau

Hey, Your Mom wants another round...

Oktoberfest Style Guidelines

Style	OG	°P	FG	IBUs	Color
Oktoberfest/Märzen	1.050-56	12.5-14	1.012-16	20-28	7-14

Commercial Example

Oktoberfest/Märzen ....Spaten Ur-Maerzen

Denkenfreudenburgerbrau—Oktoberfest

Malts	Gravity Points
3.3 lbs. (1.5kg) pale malt extract (LME) in boil	40
3.3 lbs. (1.5kg) pale malt extract (LME) at knockout	(40)
0.5 lb. (227g) CaraMunich malt	4
0.5 lb. (227g) crystal 80L malt	3
1 lb. (0.45kg) Munich malt	7

BG for 3 gallons (11.3L)	1.054	(13 °P)
OG for 5 gallons (19L)	1.056	(13.5 °P)

Hops	Boil Time	IBUs
1 oz. (28g) Tettnang (5%)	40	15
1 oz. (28g) Liberty (4%)	30	10
Total IBUs	25	

Yeast	Fermentation Schedule
White Labs WLP820	2 weeks at 45° F (7° C) in primary fermenter
Oktoberfest Lager	Lager for 6 weeks at 35° F (2° C)

Options

All-extract	6 lbs. (2.7kg) pale LME
	2 lbs. (0.9kg) amber DME

All-grain	8 lbs. (3.6kg) Vienna malt
	0.5 lb. (227g) CaraMunich malt
	0.5 lb. (227g) crystal 80L malt
	1 lb. (0.45kg) Munich malt

Mash Schedule—Multi-Rest Infusion

Rest Type	Temperature	Duration
Beta rest	140° F (60° C)	30 min.
Alpha rest	158° F (70° C)	30 min.

Summary

So there you have it—the *Reader's Digest* version of some of the classic beer styles of the world. There are many, many more. If all this talk of different malts and tastes has made you thirsty, zip on down to your local GoodBeer Store, and bring back some samples for research and development. Don't be shy—how else can you decide what your want to brew next?

DEVELOPING YOUR OWN RECIPES

Now it's time to drop the training wheels and strike out on your own. You have read about the various beer styles of the world, and you should now have a better idea of the kind of beer you like best and want to brew. Homebrewing is all about brewing your own beer. Recipes are a convenient starting point, until you have honed your brewing skills and gained familiarity with the ingredients. Do you need a recipe to make a sandwich? 'Course not! You may start out by buying a particular kind of sandwich at a sandwich shop, but soon you will be buying the meat and cheese at the store, cutting back on the mayo a little, giving it a shot of Tabasco, using real mustard instead of that yellow stuff, and *voilà*—you have made your own sandwich just the way you like it! Brewing your own beer is the same process.

This chapter will present more guidelines for using ingredients to attain a desired characteristic. You want more body, more maltiness, a different hop profile, less alcohol? Each of these can be accomplished, and this chapter will show you how.

Developing Your Own Recipes

Recipe design is easy and can be a lot of fun. Pull together the information on yeast strains, hops, and malts, and start defining the kinds of tastes and character you are looking for in a beer. Make sure you understand the signature flavors of your chosen beer style before you starting adding lots of stuff—otherwise, you will probably end up with a beer that just tastes weird. Choose a style that is close to your dream beer, and decide what you want to change about it. Change just one or two things at a time, so you will better understand the result.

To help get your creative juices flowing, here is a rough approximation of basic recipes for the common ale styles:

> Pale ale—base malt plus a half-pound of caramel malt
> Amber ale—pale ale plus a half-pound of dark caramel malt
> Brown ale—pale ale plus a half-pound of chocolate malt
> Porter—amber ale plus a half-pound of chocolate malt
> Stout—porter plus a half-pound of roasted barley

Yes, those recipes are pretty crude, but I want you to realize how little effort it takes to produce a different beer. When adding a new malt to a recipe, start out with a half-pound or less for a 5-gallon batch. Brew the recipe, and then adjust up or down depending on your tastes. Try commercial beers in each of the styles, and use the recipes and guidelines in this book to develop a feel for the flavors that the different ingredients contribute.

Read recipes listed in brewing magazines, even if they are all-grain and you are not a grain brewer. By reading an all-grain recipe and the descriptions of the malts they are using, you will gain a feel for what that beer would taste like. You will get an idea of the proportions to use. For example, if you look at five different recipes for amber ale, you will probably notice that no one uses more than one pound of any one crystal malt—all things are good in moderation. If you see an all-grain recipe that sounds good but aren't ready to brew all-grain, use the principles given in Chapter 12 to duplicate the recipe using extract and the specialty grains. You may need to use a partial mash for some recipes, but most can be reasonably duplicated without.

The choice of yeast strain is your No. 1 determinant for flavor. Take any ale recipe and change the ale yeast strain to a lager strain, and you have a lager recipe (though not necessarily an example of a particular lager style). Look at yeast strain information and determine which flavors different strains would give to the recipe. Use the calculations in Chapters 5 and 12 to estimate the IBUs and the gravity of the beer. Plan a final gravity for the beer, and decide what factors you would use to achieve it, i.e., extract brand, mash schedule, yeast strain, fermentation temperature, etc. You as the brewer have almost infinite control over the end result. Don't be afraid to experiment.

Increasing the Body

Very often, brewers say that they like a beer but wish it had more body. What exactly is "more body?" Is it a physically heavier, more dense beer? More flavor? More viscosity? It can mean all these things. In many cases, it means a higher final gravity (FG) but not at the expense of incomplete fermentation. On a basic level, adding unfermentables is the only way to increase the FG and increase the body/weight/mouthfeel of the beer. There are two types of unfermentables that can be added: unfermentable sugars and proteins.

Unfermentable sugars are highly caramelized sugars, like those in crystal malts, and long chain sugars referred to as dextrins. Dextrin malt and maltodextrin powder have already been discussed in the ingredients chapters. Dextrins are tasteless carbohydrates that hang around, adding some weight and viscosity to the beer. The effect is fairly limited, and some brewers suspect that dextrins are a leading cause of "beer farts," which result when these unfermentable carbohydrates are final-ly broken down in the intestines.

Dark caramel and roasted malts like crystal 80, crystal 120, Special "B," chocolate malt, and roasted barley have a high proportion of unfermentable sugars due to the high degree of caramelization (or charring). The total soluble extract (percent by weight) of these malts is close to that of base malt, but just because it's soluble does not mean it is fermentable. These sugars are only partially fermentable and contribute both a residual sweetness and higher FG to the finished beer.

These types of sugars do not share dextrin's digestive problems, and the added flavor and color make for a more interesting beer. The contribution of unfermentable sugars from enzymatic and caramel malts can be increased by mashing at a higher temperature (i.e., 158° F, 70° C), where the beta-amylase enzyme is deactivated. Without this enzyme, the alpha-amylase can only produce large sugars (including dextrins) from the starches, and the wort is not as fermentable. The result is a higher final gravity and more body.

Proteins are also unfermentable and are a primary contributor to the mouthfeel of a beer. Compare an oatmeal stout to a regular stout, and you will immediately notice the difference. Brewers refer to these mouthfeel-enhancing proteins as "medium-sized proteins." During the protein rest, protease breaks large proteins into medium proteins, and peptidase cleaves the ends of proteins into small peptides and amino acids. High-protein malts and adjuncts like wheat and oatmeal can substantially increase the body of the beer.

To add more body to an extract-based beer, add some caramel malt or maltodextrin powder. You can also increase the total amount of fermentables in the recipe, which will raise both the OG and FG and give you a corresponding increase in alcohol, too.

Grain brewers can add dextrin malt, caramel malt, unmalted barley, or oatmeal in addition to using the methods above. Grain brewing lends more flexibility in fine-tuning the wort than extract brewing.

Changing Flavors

What if you want a maltier-tasting beer? A bigger, more robust malt flavor is usually achieved by adding more malt or malt extract to the recipe. A 1.050 OG beer is maltier than a 1.035 OG beer. If you add more extract, be sure to increase the bittering hops a bit to keep it balanced. This brings up another way to enhance the maltiness of a beer, and that is to cut back on the flavor and aroma hop additions. You can keep the total hop bitterness and balance the same by adding more bittering hops at the beginning of the boil, but by cutting back on the middle and late hop additions, the malt flavors and aromas will be more dominant.

But what if you don't want the increased alcohol level that comes with an increase in gravity? The solution will depend on what flavor profile you are trying to achieve. If you want a stronger or crisper malt flavor, substitute a pound or two of one of the toasted malts (e.g., Vienna, Munich, amber, etc.) in place of some of the base malt to help produce the malty aromas of German bocks and Oktoberfests. Change the type of caramel malt you are using if you want to change the sweet malt character of the beer. You can add Carastan or crystal 15 or 25 malt to produce a lighter, honeylike sweetness, instead of the caramel of crystal 60 and 80, or use the bittersweet of crystal 120 and Special "B."

If the flavor profile tastes a bit flat, or you want to add some complexity to the beer, then substitute small amounts of different specialty malts for a larger single-malt addition, while keeping the same OG. For instance, if a recipe calls for a half-pound of crystal 60L malt, try using a quarter-pound each of crystal 40L and crystal 80. Or if a recipe calls for a half-pound of chocolate malt, try using just a quarter-pound of chocolate and adding a quarter-pound of toasted malt or CaraMunich. For the same strength beer, you will have more flavors.

The hop varieties and malts from different parts of the world can have a significant effect on the character of the beer, too. Sometimes these differences can be quite dramatic, and it's a sign of a really good brewer to utilize this. Tasting and chewing the ingredients before brewing with them is a useful way to make yourself aware of these differences.

Yeast, too, has a strong effect on beer flavor, and not always in ways that seem particularly yeasty. Some accentuate hops, some malt; others add deep, woody, or earthy notes, or a whiff of spicy phenol.

The best brewers use every little trick: the right malt, the right hops, technique, yeast, temperature, all working together to deliver a unified and memorable experience to the drinker.

Sugars Used in Brewing

Lots of different sugars can be used in brewing, and now that we know what the yeast want to eat and when, we can make better choices for their use. Which brings us to a good starting point— why would we want to use anything other than the sugars that come naturally from the barley? Well there are a few reasons:

- To raise the alcohol level without increasing the body of the beer
- To lighten the body of the beer while maintaining the alcohol level
- To add some interesting flavors
- To prime the beer for carbonation.

The first two are two sides of the same coin, of course, but they do illustrate two different styles of refined sugar-adjunct beer. Belgian-style strong golden ale has an OG of 1.065 to 1.080 and uses partially refined sugar syrup to achieve a brilliantly clear, high-alcohol, yet light-bodied beer. American light lager recipes have an OG of 1.035 to 1.050, and use corn sugar, cane sugar, or rice syrup solids to obtain a very light-bodied beer of average alcohol content that is perfect for a day with the lawn mower.

Various sugars have various flavors. The monosaccharides contribute no other flavor than sweetness, although apparently the soda beverage industry has a definite preference for cane sugar over beet sugar for use in soft drinks. But other natural sugars like honey and maple syrup, and processed sugars like molasses, have characteristic flavors that make a nice accent for a beer. This is what homebrewing is all about, really, taking a standard beer style and dressing it up for your own tastes. You can make a maple syrup porter, or a honey raspberry wheat, or an imperial Russian stout with hints of rum and treacle. The possibilities are myriad. On the other hand, I have coined a phrase that will serve you well in your experimentation, "The better part of flavor is discretion." A beer with 20% molasses is going to taste like fermented molasses, not beer.

And lastly, you may use sugar for priming, adding two to three gravity points of fermentable sugar per gallon to carbonate the batch. Most folks did their brewing at the boiling stage; they don't want to change their flavor profile at this stage, they simply want an unobtrusive sugar to carbonate the beer. Other brewers actually look at this last stage of fermentation with an ulterior motive; they want to add character with this final step. Whatever your goal, you can select one of several sugars to accomplish it.

Glucose-Type Sugars

The most common example of a simple brewing sugar is the corn sugar that is commonly used for priming. It is about 92% solids with 8% moisture. The solid is about 99% glucose. Corn sugar is highly refined and does not contain any corn character. Brewers seeking a cornlike character for a classic American Pilsener need to cook and mash corn grits as part of an all-grain recipe. It is known that a relatively high proportion of glucose in a wort (more than 15 to 20%) will inhibit the fermentation of maltose. The fermentation can be impaired or become stuck if the yeast is underpitched or there is a lack of free amino nitrogen (FAN) or other nutrients in the wort.

Rice syrup solids are another glucose product, and there are different types. For example, one high-glucose type is about 75% sugars (50% glucose, 25% maltose), 20% other carbohydrates (dextrins), and 5% moisture. A high-maltose type could contain only 5% glucose, 45% maltose, 45% other carbohydrates, and the same 5% moisture. Extract brewers seeking to brew a Budweiser clone can use rice syrup solids and will obtain nearly the same malt character as the real thing (assuming that all the other brewing variables are the same, also).

Sucrose-Type Sugars

Pure sucrose is the reference standard for all fermentable sugars, because it contributes 100% of its weight as fermentable extract and is 100% solids (no moisture). One pound of sucrose dissolved to form 1 gallon of solution has a gravity of 1.046, or in other words, an extract yield of 46 points per pound per gallon.

Lots of different brewing products are made from sucrose or the semi-refined by-products of sucrose. Both sugar cane and sugar beets are used to make table sugar, and the refined products are indistinguishable from one another. However, you do not get useful brewing by-products from beets, only sugar cane. Molasses is a common by-product, and it is added to refined cane sugar to make brown sugar. The fermentation of molasses produces rumlike notes and sweet flavors, but there may be sharp, harsh notes as well. Brown sugar, which only contains a small amount of molasses, will only contribute a light rummy flavor. Partially refined cane sugars like panocha or panela, Demerara, turbinado, and Barbados have better flavors than molasses, which often contains impurities from the refining process.

Here's a quote from Sykes & Ling, 1897:

> The impurities of the raw sugar derived from the beetroot are of a nauseous character, whilst those of sugarcane sugar have an agreeable, full, and luscious flavor; and so much is this the case, that the impure cane sugars are more valuable for brewing purposes than the refined, since the raw variety yield to the beer their luscious flavor.[1]

Belgian candi sugar was thought to be solid sucrose or rock candy that had been caramelized to some small degree, depending on the color. Aside from some faint caramel notes, it behaved exactly like table sugar. However, it has recently come to light (or pounded into our American heads) that the candi sugar (or *kandij zuiker* in Flemish) that the Belgians actually use in their breweries is not the solid form but rather a semi-refined syrup, which is caramelized during manufacture. It has a dark color and a strong caramel flavor. The fermentability is about 65%, based on its sugar profile, and it is about 20% water by weight. Look for this Belgian caramel syrup in your local brewing shop soon.

Invert sugar syrups, such as Lyle's Golden Syrup, are made from sucrose that has been hydrolyzed to separate the glucose and fructose. This has two effects: one, it makes the sugar more syrupy and less likely to crystallize, and two, it makes it sweeter. Invert sugar syrup is like artificial honey without the characteristic honey flavors. Golden syrup-type products tend to be a bit salty tasting due to the acid/base reactions during manufacture. Treacle is partially inverted molasses combined with other syrups. The flavor contributions from treacle can be strong, so it is best to use it in heavier-bodied beers like English strong ales, porters, and sweet stout. One-half cup per 5-gallon batch is a recommended starting point.

Maple Syrup
Maple sap typically contains about 2% sucrose. Maple syrup is standardized at a minimum of 66° Brix, and is typically composed of 95+% sucrose. Grade B syrup can contain 6% invert sugar, while Grade A Light Amber will contain less than 1%. You will get more maple flavor from the Grade B syrup. The characteristic maple flavors tend to be lost during primary fermentation, so adding the syrup after primary fermentation is over is recommended to retain as much flavor as possible. This practice will also help the beer to ferment more completely because it will not trigger maltose inhibition as discussed in Chapter 6. For a noticeable maple flavor, 1 gallon of Grade B syrup is recommended per 5-gallon batch.

Honey
The sugars in honey are 95% fermentable, typically consisting of 38% fructose, 30% glucose, 8% various disaccharides, and 3% unfermentable dextrins. Honey contains wild yeasts and bacteria, but its low water content (about 18%) keeps these microorganisms dormant. Honey also contains amylase enzymes, which can break down larger sugars and starches into fermentable sugars like maltose and sucrose. For these reasons, honey should be pasteurized before adding it to the fermenter. The National Honey Board (www.nhb.org) recommends that honey be pasteurized for 30 minutes at 176° F (80° C), then cooled and diluted to the wort gravity. To retain the most honey flavor and ensure best fermentation performance, the honey should be added to the fermenter after primary fermentation.

The NHB recommends the following percentages (by weight of total fermentables) when brewing with honey:

- 3-10%   For a subtle honey flavor in most light ales and lagers
- 11-30% For a distinct honey flavor note to develop. Stronger hop flavors, caramelized or roasted malts, spices, or other ingredients should be considered when formulating the recipe, to balance the strong honey flavors at these levels.
- 30-66% The flavor of honey will dominate the beer. These levels are associated with braggot, which is considered by the Beer Judge Certification Program Style Guidelines to have a maximum honey-to-malt ratio of 2 to 1.
- 66+%   Any brew with more than 66% honey is considered to be a form of mead, according to the BJCP.

TABLE 28
Common Brewing Sugars

Sugar	Extract Yield (ppg)	% Fermentability	Constituents	Comments
Corn sugar	42	100%	Glucose (~8% moisture)	Can be used for priming or as a wort component to increase the alcohol while lightening the body of the beer
Rice syrup solids	42	Varies by grade; high-glucose grade is ~80%	Glucose, maltose, other (~10% moisture)	Can be used for priming or as a wort component to increase the alcohol while lightening the body of the beer
Table sugar	46	100%	Sucrose	Can be used for priming or as a wort component to increase the alcohol while lightening the body of the beer
Lyle's Golden Syrup	38	100%	Glucose, fructose (18% water)	An invert sugar that has been broken down to fructose and glucose. A bit salty due to acids and bases used during processing
Molasses/treacle	36	Varies, ~90%	Sucrose, invert sugars, dextrins	Degree of fermentability is unknown, probably around 50-70%. Can cause rumlike or winey flavors
Lactose	46	—	Lactose (<1% moisture)	Lactose is an unfermentable sugar. Used in milk stouts to impart a smooth, sweet flavor
Honey	38	95%	Fructose, glucose, sucrose (~18% water)	Honey is a high-fructose mixture of sugars, which will impart honeylike flavors that depend on nectar source
Maple syrup	31	100%	Sucrose, fructose, glucose (~34% water)	Maple syrup is mostly sucrose. Grade B syrup will provide more maple flavor than Grade A syrup
Maltodextrin powder	42	—	Dextrins (5% moisture)	Maltodextrin powder contains a small amount of maltose but is mostly unfermentable. Adds mouthfeel and some body

Note: The extract of sucrose-based brewing syrups can be estimated by multiplying the "percent solids" or °Brix by the reference standard of 46 points per pound per gallon for sucrose. The extract of powdered sugars can be estimated by subtracting the percent moisture and multiplying the remainder by 46 ppg.

Toasting Your Own Malt

As a homebrewer, you should feel free to experiment in your kitchen with malts. Oven-toasted base malt adds nutty and toasty flavors to the beer, which is a nice addition for brown ale, porter, bock, and Oktoberfest. Toasting your own is easy to do, and the toasted grain can be used for both steeping and mashing. If steeped, the malt will contribute a high proportion of unconverted starch to the wort, and the beer will be hazy, but a nice nutty, toasted flavor will be evident in the final beer. There are several combinations of time and temperature that can be used to produce these special malts, so I will explain a couple of the factors that influence the flavor and describe the two methods I use.

The principal reaction that takes place when you toast malt is the browning of starches and proteins, known as the Maillard reaction. As the starches and proteins brown, various flavor and color compounds are produced. The color compounds are called "melanoidins" and can improve the stability of beer by slowing oxidation and staling reactions as the beer ages.

Since the browning reactions are influenced by the wetness of the grain, water can be used in conjunction with the toasting process to produce different flavors in the malt. Soaking the uncrushed malt in water for an hour will provide the water necessary to optimize the Maillard browning reactions. Toasting wet malt will produce more of a caramel flavor due to partial starch conversion taking place from the heat. Toasting dry grain will produce more of a toast or Grape-Nuts cereal flavor that is perfect for nut brown ales.

The malt should be stored in a paper bag for two weeks prior to use. This will allow time for the harsher aromatics to escape. Commercial toasted malts are often aged for six weeks before sale. This aging is more important for the highly toasted malts, those toasted for more than a half-hour (dry) or one hour (wet).

TABLE 29
Grain Toasting Times and Temperatures

Temperature	Dry/Wet	Time	Flavors
275° F	Dry	1 hour	Light nutty taste and aroma
350° F	Dry	15 minutes	Light nutty taste and aroma
350° F	Dry	30 minutes	Toasty, Grape-Nuts cereal flavor
350° F	Dry	1 hour	More roasted flavor, very similar to commercial brown malt
350° F	Wet	1 hour	Light, sweet, toasty flavor
350° F	Wet	1.5 hours	Toasted, malty, slightly sweet
350° F	Wet	2 hours	Strong toast/roast flavor similar to brown malt, but slightly sweet

Discretion Is the Better Part of Flavor

There comes a time in every homebrewer's development when he or she looks at an item (e.g., maple syrup, molasses, Cheerios, chile peppers, potatoes, pumpkins, loquats, ginger root, spruce tips, heather, licorice, stale bread, mismatched socks) and says, "Hey, I could ferment that!" While many of the mentioned items will indeed work in the fermenter (socks work well for dry-hopping), it is easy to get carried away and make something that no one really wants to drink a second glass of. I thought I would like spiced holiday beer—I didn't. I thought I would like a molasses porter— I didn't. I thought I would like loquat wheat beer—four hours peeling and seeding three bags of those little bastards for something I couldn't even taste!

Experimentation is fine and dandy, but be forewarned that you may not like the result. Refined sugars like molasses, candi sugar, honey, and maple syrup can taste wonderful in the right proportion—as an accent to a beer. But keep firmly in mind that you are brewing beer and not liqueur. Refined sugars often generate fusel alcohols, which can have solventlike flavors. If you want to try a new fermentable or two in a recipe, go ahead, but use a small amount so that it doesn't dominate the flavor. I feel hypocritical telling you to hold back after first saying to spread your wings and develop your own recipes. But I don't want you to spend a lot of time making a batch that is undrinkable. Just because it can be done doesn't mean it should be done. Ok, enough said.

In the next chapter, I will lead you through common problems and their causes and define some of the most common off-flavors.

[1] Sykes, W.J. and Ling, A.R. *The Principles and Practice of Brewing*, 3rd ed. (London: Charles Griffin & Co, 1907), 94.

IS MY BEER RUINED?

Common Problems - 249
Common Off-Flavors - 255

"Is My Beer Ruined?!"

This question has got to be the one most frequently asked by new brewers, and usually the answer is, "No." Depending on the cause, it might end up with an odd flavor or aroma, but you will still be able to drink it and chalk it up as another lesson on the way to brewing that perfect beer. Although a lot can potentially go wrong with a batch, most problems arise from just a couple of root causes. If the recipe was good and you used quality ingredients, there are three common culprits: poor sanitation, bad yeast, or the wrong temperature. Most problems become noticeable once the beer is in the fermenter and nothing (or something weird) is happening. Let's examine some common symptoms and their possible causes.

Common Problems

Symptom: I added the yeast two days ago, and nothing is happening.

Cause 1: Leaky bucket. Lack of fermentation can be due to several things. If the airlock is not bubbling, it may be due to a poor seal between the lid and the bucket. Fermentation may be taking place, but the carbon dioxide is not coming out through the airlock.

Cure: This is not a real problem; it probably won't affect the batch. Fix the seal, or get a new lid next time.

Cause 2: Bad yeast. When a batch is not fermenting, the most common problem is with the yeast. If dry yeast has been properly packaged and stored, it should be fully viable for up to two years. However, if you are using a yeast package that came taped to the top of a dusty can of malt extract, then the yeast may be too old or may have been subjected to poor storage conditions and will not work for you. Don't use old yeast from dusty cans.

Yeast need to be treated with care and be given the proper growing conditions. Dry yeast are dehydrated—they're parched, they're in no condition to start work. They need some nice warm water to get rehydrated in, some time to do some stretching, maybe an appetizer, and then they will be ready to tackle a full wort. If the dry yeast is just sprinkled onto the surface of the wort, some of the yeast will be up to the challenge, but most won't.

Cure: Rehydration of yeast in plain water is strongly recommended because of the principles of osmosis. Dried yeast contain adequate sugar reserves to get them going, so there is no need for sugar in the rehydration process. In a wort with a high concentration of dissolved sugar, the water that the yeast needs cannot be drawn across the cell membrane to wet it. The water is instead locked up in the wort, hydrating the sugars. A friend of mine, who insists on remaining nameless, was misled by the term "pitching," and for his first batch attempted to forcibly throw each granule of dried yeast into the wort so that it would be wetted. That batch didn't turn out very well.

Likewise, liquid yeast cultures also need their breakfast routine. They have been kept in a refrigerator and need to be warmed and fed before there will be enough active yeast to do the job properly. There are a lot more yeast cells in a dry yeast packet than in a liquid packet. The liquid packet needs to be grown in a starter to produce enough cells to take on the job of a full 5-gallon wort. Both liquid and dry yeast cultures will have a lag time from when they are pitched until they start fermenting in earnest. Aeration, the process of dissolving oxygen into the wort, provides the yeast with the oxygen they need to greatly boost their growth rate and make enough yeast cells to do the job properly.

Cause 3: Too cold. The fermentation conditions may be too cold for an otherwise healthy yeast population. Ale yeast strains vary in their temperature sensitivity but tend to go dormant below 60° F (16° C). If the yeast are rehydrated in really warm water (105° F, 41° C) and then pitched to a much cooler wort (65° F, 18° C), the large difference in temperature can thermally shock the yeast and cause a longer lag time as they adjust. Or in some cases, that otherwise normal ale fermentation temperature could cause those warm-acclimated yeast to call it quits.

Cure: Try warming the fermenter by 5° F; it may make all the difference.

Cause 4: Improper sanitation. Sanitation can be carried too far sometimes. When you were preparing the warm water for rehydrating or boiling your yeast starter, did you cool it to the proper temperature range? If the water is too cold (below 80° F, 27° C), the yeast will be sluggish and have a hard time getting rehydrated. If it is too hot (above 105° F, 41° C), then the yeast are going to get scalded and refuse to have anything to do with you and your wort. Also, if you added the yeast to the starter wort and then boiled it, well, they're dead.

Cure: Pitch new yeast.

Symptom: I added the yeast yesterday and it bubbled all day, but it's slowing down/stopped today.

Cause 1: Lack of preparation. As I stated above, yeast that are improperly prepared, whether from lack of rehydration, lack of numbers (i.e., lack of starter), or lack of aeration, will often fail to finish the job.

Cure: Pitch new yeast.

Cause 2: Too cold. Temperature can also be a major factor in fermentation performance. If the temperature of the room where the fermenter is cools down, even by only 5° F overnight, then the yeast can be slowed dramatically.

Cure: Always strive to keep the fermentation temperature constant; the yeast will thank you for it.

Cause 3: Too warm. The flip side of the coin could be that the temperature was warm, e.g., 75° F (24° C), and the yeast got the job done ahead of schedule. This often happens when a lot of yeast is pitched; the primary fermentation can be complete within 48 hours. This is not necessarily a good thing, as ferments above 70° F (21° C) tend to produce a lot of esters and phenolics that just don't taste right. The beer will still be good, just not as good as it could have been. It will depend on your tastes and the yeast strain.

Cure: Always strive to keep the fermentation temperature within the recommended range. The yeast will thank you for it.

Symptom: The last batch (did that) but this batch is (doing this).

Cause 1: Different conditions. Different yeast strains behave differently, and different ingredients can cause the same yeast to behave differently. Different temperatures can cause the same yeast working on the same ingredients to behave differently. Different yeasts working on different ingredients at different temperatures will produce different beers. Profound, eh?

Cure: Be patient; don't jump to conclusions. Go watch TV.

Cause 2: Yeast health. If you are brewing identical recipes at the identical temperatures, then a difference in fermentation vigor or length may be due to yeast health, aeration, or other factors. Only if something like odor or taste is severely different should you worry.

Cure: Wait and see.

Symptom: The airlock is clogged with gunk.

Cause: Vigorous fermentation. Sometimes ferments are so vigorous that the kraeusen is forced into the airlock. Pressure can build up in the fermenter if the airlock gets plugged, and you may end up spraying brown yeast and hop resins on the ceiling.

Cure: The best solution to this problem is to switch to a blowoff hose. Fit a large diameter hose (e.g., 1 inch) into the opening of the bucket or carboy, and run it down to a bucket of water.

Symptom: White stuff/brown stuff/green stuff is floating/growing/moving.

Cause 1: Normal fermentation. The first time you look inside your fermenter, you will be treated to an amazing sight. There will be whitish yellow-brown foam on top of the wort, containing greenish areas of hops and resins. This is perfectly normal. Even if it appears slightly slimy, it is probably normal. Only if something hairy starts growing on top of the wort should you be concerned. I remember one guy reporting a dead bat floating in his fermenter. . . . That was definitely cause for alarm.

Cure: Get a new bat.

Cause 2: Mold. A simple case of mold.

Is My Beer Ruined?

Cure: Mold can often be skimmed off with no lasting effect on the beer's flavor. Withdraw a sample of the wort with a siphon or turkey baster, and taste it. If it tastes foul, then it's not worth keeping. Otherwise, the beer was probably not harmed. Infections in beer caused by molds are not dangerous. Be meticulous in your sanitation, and you should not have any problems. Mold is indicative of a fermentation that has access to a lot of air. It is frequently encountered when brewing with fruit. If there's any yeast activity, it would maintain a blanket of carbon dioxide. Get that beer either into the bottle, or if you wish to carboy-age it for a long period, into a vessel that can be filled nearly to the brim.

Symptom: It smells like rotten eggs.

Cause 1: Yeast strain. Rotten egg odors (hydrogen sulfide) can have two common causes: the yeast strain and bacteria. Many lager yeast strains produce noticeable amounts of hydrogen sulfide during fermentation. The smell and any sulfur taste will dissipate during lagering.

Cure: Let the beer condition or lager for a few weeks after primary fermentation.

Cause 2: Bacteria. Bacterial infections can also produce sulfuric odors, and if you are not brewing a lager beer, this is a good sign that you have an infection. Fortunately, this is pretty rare, but it indicates a serious oversight in your sanitizing regime.

Cure: Let the fermentation complete, and then taste it before bottling to see if it is infected. It may be accompanied by sourness, ropiness, or other unpleasant characteristics. Toss it if it is.

Symptom: It smells sour.

Cause 1: Bacteria. In this case, it probably is. *Acetobacter* (vinegar-producing bacteria) and *Lactobacilli* (lactic acid-producing bacteria) are common contaminates in breweries. Sometimes, the infection will produce sweet smells like malt vinegar, other times, they will produce cidery smells. It will depend on which bug is living in your wort. *Acetobacter* often produce ropy strands of jelly, which can be a good visual indicator, as can excessive cloudiness, after several weeks in the fermenter (although some cloudiness is not unusual, especially in all-grain beers). *Acetobacter* is an aerobe, so its presence indicates that oxygen is getting to your beer.

Cure: If you don't like the taste, then pour it out. Lactic infections are desired in some beer styles. Be more meticulous with your sanitation, and don't suck to start siphons. Some lightly soured beers can be rescued by adding fruit.

Cause 2: Wild yeast and bacteria. Two other bugs are also common, *Brettanomyces* and *Pediococcus*. *Brettanomyces* is supposed to smell like horse sweat or a barnyard smell. I think *Brett* smells like leather, myself. *Pediococcus* can produce diacetyl (invariably as a contaminant) and acidic aromas and flavors, as well as haze.

One man's garbage can be another man's gold, though. These two cultures and *Lactobacillus* are actually essential to the Belgian lambic beer styles. Under any other circumstances, beers that taste like lambics would be discarded instead of being carefully nurtured and blended over a two-year period. Lambic beers have a pronounced tartness with fruity overtones. This type of beer is very refreshing and is excellent with heavy food.

Cure: Be meticulous in your sanitation, or investigate lambic brewing.

Symptom: It won't stop bubbling.

Cause 1: Cool temperatures. A beer that has been continually fermenting (bubbling) for a long time (more than a week for ales, more than three weeks for lagers) may not have something wrong with it. It is often due to the fermentation being a bit too cool, and the yeast are working more slowly than normal.

Cure: This condition is not a problem.

Cause 2: Gusher infection. The sustained bubbling is often due to "gusher type" infections. These infections can occur at any time and are due to wild yeasts or bacteria that eat the normally unfermentable sugars, like dextrins. The result in the fermenter is a beer that keeps bubbling until all of the carbohydrates are fermented, leaving a beer that has no body and very little taste. If it occurs at bottling time, the beer will overcarbonate and will fizz like soda pop, fountaining out of the bottle.

Cure: Improve your sanitation next time. If the beer seems to be bubbling for too long, check the gravity with a hydrometer. Use a siphon or turkey baster to withdraw a sample from the fermenter, and check the gravity. If the gravity is still high, in the teens or twenties, then it is probably due to lower than optimum temperature or sluggish yeast. If it is below 10 and still bubbling at several per minute, then a bug has gotten hold. The beer will not be worth drinking due to either the total lack of flavor or unpleasant phenols.

Saison yeast ferments very slowly, so if you're using this strain, expect much longer than normal fermentation times. Many commercial breweries using this yeast finish with a normal ale yeast.

Symptom: The fermentation seems to have stopped, but the hydrometer says 1.025.

Cause 1: Too cool. This situation is commonly referred to as a "stuck fermentation" and can have a couple of causes. The simplest cause, and probably the most common, is temperature. As previously discussed, a significant drop in temperature can cause the yeast to go dormant (and even be thermally shocked) and settle to the bottom.

Cure: Moving the fermenter to a warmer room and swirling the fermenter to stir up the yeast and get them back into suspension will often fix the problem.

Cause 2: Weak yeast/Underpitched. The other most common cause is weak yeast. Referring back to previous discussions of yeast preparation, weak yeast or low volumes of healthy yeast will often not be up to the task of fermenting a high-gravity wort. This problem is most common with higher-gravity beers, those with OGs greater than 1.078.

Cure: Add more yeast.

Cause 3: Low-attenuating extracts. Another common cause for extract kit brewers is the use of extracts high in dextrins. Two brands are known to be high in unfermentables, Laaglanders Dry Malt Extract (Netherlands) and Alexander's Pale from California Concentrate (United States). These are not bad extracts, in fact they are high quality, but their use is better suited to heavier-bodied beers like strong ales, porters, and stouts, where a high finishing gravity is desired.

Cure: In this case, the beer has fermented as far as its ingredients will allow. If you want more attenuation in the recipe, switch extract brands to one that is more attenuating, like Muntons or Briess.

Symptom: It won't carbonate.

Causes: Needs more time. Time, temperature, and yeast strain all combine to form a government committee with the charter to determine a range of times when they can expect to be 90% finished with the Carbonation/Residual Attenuation Project. This committee works best without distractions—the meetings should be held in quiet, low-light areas in a warm room. If the committee was given enough budget (priming sugar), then they should arrive at a consensus in about two weeks. If they don't get their act together within a month, then it's time to rattle their cages and shake things up a bit.

Cure: The yeast may have settled out prematurely, and the bottles need to be shaken to get the yeast back into suspension. Likewise, if the temperature is too cool in the room, moving the bottles to a warmer room may do the trick. With long-aged beers, there is sometimes not enough viable yeast left to do the job. Fresh yeast may need to be added.

Symptom: The bottles are overcarbonated.

Cause 1: Too much sugar. You used too much priming sugar.

Cure: Vent and recap all of the bottles. This may have to be done several times, as this just lets out the gas from the head space, not what is dissolved in the beer. It might be a good idea to uncap and then cover them with little squares of aluminum foil, and let them stand for several minutes/hours before recapping.

Cause 2: Bottled too soon. You bottled before fermentation was complete.

Cure: Vent and recap all of the bottles.

Cause 3: Wild yeast. A "gusher bug" has gotten into the beer. Gusher bugs (i.e., *Pediococcus* and/or wild yeasts) are a real problem, as they will keep on fermenting the beer until there is nothing left but fizzy, bitter alcoholic water. The real danger with overcarbonation is exploding bottles. Bottle grenades can be very dangerous both from flying glass and from glass slivers left in the carpet.

Cure: Refrigerate the bottles, and drink them while there is still some flavor left. I recall one story I read on the rec.crafts.brewing newsgroup where a brewer recounted how both he and his partner had each added ¾ cup of priming sugar to the batch, thinking that the other one had not. By venting and recapping all the remaining bottles after the initial explosions, they thought they had saved the batch. Then a massive storm front swept through, and the corresponding drop in barometric pressure caused the rest of the bottles to explode. Be careful!

Symptom: The (finished) beer is hazy/cloudy.

Cause 1: Chill haze. This is the No. 1 cause of cloudy homebrew. It is caused by an insufficient cold break during cooling after the boil.

Cure: Use a wort chiller.

Cause 2: Starch. If you made an all-grain beer and had incomplete conversion, or added/steeped a malt that needed to be mashed to an extract batch, then you can have residual starches in the beer that will cause cloudiness.

Cure: Check your malts to see if they need to be steeped or mashed. Watch the mash temperature, and perhaps mash longer next time.

Cause 3: Yeast. Yeast strains that have low flocculation, such as German hefeweizen, will cause the beer to be cloudy.

Cure: Use a different yeast strain if you want a clearer beer. In all cases, cloudiness can be combated by adding fining agents (e.g., isinglass, gelatin, Polyclar®, bentonite) after fermentation. When all-grain brewing, the clarity can be enhanced by adding Irish moss toward the end of the boil. See Appendix F for more info.

Common Off-Flavors

There are many flavors that contribute to the overall character of a beer. Some of these flavors have been previously described as malty, fruity, or bitter. When it comes time to figure out why a beer tastes bad, though, we need to get more specific. In this section, we will discuss several different flavors that can be perceived and what could cause each.

Acetaldehyde

A flavor of green apples or freshly cut pumpkin; it is an intermediate compound in the formation of alcohol. Some yeast strains produce more than others, but generally its presence indicates that the beer is too young and needs more time to condition.

To reduce the likelihood of acetaldehyde in your beer:
- Use a lower pitching rate.
- Don't underaerate.
- Use a cooler fermentation temperature.

To clean up acetaldehyde in the fermenter:
- Use a warmer lagering or conditioning temperature.
- Keep the beer on the yeast (i.e., don't rack too soon).
- Rouse the yeast to keep it suspended.
- Use a less flocculant yeast strain.

Alcoholic

A sharp flavor that can be mild and pleasant or hot and bothersome. When an alcohol taste detracts from a beer's flavor, it can usually be traced to one of two causes. The first problem is often hot fermentation temperatures. At temperatures above 80° F (27° C), yeast can produce too much of the higher-weight fusel alcohols, which have lower taste thresholds than ethanol. These alcohols taste harsh to the tongue, not as bad as cheap tequila, but bad, nonetheless.

To reduce the amount of fusel alcohols produced during fermentation:
- Don't overdo the aeration and yeast nutrient supplements.
- Pitch when the wort is cold.
- Ferment at a cooler temperature.
- Don't add sucrose or other refined sugars to the wort.

Astringent

Astringency differs from bitterness by having a puckering quality, like sucking on a tea bag. It is dry, kind of powdery, and is most often due to excess tannins from steeping grains too long or when the mash pH exceeds 6 due to alkaline water. It can also be a problem for hoppy pale beers brewed with alkaline (carbonate)

water. Oversparging the mash or using water that is too hot will also cause tannin extraction. Tannins can also come from overhopping with low-alpha hops. Bacterial infections can also cause astringency, i.e., vinegar tones from *Acetobacter*.

Cidery

Cidery flavors can have several causes but are often the result of adding too much cane or corn sugar to a recipe. One component of a cidery flavor is acetaldehyde, which has a green-apple character. It is a common fermentation by-product, and different yeasts will produce different levels of it, depending on the recipe and temperature. The production of excess acetaldehyde in a high refined sugar wort can also cause acetic acid to be produced by the yeast, and this is another component to overall cidery character.

If it is caused by *Acetobacter*, then there is nothing to be done about it. Keep the fruit flies away from the fermenter next time.

Diacetyl

Diacetyl is most often described as a butter or butterscotch flavor. Smell an unpopped bag of butter-flavored microwave popcorn for a good example. It is desired to a degree in many ales, but in some styles (mainly lagers) and circumstances, it is unwanted and may even take on rancid overtones. Diacetyl can be the result of the normal fermentation process or the result of a bacterial infection (i.e., *Pediococcus*). Diacetyl is produced early in the fermentation cycle by the yeast and is gradually reassimilated toward the end of the fermentation. A brew that experiences a long lag time due to weak yeast or insufficient aeration will produce a lot of diacetyl before the main fermentation begins. In this case, there is often more diacetyl than the yeast can consume at the end of fermentation, and it can dominate the flavor of the beer.

To reduce diacetyl in your beers:
- Use a higher pitching rate to limit the amount of total cell growth.
- Don't pitch warmer than fermentation temperature.
- Don't overoxygenate, and minimize oxygen exposure after fermentation starts.

To clean up diacetyl in the fermenter:
- Increase the temperature (i.e., use a diacetyl rest).
- Keep the beer on the yeast (i.e., don't rack too soon).
- Rouse the yeast to keep it suspended.
- Use a less flocculant yeast strain.

Dimethyl Sulfides (DMS)/Cooked Vegetable Flavors

Like diacetyl in ales, DMS is common in many light lagers and is considered to be part of the character. It can have a creamed corn aroma and flavor in pale beers, or a more tomatolike character in dark beers. DMS is produced in the wort during the boil by the reduction of another compound, S-methyl-methionine (SMM), which is itself produced during malting. When a malt is roasted or toasted, the SMM is reduced beforehand and does not manifest as DMS in the wort, which explains why it is more prevalent in pale lagers. In other styles, DMS is a common off-flavor that can be caused by poor brewing practices or bacterial infections.

DMS is continuously produced in the wort while it is hot and is usually removed by vaporization during the boil. If the wort is cooled slowly, these compounds will not be removed from the wort and will dissolve back in. Thus, it is important not to cover the brewpot completely during the boil or allow condensate to drip back into the pot from the lid. The wort should also be cooled quickly after the boil, either by immersing in an ice bath or using a wort chiller.

When caused by bacterial infection, DMS has a more rancid character, more liked cooked cabbage than corn. It is usually the result of poor sanitation. Repitching the yeast from an infected batch of beer will perpetuate the problem.

Estery/Fruity

Ales are supposed to be slightly fruity, and Belgian and German wheat beers are expected to have minor banana flavor components (isoamyl acetate), but sometimes a beer comes along that could flag down a troop of monkeys. Ethyl acetate (nail polish remover) is also common. Esters are produced by yeast, and different yeast strains will produce different amounts and types. Most esters in beer  are produced from ethanol, and only a small percentage are made from fusel alcohols. In general, higher fermentation temperatures produce more esters.

To reduce ester formation in your beer:
- Use sufficient aeration.
- Ferment cooler.
- Use a lower-gravity wort (below 1.055).
- Use a less-attenuable wort.
- Don't add sucrose or other refined sugars to the wort.

Grassy

Flavors reminiscent of chlorophyll and fresh-cut grass occasionally occur and are most often linked to poorly stored ingredients. Poorly stored malt can pick up moisture and develop musty smells. Aldehydes can form in old malt and can contribute green grass flavors. Hops are another source of these green flavors. If the  hops are poorly stored or not properly dried prior to storage, the chlorophyll compounds will become evident in the beer.

Husky/Grainy

These flavors are akin to the astringent flavors produced from the grain husks. These flavors are more evident in all-grain beers due to poor grain crushing or sparging practices. If the grain husks are shredded during crushing by the use of a Corona grain mill, for instance, these husk flavors are more likely to be extracted during the sparge. Follow the same procedures recommended to prevent astringency to correct the problem.

Grainy flavors can also be contributed by highly toasted malts. If you are making your own toasted malts, allow them to age at least two weeks after crushing, so the harsher aromatic compounds can dissipate. Cold conditioning the beer for a month or two will often cause these harsh compounds to settle out with the yeast.

Medicinal

These flavors are often described as medicinal, Band-Aid-like, or spicy, like cloves. The causes are various phenols that are initially produced by the yeast. Chlorophenols result from the reaction of chlorine-based sanitizers (bleach) with phenol compounds and have very low taste thresholds. Rinsing with boiled water after sanitizing is the best way to prevent these flavors. Wild (gusher) yeasts can also produce these flavors.

Metallic

Metallic flavors are usually caused by unprotected metals dissolving into the wort but can also be caused by the hydrolysis of lipids in poorly stored malts. Iron can cause metallic flavors leaching into the wort during the boil. The small amount could be considered to be nutritional if it weren't for the bad taste. In larger than trace amounts, excess metals are injurious to yeast and may also cause haze problems. Nicks and cracks in ceramic-coated steel pots are a common cause, as are high iron levels in well water. Stainless steel pots will not contribute any metallic flavors.

Aluminum pots usually won't cause metallic flavors unless the brewing water is alkaline, with a pH level greater than 9. (Not very realistic.) Shiny new aluminum pots will sometimes turn black from boiling water due to chlorine and carbonates in the water. The protective (grayish) oxides of aluminum can be enhanced by heating the clean pot in a dry oven at 350° F for about six hours.

Moldy

Molds are quickly recognized by their smell and taste. Black bread molds and mildew can grow in both wort and beer. Contamination is likely if the wort or beer is exposed to musty or damp areas during fermentation. If the infection is caught early enough, it can often be removed by skimming or cleaning of the surface before it significantly contaminates the batch. Chances are, though, that the spores have contaminated the batch, and it could crop up again.

This may be a problem for beers fermented in plastic, as these aroma chemicals are very potent and can travel through polyethylene. Make sure it's dry underneath your fermenting bucket. Could also be a result of poorly stored malt.

Oxidized

Oxidation is probably the most common problem with beer, including commercial beers. If the wort is exposed to oxygen at temperatures above 80° F (27° C), the beer will eventually develop wet cardboard or sherrylike flavors, depending on which compounds were oxidized. The oxidation of long-chain fatty acids produces 2-trans-nonenal, which tastes like cardboard and smells like old paper. See the discussion of oxygen and wort in Chapter 6.

Soapy
Soapy flavors can be caused by not washing your glass very well, but they can also be produced by the fermentation conditions. If you leave the beer in the primary fermenter for a relatively long period of time after primary fermentation is over ("long" depends on the style and other fermentation factors), soapy flavors can result from the breakdown of fatty acids in the trub. Soap is, by definition, the salt of a fatty acid, so you are literally tasting soap.

Solventlike
This group of flavors is very similar to the alcohol and ester flavors but are harsher to the tongue. These flavors often result from a combination of high fermentation temperatures and oxidation. They can also be leached from cheap plastic brewing equipment or if PVC tubing is used as a lautering manifold material. The solvents in some plastics like PVC can be leached by high temperatures. Make sure your plastics are food grade!

Skunky
Skunky or cat-musk aromas in beer are caused by photochemical reactions of the isomerized hop compounds. The wavelengths of light that cause the skunky smell are the blue wavelengths and the ultraviolet. Brown glass bottles effectively screen out these wavelengths, but green bottles do not. Skunkiness will result if the beer is left in direct sunlight or stored under fluorescent lights, as in supermarkets. Beers that use pre-isomerized hop extract and/or very little flavoring hop additions will be fairly immune to damage from ultraviolet light.

Sweaty/Goaty
I often encounter this aroma and flavor at restaurants when I order a beer from the tap. It could be that they need to clean their beer lines of mold, or it could be *Lactobacillus* or *Pediococcus* infections.

Yeasty
The cause of this flavor is pretty easy to understand. If the beer is green, is too young, and the yeast has not had time to settle out, it will have a yeasty taste. Watch your pouring method, too; keep the yeast layer on the bottom of the bottle.

If the yeast is unhealthy and begins autolyzing, it will release compounds that initially may be described as yeasty, or smell like beef bouillon, or soapy, or like a jar of B vitamins later on.

SECTION 5
APPENDICES

This final section is the closet—a place I could put extensive details and how-to's.

Appendix A—Measuring Wort Gravity discusses the use of hydrometers and refractometers. Hydrometers are an almost indispensable tool for any brewer, but they need to be corrected for temperature, and this appendix contains a correction table. Refractometers are a fancy way to measure wort gravity but are very useful. I describe how to use them and convert between Brix, Plato, and specific gravity.

Appendix B—Beer Color discusses how malt and beer color are measured, the concept of the malt color unit (MCU), and how to estimate your beer's color from the malt extracts and grains in your recipe.

Appendix C—Beer Clarity explains the various causes of haze in beer, and how to use clarifiers and finings to achieve clearer beer and a longer shelf life.

Appendix D—Building Wort Chillers explains how to go about building one of these things for yourself. A wort chiller is one of the most useful things ever invented by mankind. Chillers can also be purchased at most homebrewing shops, if you don't want to make your own.

Appendix E—Lauter Tun for Batch Sparging presents several options for building a simple mash/lauter tun from an ice chest or picnic cooler. As usual, I am probably giving you more information than you need, but my intention is to help you build it right the first time.

Appendix F—Lauter Tun Design for Continuous Sparging. This is where I take a simple subject and make it complicated. Continuous sparging efficiency depends on uniform flow. This appendix attempts to take the mystery out of uniform flow to help you design the most efficient home lautering tun possible.

Appendix G—Brewing Metallurgy is everything you never wanted to know about metals cleaning, corrosion, and joining. I am a metallurgist—I like this stuff. As my wife says, "Don't get him started!" But a lot of homebrewers build their own equipment, and this information can come in handy.

Appendix H—Conversion Factors contains tables for various metric conversions as well as brewer's units like hot water extract and °Plato.

USING HYDROMETERS AND REFRACTOMETERS

Using Hydrometers

A hydrometer measures the difference in gravity (density) by flotation. A hydrometer is used to gauge the progress of fermentation by measuring one aspect of it—attenuation. Attenuation is the degree of conversion of sugar to ethanol by the yeast. Water has a specific gravity of 1.000, and a typical beer wort has an original gravity (OG) of 1.035 to 1.060. Beers typically have a final gravity between 1.015 and 1.005. Champagnes and meads can have gravities of less than 1.000, because they contain a large percentage of ethyl alcohol, which has a specific gravity of less than 1.

Hydrometer readings are always quoted to the standard temperature 59° F (15° C). Liquid density is dependent on temperature, so hydrometer readings are adjusted to state the gravity of the liquid at this standard temperature. See Figure 4 in Chapter 1.

A hydrometer is a useful tool in the hands of a brewer who knows what wort gravity is and why he wants to measure it. Beer recipes often list the original and/or final gravities (OG and FG) to better describe the beer to the reader. For an average beer yeast, a rule of thumb is that the FG should be about one-fourth to one-fifth of the OG. For example, a typical beer OG of 1.040 should finish about 1.010 (or lower). A couple of points either way is not unusual.

It needs to be emphasized that the stated FG of a recipe is not the goal. The goal is to make a good-tasting beer. The hydrometer should be regarded as only one tool available to the brewer as a means to gauge the fermentation progress. The brewer should only be concerned about a high hydrometer reading when primary fermentation has apparently ended and the reading is about one-half of the OG, instead of the nominal one-fourth. Proper yeast preparation should prevent this problem.

Beginning brewers often make the mistake of checking the gravity too frequently. Every time you open the fermenter, you are risking infection from airborne microbes. Check the gravity when you are ready to pitch the yeast, then leave it alone until the bubbling in the airlock stops. Checking the gravity in between will not change anything, except to possibly contaminate it. Also, always remove a sample of the wort to test it. Don't stick the hydrometer into the whole batch. Use a sanitized siphon or wine thief (or turkey baster) to withdraw a sample of the wort to a hydrometer jar (tall, narrow jar), and float the hydrometer in that. There is less chance of infection, and you can drink the sample to see how the fermentation is coming along. It should taste like beer, even though it may taste a bit yeasty.

The hydrometer temperature correction table is shown below. Hydrometer readings are standardized to 15° C (59° F). When discussing specific gravities of worts and beers with other brewers, always quote the standardized value. Measure the specific gravity of your wort, take the temperature, and add the correction value (delta G) given in the table. The correction number is added to the specific gravity number, 1.0XX.

Example: If the wort temperature is 108° F, and the measured gravity of the sample is 1.042, the delta G value would be between 0.0077 and 0.0081. Rounding it off to the third decimal place gives us 0.008, which is added to 1.042, yielding 1.050 as the standardized reading.

TABLE 30
Hydrometer Temperature Corrections

° C	delta G	° F	° C	delta G	° F
0	0.0007	32.0	25	0.0021	77.0
1	0.0008	33.8	26	0.0023	78.8
2	0.0008	35.6	27	0.0026	80.6
3	0.0009	37.4	28	0.0029	82.4
4	0.0009	39.2	29	0.0032	84.2
5	0.0009	41.0	30	0.0035	86.0
6	0.0008	42.8	31	0.0038	87.8
7	0.0008	44.6	32	0.0041	89.6
8	0.0007	46.4	33	0.0044	91.4
9	0.0007	48.2	34	0.0047	93.2
10	0.0006	50.0	35	0.0051	95.0
11	0.0005	51.8	36	0.0054	96.8
12	0.0004	53.6	37	0.0058	98.6
13	0.0003	55.4	38	0.0061	100.4
14	0.0001	57.2	39	0.0065	102.2
15	0	59.0	40	0.0069	104.0
16	0.0002	60.8	41	0.0073	105.8

17	0.0003	62.6	42	0.0077	107.6
18	0.0005	64.4	43	0.0081	109.4
19	0.0007	66.2	44	0.0085	111.2
20	0.0009	68.0	45	0.0089	113.0
21	0.0011	69.8	46	0.0093	114.8
22	0.0013	71.6	47	0.0097	116.6
23	0.0016	73.4	48	0.0102	118.4
24	0.0018	75.2	49	0.0106	120.2

Using Refractometers

The benefit of using a handheld refractometer to measure wort gravity is that it only takes a couple of drops, and you can get the reading in seconds. They are very handy to have at the kettle to check your extraction when you are all-grain brewing. The only problem is that they do not measure wort specific gravity.

Refractometers measure the refraction of light passing through a solution. The more dense a solution is, the more slowly the light will travel through it, and the more the light will be refracted. Handheld refractometers are calibrated with respect to the density of sucrose solutions at 20° C (68° F). The scale in the viewing window of a refractometer is scaled in degrees Brix, which is equivalent to degrees Plato. The problem is that the wort is not made of sucrose; it is made up of several different sugars and has a slightly different refraction index than a pure sucrose solution.

There are industry standard equations that allow you to convert between the various scales with a reasonable degree of accuracy. One equation to adjust the gravity between °Brix and the °Plato of your wort is:

Wort (°Plato) = Refractometer (°Brix) ÷ 1.04

So a wort's refractometer reading of 12 °Brix is more closely 11.5 °Plato.

OK, Plato, Plato, what is °Plato? Well °Plato (like Brix) is defined as the weight percent of sucrose in solution. So, a wort of 10 °Plato is 10% by weight sucrose. The specific gravity of that sucrose solution is approximately four times the °Plato, or 1.040. But this approximation becomes less accurate after you exceed 13 °Plato. Fortunately, the American Society of Brewing Chemists has published a conversion table, and I have reproduced some of that table on the next page.

TABLE 31
Specific Gravity—°Plato Conversion

Here is a quick reference chart for converting Specific Gravity to °Plato. Balling, Plato, and Brix are basically equivalent and are the preferred gravity unit of large-scale brewers.

Specific Gravity	°Plato	Specific Gravity	°Plato
1.008	2.0	1.048	11.9
1.010	2.6	1.050	12.4
1.012	3.1	1.052	12.9
1.014	3.6	1.054	13.3
1.016	4.1	1.056	13.8
1.018	4.6	1.058	14.3
1.020	5.1	1.060	14.7
1.022	5.6	1.062	15.2
1.024	6.1	1.064	15.7
1.026	6.6	1.066	16.1
1.028	7.1	1.068	16.6
1.030	7.5	1.070	17.0
1.032	8.0	1.072	17.5
1.034	8.5	1.074	18.0
1.036	9.0	1.076	18.4
1.038	9.5	1.078	18.9
1.040	10.0	1.080	19.3
1.042	10.5	1.082	19.8
1.044	11.0	1.084	20.2
1.046	11.4		

Reference: ASBC Laboratory Methods for Craft Brewers, American Society of Brewing Chemists, St. Paul, Minn., 1997.

BEER COLOR

Ah, the many wonderful colors of beer! The pale straw of Belgian-style wit, the rich gold of Pilsener, the burnished copper hue of London ale, the rich mahogany of brown ale, the ruby-black highlights of porter, and the predawn darkness of stout—the very sight of these colors whets our imagination for the characteristic flavors of the styles. Beer color comes from the malts used—different types of malt have different characteristic colors, and these colors are expressed in the wort that is made from them. Malt extracts are just concentrated worts, and the color of the extract will depend on the malts that were mashed to make it. In addition, there are other factors in the brewing process that can also influence the color, such as Maillard reactions during the boil.

When beers are judged in a competition, beer color is often the first check a judge makes as he determines how well a beer has been brewed to style. About an inch of beer will be poured into one of the clear plastic judging cups, the beer will be swirled to dispel any bubbles on the sides, and the beer will be held to the light to gauge the color versus a color guide. Dark beers are often examined with a flashlight held behind to determine the clarity and its effect on the color. We can reasonably predict the final color of our beer by calculating the color contribution of each malt, malt extract, and adjunct that we use in our recipe. All malts are analyzed for color during production, and in the case of specialty malts, are produced to a specific color range. We can use the color ratings provided by the manufacturers to determine whether our recipe will meet the range for the intended style. Typical color ratings for several malts, malt extracts, and adjuncts are given in Tables 32 and 33.

TABLE 32
Specified Colors for Unhopped Malt Extracts*

Extract Type	Cooper's	Munton & Fison**
Wheat LME	4.5 °L	<5 °L
Extra light LME	—	2-3.5 °L
Light DME	3 °L	3.5-6 °L
Light LME	3.5 °L	4-6 °L
Amber DME	—	12-22 °L
Amber LME	16 °L	8-10 °L
Dark DME	—	22-35 °L
Dark LME	66 °L	25-30 °L

* Information taken from the manufacturers' websites

** Converted from EBC

TABLE 33
Some Typical Color Ratings of Common Malts and Adjuncts

Fermentable	°SRM Rating
2-row lager malt	1.5 °L
Wheat malt	2 °L
Pale ale malt	3 °L
Vienna malt	4 °L
Munich malt	10 °L
Biscuit malt	25 °L
Crystal 40	40 °L
Crystal 60	60 °L
Crystal 120	120 °L
Chocolate malt	350 °L
Black patent malt	500 °L
Flaked barley	1.5 °L
Flaked corn	1 °L
Flaked rice	1 °L
Flaked rye	2 °L
Flaked wheat	2 °L
Torrified wheat	1.5 °L
Maltodextrin powder	0 °L
Dextrose, glucose, sucrose, fructose	0 °L

The Basis of Color Rating

Historically, the color of beer and brewing malts has been rated as degrees Lovibond (°L). This system was created in 1883 by J.W. Lovibond and consisted of glass slides of various shades that could be combined to produce a range of colors. A standard sample of beer or wort would be compared to combinations of these slides to determine the rating. Malt color is determined by conducting a Congress mash (a standardized method) of the malt and measuring the wort color. This system was later modified to the Series 52 Lovibond scale, which consisted of individual slides or solutions for specific Lovibond ratings, but the system still suffered from inconsistency due to fading, mislabeling, and human error.

In 1950 the American Society of Brewing Chemists (ASBC) adopted the utilization of optical spectrophotometers to measure the absorptance of a specific wavelength of light (430 nanometers) through a standard-sized sample. A darker wort/beer absorbs more light and yields a higher measurement. This method allowed for consistent measurement of samples, and the Standard Reference Method (°SRM) for determining color was born. The SRM method was originally set up to approximate the Series 52 Lovibond scale, and the two scales can be considered to be nearly identical for most of their range. However, the resolution of a spectrophotometer diminishes greatly as the worts darken and very little light can penetrate the sample to reach the detector. To accommodate dark worts, the sample is diluted, and the measurement is scaled to assign an undiluted value. Unfortunately, dilutions have been shown to be nonlinear for beers made from highly colored malts. [1]

When provided with consistent, precise references, the human eye can distinguish very narrow differences in color, because it can see a variety of wavelengths of visible light as opposed to the information conveyed by a single wavelength. There is less variation in a single wavelength measurement, but there is also a corresponding loss in range. For this reason, the Series 52 Lovibond scale is still in use today, in the form of precision visual comparators, and is most often used to determine the rating of dark/roasted malts. The use of the comparator is most prevalent in the malting industry, and thus the color of malts is discussed as °L, while beer color is discussed as °SRM, though the basis (absorptance at 430 nm) is the same.

Prior to 1990, the European Brewing Congress (EBC) used a different wavelength for measuring absorptance, and conversion between the two methods was an approximation. Today, the EBC scale uses the same wavelength for measurement but uses a smaller sample glass. The °EBC rating for a malt or beer is not equivalent to the °L rating. If you are converting from EBC units, it is probably a good idea to check with the manufacturer to see which EBC method/wavelength it is using. Some malt manufacturers have reportedly not upgraded to the new standard. The current EBC scale for rating beer color is about twice the °SRM rating. The actual conversion factor between the two methods is 1.97, but to argue whether an Irish stout with an EBC rating of 90 is 45 or 45.6 °SRM is pointless.

Color swatches to illustrate seven levels of beer color are shown on the inside of the front cover. These color swatches for °SRM colors are taken from Promash Brewing Software[1], version 1.8, and are representative of beer that has been poured to a depth of about 1.5 inches in a typical 6-ounce clear plastic judging cup, swirled to de-gas, and held up to good lighting against a white background.

The main constituents of color in malts are the melanoidins produced by Maillard or browning reactions. Browning reactions between sugars and amino acids occur whenever food is heated—think toast. Different heating methods with different sugars and amino acids will produce different colors—from amber, to red, to brown, to black. Thus, the wide spectrum of beer color is due to the variety of germination and kilning procedures used in the production of malts. The final color of a beer can be estimated from a recipe by adding up the melanoidin contributions in the form of malt color units (MCU). An MCU is like an alpha acid unit (AAU) for hop bitterness (IBU) calculations. The color rating of the malt (°L) is multiplied by the weight (pounds) used in the recipe, just like the weight of a hop addition is multiplied by its alpha acid rating. To estimate the °SRM color of a beer, the MCUs are divided by the recipe volume and multiplied by a constant that is like the percent utilization in the IBU calculation. For light-colored beers (yellow/gold/light amber) the relationship between °SRM and MCU is approximately 1 to 1.

As a brief example, if 8 pounds of two-row lager malt (2 °L) and 2 pounds of Vienna malt (4 °L) are used for a 5-gallon batch, the estimated color would be (8 x 2 + 2 x 4) / 5 = 4.8, or about 5 °SRM. Unfortunately, this simple model does not work when the MCUs exceed 15. (See Figure 167.) Linear models have been proposed by Mosher and Daniels, but data for the full spectrum of beer color may be better fit by an exponential curve, such as the one described by Morey's equation.

Proposed Models for Beer Color as a Function of MCU

°SRM = MCU	(traditional)
°SRM = 0.3 x MCU + 4.7	Mosher[2]
°SRM = 0.2 x MCU + 8.4	Daniels[3]
°SRM = 1.49 x MCU^0.69	Morey[4]

The fault of the linear models proposed by Mosher and Daniels is that there is a lower limit for beer color at 4.7 and 8.4 °SRM, respectively. Obviously, there are beer styles such as Belgian-style wit, Pilsener, and American light lager that are lighter than these limits. An exponential equation fits the data better, because the function is nearly equal to MCU at low MCU values, but as the MCUs go to higher values (corresponding to brown ales, porters, and stout), the actual color diverges from the MCU = °SRM line and increases at a lower rate, as depicted by the linear models of Mosher and Daniels. A beer with an MCU of 200 compared to one with a rating of 100 is still just "very dark," instead of twice as dark, as the °SRM = MCU model would have you believe. Even expert beer judges cannot discern a difference between color values greater than 40 °SRM.

Another aspect of beer color that needs to be mentioned is "hue." Different beers with the same °SRM rating can actually be different hues, because the measurement is based on the absorptance of a single wavelength of (blue-violet) light. And actually, it isn't the absorptance of the light that's measured, but how much of the light that gets through the sample to the detector. The human eye sees all the visible wavelengths and will perceive other colors transmitted/reflected from the sample that the spectrophotometer detector will not. This drawback in the current ASBC method was noted in a recent brewing study at the University of California at Davis.[5] In the study, four beers—two lagers, a pale ale, and a stout—were diluted to the same rating (3.5 to 3.6 °SRM). A group of 31 people were presented with 10 pairings of these diluted beers and asked to determine if they were the same or were different. The results clearly showed that the panelists could correctly determine a difference in color between different beers, except in the case of the two lagers, which were perceived as being the same. The original color of the undiluted all-malt lager was 8 °SRM, and the undiluted color of the other lager, containing cereal adjuncts, was 4 °SRM. The pale ale was 25 °SRM. There was virtually no difference (less than 1 °) between the ASBC method and a Series 52 Lovibond Comparator (Tintometer Ltd., Salisbury, U.K.) in the undiluted color results for each of the three paler beers. The stout was the exception, with the comparator measuring 115 °L and the spectrophotometer measuring 86 °SRM. This difference illustrates the drawback mentioned earlier of the ASBC method for determining the color of very dark malts and beers.

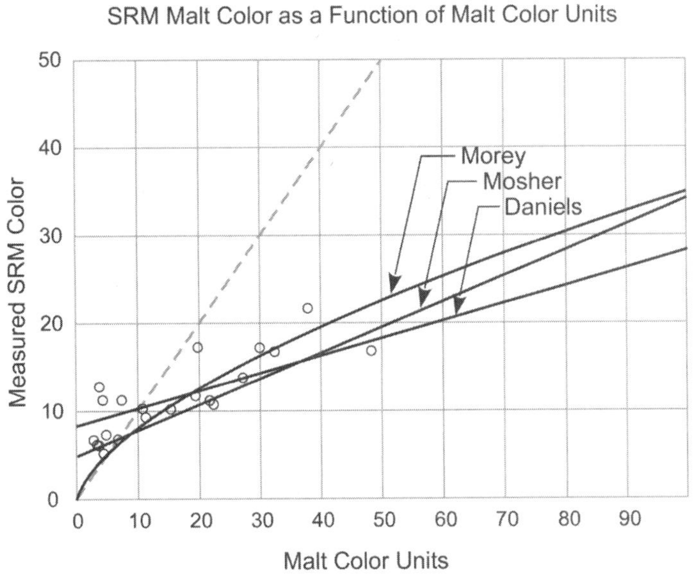

SRM Malt Color as a Function of Malt Color Units

Figure 167 A comparison of four models for final beer color. The dashed line is a reference for the case if °SRM = MCU. Lines for each of the suggested color models are shown in comparison to actual data. Analysis of commercial as well as homebrewed beer has shown that the measured color tapers off, even as the malt color contributions increase dramatically. (The data shown here is from the article "Beer Color Demystified—Part III: Controlling and Predicting Beer Color," by Ray Daniels, *Brewing Techniques*, Vol. 3, No. 6, 1995.)

Other Color Factors

The color of the malts is not the only factor that determines a beer's final color. Other variables, such as boil time, heating method, hopping rate, yeast flocculation, clarity, age/oxidation, etc., will affect the absorptance of light and the perceived color. Long boil times over high heat will promote the Maillard reactions of sugars and proteins that darken the wort. The oxidation of polyphenols (tannins) from grain husks or hop cones also contributes to wort darkening. Wort that has been over-sparged or heavily hopped (like that for an India pale ale) will have a greater propensity for darkening as it ages. Wort will also lighten during the boil and subsequently during chilling, as proteins combine with polyphenols to form the hot and cold break. Other color-carrying compounds will settle out during fermentation, as the yeast flocculates. And of course, the overall clarity of a beer will affect the degree to which light is absorbed and its perceived color—cloudy beers appear darker and will measure darker if the beer is not clarified by centrifuge or filtering.

These other factors that affect beer color are diverse and significant enough that the actual color could be plus or minus 20% of the calculated value. That being the case, a simplified exponential equation of °SRM = 1.5 x MCU^0.7 is just as valid as the derived values of Morey's equation. My purpose in stating this isn't to propose a new model, but instead to point out the inherent limits of any model for beer color. None of the three models is necessarily any more correct than another, although Morey's may be more forgiving for very light beer styles. Hopefully this caveat will prevent the more technical readers of this appendix from trying to calculate color to the fourth decimal place.

Estimating Beer Color

To plan the color of your recipe, calculate the MCU values for each of your malts and grains, and then apply the result to one of the color models. To do this, multiply the malt's Lovibond rating by the number of pounds that you are going to use, and divide by the recipe volume. See above for the color model equations. Let's look at some examples.

BJCP Style Guidelines for California Common Beer

OG =	1.044-1.055
FG =	1.011-1.014
IBU =	35-45
Color =	8-14 °SRM

No. 4 Shay Steam—California Common Beer

Recipe OG = 1.048

Recipe Malts	Color Rating	MCUs	MCU		Mosher	Daniels	Morey
6 lbs. light LME	5°L	6	12		8	11	8
0.75 lb. crystal 40°L malt	40°L	6					
0.25 lb. maltodextrin powder	0°L	0					

Comment: In this example, the recipe malts yield an °SRM color rating within the BJCP guidelines for all three color models. The brewer can be confident that the entry would not be marked down for color.

BJCP Style Guidelines for Brown Porter

OG =	1.040-1.050
FG =	1.008-1.014
IBU =	20-30
Color =	20-35 °SRM

BJCP Style Guidelines for Robust Porter

OG =	1.050-1.065
FG =	1.012-1.016
IBU =	25-45
Color =	30+ °SRM

Port O'Palmer—Porter

Recipe OG = 1.048

Recipe Malts	Color Rating	MCUs	MCU		Mosher	Daniels	Morey
6 lbs. light LME	5 °L	6	72		26	23	28
0.5 lb. crystal 60°L malt	60 °L	6					
0.5 lb. chocolate malt	350 °L	35					
0.25 lb. black patent malt	500 °L	25					

Comment: In this example, the recipe malts yield an °SRM color rating and an OG within the BJCP guidelines for Brown Porter, although the use of black patent malt adds some roast character that is more appropriate to the Robust Porter category. In this case, the brewer can use color modeling to adjust the recipe to firmly place it in the Robust Porter category, if he or she wishes. Both the OG and the color would need to be increased by a few points. There are lots of options to do this; here are three:

1. Add 1.5 pounds of dark DME. This will add about 12 points to both the OG and the MCU total, giving color estimates of 30, 25, and 32, respectively. The drawback to this approach is that the OG has increased significantly to 1.060 without changing the color very much.

2. Increase the half-pound of chocolate malt to 1 pound. This will change the MCU total to 107, without changing the OG much, giving estimates of 37, 30, and 37, respectively. Still need to increase the gravity, though. . . .

3. Increase the light LME from 6 to 7 pounds, and increase the chocolate malt to 1 pound. The MCU total only changes by 1 point from the previous option, keeping the total color almost exactly the same. However, the extra pound of extract increases the OG to 1.055, which is respectable for a Robust Porter.

Summary

Hopefully this appendix has given you a good understanding of how beer color is measured and how it can be estimated to help your brewing. It is also important to remember that final beer color is driven by many factors from all parts of the brewing process, and that these are not factored into the color models. You will need to examine your equipment, your processes, and your beers to determine which model works best for you, just as in the case of hops and IBU calculations. These tools are not the end, they are the means to an end, and the proof is in the beer. Good Brewing.

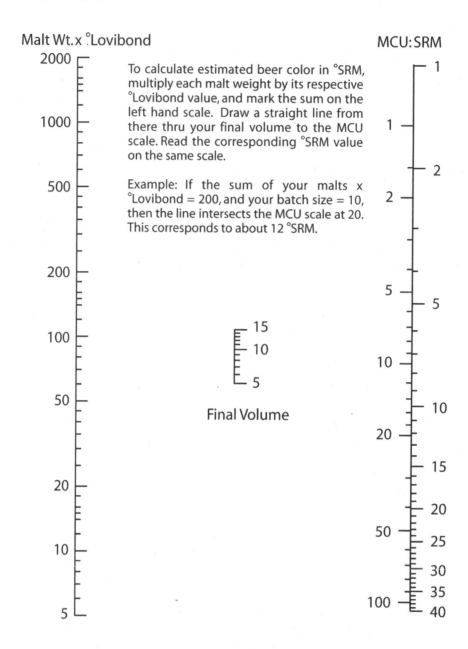

Malt Wt. x °Lovibond

To calculate estimated beer color in °SRM, multiply each malt weight by its respective °Lovibond value, and mark the sum on the left hand scale. Draw a straight line from there thru your final volume to the MCU scale. Read the corresponding °SRM value on the same scale.

Example: If the sum of your malts x °Lovibond = 200, and your batch size = 10, then the line intersects the MCU scale at 20. This corresponds to about 12 °SRM.

Final Volume

MCU:SRM

Figure 168 Nomograph for calculating °SRM from malt color units (MCUs). To use, multiply weight of the grain (pounds) by its color rating in °Lovibond, and mark the number on the L*lbs. scale. Draw a line from there through the batch size number (e.g., 5 gallons) to the MCU scale. This is the MCU contribution for that particular grain. You will need to add up the MCUs for all the malts in the grain bill and mark that total on the MCU scale to read off the calculated °SRM. This nomograph utilizes the Morey color model.

Author's Note: This work was originally published as a feature article in *Brew Your Own*, Volume 9, No. 3, 2003.

[1] Donovan, J., Promash Brewing Software, v. 1.8, Sausalito Brewing Co., Santa Barbara, Calif., 2003.

[2] Mosher, R., *The Brewer's Companion*, p. 34, Alephenalia Publications, Seattle, Wash., 1994.

[3] Daniels, R., *Designing Great Beers*, p. 57-62, Brewer's Publications, Boulder, Colo., 1996.

[4] Morey, D., "Approximating °SRM Beer Color", hbd.org/babble/Color.htm.

[5] Smythe, J.E., Bamforth, C.W., "Shortcomings in Standard Instrumental Methods for Assessing Beer Color," *J. Am. Brew. Chem.*, 58 (4): 165-166, 2000.

BEER CLARITY

What Is Beer Haze, and Why Do We Care?

Last month you planned and brewed what should be your best beer yet, and today is the first pour. Your recipe used: a new brand of malt extract/new specialty grain/wheat, and you added: dry hops/fruit/spices to the secondary fermenter to give it that extra flavor you were looking for. The guys at the homebrew shop had tried pulling your leg when you told them the recipe, suggesting that you add seaweed to the boil, and put fish guts and Jell-O™ in the fermenter. What a bunch of kidders, you didn't believe a word of it!

And now you pour your best beer and, and . . . it's cloudy!? What happened?!

There are several possible causes of cloudy or hazy beer. Maybe it's simply that your yeast has not flocculated (settled out) yet. You could try cold conditioning the beer for a few days to see if that helps. You might have a wild yeast or bacterial infection, or it could be haze due to unconverted/insoluble starch, or fruit pectin, or it could be a polyphenol/protein haze. How can you tell? What can you do about it? There is not much you can do about infections except dump the batch. Hazes due to starches represent a food source to many wild yeasts and bacteria and will cause flatulence as the starches are broken down in your gut. Fruit pectin haze can be combated by the use of pectic enzyme or by changing how you prepare your fruit for the fermenter. Finally, proteins and polyphenols from the malt and hops can combine to form both temporary and permanent hazes.

Everyone is used to seeing crystal-clear American light lager beer and assumes that this is how clear every beer should be. Wrong! In fact, the low-protein, high-adjunct beers of the United States are some of the clearest beers in the world, if not *the* clearest. The ingredients have a lot to do with it, but the other half of the equation is the filtering capability that large commercial breweries have

available to them. Filtering systems for homebrewers are available but require that you keg the beer and force-carbonate, because the yeast is filtered out, too.

But other than aesthetics, why should you care about cloudy beer? You can't taste haze . . . or can you? Haze can often be an indicator of another problem, as in the case of bacterial infections. Bacteria often cause clouding of the beer and characteristic off-flavors. For instance, *Pediococcus damnosus* is a commonly feared brewery infection that generates high amounts of diacetyl. *Lactobacillus* bacteria can produce a variety of flavors—some of which are pleasant, as in lambic beers—in addition to the tartness of lactic acid. Other lacto strains will produce excessive amounts of diacetyl like the *Pediococcus* bacteria. A third type of haze-causing bacteria are coliforms, and these bacteria will often produce vegetal off-flavors, reminiscent of parsnips and old celery. These types of hazes will most likely develop in the bottle after fermentation, and the sudden appearance of haze can be an indicator that something has gone wrong.

But most haze in an otherwise good beer is caused by a combination of protein and polyphenols. Millions of dollars are spent annually researching and combating this type of haze. Why? Because the polyphenols that contribute to haze are part of a chemical equilibrium that contributes to oxidative staling reactions. You may be wondering just what a polyphenol is. You may have heard of them in terms of being an off-flavor in beer—sometimes having spicy, plastic, or medicinal flavors. No, actually those are phenols (hydroxyl group attached to an aromatic hydrocarbon) that have characteristic off-flavors. Polyphenols are polymers of phenol compounds. You may have heard that polyphenols are tannins. Actually it's the other way around—tannins are a large type of polyphenol. And you have probably heard that oversparging and/or having the wrong mash pH will leach tannins into your wort. This is indeed true; tannins and other polyphenols can be extracted from the malt husks and from the papery hop cones. There will always be some level of polyphenols in the beer, but it's like complaining about having sand in the desert. Unless there is a sandstorm, you just accept it and work around it. If you think of phenols as being like Lego blocks, you will get an idea of the size range, and how small polyphenols can link up to form large polyphenols and tannins. The most common manifestation of protein-polyphenol haze is "chill haze," which is formed by small polyphenols cross-linking with protein. These complexes are insoluble when the beer is chilled but don't have enough mass to settle out effectively. These chill haze complexes dissolve back into solution when the beer is warmed to room temperature.

Larger polyphenols form larger protein complexes and can settle out as hot and cold break, while the smaller polyphenols are carried over into the final beer. As mentioned earlier, these small polyphenols can grow by polymerization, especially in the presence of oxygen. If a beer with chill haze was poorly handled during bottling, the oxygen can cause the chill haze to become permanent haze.

It was interesting to note, while searching the abstracts in the professional brewing journals, that haze seems to have become a bigger problem in the past ten years. While this increase could simply be attributed to growth in the craftbrewing industry and a tighter focus on quality, a better explanation might be that there is also more awareness and control of oxidation in the wort production process. A reduction in wort oxidation will result in less polymerization of the smaller polyphenols, such that fewer polyphenols and tannins are precipitated in the break material during boiling and cooling. Thus, more polyphenols survive into the packaged beer, where they contribute to chill haze. In other words, a beer produced thirty years ago with little regard to hot-side aeration may have been more prone to staling and had a shorter shelf life, but it was probably clearer than comparable beers today.

Fixing Haze in the Recipe

To reduce the haze in your brewing, you can try to reduce the protein levels, reduce the polyphenols, or a bit of both. You can make the reductions by tweaking the recipe or by using clarifiers and finings. Each option has its pros and cons. To reduce proteins and/or polyphenol in the recipe, you can change from an all-malt recipe to one that uses a percentage of low-protein adjunct like corn, rice, or refined sugar, as exemplified by American light lager, Belgian-style tripel, and Belgian-style strong ale. Using wheat or wheat extract in a recipe to reduce polyphenols (wheat doesn't have a husk) can be a double-edged sword. At low levels, 5 to 12% of fermentables, the high protein levels in wheat can cause extensive haze, but as the percentage of wheat increases to 40%, the total polyphenol levels are substantially decreased, and the beer is very clear.

Hops are another source of polyphenols in a recipe. A lot of brewers swear by the exclusive use of low-alpha aroma hops for bittering, justly claiming a more refined hop character in the beer. The downside to this is the greater proportion (up to four times) of hop cone material in the wort and the large amount of polyphenols that will be extracted from it during the boil. I brew an American wheat extract beer that tends to be hazy due to the wheat gluten. The last time I brewed it, I switched from using Nugget (12% alpha acids) as my bittering hop to using all Liberty (3.5% alpha acids). That batch had a superb hop character that was as rich as royalty, and a creamy head that needed a spoon to clean the glass, but it was hazier than previous batches. A study by McMurrough, et al.[1], showed that 70% of malt polyphenols can survive the hot and cold break, while only 20% of hop polyphenols do. The message here for reducing the polyphenols and proteins that cause haze is to achieve a good hot break, perhaps aided by Irish moss, and use a wort chiller to get a good cold break.

If you are an all-grain brewer, your malts and the way you mash and sparge can affect your polyphenol levels, too. The Crisp Malting Group has developed a special barley strain and a resulting pale ale malt called Clarity that has extremely low polyphenol levels. Greg Beron of Culver City Brewing Supply in Los Angeles brewed a blonde ale using nine pounds of the malt plus some specialty grains without using other clarifiers, and the beer came out brilliantly clear. The local members of the Pacific Gravity brewing club gave the batch high marks. Your sparging method can also affect the total polyphenol levels. While the first runnings have been shown to generate the highest concentration of the small polyphenols, it is also known that the last runnings of a continuous sparge contain the highest proportion of tannin-type polyphenols extracted from the husks. This is due to the rise of the mash pH, as the buffering power of the malt acids is rinsed away from the grain bed. By using a batch sparge—where the final runnings typically don't fall below 1.020, or a no-sparge technique—where there is no rinsing to change the mash pH, you can prevent excessive tannin extraction into your wort.

Fixing Haze With Clarifiers and Finings

Now we come to the seaweed, fish guts, and Jell-O. You can add clarifiers to your wort and beer that will chemically and electrostatically pull haze formers out of solution and allow them to settle to the bottom. Irish moss and isinglass are the most common clarifiers used by homebrewers.

Irish Moss

Irish moss is a type of red seaweed called carrageen that preferentially attracts large proteins. Irish moss is the only clarifier that you add to your boil. All other clarifiers are added after fermentation. Irish moss is added during the last 20 minutes of the boil, where it greatly enhances the clumping

and precipitation of the hot break proteins that would otherwise contribute to haze and staling reactions. In the past, it was generally accepted that the proteins that caused haze were different from the proteins that were responsible for head retention. However, more recent studies[2] show that the proteins are similar enough that any attempt to eliminate haze-forming proteins via enzymes or non-specific protein-absorbing additives like bentonite will also affect the head retention and body of the beer. What this means to you is that any suggestions you may receive about adding a protein rest to your mash schedule or enzyme clarifiers to your wort are probably not good ideas. In addition, misuse of the right clarifiers can also be trouble. If too much Irish moss is used in the boil, the smaller proteins responsible for head retention can be affected and could reduce the free amino nitrogen (FAN) that the yeast need for nutrition. For this reason, it is not recommended for use with malt extract/adjunct worts. It is commonly available as dry flakes that are rehydrated before use. A typical dose is 1 teaspoon of flakes for 5 gallons of boil volume, or one-eighth gram per liter of boil. Another form of Irish moss is a product called Whirlfloc from Australia. It is a large tablet that you simply drop into your wort. Each tablet is good for a 5-gallon batch. People have reported excellent results using Whirlfloc.

Isinglass

The other popular fining agent is isinglass, commonly used in English cask ales. Composed almost entirely of the protein collagen, it is obtained by cleaning and drying the swim bladders of the sturgeon, cod, hake, and other fishes. It is an excellent clarifier for yeast. While it is able to bind and settle some of the larger proteins, it is not very effective for reducing chill haze. Isinglass is sold as dehydrated powder to be used at 30 to 60 milligrams/liter dosage, but it is most commonly available for homebrewers as a ready-to-use liquid. To use it, add it to the fermenter after fermentation has finished, or to the bottling bucket when you add your priming sugar solution, but do not attempt to heat it up, because it is easily denatured. Two ounces of liquid will treat 5 gallons of beer.

(Seriously, you have to wonder whose idea this was. "Igor, go get me some fish guts to add to the beer. What! Nothing fresh? Well, just scrape some of that dried stuff off the cutting board there. . . .")

Gelatin

Gelatin is a by-product of the collagen extraction process from cow hooves and pigskin. It is not as effective as collagen at settling the yeast mass, needing about three times as much to do the same job. But it is much less expensive. Gelatin is mixed and combined with the beer in the same way as isinglass, but at levels of 60 to 90 milligrams/liter.

PVPP/Polyclar

Polyvinylpolypyrrolidone, also known as povidone, is a micronized white powder, with a high surface-area-to-volume ratio that readily absorbs polyphenols, including tannins. The necessary contact time is only a few hours. Commercially, it is the most popular clarifier and stabilizer. About 6 to 10 grams per 20 liters/5 gallons is added after fermentation, prior to bottling. It is commonly combined with cooled boiled water to form a slurry that is gently added to the fermenter. The slurry needs to be mixed thoroughly with the beer and allowed to settle out (less than one day). Then the beer should be racked off the sediment and bottled or kegged. This material is not approved by the Food and Drug Administration for ingestion. Commercial breweries remove it by filtration.

Silica Gel

Silica hydrogels and xerogels are the other half of the one-two punch that commercial brewers use to control haze and improve shelf life. Where PVPP works to bind polyphenols, silica gel binds to proteins. In fact, it binds preferentially to haze-active proteins, because chemically it reacts with the same sites on the proteins that the polyphenols do. Silica gel is used at the same 6 to 10 grams per 20 liters/5 gallons rate and with the same procedure as Polyclar®. Silica gel and PVPP work synergistically to reduce haze more than each would alone. A combined product called Polyclar Plus is available to commercial breweries; I don't know if it has been packaged for a homebrewing scale. This material is not approved by the FDA for ingestion. Commercial breweries remove it by filtration. Allowing the material to settle and carefully racking away from the sediment should be sufficient.

Summary

Beer haze can have many possible causes, but a hazy beer that tastes good is probably suffering protein/polyphenol haze. Haze is usually treatable by the use of different ingredients, including malt and hop varieties, as well as by additives like clarifiers and finings. Hopefully, this discussion has helped you understand how these hazes form and how to best address the cause and solution in your own brewery.

TABLE 34
Clarifier Summary

Clarifier	Purpose	Amount	Comments
Irish moss	Protein coagulant	1 teaspoon per 5 gallons	A good clarifier for almost all worts, though not recommended for high-adjunct or extract-based worts
Whirlfloc	Protein coagulant	1 tablet per 5 gallons	A good clarifier for almost all worts, though not recommended for high-adjunct or extract-based worts
Isinglass	Yeast flocculent	15-60 mg/L or 2 fl. oz. per 5 gal.	Most effective for settling yeast. Will also settle some protein haze
Gelatin	Yeast flocculent	60-90 mg/liter	Only about one-half to one-third as effective as isinglass
Polyclar/PVPP	Polyphenol binder	6-10 grams/5 gallons	A non-aerated slurry should be mixed into the beer before bottling and allowed to settle out. Should take a day at most
Silica gel	Protein binder	6-10 grams/5 gallons	A non-aerated slurry should be mixed into the beer before bottling and allowed to settle out. Should take a day at most

Author's Note: This work was originally published as a feature article in *Zymurgy* 26, no. 5 (2003).

---

[1] McMurrough, L., et al., "Interaction of Proteases and Polyphenols in Worts, Beers, and Model Systems," *Journal of the Institute of Brewing* 91 (1985), 93-100.

[2] Ishivashi, Y., et al., "Development of a New Method for Determining Beer Foam and Haze Proteins by Using the Immunochemical Method," ELISA, *Journal of the American Society of Brewing Chemists* 54 (1996), 177-182. Bamforth, C.W., "Beer Haze," *Journal of the American Society of Brewing Chemists* 57:3 (1999), 81-90.

BUILDING WORT CHILLERS

Wort chillers are copper heat exchangers that help cool the wort quickly after the boil. There are two basic types, immersion and counterflow. The first works by circulating cold water through the tubing, which is then submerged in the hot wort. The counterflow version works by running the hot wort through the tubing, while cold water runs outside in the opposite direction. The basic material for both types is ⅜-inch diameter soft copper tubing. Half-inch diameter tubing also works well,

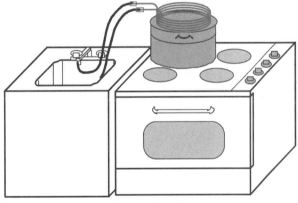

Figure 169 Immersion chilling on the stove

especially for large-scale immersion chilling, but ⅜-inch is the most common. Do not use less than ⅜-inch, because the restricted water flow impairs cooling efficiency.

Immersion Chillers

Immersion chillers are the simplest to build and work very well for small boils done on the stove in the kitchen. An immersion chiller is easy to construct. Simply coil about 30 to 50 feet of soft copper tubing around a pot or other cylindrical form. Springlike tube benders can be used to prevent kinks from forming during bending. Be sure to bring both ends of the tube up high enough to clear

Figure 170 Immersion wort chiller

the top of your boiling pot. Attach compression-to-pipe-thread fittings to the tubing ends. Then attach a pipe-thread to a standard garden hose fitting. This is the easiest way to run water through the chiller without leaking. The cold water "in" fitting should connect to the top coil, and the hot water "out" should be coming from the bottom coil for best chilling performance. An illustration of an immersion chiller is shown at left and in Figure 55 on p. 84.

The advantages of an immersion chiller are that it is easily sanitized by placing it in the boil, and it will cool the wort before it is poured into the fermenter. This allows you to separate the wort from the cold break. Make sure the chiller is clean (but not necessarily shiny) before you put it into the wort. Place it in the boiling wort during the last few minutes before the heat is turned off, and it will be thoroughly sanitized. Working with cool wort is much safer than working with hot wort. The cool wort can be poured into the fermenter with vigorous splashing for aeration without having to worry about oxidation damage. The wort can also be poured through a strainer to keep the spent hops and much of the break material out of the fermenter.

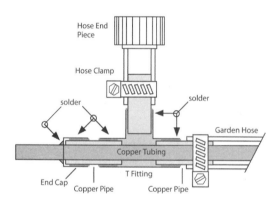

Figure 171 Suggested counterflow wort chiller design

Counterflow Chillers

Counterflow chillers are a bit more difficult to build but cool the wort a bit better. Counterflow chillers use more water to cool a smaller volume of wort faster than an immersion chiller, so you get a better cold break and clearer beer. The drawbacks are that the cold break is carried into the fermenter with the wort, it's harder to keep the inside of the chiller clean, and it's hard to keep hops and hot break material in the kettle from clogging the intake. A copper pot scrubby attached to the end of the racking cane will help.

The increased efficiency of a counterflow chiller lets you use a shorter length of tubing to achieve the same amount of wort cooling. The tube-within-a-tube chiller can be coiled into a convenient roll. The hot side of the chiller, the racking tube intake, needs to be copper or another heat-resistant material. Plastic racking canes tend to melt from the heat of the pot when the hot wort is siphoned into the chiller. Counterflow chillers are best used when there is a spigot mounted on the side of the pot, negating the need to siphon the wort.

Figure 171 shows one example for building the counterflow fittings and assembling the copper tubing inside the garden hose. First, cut off the ends of the garden hose, and slide the ³/₈-inch soft copper tubing through the hose. Apply some dishwashing detergent to help slide the tube through the hose. Next, re-coil the hose/tubing to make it more compact. Then assemble the fittings, using common ½-inch inner diameter rigid copper tube, an end cap, and sweat-type T fittings. Solder them together using lead-free silver solder and a propane torch. Reattach the hose ends via the tube clamps to the T's. Drill a ³/₈-inch diameter hole through the end cap, and slip it over the ends of the soft copper tubing, which the wort will travel through. Seal the openings for the tubing with a fillet joint soldered around the hole.

There is a company that manufactures fittings for building counterflow chillers. These fittings are known as Phil's Phittings from the Listermann Manufacturing Company (www. listermann.com). The fittings make building a counterflow chiller easy.

Hybrid Chillers

There is a third type of chiller that is a hybrid of the previous two types. This chiller has the hot wort flow through the copper tubing like a counterflow, but the cooling water bathes the coil similar to an immersion chiller. This type of chiller can be built for about the same cost as a counterflow. The basic materials are 2 feet of 6-inch diameter PVC pipe, and 20 to 30 feet of ⅜-inch copper tubing. Brass or plastic hose barbs can be used for the water fittings, but brass compression fittings should be used to attach the copper tubing to

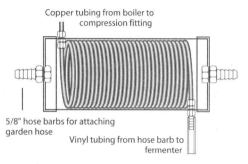

Copper tubing from boiler to compression fitting

5/8" hose barbs for attaching garden hose

Vinyl tubing from hose barb to fermenter

Figure 172 Hybrid chiller inside a PVC pipe

the hot side of the chiller. To obtain a good seal, a rubber washer and the "flat" of the compression-to-pipe-thread fitting should be on the inside of the PVC pipe. With this type of chiller, it is important to have good water flow to get a good chill. One option is to place a smaller-diameter, closed PVC pipe inside the copper coil to increase the flow of cooling water along the coils, rather than through the middle of the chiller body.

Plate Chillers

Plate chillers made from thin sheets of brazed stainless steel have recently come to the homebrewing market and are similar to what professional brewers use daily for chilling their wort. While these can't be built at home, they are very efficient, and I thought I would mention them as an available option. Plate chillers are somewhat expensive (around $100), but they work so well that the cost is justified. They can chill 10 gallons to within a few degrees of the water temperature in five minutes. They need more care in cleaning after use because they have crevices, and you cannot store them wet. Always flush them thoroughly with clean water, and dry them as well as you are able.

LAUTER TUN DESIGN FOR BATCH SPARGING

On any given day, there is at least one guy standing in front of the brass fittings at the hardware store, trying to figure out what he needs to build his mash tun. Building a mash tun from a cooler or Esky is inexpensive and the easiest way to start all-grain brewing. You can use either a rectangular chest cooler or a cylindrical beverage cooler.

Choosing a Cooler

The original home lautering system was probably the bucket-in-a-bucket false bottom championed by Charlie Papazian in *The Complete Joy of Homebrewing* (Avon Books, 1984). This setup is fairly effective and very cheap to assemble. Using two food-grade 5-gallon buckets, the inner bucket is drilled with lots of small holes to form a false bottom that holds the grain and allows the liquid to run off; the sweet wort passes into the outer bucket and is drawn off through a hole in the side.

Picnic coolers (also called cool boxes or Eskies) offer a few advantages not available with buckets, adding both simplicity and efficiency. A cooler's built-in insulation provides better mash temperature stability than a bucket can provide. Its size also allows mashing and lautering in the same vessel. Thus, all-grain brewing is as simple as pouring the grain into the cooler, adding hot water, waiting an hour, and then draining the sweet wort.

The shape of the cooler determines your grain bed depth. In general, deeper is better. If the grain bed is wide and shallow (less than 4 inches), it won't filter efficiently, and your beer will be cloudy with debris. However, if the grain bed is too deep, it increases the risk of compaction and a stuck sparge from high flow rates. My advice is to pick your cooler based on your average batch. Don't pick one larger than you really need and think that a larger one will give you more flexibility for future batches. If you pick one that is too large for the majority of your batches, your grain bed depth will be too shallow, and it won't hold the heat as well.

A 10-gallon cylindrical beverage cooler with either a false bottom or manifold works well for both 5- and 10-gallon batches The rectangular ice chest coolers also work well, and are commonly sized at 20, 24, 34, or 48 quarts (5 to 12 gallons), offering a good choice for any batch size. Many coolers have drain spigots that can be removed to make it easy to drain the wort via a bulkhead fitting. If you are using a cooler that does not have a drainage opening or spigot, lautering works just as well, if you come over the side with a vinyl hose, siphoning the wort out. You should use a stopcock or clamp to regulate the flow, and as long as you keep air bubbles out of the line, it will work great.

Everything you need to build a mash/lauter tun is readily available at a hardware store. The total investment for the cooler and all the parts to convert it into a mash/lauter tun is usually less than $50.

Rinsing vs. Draining—A Recap

Traditionally, homebrewers have sparged their mashes like the commercial brewers do: using water sprinklers or rotating sparge arms to rinse the mash uniformly for the best extraction. To get the most uniform flow through all parts of the grain bed, the mash must be kept fully hydrated with free water above the grist to help prevent settling and compaction. Lautering was typically an hourlong process of monitoring the flow rates and the runoff gravity to assure good extraction. I spent a year conducting fluid flow experiments with ground-up corncobs and food coloring, and enlisted the aid of two hydrologists and an astrophysicist, in order to gain a thorough understanding of how to optimize extraction of wort via continuous sparging. That work is collected in Appendix F.

Meanwhile, other homebrewers who were not so concerned with optimizing efficiency simply drained their mashes of the wort that was there using a slotted pipe manifold or stainless steel screen, dumped in another batch of water, drained again, and got on with their day. Frankly, I was disturbed by this flagrant disregard for technology: Sure it was easy and didn't take as much time, but where was the fun in that?! Eventually, I realized that there was room for intellectual discussion and elegance of design in batch sparging, and I joined the bandwagon.

Estimating Grain Bed Depth

In order to estimate the typical grain bed depth in a cooler, you need to know the dimensions of the cooler and the original gravity of your typical batch. And you need to know that 1 pound of dry grain has a mash volume of 42 fluid ounces, without free-standing water. (In metric units: 500 grams has a volume of 1.325 liters.)

Here is how you calculate it:

1. Multiply your typical batch size (5 gallons) by your typical OG (1.050) and divide by your typical yield in ppg (30) to determine your average grain bill.

$$5 \times 50 / 30 = 8.3 \text{ lbs.}$$

2. Multiply this weight by 42 fluid ounces per pound to determine the volume of the grain bed.

$$8.3 \times 42 = 350 \text{ fl. oz.}$$

3. Multiply the grain bed volume by 1.8 to convert it to cubic inches. (231 cubic inches/gallon)

$$350 \times 1.8 = 630 \text{ cu. in.}$$

4. Divide the grain bed volume in cubic inches by the floor area of the tun (9" x 14") to get the resultant depth.

$$630 / (9 \times 14) = 5 \text{ inches deep}$$

If you want to calculate the total volume of the mash (including freestanding water), you just need to know that any water ratio beyond 1 quart per pound only adds its own volume.

For example, 8 pounds of grain at a ratio of 2 quarts per pound would equal

$$8 \times (42 + 32) = 592 \text{ fluid ounces}$$
or 4.6 gallons.

Draining the wort, rather than rinsing the grain bed, changes the design requirements. In the steady-state flow conditions of continuous sparging, you want the flow rate to be the same at every point in the grain bed, and a false bottom is the best solution for realizing this goal. The problem with this solution is that a uniformly high outflow rate can compact the grain bed uniformly into an impenetrable layer that results in a stuck sparge. High performance comes with a high-risk price tag. If you are simply draining the wort, you don't care whether it is drained from over here or over there, as long as it drains. Extraction uniformity is achieved by stirring in the next batch of sparge water. The drainage points could be entirely along one side of the tun; it doesn't matter, as long as you can drain it.

If the grain bed is drained from a single point with a high flow rate, the grain will quickly compact around that point, and flow will cease. The more you distribute that collection point, the lower the effective flow rate will be at any of those distributed points. This is the benefit of a slotted pipe or long screen—any decrease in flow at one point can be alleviated by an increase in flow at another point. Actually, false bottoms operate the same way, but the difference is that they are more uniform and symmetrical, so that a high flow rate at one point is a high flow rate everywhere. Slotted pipes are not good enough to have that problem. Thus, slotted pipes and screens work better for draining the wort than false bottoms at high flow rates. In fact, the standard operating procedure for batch spargers seems to be to open the valve all the way and drain the tun as fast as it will go! There is no benefit to draining the wort this fast other than less time. I think it is the same rationale as for driving a fast car fast—if you got it, you might as well use it.

Batch sparging works fine with false bottoms; you just need to be aware that if you attempt to go from 0 to 60 mph in two seconds, you run a greater risk of compacting the bed. Start slowly, and you won't have any problems.

False Bottom, Pipe Manifold, or Screen?

When you design your mash/lauter tun, you need to decide how you are going to collect the wort. Are you going to rinse (continuous sparging) or drain (batch sparging)? If you are going to use continuous sparging, you will need to consider the distribution and uniformity of flow through the tun (see Appendix F), and false bottoms generally work best for this. Batch sparging and no-sparge don't require uniformity, and there are more options available. Here is a list of pros and cons for each:

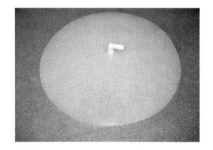

False Bottoms

Pros:

- Prefabricated false bottoms for round beverage coolers are readily available from several suppliers and are easy to assemble.
- False bottoms are always more uniform when continuous sparging than manifolds—near 100%.

Cons:

- False bottoms are tedious to fabricate yourself and difficult to fit to rectangular coolers. They should fit closely around the edges of the tun to prevent gaps that can allow sparge water to bypass the grain bed and reduce the yield.
- False bottoms are more prone to stuck sparges when the lauter flow is too fast, because they will compact the grain bed uniformly.

Manifolds

Pros:

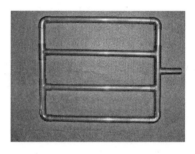

- Copper pipe manifolds are easy to build and fit to any size cooler.
- Stuck sparges are rare with manifolds, because the grain bed will not compact uniformly.
- Highly efficient configurations for continuous sparging are easily built.

Cons:

- The efficiency of manifolds varies with the pipe spacing and the grain bed depth.
- The grain bed is not lautered below the manifold, so the pipe slots should face down and be as close to the bottom of the tun as possible.
- Lots of slots to cut.

Stainless Steel Screens and Braids

Pros:

- No slots to cut.
- Screens clear very quickly during the lautering recirculation step.
- Stuck sparges are rare with screens and braids, because the grain bed will not compact uniformly.
- Prefabricated screens and braid assemblies are available from several suppliers.

Cons:

- Cutting the braid free from a rubber hose is a bit of work.
- Half-inch diameter, light-gauge steel braids can collapse from the weight of the mash and make lautering difficult. One-inch hose braids won't collapse.
- Not well suited for continuous sparging.

Siphon or Bulkhead Fitting?

You also have two options for getting the wort out of the tun: You can use a bulkhead fitting, or you can siphon out the wort. Many coolers have drain spigots that can be removed to make it easy to drain the wort via a bulkhead fitting. If your cooler does not have a drainage opening or spigot, you can buy a hole saw for your drill that will easily cut a nice hole in the cooler. Bulkhead fittings are available from several suppliers, or you can make your own. A bulkhead fitting is basically a short section of fully threaded pipe with two flat washers, two rubber washers, and two nuts for sealing around the hole that the pipe passes through. (See Figure 177.) A hose barb and vinyl tubing can be used to connect to the lautering device on the inside, and a ball valve and/or a hose barb is connected to the outside. Another suggested design using off-the-shelf fittings is detailed in Figure 180.

With the siphon method, vinyl tubing connects directly to the lautering device and just comes out over the side of the cooler. During the mash, the tubing can be coiled inside the tun with the lid on to help retain the heat. Both methods work well, although the bulkhead fitting looks spiffier and it is hard to siphon all the wort out. Whichever method you choose, you will also need a proper valve to regulate the flow rate. Ball valves are readily available in brass, chrome-plated brass, or stainless steel. Plastic stopcocks are an inexpensive option and work nicely in-line with the siphoning method. See Figure 178.

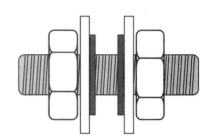

Figure 177

Figure 178

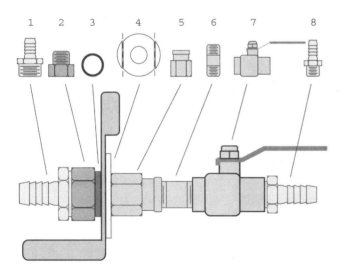

Figure 179

Figure 180 Suggested design for brass bulkhead fitting
1. ½" nylon barb to ¾" M hose fitting   5. ½" FIP to ⅜ FIP reducer
2. ¾" F hose to ½" MIP adapter (brass)   6. ⅜ MIP nipple (1.5")
3. Rubber O-ring (No. 15, ⅛ thick)   7. ⅜ ball valve (brass)
4. Washer/spacer, trimmed to fit   8. ⅜ MIP to ⅜ barb

To assemble:
1. Slip the O-ring over the male threads on #2, so it rests against the flange.
2. Apply some Teflon tape to the male threads of #2, and insert it through the spigot hole from the inside of the cooler.
3. Slip the spacer over the threads, and hand tighten #5 to make a good seal.
4. Assemble the rest of the parts in the sequence shown.

Design Options

Design Option 1—Round Cooler With False Bottom

Works for: Continuous sparging, batch sparging, no-sparge

Degree of Difficulty: Easy

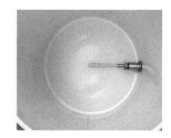

This system is probably the easiest to assemble, because it is readily available off-the-shelf. This system can lauter any beer by any method—the only caveat is that you need to watch your flow rate so that you don't compact the grain bed and get a stuck sparge.

Design Option 2—Rectangular Cooler With False Bottom

Works for: Batch sparging, no-sparge

Degree of Difficulty: Easy

Round false bottoms also work in a rectangular cooler for batch sparging, because the incongruity of the shapes doesn't matter. However, this design will not work well for continuous sparging, because the grain in the corners would not be as well rinsed as the grain in the middle of the tun. Many brewers prefer the larger, wider rectangular coolers for ease of stirring and water additions.

Design Option 3—Round Cooler With Manifold

Works for: Continuous sparging, batch sparging, no-sparge

Degree of Difficulty: Strenuous

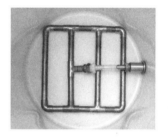

The manifold design can be optimized for distribution and uniformity, allowing flexibility for any sparging method. Soft copper tubing and compression fittings can be use to make a ring. The advantage of the manifold over the false bottom in this case is the reduced risk of a stuck sparge from uniform compaction.

Design Option 4—Rectangular Cooler With Manifold

Works for: Continuous sparging, batch sparging, no-sparge

Degree of Difficulty: Moderate

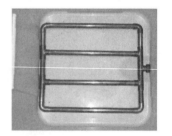

The manifold design can be optimized for distribution and uniformity, allowing flexibility for any sparging method. The slotted pipes require some time to make, but the resulting manifold is very durable. Many brewers prefer the larger, wider rectangular coolers for ease of stirring and water additions.

Design Option 5—Round Cooler With Braid

Works for: Batch sparging, no-sparge, continuous sparging

Degree of Difficulty: Moderate

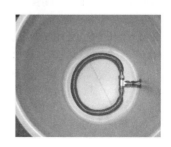

A round ring in a round cooler that divides the area evenly inside and outside the ring is actually more uniform than a false bottom of the same size. The other advantage of a ring over the

false bottom here is the reduced risk of a stuck sparge from uniform compaction.

Design Option 6—Rectangular Cooler With Braid

Works for: Batch sparging, no-sparge
Degree of Difficulty: Easy

This configuration doesn't adequately cover the floor area to work well for continuous sparging but will still work fine for the draining methods. Stainless steel braids clear quickly during the recirculation step. Many brewers prefer the larger, wider rectangular coolers for ease of stirring and water additions. The only problem is that the braid tends to move around and is hard to hold down on the bottom.

Design Option 7—Round Cooler With Screen

Works for: Batch sparging, no-sparge
Degree of Difficulty: Easy

These screen designs are the soul of simplicity and work fine for batch and no-sparge brewing. They are available as conversion kits and are easy to install. They tend to be rigid, and movement is not a problem.

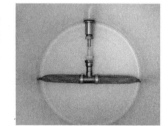

Design Option 8—Rectangular Cooler With Screen

Works for: Continuous sparging, batch sparging, no-sparge
Degree of Difficulty: Easy

These screen designs are the soul of simplicity and work fine for batch and no-sparge brewing. They are available as conversion kits and are easy to install. They tend to be rigid, and movement is not a problem.

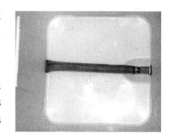

Building a Copper Pipe Manifold

A manifold can be made of either soft or rigid copper tubing. Choose a form to suit your cooler and design. In a round cooler, the best shape is a circle divided into quadrants, although an inscribed square works nearly as well. In a rectangular cooler, the best shape is rectangular with several legs to adequately cover the floor area.

Copper sweat fittings can be used to join the legs together. The fittings don't need to be soldered; simply crimping the ends slightly with a pair of pliers will provide the friction to hold the assembly together. When you cut the half-inch copper water pipe lengths to fit the cooler, don't forget to take the assembled elbow and T fitting lengths into account.

Use a standard hacksaw blade to cut the slots—they don't need to be any narrower. The slots in the pipes should only be cut halfway through and don't need to be closer than a quarter-inch apart. Even a half-inch apart is fine. The slots should face down—wort that is physically below the slots will not defy gravity and flow upwards.

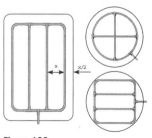

Figure 189

A wide variety of off-the-shelf brass fittings, such as hose barbs and compression fittings, can be used to connect the manifold to a siphon or bulkhead.

Building a Stainless Steel Braided Ring

The stainless steel braid from hot water hoses make good lautering screens. They are a bit of work to cut and disassemble, however, so here is one suggestion for making one.

Parts List:

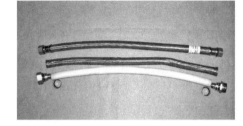

- 24-inch x 1-inch diameter water heater connector
- ⅝-inch compression T brass fitting (with included ferrules)
- 2 1-inch lengths of ½-inch diameter copper tubing

Procedure:

Figure 190

1. Clamp one of the end fittings in a shop vise.
2. Cut all the way through the metal sleeve that binds the hose braid to the end fittings with a hacksaw. This way, the ends are evenly trimmed and won't fray.
3. Pull the hose off the fitting in the vise.
4. Clamp the other end, and repeat.
5. Now, axially compress the braid to work it loose, and slide it off the hose. See Figure 190.
6. Pull/compress the ends of the braid to make it narrow, and slide one of the copper tubing pieces onto each end of the braid. Let the end of the braid extend about one-eighth inch beyond the tubing.
7. Slide a compression T nut over each end of the braid onto the copper pipe.
8. Insert a ferrule into each end of the braid. See Figure 191.

9. Slide the assembly snugly into the T, and tighten the nut so that it crimps down on the copper pipe.
10. Do the same to the other side, and now you have a braided ring manifold that won't come apart in the mash. This ring can now be connected to a bulkhead or siphon like the other systems.

A ring that divides the area equally in half (half the area is inside/outside ring) is nearly as effective as a false bottom for uniformity of sparge flow during continuous sparging. Flow uniformity doesn't really matter for batch sparging, but it's nice to have. See Appendix F for more information on uniform fluid flow during lautering.

Figure 191

Home Mashing Setups

To properly conduct a mash, you need room. You need to be able to heat the mash water and sparge water, and boil the entire 6 to 7 gallons of wort. Many brewers find that an electric stove is not up to the task, unless they can sit the pot on two burners at once. A gas stove will usually do the job, but it is often more economical (i.e., less hassle) to buy

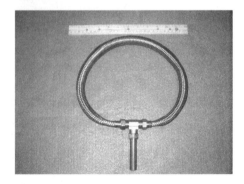

Figure 192

a propane burner. The total investment for a home canning- or crab cooker-type propane burner is usually less than $100, including the propane tank.

If you are using single-temperature infusion mashes or two-step infusion mashes in a cooler, you will only need one burner, but you will need two brewpots that can hold 5 to 8 gallons. When my wife kicked me and my mess out of the kitchen, I built a three-tier, gravity-fed system with three propane burners to provide the heat. (See Figure 193.) This is a very popular setup among "enthusiasts" like myself. The vessels are commonly converted stainless steel beer kegs from legitimate resellers like Sabco Industries. A cooler can be used in place of the middle mash tun, reducing the need for a third burner. Other setups make use of a pump to transfer the water to the hot water tank and use only the one burner under the boil kettle. There are many ways to design your own brewery.

Figures 193 and 194 This is my hot water tank that feeds the sparge. It is a converted stainless steel beer keg with the top cut out and fittings installed. A thermometer is shown in front, and the sight tube along the left side shows how much water is being used. The keg sits on top of a propane burner, which is very handy when heating 6-plus gallons of water. Another propane burner fires the boiling kettle. Full volume boils for a 5-gallon batch can be difficult on a kitchen stove; propane is an economical alternative. You could also fill another cooler with your sparge water and drain it to your lauter tun. Many homebrewers do it that way.

LAUTER TUN DESIGN FOR CONTINUOUS SPARGING

Continuous sparging is all about understanding steady-state flow. We need to understand how the sparge water is going to flow through the grain bed, so we can predict where the grain will be rinsed of sugar and where it won't be. Before I lead you through all the theory and explanations, let me cut to the chase and tell you how it works best:

- Use a false bottom or a large multi-pipe manifold to maximize coverage of the floor of the lauter tun.
- Regulate the flow with a valve to achieve a slow flow rate—no greater than 1 quart per minute—to prevent compacting the grain bed.
- Maintain an inch of water over the grain bed during the lauter to ensure fluidity and free flow.

To explain why false bottoms work best, I have to turn to fluid dynamics and some mathematical models that a friend put together for me. As I mentioned in the last appendix, I spent a year conducting fluid flow experiments with ground-up corncobs and food coloring in an aquarium in order to understand how slotted pipes worked under continuous sparging. Those experiments demonstrated that the flow converged to the pipe, and that all points along a slotted pipe drained at the same rate, regardless of distance to the drain. See Figure 195.

To explain these observations, I posted on the Homebrew Digest asking for someone with good math skills to contact me to help me figure out a model. A few weeks later I was picking up a hose barb at Home Depot and noticed a guy standing in front of the brass fittings with a cooler next to

him. Turned out that he was an astrophysicist at Cal Tech, and he offered to check the library for a book on fluid dynamics. He found a book, read it, and put together a computer model based on Darcy's Law and Laplace's Equation that could quantify the flow in a lauter tun as a histogram. See the sidebar, "Fluid Mechanics," on p. 300. As you may imagine, this came in handy for comparing manifolds and false bottoms. The next sections explain how we used the model to understand lauter tun flow.

Fluid Mechanics

To extract the wort from all regions of the grain bed, there must be fluid flow from all regions to the drain. In a perfect world, the wort would separate easily from the grain, and we could simply drain the grain bed and be done. But it is not a perfect world, and we must rinse or sparge the grain bed to get most of the sugars, and some sugar is still left behind. If some regions of the grain bed are far from the drain and experience only 50% of the sparge flow, then only 50% of the wort from those regions will make it to the drain. Fluid mechanics allows us to model the flow rates for all regions of the grain bed and determine how well a grain bed is rinsed. These differences can be quantified, enabling us to compare different lauter tun configurations.

To illustrate, let's look at a cross section of a 10-inch-wide by 8-inch-deep lauter tun using a single pipe manifold. See Figure 196a. For every unit volume of water that rinses the grain bed, grain at the top of the grain bed will experience "unit" or 100% flow. As the flow moves deeper into the grain bed, it must converge to the single drain. This means that the region immediately above the drain can experience ten times the unit flow, while a region off to the side will only experience a tenth of the unit flow. A vector flow plot for two pipes in Figure 196b demonstrates the same behavior, although the convergence effect is less. Figure 197 shows the flow rate distribution for the single pipe manifold. For purposes of illustration, unit flow (the big white upper area) is drawn

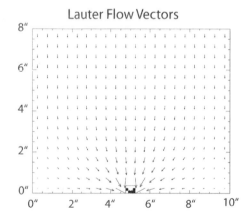

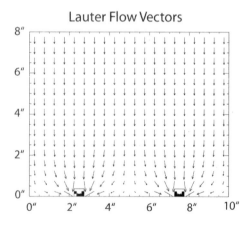

Figure 196 These pictures show the flow vectors in a lauter tun consisting of a single pipe and double pipes. The size of the arrows indicates the relative speed of the flow. Note how the flows converge to the pipes, leaving low flow areas in the corners. This same behavior has been observed when flowing food coloring dye through a grain bed in a glass aquarium.

within the bounds of ±10% of actual unit flow, and lines for 50%, 90%, 110%, and 200% of unit flow are shown. Figures 196 and 197 convey the same idea, but Figure 197 lets us quantify the percentages of flow for this grain bed. A histogram (Figure 198) can be constructed from this data that summarizes the flow distribution, and we can use the histogram to measure two aspects of lautering performance—efficiency and uniformity. Figures 199 and 200 illustrate how these flows and histogram compare to a false bottom. The differences will be explored more fully in the next couple of sections, as we look at the concepts of lauter efficiency and uniformity.

1-pipe flow rates

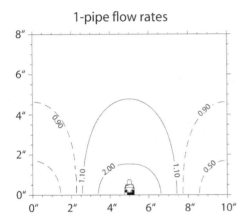

Figure 197 Darcy's Law allows us to quantify the flow velocity at any point within the lauter tun. The lines show the boundaries for 50, 90, 110, and 200% of unit flow velocity. The area above the flow lines is a region of uniform flow.

False bottom flow rates

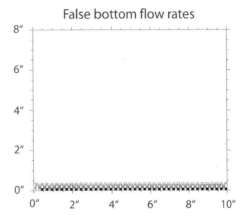

Figure 199 As in Figure 197, the lines for 50, 90, 110, and 200% of unit flow are shown, but the convergence zone is so small that you can't pick them out. This false bottom model represents ⅛-inch holes on ¼-inch centers.

1-pipe histogram

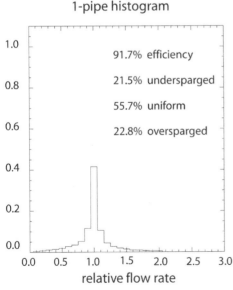

91.7% efficiency

21.5% undersparged

55.7% uniform

22.8% oversparged

relative flow rate

Figure 198 Histogram showing the relative amounts of different percentages of unit flow as described by Figure 197

False bottom histogram

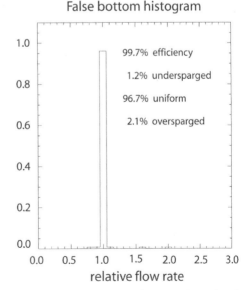

99.7% efficiency

1.2% undersparged

96.7% uniform

2.1% oversparged

relative flow rate

Figure 200 As expected, the histogram shows that the vast majority of the grain bed lies within the big, white uniform region above the convergence zone.

Fluid Mechanics

For fluid flow through porous material, Darcy's Law states that flow velocity is proportional to pressure variations and inversely proportional to the flow resistance. The resistance (or, inversely, the permeability) to flow is determined by the media—in our case, the grist. By combining this velocity/pressure relationship with a statement that water is conserved (i.e., water is not created or destroyed), we can form a numerical model that describes the fluid flow throughout the tun.

Darcy's Law: $\mathbf{u} = -K/\mu \, \nabla p$

where p is the pressure (actually, the velocity potential), μ is the absolute (or shear) viscosity, K is the permeability, and $\mathbf{u}$ is the Darcean velocity (bulk flow velocity).

Conservation of water: $\nabla \cdot u = 0$

Combination: $\nabla^2 p = 0$ (Laplace's equation)

Assuming K and μ are constant everywhere, this equation holds true everywhere except the top of the tun, where water is added, and the pipe slot, where liquor flows out of the tun. The tun walls are rigid (they can support any pressure), and nothing flows through the walls.

Efficiency

Earlier we stated that 50% of the unit flow rate would only extract 50% of the sugar. However, we cannot say that a 200% flow rate will extract 200% of the sugar. If we assume that 100% of the unit flow rate extracts 100% of the sugar, then there is no more sugar to extract, and higher flow rates do not extract anything further, except possibly tannins. If we add up all the extraction from the different flow regions of the grain bed, we can determine the efficiency percentage for that configuration.

For example, if a single pipe manifold system lautered 5% of the grain bed at 40% of unit flow, 10% at 60% flow, 15% at 80% flow, and 70% of the grain bed at 100% of unit flow or greater, the efficiency of that tun would be calculated as 90%:

(5 x 40 + 10 x 60 + 15 x 80 + 70 x 100 = 90%).

A "perfect" false bottom would lauter the entire grain bed with 100% of unit flow, because every region would have equal access to the drain, and would be 100% efficient. The computer model estimates a real false bottom (eighth-inch holes on quarter-inch centers) to be 99.7% efficient. (See Figure 200.)

Uniformity

While efficiency gives a measure of the extract quantity, the uniformity gives a measure of its quality. To discuss uniformity, we look at three percentages of flow: flow less than 90%, flow between 90 and 110%, and flow greater than 110%. With these three percentages, we can compare different configurations that have similar efficiency and determine if one configuration is more uniform than another. Flow values between 90 and 110% are considered "uniformly sparged," with values less than 90% being undersparged and values greater than 110% oversparged. Generally, the percentage of oversparging is roughly the same as the percentage of undersparging for any one configuration.

Returning to our single pipe manifold example, let's look at the histogram in Figure 197. From the histogram we can determine that only 56% of the grain bed is uniformly sparged, with 21% being undersparged and 23% over. This means 23% of the grain bed is subject to tannin extraction. But these percentages can be adjusted dramatically by tweaking a few variables.

Factors Affecting Flow

(My thanks to Brian Kern, an astrophysicist and brewer from Cal Tech, who co-developed this material with me.)

The computer model analyzed 5,184 configurations of lauter tun and manifold in order to determine the primary factors for flow efficiency and uniformity. In descending order, the factors are:

- interpipe spacing
- wall spacing
- grain bed depth.

The analysis also determined that the pipe slots should always face down, being as close to the bottom as possible, because wort is not collected from below the manifold.

Interpipe spacing. By increasing the number of pipes across the width of the tun, you are effectively decreasing the interpipe spacing. Interestingly, analysis of the models (see Figures 202 to 205) showed a nearly linear relationship between pipe spacing and both efficiency and uniformity, which peaks at a center-to-center pipe spacing of four times the pipe diameter. For a half-inch pipe, maximum efficiency and uniformity occur at a center-to-center spacing of 2 inches. Although optimum, it is not necessary for the pipes to be that close; the relationship between spacing and efficiency/uniformity starts to flatten out at 3 inches, or six times the pipe diameter. As can be seen in Table 35, only 1 to 2% gains are realized by decreasing the pipe spacing from 3 to 2 inches, although when the grain bed is shallow (4 inches), the differences approach 5%.

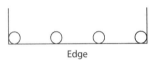

Wall spacing. The next most significant factor is the spacing of the pipes with respect to the walls of the tun. There are three ways to do this (see Figure 201).

- Edge spacing—the two outermost pipes are placed flush against the walls, and any other pipes are spaced evenly between them.
- Even spacing—the spacing between the outer pipes and the walls is the same as the interpipe spacing.
- Balanced spacing—the spacing between the outer pipes and the walls is half of the interpipe spacing.

Figure 201

TABLE 35
Effects for Pipe Spacing (10-inch-wide by 8-inch-deep grain bed)

No. of Pipes	C-C Spacing	Efficiency	Under	Uniform	Over
1	10.00	91.7%	21.5%	55.7%	22.8%
2	5.00	96.2%	9.6%	79.7%	10.7%
3	3.33	97.8%	5.5%	89.0%	5.5%
4	2.50	98.6%	3.4%	92.1%	4.5%
5	2.00	98.9%	2.7%	93.0%	4.3%

As you can see in Table 36, balanced spacing is the most efficient. This spacing places the wall at half of the interpipe spacing, so that flow velocity is symmetrical around every pipe in the manifold, and the manifold draws as uniformly as possible from the grain bed. Another way of looking at this variable is to say that balanced spacing covers the greatest area, with the closest interpipe spacing, using the least number of pipes, for a given tun width. This factor is most significant for

large interpipe spacings; at closer spacings, the uniformity difference between balanced and edge spacing is smaller (5% or less). But with edge spacing, you need to be aware of the propensity for preferential flow down the walls to the drain. This phenomenon is often referred to as "channeling."

Fluid mechanics describes a "boundary effect," in which the flow resistance decreases at the wall, due to a lack of interlocking particles, as a function of particle size. The boundary layer for crushed malt is about 1/8-inch wide. Likewise, if the edges of a false bottom do not conform to the tun walls, the flow will divert into the gaps. These low-resistance paths can result in some percentage of the sparge water bypassing the grain bed, which decreases the yield from each volume of wort collected. This implies that balanced spacing is preferable to edge spacing for manifolds, and false bottoms should be fitted closely to the tun to minimize the effect.

TABLE 36
Effects for Wall Spacing (10-inch-wide by 8-inch-deep grain bed)

No. of pipes	Wall Spacing	Efficiency	Under	Uniform	Over
2	Balanced	96.2%	9.6%	79.7%	10.7%
2	Even	94.5%	14.1%	66.6%	19.3%
2	Edge	92.0%	20.4%	56.9%	22.7%
3	Balanced	97.8%	5.5%	89.0%	5.5%
3	Edge	96.4%	9.0%	80.3%	10.7%
3	Even	96.2%	9.7%	76.3%	14.0%
4	Balanced	98.6%	3.4%	92.1%	4.5%
4	Edge	98.0%	4.9%	89.9%	5.2%
4	Even	97.1%	7.1%	84.3%	8.6%
5	Balanced	98.9%	2.7%	93.0%	4.3%
5	Edge	98.6%	3.4%	92.0%	4.6%
5	Even	97.7%	5.3%	87.6%	7.1%

Grain bed depth. The depth of the grain bed is the final significant factor—not the total depth of the grain and sparge water, only the depth of the grain itself. For both false bottoms and manifolds, the amount of flow convergence depends only on the drain size and spacing. The size of the convergence does not change significantly with depth (pressure). The ratio of underflow, uniform flow, and overflow within the convergence zone are nearly constant, and the size (height) of the convergence zone is nearly constant. In the case of false bottoms, the drain features are quite small, so the convergence zone is narrow (less than a half-inch, in our model). But the drain features of manifolds are larger and more spread out, so the convergence zone is large and affects a larger proportion of the mash.

In other words, increasing the grain bed depth changes the proportion of the grain bed that is outside the convergence zone, which increases the proportion of uniform flow, which increases the extraction efficiency as a whole. Thus, the efficiency of false bottoms (small zones) are not significantly affected by grain bed depth, while manifolds (large zones) are, although you can minimize it by decreasing the pipe spacing to reduce the height of the convergence zone.

TABLE 37
Effects for Grain Bed Depth (10-inch-wide grain bed)

No. of pipes	Depth	Efficiency	Under	Uniform	Over
1	4"	83.2%	43.8%	13.4%	42.8%
1	6"	88.9%	29.9%	38.4%	31.7%
1	8"	91.7%	21.5%	55.7%	22.8%
1	10"	93.3%	17.2%	64.5%	18.3%
1	12"	94.4%	14.3%	70.4%	15.3%
1	24"	97.2%	7.2%	85.1%	7.7%
1	48"	98.6%	3.6%	92.5%	3.8%
5	4"	97.8%	5.4%	86.1%	8.5%
5	6"	98.5%	3.6%	90.7%	5.7%
5	8"	98.9%	2.7%	93.0%	4.3%
5	10"	99.1%	2.2%	94.4%	3.4%
5	12"	99.2%	1.8%	95.3%	2.9%
5	24"	99.6%	0.9%	97.7%	1.4%
5	48"	99.8%	0.5%	98.8%	0.7%

For example: If you had only one pipe in a 10-inch-wide tun with an 8-inch-deep grain bed, the convergence zone is about 3.5 inches deep, and the percentage of uniform flow is 55.7%. If the grain bed is 48 inches deep, the convergence zone is still about 3.5 inches, but the percentage of uniform flow is now 92.5%. With five pipes, the zone height is 0.5 inches, and 90% of the flow is uniform at 8-inch depth. When you build a manifold lautering system, both the pipe spacing and wall spacing affect the actual size of the convergence zone, and the grain bed depth affects its relative size. To get the best performance from a manifold system you should optimize all three factors.

To summarize:

- Design the manifold to have an interpipe spacing of 2 to 3 inches, closer to 2 being better.
- Use balanced spacing to get the best results with the fewest pipes.
- Choose a cooler that will give a good grain bed depth for your typical batch. I recommend a depth of 6 to 12 inches.

The following four plots summarize the analysis of all the numerical models for pipe spacing, wall spacing, and depth for half-inch diameter pipes. Each plot shows the behavior of the stated quantity as a function of center-to-center pipe spacing, and as a function of grain bed depth. The relationships are nearly linear except at close pipe spacings and shallow grain bed depths.

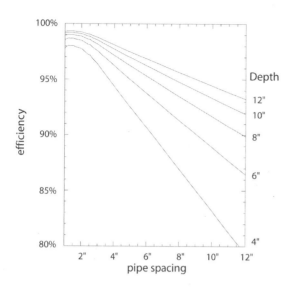

Figure 202 Lautering efficiency as a function of pipe spacing and grain bed depth

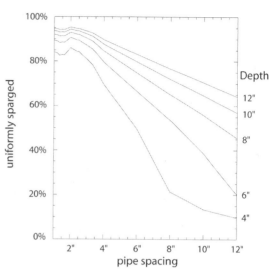

Figure 203 Lauter flow uniformity as a function of pipe spacing and grain bed depth

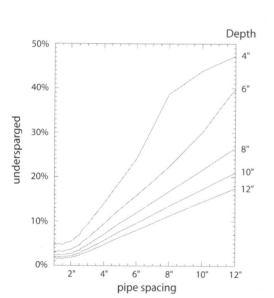

Figure 204 Lauter flow below 90% as a function of pipe spacing and grain bed depth

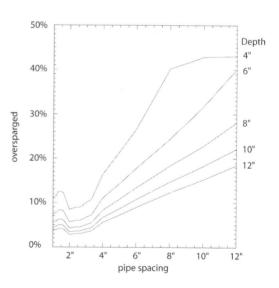

Figure 205 Lauter flow above 110% as a function of pipe spacing and grain bed depth

Designing Pipe Manifolds for Continuous Sparging

Now that you know how to design a copper pipe manifold, let's build one. A manifold can be made of either soft or rigid copper tubing. Choose the form to suit your cooler and design. In a round cooler, the best shape is a circle divided into quadrants, although an inscribed square seems to work just as well. See Figure 189 (p. 293). In a rectangular cooler, the best shape is rectangular with several legs to adequately cover the floor area. When designing your manifold, keep in mind the need to provide full coverage of the grain bed while minimizing the total distance the wort has to travel to reach the drain.

In addition, it is very important to avoid channeling of the water down the sides, which will happen if you place the manifold too close to the walls. The distance of the outer manifold tubes to the cooler wall should be half of the manifold tube spacing or slightly greater. This results in water along the wall not seeking a shorter path to the drain than wort that is dead center between the tubes.

The transverse tubes in the rectangular tun should not be slotted. The longitudinal slotted tubes adequately cover the floor area, and the transverse tubes are close enough to the wall to encourage channeling. The slots should face down—any wort physically below the slots will not be collected. In a circular tun, the same guidelines apply, but if you are using an inscribed square, the transverse tubes can be slotted where they are away from the wall.

Designing Ring Manifolds for Continuous Sparging

Ring-shaped manifolds or stainless steel braids are an elegant-looking system for round beverage coolers, but how efficient are they? It turns out that they are pretty good if we apply the balanced spacing concept. For a single ring, balanced spacing means having an equal volume inside and outside the ring. The diameter of the ring that divides the tun volume in half is expressed mathematically by the equation:

$$D_{ring} = 0.707 \, D_{tun}$$

The following charts plot the efficiency quantities of rings and false bottoms in a Sankey keg as a function of diameter. The total diameter of a Sankey keg is 15 inches. The half-volume diameter is 10.6 inches. It is interesting to note that a single ring is more efficient than a false bottom until the false bottom diameter is at least 80% of the tun diameter. These ratios hold true for any tun diameter. If more rings were added in a balanced spacing manner, the efficiency would improve and approach that of false bottoms, just like rectangular manifolds in rectangular coolers.

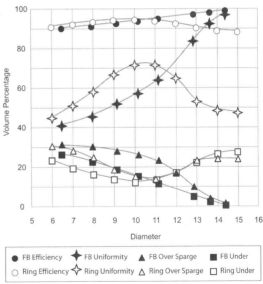

Figure 206

How to Continuous Sparge

Extraction efficiency is determined by measuring the amount of sugar extracted from the grain after lautering and comparing it to the theoretical maximum yield. In an optimum mash, all the available starch is converted to sugar. This amount varies depending on the malt, but it is generally 37-ish points per pound per gallon for a two-row barley base malt. This means that if 1 pound of this malt is crushed and mashed in 1 gallon of water, the wort will have a specific gravity of 1.037. Most brewers would get something closer to 1.030. This difference represents an extraction efficiency of 80%, and the difference could be attributed to poor conversion in the mash, but it can also be caused by lautering inefficiency.

Our goal in the continuous sparging process is to rinse all the grain particles in the tun of all the sugar. To do this we need to focus on two things:

- Keep the grain bed completely saturated with water.
- Make sure that the fluid flow through the grain bed to the drain is slow and uniform.

By keeping the grain bed covered with at least an inch of water, the grain bed is in a fluid state and not subject to compaction by gravity. Each particle is free to move, and the liquid is free to move around it. Settling of the grain bed due to loss of fluidity leads to preferential flow and poor extraction.

Continuous sparging depends on being able to rinse the sugars from the grist, and a big part of this process is diffusion. If you rinse quickly, you will end up with mostly sparge water in your boiler, because the sugar won't have time to diffuse into the sparge water as it flows past.

Continuous Sparging Procedure

In general, the equipment setup for continuous sparging is the same as for batch sparging. But you can make it easier on yourself by using another cooler as a hot water tank and feeding the sparge water continuously with a valve and hose. If your grain bed is shallow, you may want to direct this flow onto a coffee can lid to keep it from stirring up and clouding the wort. Rotating sparge arms and drip coils are another convenient way to deliver the sparge water to the tun. However you do it, you need to maintain an inch of free water over the grain bed to keep it fluid.

A surface layer of fine grain particles and protein, called *top dough* or *teig*, will tend to form on top of the grain bed during continuous sparging, and this layer should either be removed or broken up, so it doesn't form an impermeable cap that will prevent the grain under it from being rinsed properly. Commercial breweries use rotating rakes to avoid this problem and prevent channeling. Their lauter tuns are typically 3 feet deep or more, and they can run the rakes within a few inches of the false bottom to ensure good extraction without losing clarity. Homebrewing lauter tuns are typically only 4 to 12 inches deep, so it is harder to stir without causing turbidity in the wort, but stirring the upper levels of the grain bed during the lauter will help extraction. Here is the general procedure:

1. Recirculate. Open the outflow valve slowly, and drain some wort into a quart pitcher. The wort will be cloudy with bits of grain. Close the valve, and gently pour the wort back into the grain bed, recirculating the wort. Repeat this procedure until the wort exiting the tun is pretty clear (like unfiltered apple cider). It will be dark amber and hazy, but not cloudy. It should only take a couple of quarts.

2. Lauter. Once the wort has cleared, begin adding sparge water, and drain the wort carefully into your boiling pot. Fill the pot slowly at first, and allow the level to cover the outlet tube. Be sure to have a long enough tube so that the wort enters below the surface and does not splash. The splashing of hot wort before the boil can cause long-term oxidation damage to the flavor of the beer.

The sparge water can be added either with a hose from a hot water tank or by pouring in a couple of quarts at a time with a pitcher. Pour it onto a coffee can lid if necessary, and be sure to maintain at least an inch of free water above the grain bed. Watch the outflow rate; you do not want to lauter too fast, as this could compact the grain bed and you would get a stuck sparge. A maximum rate of 1 quart per minute is recommended. Continue adding sparge water and draining the wort into your pot.

3. Stuck sparge? If the wort stops flowing, even with water above the grain bed, then you have a stuck sparge. There are two ways to fix it: (a) Blow back into the outlet hose to clear any obstruction; or (b) Close the valve and add more water, stirring to dilute and resuspend the mash. You will need to recirculate again. Stuck sparges are an annoyance but usually not a major problem.

4. Gauge your progress. An advantage to brewing a dark beer is that you can see the color of the wort change as you lauter. It will get a lot lighter when most of the sugars are extracted. If you lauter too fast, you will not rinse the grains effectively, and you will get poor extraction. So, watch your wort volume, runoff color, and check the runoff gravity with your hydrometer periodically as you near your boiling volume. You will want to collect about 1 to 1.5 gallons more than your batch size and boil down to your target gravity. If you oversparge, the mash pH will rise abruptly, as the runnings gravity will fall below 1.012, and tannin extraction is likely. Hopefully, you will have collected enough wort before your runnings fall below 1.012. This rise in wort pH as a function of gravity depends greatly on the mash chemistry. In a distilled water mash, the pH could be expected to rise when the gravity falls below 1.020.[1] In water that has a calcium level between 100 and 200 ppm, the wort pH won't rise significantly even when the runnings fall below 1.008.

[1] Taylor, D.G., "The Importance of pH Control During Brewing," *MBAA Tech Quarterly* 27:4 (1990), 131-136.

BREWING METALLURGY

This appendix may contain a lot more detail than most brewers need, but being a metallurgist, I frequently get asked about metals usage in brewing, so I thought my book would be a good place to write it all down for reference. The three main topics are: cleaning, corrosion, and joining. I will discuss how to best clean the various metals and how the different metals corrode. Homebrewers make a lot of their own equipment from off-the-shelf parts at the hardware store, but you should be aware that building an item from dissimilar metals could accelerate corrosion. Likewise, the joining of metals can present a challenge, so I will provide tips for soldering, brazing, and welding.

The primary concern in brewing is flavor. We want to taste the beer, not the materials or processes used in production. While some metals, like aluminum, iron, and carbon steel will merely taste bad, other metals can be toxic to yeast and people if the concentrations are high enough. The last section of this appendix lists toxicity information for the metals commonly found in brewing and plumbing.

General Information and Cleaning

Aluminum

Aluminum is a good choice for brewpots and actively heated mash/lauter tuns. It has high heat conductivity, which helps prevent hot spots and scorching of the wort or mash, and is less expensive than stainless steel. The aluminum alloys most commonly used for cookware are alloys 3003 and 3004, which have very high corrosion resistance. Under the conditions of temperature and pH (4 to 8.5) normally encountered in brewing, aluminum (by itself) will not corrode and should not contribute any metallic flavor to your beer. However, when using aluminum for a brewing pot, do not clean the metal shiny bright between uses, or you may get a metallic off-flavor. Like all metals, aluminum depends on a passive surface oxide for corrosion resistance, and scouring the metal shiny bright will remove the passive film. Allow it to grow dull and gray with use. To encourage a passive film in a brand new pot, wash it thoroughly, dry it thoroughly, and then put it in your oven (dry) at 350° F for about 10 minutes. This will help the anhydrous oxide layer to thicken. To clean aluminum, I recommend percarbonate-based cleaners like Straight-A and PBW, or unscented dishwashing detergent like Ivory. Do not use bleach, because it can cause pitting of the aluminum.

Aluminum will corrode if placed adjacent to another metal like copper in wort or beer, but even this most aggressive situation is usually insignificant in homebrewing. I will discuss this in the galvanic corrosion section later.

Copper

Copper has a long history in brewing. It has high heat conductivity, is easy to form, and was traditionally used for making the brewing kettles or "coppers." These days, professional brewers typically choose stainless steel because it is stronger, more inert, and easier to maintain. But for the homebrewer, copper and brass are still the cheapest and best choices for wort chillers and fittings.

Copper is relatively inert to both wort and beer. With regular use, it will build up a stable oxide layer (dull copper color) that will protect it from any further interaction with the wort. Only minimal cleaning to remove surface grime, hop bits, and wort protein is necessary. There is no need to clean copper shiny bright after every use or before contact with your wort. It is better if the copper is allowed to form a dull copper finish with use.

However, you need to be aware that copper can develop a toxic blue-green oxide called verdigris. Verdigris includes several chemical compounds—cupric acetate, copper sulfate, cupric chloride, etc.—and these blue-green compounds should not be allowed to contact your beer or any other food item, because they are readily soluble in weakly acidic solutions (like beer) and can lead to copper poisoning.

To clean heavy oxidation (black) and verdigris, use vinegar or oxalic acid-based cleansers like Revere Copper and Stainless Steel Cleaner.

For regular cleaning of copper and brass, unscented dish detergent or sodium percarbonate-based cleaners are preferred. Cleaning and sanitizing copper wort chillers with bleach solutions is not recommended. Oxidizers like bleach and hydrogen peroxide attack copper. These cleaning agents will quickly cause copper and brass to blacken as oxides form. These black oxides do not protect the surface from further corrosion, and since they are formed under alkaline conditions, they are quickly dissolved by the acidic wort. If a wort chiller is cleaned or sanitized with bleach, the yeast will be exposed to potentially harmful levels of dissolved copper. Under normal brewing conditions, no off-flavors are associated with copper, as almost all of it is removed from solution by the yeast.

Brass

Brass is a group of alloys made from copper and zinc with some lead thrown in for machinability. The lead percentage varies, but for the alloys used in plumbing fittings it is 3% or less. Lead does not alloy or mix with the copper and zinc in brass, but instead exists as tiny globules (like bananas in Jell-O). These globules act as a lubricant during machining and result in a microthin film of lead being smeared over the machined surface. It is this lead that can be dissolved off by the wort. While this teeny, tiny amount of lead is not a health concern, most people would be happier if it wasn't there at all.

Fortunately, this surface lead is very easy to remove by soaking the parts in a solution of vinegar and hydrogen peroxide. You can get these at the grocery store or drugstore. You can use white distilled vinegar or cider vinegar; just check the label to be sure it is 5% acid by volume. The hydrogen peroxide should be 3% by volume. To make the solution, mix them at a 2-to-1 volume ratio of vinegar to peroxide. Simply immerse the parts in the solution, and watch for the color of the parts to change. The process takes less than 5 minutes to clean and brighten the surface. The color of the brass will change to buttery yellow-gold when the lead is removed. If the solution starts to turn blue or green, and/or the parts start darkening, it means that the parts have been soaking too long, the peroxide is used up, and the copper is dissolving, which will expose more lead. Make up a fresh solution and soak the parts again. This treatment only needs to be done once before the first use of the parts.

While zinc is an important nutrient for yeast, it can be too much of a good thing. Corrosion of brass can cause soapy or goaty flavors plus increased acetaldehyde and fusel alcohol production when zinc concentrations exceed 5 ppm. But like copper, brass is usually stable in wort and will turn dull with regular use as it builds up a passive oxide layer. Brass should be treated like copper for normal cleaning.

Carbon Steel

Carbon steel is predominantly iron, alloyed with carbon and other trace elements. In homebrewing it is commonly used for porcelain-enamel cookware and as rollers in grain mills. Many homebrewers get started in the hobby with an enamelware brewpot, because it is inexpensive. The drawback with these pots is that the porcelain can become cracked or chipped with use, exposing the steel to the wort. While a little extra iron/rust in your diet won't hurt you, it will taste bad and form haze. There is no practical way to fix these flaws in the porcelain, and the steel will rust between uses. A rusty pot will cause metallic, bloodlike off-flavors in the wort.

Many brewers like to build their own roller mills for crushing grain. Carbon steel is not stainless steel and needs to be protected against rusting by oiling or plating. If the roller steel is kept clean and dry between crushes, then it usually won't rust. It can be cleaned with a nylon or brass wire brush to remove any light rusting that may occur. Cleaning with steel wool or a steel wire brush will actually promote corrosion.

You can improve the corrosion resistance of carbon steel slightly by rubbing it with vegetable oil and buffing it off like car wax. By doing this, you protect the surface oxides from hydration, producing a black oxide rather than rust. The black oxide is more adherent and will eventually cover the entire surface, inhibiting further corrosion. The oil will become more waxlike, too, as the volatile components vaporize over time. This oxide/wax coating has limited corrosion resistance, and direct contact with water will usually induce red rust. The rust can be cleaned away as described above to restore the more passive surface.

Stainless Steel

Stainless steels are iron alloys containing chromium and nickel. The most common type of stainless steels used in the food and beverage industry are the 300 series, which typically contain 18% chromium and 8% nickel. The specific alloys that are most often used are AISI 304 and 316, which are very corrosion resistant and are basically inert to beer. The presence of chromium and its oxides inhibit rust and corrosion. Stainless steel is referred to as being "passivated" when the protective chromium oxide surface layer is unbroken. If this oxide layer is breached by iron (from a wire brush or drill bit) or dissolved by chemical action (like bleach), or compositionally altered by heat (brazing or welding), it will rust. The problem with stainless steel corrosion is usually not an off-flavor but more often a hole in a valuable piece of equipment.

If the protective oxide layer is compromised, stainless steel can be repassivated by thoroughly cleaning to remove the contamination. Usually this cleaning involves dipping the steel in nitric or citric acid to dissolve free-iron or heavy oxides. But before you head out to buy acid, let me emphasize that you do not need it to passivate your stainless steel. The key to achieving a passive surface is getting the steel clean and free of contaminants. The easiest way to do this at home is to use a kitchen cleanser made for cleaning stainless steel cookware. Three examples are Bar Keepers Friend Cleanser and Polish, Kleen King Stainless Steel and Copper Cleaner, and Revere Copper and Stainless Steel Cleaner. The active ingredient in these cleansers is oxalic acid, and it serves the same cleaning purpose as nitric acid. Once the surface has been cleaned to bare metal, the passive oxide layer will reform immediately. These cleansers also work very well for cleaning copper.

What this means is that you can perform cutting, grinding, soldering, or welding on your stainless steel, and with just a few minutes of work with cleanser and a green scrubby, it will be passive again. Be sure to rinse thoroughly with clean water afterward, so you don't leave any acid behind. Do not use steel wool or even a stainless steel scrubby; they will cause rust.

As you may be realizing, stainless steel is not invulnerable. Unfortunately, people tend to assume it is and then are shocked when it does corrode. Stainless steel has an Achilles heel, and that weakness is chlorine, which is common in cleaning products. Chlorine can dissolve the protective oxides, exposing the metal surface to the environment. Let's suppose you are sanitizing a corny keg with bleach. If there is a scratch or a rubber gasket against the steel that creates a crevice, then these secluded areas can lose their passivation. Inside the crevice, on a microscopic scale, the chlorides can combine with the oxygen from the oxide to form chlorite ions. That crevice becomes a tiny, highly active site compared to the more passive stainless steel around it, so it corrodes. This mechanism is known as crevice corrosion.

The same thing can happen at the water's surface if the keg is only half full. In this case, the steel above the water line is in air, and the passive oxide layer is stable. Beneath the surface, the oxide layer is less stable due to the chloride ions, but it is uniform. With a stable area above, and a less stable but very large area below, the water line becomes the "crevice." Usually this type of corrosion will manifest as pitting or pinholes. The mechanism described is accelerated by localization, so a pit is most often the result. It can cause pinholes in kegs half-filled with bleach solution within a few hours.

Bio-fouling (trub deposits) and beerstone scale (calcium oxylate) can cause corrosion by a similar mechanism. The metal underneath the deposit can become oxygen depleted via biological or chemical action. When this happens, it will lose passivation and become pitted. This is why the removal of beerstone from stainless steel storage or serving tanks is important. The dairy industry has the same problem with calcium oxylate and uses phosphoric acid to dissolve the buildup. Phosphoric acid is a good choice, as it does not attack the steel. Do not use swimming pool (muriatic) acid to dissolve beerstone or clean stainless steel. The acid used for swimming pools is actually hydrochloric acid, which is very corrosive to stainless steel.

A second way that chlorides can cause corrosion of stainless is by concentration. This mode is very similar to the crevice mode described above. By allowing chlorinated tap water to evaporate and dry on a steel surface, the chlorides become concentrated. The next time the surface is wetted, dissolution of the oxides at that spot will occur quickly, creating a shallow pit. The next time the keg is allowed to dry, that pit will probably be one of the last sites to dry, causing chloride concentration again. At some point in the life of the keg, that site will become deep enough for crevice corrosion to take over, and the pit will corrode through.

To prevent the stainless steel from being attacked and pitted by the use of chlorinated cleaning products like bleach, follow these three simple guidelines:

- Do not allow the stainless steel vessel to sit for extended periods of time (hours, days) filled with bleach water or another chlorinated cleaning solution.
- If you use bleach for cleaning, rinse the vessel thoroughly with water and dry it to prevent evaporation concentration.
- Use percarbonate-based cleaning products like PBW, Straight-A, B-Brite and One-Step, which won't attack the protective oxide layer.
- Some of the chemical company guys also recommend a final rinse with an acidic product such as phosphoric acid rinse or sanitizer, although this is a belt-and-suspenders solution.

Galvanic Corrosion

All corrosion is basically galvanic (an overgeneralization). The electrochemical difference between two metals in an electrolyte causes an electric current to flow and causes one of the metals to ionize. These ions combine with oxygen or other elements to create corrosion products. Cleaning off the corrosion products will not solve the problem. The cause of the corrosion is usually the environment (electrolyte) and the metals themselves. Think back to your high school chemistry class, and I will explain. An electrolyte can be defined as any liquid containing dissolved ions or salts, like tap water or seawater. Metals will corrode faster in strong electrolytes (seawater) than in weak electrolytes (tap water). Sticking a copper wire and a nail in a potato will give a different voltage (and therefore a different corrosion rate) than putting them in a glass of beer. And the ratio of the surface areas directly affects the corrosion rate, too.

Because the galvanic corrosion potential of two metals depends on several factors, including electrolyte and surface area, the standard electrolyte for comparing galvanic potential is seawater. A galvanic series lists the corrosion potential of different metals from most active to most passive. When two metals are placed in contact with one another in the electrolyte, the most active metal of the pair will corrode. The separation of the two metals in the series gives an indication of the aggressiveness of the corrosion, all other factors being equal.

The surface area factor works like this: If you have an active metal coupled to a passive metal, and the passive metal has a larger surface area than the active metal, the corrosion of the active metal will be increased. If the active metal area is larger than the area of the passive metal, the corrosion of the active metal will decrease significantly. In either case, most of the corrosion will take place at the interface of the two metals.

TABLE 38
Galvanic Series in Seawater

Most Active
Magnesium
Zinc
Galvanized Steel
Aluminum (3003, 3004, pure)
Cadmium
Carbon Steel and Cast Iron
Unpassivated Stainless Steels
Lead-Tin Solder
Lead
Tin
Brass
Copper
Bronze
Passivated Stainless Steels
Silver Solder
Silver
Titanium
Graphite
Gold
Platinum
Most Passive

This means is that if you have small area of aluminum in contact with a large area of brass, the aluminum will corrode quickly. But if you mount a small brass fitting on an aluminum pot, very little corrosion of the aluminum will take place, because of the large difference in surface areas. Brass, copper, stainless steel, and silver solder are close enough together on the galvanic series that there is not much potential for corrosion between them. In my own experience, I have had brass and copper fittings mounted or soldered to my stainless steel converted kegs for the past six years and have not seen any corrosion to speak of. Randy Mosher, the "buck a pound brewery" guy, has used copper-to-stainless brazed with silver braze and welded with aluminum bronze for several years with no problems, either.

This brings up the deciding factor in galvanic corrosion situations—exposure time. As homebrewers, our equipment is not operated seven days a week. The equipment is only exposed to an electrolyte for a few hours at time, every couple of weeks or so. This is not much exposure compared to a professional brewery or other industrial corrosion situations. So, even if we design and build equipment with galvanic couples, the useful life of our equipment is pretty long.

Soldering, Brazing, and Welding

Soldering. Soldering is the only nonmechanical joining process you need 90% of the time when you are building homebrewing equipment. The other 10% usually consists of welding a stainless steel nipple onto a converted stainless steel keg (more on this later). Soldering with lead-free silver plumbing solder allows you to join any of the metals we've discussed, although I would not advise soldering brass or copper to aluminum because of the increased galvanic effect.

The most common difficulty encountered when trying to solder to stainless steel is lack of wetting—the solder just balls up and sits there. This is caused by not having the proper flux. The surface oxides that protect stainless steel also make it difficult for the solder to wet it. Look for a water-soluble flux that contains hydrochloric acid or zinc chloride. The second-most common difficulty is getting the parts hot enough. Most of the time a propane torch is sufficient, but sometimes a methylacetylene-propadiene (MPS)-type gas (e.g., MAPP gas) is needed if the parts are very large. MPS gas burns hotter than propane but not as hot as acetylene and does not need special equipment. A good strategy is to "tin" one of the parts with solder beforehand to create a pre-wetted surface. Flux is then applied to the other parts, and the joint is fitted together and heated. In this way, the surfaces are protected from oxidation until the solder can melt and make the joint. Once hot, more solder can be fed into the joint to finish it.

Brazing. Brazing is exactly like soldering, except the filler metals are stronger and melt at higher temperatures. Unless you are going to butt braze a nipple onto the side of a keg, there is no real reason to use brazing instead of soldering. Brazing provides for a stronger joint, but usually the strength of soldering is more than adequate. A problem with brazing stainless steel is that the brazing temperatures are right in an embrittling temperature range of 800 to 1600° F (425 to 870° C). These temperatures allow the chromium to diffuse away from the grain boundaries to form chromium carbides, depleting that area of chromium and creating un-stainless steel. In other words, it will crack and rust. Steel that has been exposed to these temperatures is referred to as being "sensitized." This situation soon leads to localized corrosion and rapid cracking of the grain boundaries. All exposure to these temperatures is cumulative, and the resulting chromium diffusion cannot be corrected in any practical manner for homebrewers. It is much better to just avoid these temperatures and prevent it from occurring.

Welding. If you need a really strong joint in stainless steel, the best method is welding, and the best welding method for adding nipples to converted kegs or pots is gas tungsten arc welding (GTAW), also known as TIG welding. TIG welding has the advantage of a small weld head, lower heat input is required, and filler metal is optional. The other common welding methods for stainless steel: gas metal arc welding (GMAW) also known as MIG, and shielded metal arc welding (SMAW) or "Stick Arc." These processes are not as well suited for welding thin sections. Although MIG is probably the most common process for welding stainless steel, the large weld head must be held close to the work, and this decreases its effectiveness in tight areas.

It is pretty easy to check the Yellow Pages under "Welding" and find a local stainless steel welder to do the job for you. You will most likely not exceed their one-hour minimum charge. In fact, when I had nipples put on three kegs a few years ago, I was only charged $25 for the bunch. (OK, it has now been more than ten years ago.) One thing to keep in mind after welding is that the bluish or straw-colored area around the weld joint is no longer passivated. The heat has created different oxides that can corrode, so you will need to use the stainless steel cleansers mentioned earlier to clean the discoloration away to bare metal so it can repassivate itself.

Note: Do NOT weld galvanized or cadmium-plated steel parts. These metals vaporize easily and can cause metal-fume fever as well as acute toxicity from inhalation. In fact, cadmium has no place in the brewery at all due to its high toxicity. Galvanized parts for stands, etc., can be welded if the zinc coating is first sanded/ground off within a half-inch of the weld area.

Hopefully this appendix has given you the information you need to help choose your materials and processes for gadget building. The points to remember are:

- Metals depend on passive surface oxides for corrosion protection.
- Cleaning metals shiny bright may lead to off-flavors.
- Soldering will usually do the job, and if not, welding is easily hired out.

Toxicity of Metals

While many people are aware of the general toxicity of lead and cadmium, most people don't know how they are toxic. In all cases of acute heavy metal poisoning by ingestion, the symptoms are nausea and vomiting. Chronic (long-term) poisoning symptoms are more varied but often involve skin discoloration, weakness, and anemia. The following information comes from two books on industrial hygiene, and much of the data is from standard Food and Drug Administration animal testing. The notation "LD50" means that half of the (mice) in the test were killed by the test dosage, and the dosage is stated as milligrams ingested per kilogram of body weight.

Aluminum

Usage: Cookware and tubing. Galvanically active

There was a concern ten years ago that the use of aluminum in cooking and the ingestion of aluminum contributed to Alzheimer's disease. The medical study that generated the controversy was later found to have been flawed due to contamination of the test samples. An independent experiment conducted by Jeff Donaghue and reported in *Brewing Techniques* showed that in side-by-side aluminum vs. stainless steel boils of wort from a single mash, there was no detectable difference in the amount of aluminum between the samples either before or after fermentation. The amount of aluminum in the wort boiled in the aluminum pot was less than the detection limit for the test—0.4 milligrams per liter or 0.4 ppm.[1] If you drank 20 liters (5 gallons) of that beer, you would only ingest 20 milligrams of aluminum, about the same amount as a single buffered aspirin tablet and half of what you would get from a single antacid tablet.

Acute toxicity: Aluminum chloride—770 milligrams per kilogram body weight LD50

Chronic toxicity: No data

Cadmium

Usage: Cadmium is an ingredient in some solders and brazing alloys, none of which are approved for use with food. Cadmium is also used as an industrial protective coating for steel (most common in nuts and bolts), like galvanizing, but it has a more golden color. Galvanically active.

Acute toxicity: Symptoms are exhibited upon ingestion of 14.5 milligrams, which causes nausea and vomiting. A case where a 180-pound man ingested 326 milligrams was not fatal. The presence of copper or zinc at the time of ingestion will lessen the absorption of cadmium into the body, and reduce the toxic effects. Cadmium is easily vaporized during welding and can cause acute toxicity from inhalation.

Chronic toxicity: A study with rats found a 50% reduction in hemoglobin over 3 months when rats drank water containing 50 ppm. Other rats drinking water with 0.1 to 10 ppm for one year showed no change in hemoglobin levels.

Chromium

Usage: Secondary constituent of stainless steel. Used as electroplated coating for carbon steel. Galvanically passive.

The Chromium 6 ion that received so much publicity in the 1990s is not encountered in homebrewing. Chromium 6 is electrically generated in solution during chromium electroplating and is a wastewater contaminant. Chromium 6 is not generated by water sitting in contact with electroplated chromium or by the galvanic corrosion of stainless steel.

Acute toxicity: Soluble chromates are of very low toxicity when ingested, 1,500 milligrams per kilogram body weight before symptoms are seen. Chromium is most toxic when inhaled as fumes or dust. Chromium is not vaporized during typical welding of stainless steel.

Chronic toxicity: No documented evidence of long-term toxicity from soluble chromates.

Copper

Usage: Rigid and flexible tubing for plumbing and refrigeration systems. Galvanically passive.

Copper is an essential nutrient, and the average daily intake is 2 to 5 milligrams. Ninety-nine percent is excreted from the body in the feces.

Acute toxicity: 200 milligrams per kilogram body weight of copper salts is the lowest lethal dose.

Chronic toxicity: While dosages are not recorded, chronic poisoning symptoms include headache, fever, nausea, sweating, and exhaustion. Sometimes hair, fingernails, skin, and bones will turn green.

Iron

Usage: Primary constituent of carbon steel and stainless steel. Galvanically active.

While iron is an essential nutrient, overdoses of iron supplements are very dangerous.

Acute toxicity: Ferric chloride—400 milligrams per kilogram LD50. Symptoms of iron toxicity include headache, nausea, vomiting, anorexia/weight loss, and shortness of breath. Skin might turn gray.

Chronic toxicity: No data on dose. 10 milligrams per day is the U.S. Recommended Daily Allowance for men, 12 milligrams per day for women.

Lead

Usage: Tertiary constituent of brass; used in plumbing fixtures, fittings, and non-food-grade solders.

Acute toxicity: The oral dose of soluble lead needed to kill a guinea pig is 1,330 milligrams per kilogram body weight.

Chronic toxicity: Lead slowly accumulates in the body. Normal intake from environmental sources averages 0.3 milligrams a day. Ninety-two percent is excreted. Blood tests are a good indicator of lead exposure. Normal blood lead levels in adults are between 3 and 12 micrograms per 100 grams of whole blood. Adverse effects are not seen until a person has a blood lead level of more than 20 micrograms/100 grams whole blood for several years. The more serious symptoms are not seen until blood levels test higher than 50 micrograms for a period of 20 years, or from a single massive dose. The symptoms of lead poisoning range from loss of appetite, metallic taste in the mouth, to anxiety, nausea, weakness, headache, to tremors, dizziness, hyperactivity, to seizures, coma, and death from cardiorespiratory failure. Men will also suffer from impotence and sterility.

Zinc

Usage: Zinc is a secondary constituent of brass. It is an essential nutrient and the RDA is 15 milligrams.

Acute toxicity: Mass poisonings have been repeatedly reported from drinking acidic beverages from galvanized containers (e.g., wine punch in trash cans). Fever, nausea, stomach cramps, vomiting, and diarrhea occurred three to twelve hours after ingestion. The lowest lethal dose in guinea pigs is 250 milligrams per kilogram. Zinc is easily vaporized during welding and can cause acute toxicity from inhalation. Short-term symptoms mimic the flu and are indeed called "welder's flu" and "metal fume fever."

Chronic toxicity: No apparent injury in rats from 0.5 to 34 milligrams of ZnO for periods of one month up to one year.

References:

Casarett and Doull's Toxicology, 2nd ed. (New York: MacMillan Publishing Co.), 1980.

Patty's Industrial Hygiene and Toxicology, 3rd ed., vol. 2A. (New York: John Wiley and Sons), 1981.

Owen, Charles A. *Copper Deficiency and Toxicity*. (Park Ridge, N.J.: Noyes Publications), 1981.

My thanks to Mike Maag, industrial hygienist with the Virginia Department of Labor and Industry, for helping me track down this information.

[1] Donaghue, "Testing Your Metal—Is Aluminum Hazardous to Your Beer?" *Brewing Techniques*, 3:1 (January/February 1995), 62.

METRIC CONVERSIONS

The tables given in this section are intended to provide a quick reference for metric users of the book who don't have a calculator handy.

TABLE 39
Ounces Conversion

Ounces are bound to be confusing for the metric world. This table converts both fluid and avoirdupois ounces into milliliters and grams. (By the way, 1 cup = 8 fluid ounces.)

Fluid Ounces	Milliliters	Ounces	Grams
1	30	0.25	7
2	59	0.5	14
3	89	0.75	21
4	118	1	28
5	148	1.25	35
6	177	1.5	43
7	207	1.75	50
8	237	2	57
9	266	2.25	64
10	296	2.5	71
11	325	2.75	78
12	355	3	85
13	385	3.25	92
14	414	3.5	99
15	444	3.75	106
16	473	4	114

Appendix H

TABLE 40
Temperature Conversion

Find the value in the Number column that you want to convert and read the equivalent in either unit.
6° F = -14° C. 6° C = 43° F.

°F	Number	°C	°F	Number	°C
32	0	-18	162	72	22
36	2	-17	165	74	23
39	4	-16	169	76	24
43	6	-14	172	78	26
46	8	-13	176	80	27
50	10	-12	180	82	28
54	12	-11	183	84	29
57	14	-10	187	86	30
61	16	-9	190	88	31
64	18	-8	194	90	32
68	20	-7	198	92	33
72	22	-6	201	94	34
75	24	-4	205	96	36
79	26	-3	208	98	37
82	28	-2	212	100	38
86	30	-1	216	102	39
90	32	0	219	104	40
93	34	1	223	106	41
97	36	2	226	108	42
100	38	3	230	110	43
104	40	4	234	112	44
108	42	6	237	114	46
111	44	7	241	116	47
115	46	8	244	118	48
118	48	9	248	120	49
122	50	10	252	122	50
126	52	11	255	124	51
129	54	12	259	126	52
133	56	13	262	128	53
136	58	14	266	130	54
140	60	16	270	132	56
144	62	17	273	134	57
147	64	18	277	136	58
151	66	19	280	138	59
154	68	20	284	140	60
158	70	21	288	142	61

TABLE 41
Volume Conversion

Find the value in the Number column that you want to convert and read the equivalent in either unit. 2 liters = 2.11 quarts. 2 quarts = 1.89 liters.

Quarts	Number	Liters	Quarts	Number	Liters
0.53	0.50	0.47	11.10	10.50	9.93
1.06	1.00	0.95	11.63	11.00	10.41
1.59	1.50	1.42	12.16	11.50	10.88
2.11	2.00	1.89	12.68	12.00	11.35
2.64	2.50	2.37	13.21	12.50	11.83
3.17	3.00	2.84	13.74	13.00	12.30
3.70	3.50	3.31	14.27	13.50	12.77
4.23	4.00	3.78	14.80	14.00	13.24
4.76	4.50	4.26	15.33	14.50	13.72
5.29	5.00	4.73	15.86	15.00	14.19
5.81	5.50	5.20	16.38	15.50	14.66
6.34	6.00	5.68	16.91	16.00	15.14
6.87	6.50	6.15	17.44	16.50	15.61
7.40	7.00	6.62	17.97	17.00	16.08
7.93	7.50	7.10	18.50	17.50	16.56
8.46	8.00	7.57	19.03	18.00	17.03
8.98	8.50	8.04	19.55	18.50	17.50
9.51	9.00	8.51	20.08	19.00	17.97
10.04	9.50	8.99	20.61	19.50	18.45
10.57	10.00	9.46	21.14	20.00	18.92

TABLE 42
Weight Conversion

Find the value in the Number column that you want to convert and read the equivalent in either unit. 1.5 kilograms = 3.3 pounds. 1.5 pounds = 0.68 kilograms.

Pounds	Number	Kilos	Pounds	Number	Kilos
0.55	0.25	0.11	12.65	5.75	2.61
1.10	0.50	0.23	13.20	6.00	2.73
1.65	0.75	0.34	13.75	6.25	2.84
2.20	1.00	0.45	14.30	6.50	2.95
2.75	1.25	0.57	14.85	6.75	3.07
3.30	1.50	0.68	15.40	7.00	3.18
3.85	1.75	0.80	15.95	7.25	3.30
4.40	2.00	0.91	16.50	7.50	3.41
4.95	2.25	1.02	17.05	7.75	3.52
5.50	2.50	1.14	17.60	8.00	3.64
6.05	2.75	1.25	18.15	8.25	3.75
6.60	3.00	1.36	18.70	8.50	3.86
7.15	3.25	1.48	19.25	8.75	3.98
7.70	3.50	1.59	19.80	9.00	4.09
8.25	3.75	1.70	20.35	9.25	4.20
8.80	4.00	1.82	20.90	9.50	4.32
9.35	4.25	1.93	21.45	9.75	4.43
9.90	4.50	2.05	22.00	10.00	4.55
10.45	4.75	2.16	22.55	10.25	4.66
11.00	5.00	2.27	23.10	10.50	4.77
11.55	5.25	2.39	23.65	10.75	4.89
12.10	5.50	2.50	24.20	11.00	5.00

TABLE 43
Extract Conversion

A quick reference chart for converting between points/pound/gallon and Hot Water Extract (Liter Degrees/Kilogram). 1 PPG = 8.3454 HWE

PPG	HWE	PPG	HWE
1	8	24	200
2	17	25	209
3	25	26	217
4	33	27	225
5	42	28	234
6	50	29	242
7	58	30	250
8	67	31	259
9	75	32	267
10	83	33	275
11	92	34	284
12	100	35	292
13	108	36	300
14	117	37	309
15	125	38	317
16	134	39	325
17	142	40	334
18	150	41	342
19	159	42	351
20	167	43	359
21	175	44	367
22	184	45	376
23	192	46	384

REFERENCES

The references used in the preparation of this book are listed by chapter. If a chapter does not have a listing, it indicates that the material is general knowledge and is available from several sources.

Section I—Brewing With Malt Extract

Chapter 2—Brewing Preparations

Liddil, J., Palmer, J., "Ward Off the Wild Things: A Complete Guide to Cleaning and Sanitation," *Zymurgy*, Vol. 13, No. 3, 1995.

Palmer, J., "Preparing for Brew Day, *Brewing Techniques*," Vol. 4, No. 6, 1996.

Talley, C., Five Star Affiliates Inc. discussion, 2005.

Theiner, E., Logic Inc., discussion, 2005.

Chapter 3—Malt Extract and Beer Kits

Hansen, B., Briess Malt & Ingredients Co., discussion, 2004.

Henry, M., Coopers Brewing Products Co., discussion, 2003.

Janes, A., Muntons PLC, discussion, 2003.

Jiranek, V., Meneses, F.J., and Henschke, P.A., "Survey Of Industrial Strains Of Saccharomyces Cerevisiae Reveals Numerous Altered Patterns Of Maltose And Sucrose Utilization," *J. Inst. Brew.* 108 (3), 310–321, 2002.

Lodahl, M., Malt Extracts: Cause for Caution, *Brewing Techniques*, Vol. 1, No. 2, 1993.

Noble, R., International DiaMalt Co. Ltd., discussion, 2003.

Chapter 4—Water for Extract Brewing

DeLange, A.J., "Experiments in Removing Chlorine and Chloramine from Brewing Water," *Brewing Techniques*, Vol. 7, No. 2, 1999.

Chapter 5—Hops

Brynildson, M., "Hops and Dry-Hopping, A Craftbrewers Perspective" presentation at the SoCal Homebrewers Festival, Temecula, Calif., 2005.

Daniels, R., *"Designing Great Beers,"* Brewers Publications, Boulder, Colo., 1996.

DeKeukeleire, D., et. al., "The Oxygenated Sesquiterpenoid Fraction of Hops in Relation to the Spicy Hop Character of Beer," *J.Inst.Brew.* 108(1):86-93, 2002.

Garetz, M., *"Using Hops: The Complete Guide to Hops for the Craft Brewer,"* HopTech, Danville, Calif., 1994.

High Quality Hops From the Yakima Valley Varietal Information, Yakima Chief Inc., Sunnyside, Wash., 2003.

Hopsteiner Varietal Information, S.S. Steiner, Inc., New York, 2003.

Moir, M, "Hops–A Millenium Review," *J.Am.Soc.Brew.Chem* 58(4): 131-146, 2000.

Neve, R.A., *Hops*, Chapman and Hall, London, 1991, pp. 26-46.

Olsen, R., et. al., *Hop Variety Characteristics*, Hopunion CBS, LLC., Yakima, Wash., 2003.

Pyle, N., Ed., *The Hop FAQ*, www.realbeer.com/hops/FAQ.html, 1994.

Tinseth, G., discussion, 1995.

Tinseth, G., *The Hop Page*, www.realbeer.com/hops/, 1995.

Chapter 6—Yeast

Aquilla, T., The Biochemistry of Yeast, *Brewing Techniques*, Vol. 5, No. 2, 1997.

Cone, C., Lallemand Inc., (retired), discussion, 2003.

Doss, G., "Achieving Optimum Cell Growth and Fermentation Management," presentation at the Craftbrewers Conference, Philadelphia. Pa., 2005.

Doss, G., Wyeast Laboratories Inc., 2005.

Fischborn, T., Lallemand Inc., discussion, 2005.

Logsdon, D., Wyeast Laboratories Inc., discussion, 2001.

McConnell, D., Yeast Culture Kit Co., discussion, 1995.

Moline, R., Lallemand Inc., discussion, 1999.

Raines, M.B., discussion, 1995.

Reichwage, R., G.W. Kent Inc., discussion, 1995.

Villa, K. Coors Brewing Co., discussion, 2000.

Weix, P., Ed., *The Yeast FAQ*, ftp://ftp.stanford.edu/pub/clubs/homebrew/beer/docs/, 1994.

White, C., White Labs Inc., discussion, 2005.

Chapter 7—Boiling and Cooling

Barchet, R., "Cold Trub: Implications for Finished Beer, and Methods of Removal," *Brewing Techniques*, Vol.2, No. 2, 1994.

Barchet, R., "Hot Trub, Formation and Removal," *Brewing Techniques*, Vol. 1, No. 4, 1993.

Fix, G., discussion, 1994.

Kunze, W., *Technology Brewing and Malting, Intl. Ed.*, VLB Berlin, 1999.

Chapter 8—Fermentation

Alexander, S., discussion, 1997.

Casey, G., "Origins & Controlling Esters & Higher Alcohols in Beer," presented at Rocky Mountain Microbrewing Symposium, Colorado Springs, Colo., 2005.

Cone, C., Lallemand Inc., (retired), discussion, 2003.

Doss, G., "Achieving Optimum Cell Growth and Fermentation Management," presentation at the Craftbrewers Conference, Philadelphia. Pa., 2005.

Doss, G., Wyeast Laboratories Inc., 2005.

Fischborn, T., Lallemand Inc., discussion, 2005.

Fix, G., Fix, L., *An Analysis of Brewing Techniques*, Brewers Publications, Boulder, Colo., 1997.

Fix, G., *Principles of Brewing Science,* 2nd Ed., Brewers Publications, Boulder, Colo., 1999.

Korzonas, A., discussion, 1997.

Kunze, W., *Technology Brewing and Malting, Intl. Ed.*, VLB Berlin, 1999.

Lewis, M.J., Young, T.W., *Brewing,* 2nd Ed., Kluwer Academic/ Plenum Publishers, New York, 2002.

Logsdon, D., Wyeast Laboratories Inc., discussion, 2001.

Palmer, J., "Conditioning – Fermentation's Grand Finale," *Brewing Techniques*, Vol. 5, No. 3, 1997.

Chapter 9—Fermenting Your First Beer

Chapter 10—What Is Different About Brewing Lager Beer?

Casey, G., "Origins & Controlling Esters & Higher Alcohols in Beer," presented at Rocky Mountain Microbrewing Symposium, Colorado Springs, Colo., 2005.

Doss, G., "Achieving Optimum Cell Growth and Fermentation Management," presentation at the Craftbrewers Conference, Philadelphia. Pa., 2005.

Doss, G., Wyeast Laboratories Inc., 2005.

Fischborn, T., Lallemand Inc., discussion, 2005.

Logsdon, D., Wyeast Laboratories Inc., discussion, 2004.

Noonan, G., *New Brewing Lager Beer*, Brewers Publications, Boulder, Colo., 1996.

White, C., White Labs Inc., discussion, 2005.

Chapter 11—Priming and Bottling

Derdelinckx, G., et. al., "Refermentation in Bottles and Kegs: A Rigorous Approach," *Brauweld Intl.*, Vol. 11, pp. 156-164, 1992.

Draper, D., discussion, February, 1996.

Fix, G., Fix, L., *An Analysis of Brewing Techniques*, Brewers Publications, Boulder, Colo., 1997.

Noonan, G., *New Brewing Lager Beer*, Brewers Publications, Boulder, Colo., 1996.

Palmer, J., "Sweetness: Brewing Sugars and How to Use Them," *Brew Your Own*, Vol. 10, No. 2, 2004.

Venezia, D., Venezia & Co., discussion, 1998.

Section II—Brewing With Extract-and-Specialty-Grain

Chapter 12—What Is Malted Grain?

Briggs, D.E., Hough, J.S., Stevens, R., and Young, T.W., *Malting and Brewing Science,* Vol. 1, Chapman & Hall, London, 1981.

Briggs, D.E., *Malts and Malting*, Blackie Academic & Professional, London, 1998.

Broderick, H.M., ed., *The Practical Brewer – A Manual for the Brewing Industry*, Master Brewers Association of the Americas, Madison, Wis., 1977.

Fix, G., Fix, L., *An Analysis of Brewing Techniques*, Brewers Publications, Boulder, Colo., 1997.

Gruber, M.A., "The Flavor Contributions of Kilned and Roasted Products to Finished Beer Styles," *Tech. Q. Master Brew. Assoc. Am.,* 38(4) 227-233, 2001.

Hansen, B. Briess Malt & Ingredients Co., discussion, 2004.

Kuske, D., Specialty Malts, Briess Malt & Ingred. Co., MBAA Short Course, Chilton, Wis., 2005

Lewis, M.J., Young, T.W., *Brewing, 2nd Edition*, Kluwer Academic/ Plenum Publishers, New York, 2002.

Maney, L., discussion, 1999.

Noonan, G., *New Brewing Lager Beer*, Brewers Publications, Boulder, Colo. 1996.

Papazian, C., *The Homebrewers Companion*, Brewers Publications, Boulder, Colo. 1994.

Wahl, R., Henrius, M., *The American Handy Book of the Brewing, Malting, and Auxiliary Trades,* Vol. 1, Chicago, 1908.

Chapter 13—Steeping Specialty Grains

Gruber, M.A., "Cold Water Extraction of Dark Grains," *Zymurgy*, Vol. 25, No. 1, 2002.

Palmer, J., "Beginner's Guide to Using Grain in Extract Recipes," *Brewing Techniques*, Vol. 4, No. 5, 1996.

Section III—All-Grain Brewing

Chapter 14—How the Mash Works

Bamforth, C.W., "Barley and Malt Starch in Brewing: A General Review," *Tech. Q. Master Brew. Assoc. Am.,* 40(2), pp. 89-97, 2003.

Bamforth, C.W., "pH in Brewing: An Overview," *Tech. Q. Master Brew. Assoc. Am.,* 38(1): 1-9, 2001.

Briggs, D.E., *Malts and Malting*, Blackie Academic & Professional, London, pp. 154-184, 1998.

Briggs, D.E., Hough, J.S., Stevens, R., and Young, T.W., *Malting and Brewing Science,* Vol. 1, Chapman & Hall, London, 1981.

Briggs, D.E., Hough, J.S., Stevens, R., Young, T.W., *Malting and Brewing Science,* Vol. 1, Chapman & Hall, London, pp. 235-280, 1981.

Eglinton, J.K., Langridge, P., Evans, D.E., "Thermostability Variation in Alleles of Barley Beta Amylase," *J. Cereal Sci.,* 28: 301-309, 1998.

Evans, D.E., Collins, H., Eglinton, J., Wilhemson, A., "Assessing the Impact of the Level of Diastatic Power Enzymes and Their Thermostability on the Hydrolysis of Starch During Wort Production to Predict Malt Fermentability," *J. Am. Soc. Brew. Chem.*, 63(4): (galley proof), 2005

Evans, D.E., van Wegan, B., Ma, Y., and Eglinton, J., "The Impact Of The Thermostability Of Alpha Amylase, Beta Amylase And Limit Dextrinase On The Potential Wort Fermentability," *J. Am. Soc. Brew. Chem.* 61: 210-218, 2003.

Fix, G., *Principles of Brewing Science,* 2nd Ed., Brewers Publications, Boulder, Colo. 1999.

Jones, B.L, Marinac, L., "The Effect of Mashing on Malt Endoproteolytic Activities," *J. Agric. Food Chem.* 50:858-864, 2002.

Jones, B.L,. Budde, A.D., "Effect of Reducing and Oxidizing Agents and pH on Malt Endoproteolytic Activities and Brewing Mashes," *J. Agric. Food Chem.,* 51: 7504-7512, 2003.

Jones, B.L., "The Endogenous Endoprotease Inhibitors of Barley and Malt and Their Roles in Malting and Brewing," *J. Cereal Sci.,* 42: pp. 271-280, 2005.

Jones, B.L., Budde. A.D., "How Various Malt Endoproteinase Classes Affect Wort Soluble Protein Levels," *J. Cereal Sci.,* 41:pp 95-106, 2005.

Jones. B.E., "Endoproteases of Barley and Malt: A Review," *J. Cereal Sci.* 42: 139-156, 2005.

Kunze, W., *Technology Brewing and Malting,* 2nd Ed., T. Wainwright, Ed., VLB, Berlin, pp.190-200, 1999.

Kuroda, H., Maeba, H., Takashio, M., "Enzymes that Transform Linoleic Acid into Di- and Trihydroxyoctadecenoic Acids in Malt," *Tech. Q. Master Brew. Assoc. Am.,* 40(1) pp 11-16, 2003.

Lewis, M.J., Young, T.W., *Brewing,* 2nd Ed., Kluwer Academic/ Plenum Publishers, New York, 2002.

Lewis, M.J., Young, T.W., *Brewing,* 2nd Ed, Kluwer Academic/Plenum Publishers, New York, pp. 233-250, 2001.

MacGregor, A.W., Bazin, S.L, and Izydorczyk, M.S., "Gelatinization Characteristics and Enzyme Susceptibility of Different Types of Barley Starch in the Temperature Range 48-78°C," *J. Inst. Brew.* 108: 43-47. 2002.

Maney, L., discussion, 1999.

Moll, M., *Beers and Coolers,* Intercept LTD, Andover, Hampshire, England, 1994.

Muller, R., "Factors Influencing the Stability of Barley Malt Beta-Glucanase During Mashing," *J. Am. Soc. Brew. Chem.* 53(3): 136-140, 1995.

Muslin, E. H., Karpelenia, C.B., Henson, C.A., "The Impact of Thermostable Alpha Glucosidase on the Production Of Fermentable Sugars During Mashing," *J. Am. Soc. Brew. Chem.* 61:142-145, 2003.

Noonan, G., *New Brewing Lager Beer,* Brewers Publications, Boulder, Colo. 1996.

Osman, A.M., "The Advantages of Using Natural Substrate-Based Methods in Assessing the Roles and Synergistic and Competitive Interactions of Barley Malt Starch-Degrading Enzymes." *J. Inst. Brew.* 108:204-214, 2002.

Sissons, M.J., Taylor, M., Proudlove, M. "Barley Malt Limit Dextrinase: Its Extraction, Heat Stability, and Activity during Malting and Mashing." *J. Am. Soc. Brew. Chem.* 63:104-110, 1995.

Sjoholm, K., Macri, L.J., MacGregor, A.W., "Is There a Role for Limit Dextrinase in Mashing?" Proc. *Cong. Eur. Brew. Conv.* 25:277-284, 1995.

Stenholm, K., Home, S. "A New Approach to Limit Dextrinase and Its Role in Mashing." *J. Inst. Brew.* 105:205-210, 1999.

Stenholm, K., Home, S. Pietila, K., Macri, L.H., MacGregor, A.W., "Starch Hydrolysis in Mashing," *Proc. Congr. Eur. Brew. Conv.* 26:142-145, 1997.

Yu-Lai Jin, Speers, R.A., Paulson, A.T., Stewart, R.J., "Barley Beta Glucans and Their Degradation During Malting and Brewing," *Tech. Q. Master Brew. Assoc. Am.* 41(3) 231-240, 2004.

Chapter 15—Understanding the Mash pH

Daniels, R., *Designing Great Beers*, Brewers Publications, Boulder, Colo. 1997.

DeLange, A.J., discussion, 1998.

DeLange, A.J., "Experiments in Removing Chlorine and Chloramine From Brewing Water," unpublished, 2001.

DeLange, A.J., "Understanding Alkalinity and Hardness – Part I," unpublished, 1999.

DeLange, A.J., "Understanding Alkalinity and Hardness – Part II," unpublished, 2001.

Hanghofer, H., discussion, 1998.

Chapter 16—The Methods of Mashing

Alexander, S., discussion, 2005.

DeLange, A.J., discussion, 2005.

Brynildson, M., Firestone Walker Brewing Co, discussion, 2004.

Fix, G., *Principles of Brewing Science,* 2nd Ed., Brewers Publications, Boulder, Colo. 1999.

Hansen, B., Briess Malt & Ingredients Co., discussion, 2004.

Kunze, W., *Technology Brewing and Malting,* 2nd Ed., T. Wainwright, ed., VLB, Berlin, pp.190-200, 1999.

Mosher, R., *Radical Brewing*, Brewers Publications, Boulder, Colo., 2004.

Noonan, G., *New Brewing Lager Beer*, Brewers Publications, Boulder, Colo., 1996.

Chapter 17—Getting the Wort Out (Lautering)

Bonham, L.K., No-Sparge Brewing—An Old Technique Revisted, *Brewing Techniques*, Vol. 6, No. 4, 1998.

Conn, D., discussion, 2005.

Donovan, J., *Mechanics of No-Sparge Brewing*, www.promash.com/nosparge.html, 2000.

Gregory, G., discussion, 1998.

Hansen, B., Briess Malt & Ingredients Co., discussion, 2005.

Obenauer, D., CrankandStein Co., discussion, 2005.

Palmer, J., Prozinski, P., "Fluid Dynamics—A Simple Key to the Mastery of Efficient Lautering," *Brewing Techniques*, Vol. 3, No. 4, 1995.

Richman, D., discussion, April, 1995.

Schwartz, K., *A Formulation Procedure for No-Sparge and Batch-Sparge Recipes*, http://home.elp.rr.com/brewbeer/files/nbsparge.html, 1998.

Chapter 18—What to Expect When You're Extracting

Palmer, J., "What to Expect When You're Extracting," *Zymurgy*, Vol. 26, No. 1, 2003.

Chapter 19—Your First All-Grain Batch

Section IV—Recipes, Experimentation, and Troubleshooting

Chapter 20—Some of My Favorite Beer Styles and Recipes

Bergen, R., "A Stout Companion," *Brewing Techniques*, Vol. 1, No. 4, 1993.

Bergen, R., "American Wheat Beers," *Brewing Techniques*, Vol. 1, No. 1, 1993.

Bergen, R., "California Steaming," *Brewing Techniques,* Vol. 2, No. 1, 1994.

Bergen, R., "Porters – Then and Now," *Brewing Techniques*, Vol. 1, No. 3, 1993.

Daniels, R., *Designing Great Beers*, Brewers Publications, Boulder, Colo. 1997.

Fix, G., L., *Vienna, Marzen, Oktoberfest*, Brewers Publications, Boulder, Colo. 1991.

Foster, T., *Pale Ale*, Brewers Publications, Boulder, Colo. 1990.

Foster, T., *Porter*, Brewers Publications, Boulder, Colo. 1992.

Jackson, M, *New World Guide to Beer*, Courage Books, Philadelphia, Pa. 1988.

Lewis, M., *Stout*, Brewers Publications, Boulder, Colo. 1995.

Miller, D., *Continental Pilsener*, Brewers Publications, Boulder, Colo. 1990.

Mosher, R., *Radical Brewing*, Brewers Publications, Boulder, Colo., 2004.

Renner, J., discussion, November, 1995.

Richman, D., *Bock*, Brewers Publications, Boulder, Colo. 1994.

Slosberg, P., "The Road to an American Brown Ale," *Brewing Techniques*, Vol. 3, No. 3, 1995.

Tomlinson, T., "India Pale Ale, Part 1: IPA and Empire," *Brewing Techniques*, Vol. 2, No. 2, 1994.

Tomlinson, T., "India Pale Ale, Part 2: The Sun Never Sets," *Brewing Techniques*, Vol. 2, No. 3, 1994.

Chapter 21—Experiment!

Mosher, R., *The Brewers Companion*, Alephenalia Publishing, Seattle, Wash. 1995.

Chapter 22—Is My Beer Ruined?

Gold, Elizabeth, ed. *Evaluating Beer*, Brewers Publications, Boulder, Colo. 1993.

Maney, L., discussion, 1999.

Papazian, C., *The Homebrewers Companion*, Brewers Publications, Boulder, Colo. 1994.

Section V—Appendices

Appendix A—Using Hydrometers

Appendix B—Beer Color

Daniels, R., *Designing Great Beers*, Brewer's Publications, Boulder, Colo. 1996

Daniels, R., "Beer Color Demystified—Part III: Controlling and Predicting Beer Color," *Brewing Techniques*, Vol.3, No.6, 1995

Donovan, J., *Promash Brewing Software*, v. 1.8, Sausalito Brewing Co., Santa Barbara, Calif., 2003 www.promash.com

Morey, D., *Approximating °SRM Beer Color*, hbd.org/babble/Color.htm

Mosher, R., *The Brewer's Companion*, Alephenalia Publications, Seattle,Wash. 1994

Palmer, J., "Raise the Colors," *Brew Your Own*, Vol. 9, No. 3, 2003.

Smythe, J.E., Bamforth, C.W., "Shortcomings in Standard Instrumental Methods for Assessing Beer Color," *J. Am. Brew. Chem.*, 58 (4): 165-166, 2000

Appendix C—Beer Clarity

Bamforth, C.W., "Beer Haze," *J. Am. Soc. Brew. Chem.* 57(3):81-90, 1999.

Fix, G.J, Fix, L.A., *An Analysis of Brewing Techniques*, Brewers Publications, Boulder, Colo., 1997.

Goldammer, T., *The Brewers Handbook*, KVP Publishers, Clifton, Va., 1999.

Ishivashi, Y. et al, "Development of a New Method for Determining Beer Foam and Haze Proteins by Using the Immunochemical Method," ELISA, *J. Am. Soc. Brew. Chem.* 54:177-182, 1996.

McMurrough, L. et al, "Interaction of Proteoses and Polyphenols in Worts, Beers, and Model Systems," *J. Inst. Brew.* 91:93-100, 1985.

Palmer, J., "I Can See Clearly Now," *Zymurgy*, Vol. 26, No. 5, 2003.

Appendix D—Building Wort Chillers

Appendix E—Lauter Tun Design for Batch Sparging

Palmer, J., "How to Build a Mash/Lauter Tun," *Zymurgy*, Vol. 25, No. 2, 2002.

Appendix F—Lauter Tun Design for Continuous Sparging

Kern, B.D., discussion, 2001.

Palmer, J., Kern, B.D., "Lauter Dynamics: Design Priorities Based on Fluid Flow Studies, Part I," *Zymurgy*, Vol. 24, No. 4, 2001

Palmer, J., Kern, B.D., "Lauter Dynamics: Design Priorities Based on Fluid Flow Studies, Part II," *Zymurgy*, Vol. 24, No. 5, 2001

Appendix G—Brewing Metallurgy

Casarett and Doull's Toxicology, 2nd Ed., MacMillan Publishing Co., New York, 1980.

Owen, Charles, A., *Copper Deficiency and Toxicity*, Noyes Publications, Park Ridge, New Jersey, 1981.

Patty's Industrial Hygiene and Toxicology, 3rd Ed., Vol. 2A, John Wiley and Sons Inc., New York, 1981.

Appendix H—Conversion Tables

Briggs, D.E., Hough, J.S., Stevens, R., and Young, T.W., *Malting and Brewing Science*, Vol. 1, Chapman & Hall, London, 1981.

GLOSSARY

One of the first things a new brewer asks is, "What do I need to buy to get started?" and "What does that word mean?" For guidance to simple starter equipment setups for homebrewing, see the List of Equipment on p. 6-7. The glossary is divided into two groups—Basic and Advanced—to help you get started right away without burying you in details.

Basic Terms

The following fundamental terms will be used throughout this book.

Aerate—To mix air into solution to provide oxygen for the yeast.

Ale—A beer brewed from a top-fermenting yeast with a relatively short, warm fermentation.

Alpha Acid Units (AAU)—A homebrewing measurement of hops. Equal to the weight in ounces multiplied by the percent of alpha acids.

Attenuation—The degree of conversion of sugar to alcohol and CO_2.

Beer—Any beverage made by fermenting a wort made from malted barley and seasoned with hops.

Blow-off—A type of airlock arrangement consisting of a tube exiting from the fermenter, submerging into a bucket of water, that allows the release of carbon dioxide and removal of excess fermentation material.

Cold Break—Proteins that coagulate and fall out of solution when the wort is rapidly cooled prior to pitching the yeast.

Conditioning—A term for secondary fermentation in which the yeast refine the flavors of the beer. Conditioning continues in the bottle as long as there are active yeast present. Also, conditioning refers to the level of carbonation and quality of mouthfeel of a beer during judging.

Fermentation—The total conversion of malt sugars to beer, defined here as three phases: adaptation, primary, and secondary.

Gravity—Like density, gravity describes the concentration of malt sugar in the wort. The specific gravity of water is 1.000 at 59 °F. Typical beer worts range from 1.035-1.055 before fermentation (the "Original Gravity").

Hops—Hop vines are grown in cool climates, and brewers make use of the cone like flowers. The dried cones are available in pellets, plugs, or whole.

Hot Break—Proteins that coagulate and fall out of solution during the wort boil.

International Bittering Units (IBU)—A more precise method of measuring hops. Equal to the AAU multiplied by factors for percent utilization, wort volume, and wort gravity. An IBU is defined as 1 milligram of isomerized alpha acid per liter of beer.

Kraeusen (kroy-zen)—Refers to the foamy head that builds on top of the beer during fermentation. Also an advanced method of priming.

Lag Time—The period of adaptation and rapid aerobic growth of yeast upon pitching to the wort. The lag time typically lasts from 2 to 12 hours.

Lager—A beer brewed from a bottom-fermenting yeast and given a long cool fermentation. Lager beer is characterized by a lack of esters, maltier flavor, and high clarity.

Pitching—Term for adding the yeast to the fermenter.

Primary Fermentation—The vigorous fermentation phase marked by the evolution of carbon dioxide and kraeusen. Most of the total attenuation occurs during this phase.

Priming—The method of adding a small amount of fermentable sugar prior to bottling to give the beer carbonation.

Racking—The careful siphoning of the beer away from the trub to another fermenter or bottles.

Sanitize—To reduce microbial contaminants to insignificant levels.

Secondary Fermentation—A period of settling and conditioning of the beer after primary fermentation and before bottling.

Sterilize—To eliminate all forms of life, especially microorganisms, either by chemical or physical means.

Trub (trub or troob)—The sediment at the bottom of the fermenter consisting of hot and cold break material, hop bits, and dead yeast.

Wort (wart or wert)—The malt-sugar solution that is boiled prior to fermentation. The wort before boiling is called "sweet wort," after boiling (with hops) it is called "bitter wort."

Zymurgy—The science of brewing and fermentation.

Advanced Terms

The following terms are more advanced and are more likely to come up as you progress in your homebrewing skills and experience.

Acrospire—The beginnings of the plant shoot in germinating barley.

Adjunct—Any non-enzymatic fermentable. Adjuncts include unmalted cereals such as flaked barley or corn grits, syrups, and refined sugars.

Aerobic—A process that utilizes oxygen.

Aldehyde—A chemical precursor to alcohol. In some situations, alcohol can be oxidized to aldehydes, creating off-flavors.

Aleurone Layer—The living sheath surrounding the endosperm of a barley corn, containing enzymes.

Alkalinity—The condition of pH between 7 and 14. The chief contributor to alkalinity in brewing water is the bicarbonate ion (HCO^3_{-1}).

Amino Acids—An essential building block of protein, being composed of an organic acid containing an amine group (NH_2).

Amylase—An enzyme group that converts starches to sugars, consisting primarily of alpha and beta amylase. Also referred to as the diastatic enzymes.

Amylopectin—A branched starch chain found in the endosperm of barley. It can be considered to be composed of amylose.

Amylose—A straight-chain starch molecule found in the endosperm of barley.

Anaerobic—A process that does not utilize oxygen or may require the absence of it.

Apparent Attenuation—The percent reduction in the specific gravity of the beer due to fermentation. %AA = OG-FG/OG.

ASBC—Abbreviation for American Society of Brewing Chemists, a professional organization that determines standards and test methods for brewing materials and processes.

Autolysis—When yeast run out of nutrients and die, the cell ruptures, producing off-flavors.

°Balling, °Brix, or °Plato—These three nearly identical units are the standard for the professional brewing industry for describing the amount of available extract as a weight percentage of cane sugar in solution, as opposed to specific gravity, e.g., 10 °Plato is equivalent to a specific gravity of 1.040.

Beerstone—A hard organo-metallic scale that deposits on fermentation equipment, chiefly composed of calcium oxalate.

Biotin—A colorless crystalline vitamin of the B complex, found especially in yeast, liver, and egg yolk.

Buffer—A chemical species, such as a salt, that by disassociation or reassociation stabilizes the pH of a solution.

Cellulose—Similar to a starch but organized in a mirror aspect; cellulose cannot be broken down by starch enzymes and vice versa.

Decoction—A method of mashing whereby temperature rests are achieved by boiling a part of the mash and returning it to the mash tun.

Dextrin—A complex sugar molecule, left over from diastatic enzyme action on starch.

Diacetyl—A vicinal diketone and common fermentation byproduct that has a buttery or butterscotch aroma and flavor. Diacetyl is cleaned up by the yeast during secondary fermentation.

Diastatic Power—The amount of diastatic enzyme potential that a malt contains.

Dimethyl Sulfide (DMS)—A background flavor compound that is desirable in low amounts in lagers, but at high concentrations tastes of cooked vegetables like corn or cabbage. Actually this is only one of a group of sulfur compounds that contribute to these aromas and flavors. Others are dimethyl disulfide, dimethyl trisulfide, diethyl sulfide, etc.

EBC—Abbreviation for European Brewing Congress. This is a unit for color based on optical spectrophotometry to measure the absorptance of a specific wavelength of light (430 nanometers) through a standard-sized sample. The EBC uses a different sized sample glass than the ASBC, and the conversion factor between EBC and SRM units is EBC = 1.97*SRM.

EBU—Abbreviation for European Bitterness Units. Equivalent to IBU.

Endosperm—The nutritive tissue of a seed, consisting of carbohydrates, proteins, and lipids.

Enzymes—Protein-based catalysts that effect specific biochemical reactions.

Esters—Aromatic compounds formed from alcohols by yeast action. Typically smell fruity.

Ethanol—The type of alcohol in beer, formed by yeast from malt sugars.

Extraction—The soluble material derived from barley malt and adjuncts. Not necessarily fermentable.

Fatty Acid—Any of numerous saturated or unsaturated aliphatic monocarboxylic acids, including many that occur in the form of esters or glycerides, in fats, waxes, and essential oils.

Fine Grind, Dry Basis (FGDB)—A measure (percentage by weight) of the total soluble extract or maximum extraction achievable for a particular malt in a laboratory mash and lauter. This number, when applied to the reference standard sucrose, is the basis for both ppg and HWE.

Finings—Ingredients such as isinglass, bentonite, Polyclar, and gelatin that improve clarity by helping the yeast, suspended proteins, and polyphenols to flocculate and settle out of the beer after fermentation.

Flocculation—The state of being clumped together. In the case of yeast, it is the clumping and settling of the yeast out of solution.

Fructose—Commonly known as fruit sugar, fructose is an isomer of glucose and differs by having a ketone group rather than an aldehydic carbonyl group attachment.

Fusel Alcohol—A group of higher molecular weight alcohols that esterify under normal conditions. When present after fermentation, fusels have sharp solvent like flavors and are thought to be partly responsible for hangovers.

Gelatinization—The process of rendering starches soluble in water by heat or by a combination of heat and enzyme action, is called gelatinization.

Germination—Part of the malting process where the acrospire grows and begins to erupt from the hull.

Glucanase—An enzyme that acts on beta glucans, a type of gum found in the endosperm of unmalted barley, oatmeal, and wheat.

Glucose—The most common type of sugar, a single sugar six-carbon molecule. Also known as blood sugar, corn sugar, and dextrose.

Grist—The term for crushed malt before mashing.

Hardness—The hardness of water is equal to the concentration of dissolved calcium and magnesium ions. Usually expressed as ppm of calcium carbonate ($CaCO_3$).

Hopback—A vessel that is filled with hops to act as a filter for removing the break material from the finished wort.

Hot Water Extract (HWE)—The international unit for the total soluble extract of a malt, based on specific gravity. HWE is measured as liter degrees per kilogram, and is equivalent to points/pound/gallon (ppg) when you apply metric conversion factors for volume and weight. The combined conversion factor is 8.3454 x ppg = HWE.

Hydrolysis—The process of dissolution or decomposition of a chemical structure in water by chemical or biochemical means.

Infusion—A mashing process where heating is accomplished via additions of boiling water.

Invert Sugar—A mixture of glucose and fructose found in fruits or produced artificially by the inversion of sucrose (e.g., hydrolyzed cane sugar). Stable in syrup form.

Irish Moss—An emulsifying agent, Irish moss promotes break material formation and precipitation during the boil and upon cooling. Irish moss promotes clarity but is not a fining agent, because it is used before fermentation. Irish moss is sold as dehydrated flakes and should be rehydrated before use. Use by adding it to the boil during the last 15 minutes. Recommended dose (as flakes) is 2-3 tsp/5 gallons, or 1/16-1/8 grams per liter.

Isinglass—The clear swim bladders of a small fish, consisting mainly of the structural protein collagen, act to absorb and precipitate yeast cells via electrostatic binding. Isinglass is used as a fining agent after primary fermentation in the fermenter or keg.

Lactic Acid—A tart, sour, but not vinegary acid that is produced by bacterial fermentation. While usually a contaminant and off-flavor, it is a hallmark of some styles, including lambics and Berliner weisse.

Lactose—An unfermentable sugar, lactose comes from milk and has historically been added to stout, hence milk stout.

Lauter—To strain or separate. Lautering acts to separate the wort from grain via filtering and sparging.

Lipid—Any of various substances that are soluble in nonpolar organic solvents, including fats, waxes, phosphatides, cerebrosides, and related and derived compounds. Lipids, proteins, and carbohydrates compose the principal structural components of living cells.

Liquefaction—As alpha amylase breaks up the branched amylopectin molecules in the mash, the mash becomes less viscous and more fluid, hence the term liquefaction of the mash and alpha amylase being referred to as the liquefying enzyme.

Liter Degrees per Kilogram—The international unit for extract potential from a malt or malt extract based on specific gravity of the solution. Equivalent to points per pound per gallon with a conversion factor of 1 L°/kg = 8.345 ppg.

Lovibond—A unit of malt color measurement, based on standard solutions. The low end (<35) is equivalent to the Standard Reference Method (SRM) for all practical purposes.

Lupulin Glands—Small, bright yellow nodes at the base of each of the hop petals, which contain the resins utilized by brewers.

Maillard Reaction—A browning reaction caused by external heat wherein a sugar (glucose) and an amino acid form a complex, and this product has a role in various subsequent reactions that yield pigments and melanoidins.

Maltose—The preferred food of brewing yeast. Maltose consists of two glucose molecules joined by a 1–4 carbon bond.

Maltotriose—A sugar molecule made of three glucoses joined by 1–4 carbon bonds.

Mash—The hot water steeping process that promotes enzymatic breakdown of the grist into soluble, fermentable sugars.

Melanoidins—Strong flavor compounds produced by browning (Maillard) reactions.

Methanol—Also known as wood alcohol, methanol is poisonous but cannot be produced in any significant quantity by the beermaking process.

Modification—An inclusive term for the degree of degradation and simplification of the endosperm and the carbohydrates, proteins, and lipids that comprise it.

Peptidase—A proteolytic enzyme that breaks up small proteins in the endosperm to form amino acids.

pH—A negative logarithmic scale (1-14) that measures the degree of acidity or alkalinity of a solution for which a value of 7 represents neutrality. A value of 1 is most acidic, a value of 14 is most alkaline.

Phenol—A group of compounds consisting of a hydroxyl group (-OH) attached to an aromatic hydrocarbon group that have various medicinal and plastic flavors.

Points per Pound per Gallon (PPG)—The U.S. homebrewers' unit for total soluble extract of a malt, based on specific gravity of the solution. The unit describes the change in specific gravity (points) per pound of malt, when dissolved in water to create a specific volume (gallons). Ppg is mathematically equivalent to gallon•points/pound, which is equivalent to the metric liter•degrees/kilogram. 8.345 ppg = 1 L°/kg.

Polyphenol—A polymer of phenols that contributes to haze and staling reactions.

ppm—The abbreviation for parts per million and equivalent to milligrams per liter (mg/l). Most commonly used to express dissolved mineral concentrations in water.

Protease—A proteolytic enzyme that breaks up large proteins in the endosperm that would cause haze in the beer.

Proteolysis—The degradation of proteins by proteolytic enzymes, e.g., protease and peptidase.

Saccharification—The conversion of soluble starches to sugars via enzymatic action.

Sparge—To sprinkle. To rinse the grain bed during lautering.

SRM—Abbreviation for Standard Reference Method. In 1950, the American Society of Brewing Chemists (ASBC) adopted the utilization of optical spectrophotometers to measure the absorptance of a specific wavelength of light (430 nanometers) through a standard-sized sample.

Sterols—Any of various solid steroid alcohols widely distributed in plant and animal lipids.

Sucrose—This disaccharide consists of a fructose molecule joined with a glucose molecule. It is most readily available as cane sugar.

Tannins—Astringent large polyphenol compounds that can cause haze and/or join with large proteins to precipitate haze from solution. Tannins are most commonly found in the grain husks and hop cone material.

INDEX

Entries listed in **boldface** refer to illustrations or captions.